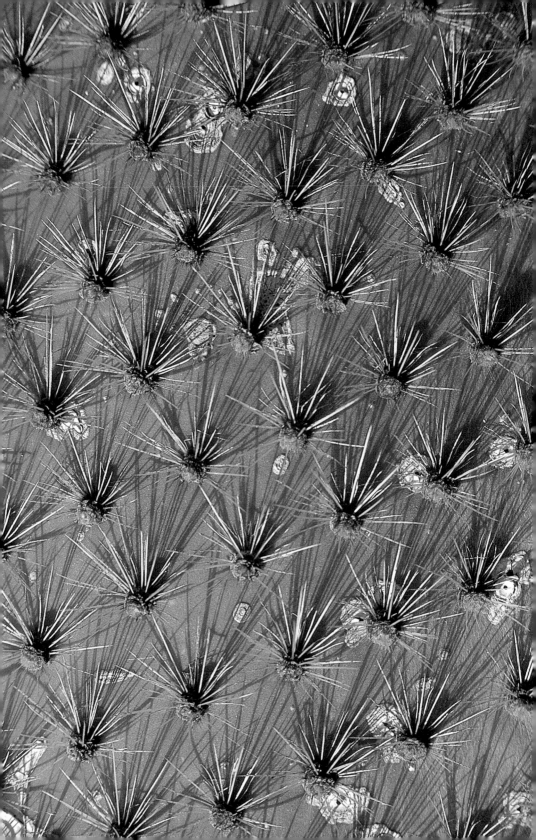

INSIGHT GUIDES

Created and Directed by Hans Höfer

ECUADOR

Edited by Tony Perrottet
Update Editor: Andrew Eames
Principal photography by Eduardo Gil

Editorial Director: Brian Bell

Houghton Mifflin

APA PUBLICATIONS

This small Andean nation, with its stable politics, friendly people and astounding diversity of landscapes, has understandably long been a favorite of travelers, and not just because of the Galápagos, one of the wonders of the natural world. Ecuador has much more to offer: no more than a short hop from the tranquil colonial capital city of Quito are the world's highest active volcano, vibrant Indian markets, palm-fringed Pacific beaches and the teeming jungles of the Amazon basin.

Such a complex destination lends itself perfectly to the approach taken by the 190-title award-winning Insight Guides series, created in 1970 by **Hans Höfer,** founder of Apa Publications and still the company's driving force. Each book encourages readers to celebrate the essence of the place rather than try to tailor it to their expectations, and is edited in the belief that, without insight into a people's character and culture, travel is more likely to narrow than to broaden the mind.

Höfer

A pa's editor-in-chief for the South American region, **Tony Perrottet,** decided to put together the original edition of *Insight Guide: Ecuador* himself. An Australian-born journalist, Perrottet studied history at Sydney University before being lured to South America by tales of relatives who worked on sheep stations in Patagonia. He first visited Ecuador in 1986, exploring remote Andean communities and canoeing the tributaries of the Amazon in search of material. Now based New York City, Perrottet has written and photographed for dozens of international publications. Aside of from the overall editing of this book, Perrottet wrote the Galápagos chapter and contributed some photographs.

The major contributor to the book,

Meisch

US-born writer **Lynn Meisch,** has spent more than nine years in the Andes, much of that time in Ecuador doing research on crafts and traditional costume. Meisch tackled everything from Andean music, Otavaleño weaving, Ecuadorian cuisine and the Avenue of the Volcanoes to the latest in Ecuadorian modern art. She is also author of the respected *Traveler's Guide to El Dorado and the Inca Empire* and *Otavalo: Weaving Costume and the Market.*

Fellow anthropologist **Les Field** turned his attention towards Ecuador's Oriente and coast. Californian born and raised, Field brought together the latest in academic research for his chapters on the Peoples of the Amazon and Ecuador's near-unknown pre-Columbian cultures.

One of the few full-time foreign correspondents based in Ecuador is **Sally Burch**. Brought up in Great Britain and now married to an Ecuadorian businessman, Burch brought her deft journalistic touch to the chapter on oil exploration, while her pointed observations gleaned from years of people-watching were put to effective use in the chapter on the Ecuadorians. Burch also contributed the book's geographical introduction, *Coast, Sierra and Jungle.*

Sean Doyle came to Latin America as part of his peregrination around the world, exploring everything from the markets of Rajasthan to the jazz bars of Copenhagen. For this book, Doyle contributed the chapters on Ecuadorian history, (so-called) Panama hats and the North Coast.

Making a return to Insight Guides after work on the South America and Peru books is journalist **Mary Dempsey**. Born in Toronto and raised in the US Midwest, Dempsey developed "an incurable case of wanderlust" while studying journalism and political sci-

Burch

Doyle

Dempsey

Perrottet

Rachowiecki

Wagenhauser

Gil

ence. Having visited Ecuador many times as correspondent for *TravelAge* magazine, Dempsey was perfectly qualified to contribute the chapters on Quito and Guayaquil.

A familiar name to travelers in Ecuador is **Rob Rachowiecki**, author of two other books on the country. Rachowiecki, an Englishman, arrived in Quito in 1981 with US$150, a backpack and no ticket home. Although he now lives in Tucson, Arizona, Rachowiecki returns to lead tours into the Amazon and to the Galápagos for Wilderness Travel, based in California. For this book, Rachowiecki has written chapters on the Oriente, Western Lowlands and birdwatching.

Contributing the chapter on adventure travel is the energetic former head of the South American Explorer's Club, **Betsy Wagenhauser**, native of Texas. Wagenhauser has climbed dozens of Ecuador's highest peaks, cycled its highways and rafted many of its mountain rivers.

Writer **Joseph Hooper** journeyed from his New York home to the middle of the Amazon to meet Randy Borman, profiled in the chapter *Gringo Chief*. When not traipsing along rainforest paths with Cofan *indígenas*, Hooper writes features for *Esquire, M, Inc.* and the *New York Times* magazine.

Additional research for many chapters was done by German-born **Gerhard Ponemunski**, a long-time resident of Ecuador. The Travel Tips section was largely compiled by Ponemunski, with additional information from Australian writer **Lesley Thelander**.

The chief photographer for the book is Argentine-born **Eduardo Gil**. Gil studied sociology and worked as a pilot before dedicating himself to photography. Director of the prestigious Buenos Aires Cultural Center, Gil has exhibited in galleries across Latin America, Europe and New York – and

has contributed to the Insight Guides to Peru, Buenos Aires, South America, Chile and Cuba.

Readers of *Insight Guide: Brazil* and *Insight Guide: Rio* will be familiar with the work of **John Maier**, currently staff photographer with *Time* magazine.

The extraordinary wildlife photographs from the Galápagos were taken by the renowned island resident **Tui de Roy**. The equally stunning wildlife photography from the Oriente was done by Liechtenstein-born photographer **André Bartschi**.

Many intimate portraits of indigenous life were taken by Scotsman **Eric Lawrie**. Having spent many years in Yemen before deciding that Latin America was more to his liking, Lawrie specializes in photographing the Sierra and its people.

Guayaquil-born **Bolo Franco** turned his local knowledge to good use with shots of the tropical coast.

North American **Donna Elmendorf** spent time as babysitter for Mick Jagger's daughter and a freelance travel photographer before finding herself on the US Embassy staff in Quito. Her extensive travel experiences in Ecuador are here represented by a wide range of photographs.

Thanks must also go to **Gustavo Davila Jarrin** of CETUR, **Patricio Torres** of Ecuatoriana and **Mariano Proano** of Metropolitan Touring for their help.

This latest edition has been extensively revised and updated, under the guidance of managing editor **Andrew Eames**. Essential work on the ground was carried out by British-born **Jane Letham** and US-born **Mark Thurber**, both Quito-based. He is a geologist and guide. she works for the South American Explorers Club, and has traveled extensively through South America. New pictures were provided by **Harry Walker**.

Lawrie

Letham

Thurber

CONTENTS

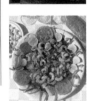

Preceding pages: typical Ecuadorian weave; fabric of nature.

The Republic of Ecuador took its name in the early 1800s from the equatorial line that runs through its heart – a geographical peculiarity that would long remain, as far as the rest of the world was concerned, Ecuador's major claim to fame. When outsiders did consider Ecuador, it was as a kind of giant natural laboratory. The French scientist La Condamine, the German Alexander von Humboldt, the Englishmen Charles Darwin and Edward Whymper, all published adventure-spiced volumes from their travels in Ecuador, recounting a land of fantastic animals, ice-capped volcanoes and impenetrable Amazonian jungles.

Ecuador comes into the world's eye no more often today – a fact that many Ecuadorians feel thankful for, considering the chaos that has racked many of the country's neighbors. Politically one of the most stable countries in Latin America, Ecuador is also amongst the safest to travel around, and even minor nuisances such as pickpocketing are almost unheard-of events.

Having largely avoided the most bitter extremes of poverty that afflict other Andean countries such as Bolivia and Peru, Ecuadorians remain an approachable and easygoing people. They include descendents of the Spanish conquistadors and original pre-Columbian inhabitants, many of whom still speak Quichua and maintain traditions from Inca times and before. Divided into 10 distinctly different communities, they prefer to be called *indígenas* (natives) rather than the Spanish *indio* (or even 'Indian' in English), and are remarkably open to foreigners, given the history of repression that has marked their country's evolution.

Add to this cultural wealth Ecuador's compact diversity – although only half the size of France, it contains the snow-capped Andes, the Pacific coast and expanses of Amazon jungle – and you begin to see why Ecuador is rapidly earning a reputation for being one of the most popular new destinations in South America.

COAST, SIERRA AND JUNGLE

Straddled across the Andes on the most westerly point of South America, Ecuador is about half the size of France (271,000 sq. km or 103,000 sq. miles) making it the smallest of the Andean countries.

The Andean mountain chain divides the country into three distinct regions: the coastal plain or Costa, the mountains or Sierra and the eastern jungle or Oriente. The fourth region is the Galápagos Islands, situated in the Pacific Ocean some 1,000 kilometers (620 miles) due west from the mainland. The striking geographical and cultural contrasts between these regions in one small country are what make Ecuador such a fascinating place to visit.

Due to the geological fault which runs along the west coast of South America, earth tremors are fairly frequent. Ecuador has suffered a few major earthquakes; the last one of importance, in March 1987, destroyed 40 kilometers (25 miles) of the pipeline that transports oil from the Oriente, precipitating a serious economic crisis.

Contrasting climates: The Costa extends the length of the coast, between sea and mountains, varying in width from 20 to 180 kilometers (12 to 112 miles). The low-lying areas and marshlands frequently become flooded, making access difficult in the rainy season. To the north, a chain of hills rises to a height of 800 meters (2,560 ft).

The shore-line offers long stretches of relatively unspoilt sandy beaches, lined with coconut palms, and a warm sea all year round. The river estuaries harbor mangrove swamps, important breeding grounds for land and marine wildlife, though many of these are being cut back to make way for shrimp farms. Further inland, particularly on the fertile lowlands irrigated by the Guayas and Daule rivers, extend plantations of bananas, sugar-cane, cacao and rice.

The Andes are formed by two parallel chains of mountains, joined at intervals by transversal foothills. Between these lie the valleys of the Sierra, from each of which a river flows east or west. These valleys have

<u>Right</u>, the awesome Mount Chimborazo.

been populated and farmed for many centuries. From the valley floor, a patchwork quilt of small fields extends far up the mountain side, demonstrating the intensive use made of every available inch of land.

Interspersed along both chains of the northern Sierra loom the eternal snowy peaks of mountains and volcanoes. The route followed by the Pan-American highway, through valleys and over passes, was dubbed the "Avenue of the Volcanoes" by the 18th century German explorer Alexander von Humboldt. Mt Chimborazo, in the central region, is the highest mountain in Ecuador, (6,310 meters/20,190 ft). A little further north is Cotopaxi, at 5,897 meters (18,870 ft) the highest active volcano in the world. In several locations, springs of hot water spurt from the mountain sides, making excellent bathing places. To the south the mountains are much lower.

The equatorial forest of the Oriente begins on the eastern slopes of the Andes. The rivers formed in the mountains of Ecuador by the melting snows of the volcanoes are the main affluents of the Amazon, the longest being the Napo (855 km/530 miles). The swift-flowing rivers are also the main means of transport, given the lack of roads. Together with the abundant vegetation of the forests, they offer both magnificent scenery and a fruitful terrain for adventure.

Little by little, however, the incursion of settlers from the west, including business interests (oil, timber, agricultural concerns, etc) and the building of new roads, is affecting the ecology of the region and destroying much of the virgin forest.

The Republic of Ecuador also claims 175,000 sq. km (66,500 sq. miles) of Amazonian territory which was invaded by Peru in 1941, and which still appears on all national maps. Ecuador does not recognise the 1942 treaty it signed in Rio de Janeiro while under occupation, and considers it partly inapplicable, which causes frequent tension with its southern neighbor.

The Galápagos Islands, home to the famous giant tortoises that share their name, consist of 13 islands and 40 to 50 islets, some of which are no more than large rocks. The largest island, Isabela, measures more than 4,000 sq. km (1,520 sq. miles).

Left, sealion in the Galápagos Islands.

Originally formed of more than 2,000 volcanoes, several of which are still active, the archipelago is considered to have evolved in isolation, which makes its wildlife particularly interesting from the view point of evolutionary history. A dramatic fire in the early 1990s fortunately left most of this intact.

Land of two seasons: Being right on the equator, Ecuador has no real summer or winter. It has two seasons: July and August are normally dry, and sometimes referred to as "summer", while the "winter" or rainy season is more intense between December and May. The other months alternate rainy and dry periods.

The lowlands of Costa and Oriente are hot and humid (above 25°C or 80°F); on the coast it is hotter in the rainy season, while the jungle has heavy rainfall most of the year. The Galápagos Islands have a hot, arid climate. In the mountains, on the other hand, the climate is reminiscent of spring-time: hot and dry in the sun, cool in the shade, but never a sticky heat. When it rains in the Andes it can get quite chilly. There is a particularly luminous quality to the daylight in the Sierra which attracts artists.

The variations in altitude and physiognomy over short distances create a series of micro-climates with widely differing temperatures and rainfall and distinct vegetation. This makes it possible to produce a variety of fruits, vegetables and grains.

The distinct ecological zones of this country also account for the broad variety of wildlife. For example, of the 2,600 species of birds existing in this part of the world, 1,500 can be found in Ecuador.

Range of cultures: The population of Ecuador totals around 11 million inhabitants, half of whom live in the cities. Population growth is rapid: around 2.7 percent annually.

The country is divided into 21 provinces, many of them named after mountains (Chimborazo, Cotopaxi, Pichincha) or rivers (Guayas, Napo, Esmeraldas). The capital city is Quito, situated in the northern Sierra, at an altitude of 2,700 meters (9,000 ft). It has one and a quarter million inhabitants. Guayaquil, the largest city with more than 1.7 million inhabitants, is a sea-port in the center of the agro-exporting region, and is the economic nerve-center of the country.

Left, rainforest in the Amazon basin.

The archaeology of the Americas shines, in the public mind, with just a few stars: the Incas of Peru, the Aztecs of central Mexico and the Maya of southern Mexico and Guatemala. The many pre-Colombian cultures (i.e. those that flourished before the arrival of the Spanish) beyond those centers are little known, despite some astonishing recent discoveries.

Ecuador comprises one of those *tierras incognitas*, even though it boasts a fabulously rich archaeological heritage. Because of the close proximity between coast, Sierra and Amazonia in Ecuador, experts are able to study most clearly the movements that shaped civilization on the entire continent. It is becoming clear that many key developments defining pre-Colombian South America actually took place in Ecuador.

The oldest pottery in all of the Americas has been found here. Cultures have been discovered that worked in platinum, a metal unknown in Europe until the mid-1800s. Ancient trade links have been established between Ecuador, Mexico and Amazonia. And it seems likely that pre-Colombian Ecuadorians sailed to and explored the Galápagos Islands.

The remotest past: The first human beings who came to Ecuador were hunters and gatherers. The approximate time period of their arrival is still bitterly debated, but it is certain that human beings have been in the Andes for 15,000 years, very probably for 30,000 years, and perhaps for as long as 50,000 years. Notwithstanding this debate, the crucial question here in Ecuador surrounds the gradual, all-important transformation from the hunting and gathering way of life to what the archaeologists would call the "formative lifestyle".

While hunters and gatherers maintain a nomadic existence, formative cultures feature permanent settlements and communities. Most archaeologists believe that this transformation in the Americas occurred over

a 2,000 or 3,000-year period, starting around 3000 BC in the most advanced areas. To the great surprise of many archaeologists, the earliest pottery and other evidence of formative cultures in the whole of South America has been found on the coast of Ecuador, from a culture known as Valdivia.

The Valdivian culture stretched along the Ecuadorian coast of the modern day province of Manabi, with its extensive, ecologically rich mangrove swamps, reaching inland to the drier hilly country. The earliest

Valdivian site, dating back perhaps to 3500 BC, is called Loma Alta. A range of extraordinary pottery has been found at this site, decorated with different carved motifs and a variety of colored clays. The Valdivian potters also formed multi-colored female figurines that turn up in late strata in the archaeological sites.

In Real Alto, a large Valdivian town continuously inhabited for over 2,000 years, archaeologists have found the remains of over 100 household structures, each of which may have housed 20 or more persons. By 1500 BC, the Real Alto people had built ceremonial temples on the tops of hills in the

Preceding pages: gold earrings and bracelets from the Carchi culture, 500–1400 BC. **Left,** Jama Coaque figurine, 500 BC. **Right,** priapic pottery from the Carchi culture.

center of their town, where complex rituals obviously took place. An abundance of female figurines have been found here, displaying sculpted hair, and long, slender legs.

The ancient Japanese in Ecuador?: The problem for the archaeologists and historians of pre-Colombian South America was not that the earliest and most advanced formative culture was found in Ecuador, although that surprised them. The real problem was that the Valdivian culture could not have appeared out of nowhere, with highly developed pottery, cultivation, and social organization firmly under its belt. There must have been a long line of precursors, of trial-and-error development which led up to these cultural achievements.

The evidence to show that these developments occurred on the coast of Ecuador, ultimately giving birth to Valdivia, is not completely convincing. Investigations have uncovered pottery older than Valdivia on the coast. Yet supporting data linking these oldest clay chips to Valdivia is lacking.

The famous Ecuadorian archaeologist, Emilio Estrada, at first alone, but later with the collaboration of Smithsonian Institute archaeologists Betty Meggers and Clifford Evans, postulated that Valdivia's origins were to be found on the Japanese island of Kyushu. The Jomon culture, which existed on Kyushu around 3000 BC, produced pottery strikingly similar to the pots found in the Valdivian sites – curved and zig-zag lines, wedge shapes and combinations of ridges, lines, dots and grooves. Estrada was encouraged by finds from later cultures, such as Guangala and Bahia, also on the coast, which revealed figurines with astonishing similarity to Asian Buddhas, as well as clay models of buildings that look like pagodas.

The heroic and well-publicized voyages of Thor Heyerdahl also encouraged these archaeologists, even though Heyerdahl's rafts sailed from Peru to Polynesia, not from Japan to Ecuador. The acceptance of the Jomon-Valdivia connection was wholehearted in some quarters. Indeed, visitors to the Museum of the Banco Central, Quito's most important archaeological museum, will encounter this theory as a nearly proven fact, presented as the most up-to-date hypothesis by the museum's guides.

But the Jomon theory has actually been largely discarded. No single phase in the development of Valdivian pottery corresponds to a particular phase in the Jomon cultural development. In fact, the decorative motifs common to both Jomon and Valdivia are found all over the world because the techniques that produced these motifs are precisely those which potters choose almost automatically when they experiment with the results of applying a finger, a bone tool, a leaf or a stone to the wet clay.

On a deeper level, the critique of Estrada *et al* strikes an important chord for all archaeological studies in the Americas. There seems to be an irresistible tendency to assume that technological and artistic advances originated in the "discovery" of these lands by Asians or Europeans. The most vulgar expression of this tendency is to be found in the still-popular Van Daniken phenomenon, which connects advanced pre-Colombian civilizations with extraterrestrials.

Origins in the Amazon: In the Oriente region of Ecuador, as elsewhere in Amazonia, the persistent presence of hunting and gathering peoples has led many observers to regard Amazonia as an historical backwater, incapable of supporting large populations and advanced civilizations. The first hint that this could not be the case came from agricultural scientists investigating the domestication of manioc; they concluded that manioc was domesticated in the Amazon basin at least 8,000 years ago.

Archaeologists have concluded that large cities (of more than 10,000 people) supported by manioc cultivation grew up on the Amazon's fertile flood-plain as well as in the jungles on the eastern slope of the Ecuadorian and Peruvian Andes. These new historical concepts regarding Amazonia view modern tribes as being descended from the inhabitants of these undiscovered cities, the survivors of the plagues, wars and forced dislocations caused by the Spanish Conquest.

The cultures of the Amazonian cities, which archaeologists are now starting to find in Ecuador and Peru, gave pottery and manioc to South America. Manioc, along with corn (which came to Ecuador from Central America by way of trade), formed the agricultural foundation for a series of advanced coastal Ecuadorian cultures, starting with Valdivia, according to the new view. The Andes, or Sierra, at first acted as a thoroughfare between the Amazon and the coast.

An important site near Cuenca, called Cerro Narrio, is situated at the crossroads of a natural, easy route, following the drainages of the Pastaza and Paute rivers. Beginning around 2000 BC, Cerro Narrio may have been a key trading center, where exchanges of technologies, products, and ideas from the coast, Amazonia, and the Sierra took place. Ceramics bearing an unmistakable design relationship to those of coastal cultures have been found at Cerro Narrio, but archaeologists are unable to determine whether these pots were imported from the coast or were made at Cerro Narrio by potters who had come from the coast to live in the Sierra.

Archaeologists now believe that a number

Flowering in coast and Sierra: Following the establishment of formative cultures and of wide-ranging trade and exchange networks, stretching from Mexico to Peru and from the Amazon to the coast, archaeologists describe a period of "regional development" (500 BC–AD 500) followed by a period of "integration" (500–AD 1500). The final period culminated in the conquest of all of what is now Ecuador by the Inca Empire, which undertook an extensive program of city building and artistic creativity in Ecuador, before being itself destroyed by the Spaniards. A grand flowering of cultural activity preceded the Inca conquest of Ecuador, and the abundance of distinctive and particular phases,

of important items were traded between coast, Sierra and jungle. Coastal societies collected spondylus shells, which were processed into beads in the Sierra and traded in Amazonia, where the shell design appears on much of the pottery that has been discovered. The Sierran societies domesticated the potato for trade, as well as coca – crucial in rituals in the whole area. Meanwhile, Amazonian societies were renowned for their ritual vessels, made for more than 3,000 years, and for their hallucinogenic concoctions.

<u>**Above**</u>, **Pre-Columbian copper pieces found in the Sierra.**

especially on the coast, is overwhelming. The extraordinary achievement of these coastal cultures is embodied in the goldwork and sculpture of the La Tolita and Manta civilizations.

The La Tolita culture reached its zenith around 300 BC and its star shone for perhaps 700 years on the coast of northern Ecuador and southwestern Colombia. The key site is a small, swampy lowland island in the mouth of the Santiago River in the coastal province of Esmeraldas. Now inhabited by Afro-Ecuadorean fisherfolk, La Tolita came to the attention of Westerners in the 1920s, when several European explorers announced that an unprecedented number of gorgeous and finely crafted objects of gold were being found regularly on the island.

The merciless pillage of these priceless objects went on for years, and was even industrialized by a prospector named Yanuzelli, who mechanized the milling of thousands of tons of sand from which gold artifacts were extracted and then melted down into ingots. Yanuzelli converted perhaps 800 kilos of artifacts into ingots, yet even today many gold objects are found on La Tolita.

The magnificent mask of the Sun God, with its ornately detailed fan of sunrays, is the symbol of Ecuador's Banco Central and was found on La Tolita. So much gold has

been uncovered on La Tolita that archaeologists believe that the island was a sacred place, a pre-Colombian Mecca or Jerusalem, a city devoted to the production of holy, gold images, a city of goldsmiths. It may have been the destination of pilgrims from the coast, the Sierra and possibly Amazonia, who went there to obtain the sacred symbols of an ancient cult that influenced most of what is now Ecuador.

The skill and aesthetic of La Tolita goldwork is matched by the sculpture found on the island. The freestanding, detailed figures in active poses of motion make La Tolita sculpture completely unique in pre-Colom-

bian art. The sculptures depict both deities and mortal humans, the latter displaying deformities and diseases, or experiencing emotions of joy, sadness, or surprise.

Unique skills: La Tolita artisans also excelled in a metal-craft unknown even in Europe until the 1850s. Metalsmiths on the island worked in platinum, creating intricate masks, pendants, pectorals, and nose-rings in a metal with a very high melting point. Archaeologists have long puzzled over just how La Tolita metalsmiths were able to work in platinum, with only relatively rudimentary tools and technology. One theory hypothesizes that by combining pure platinum with bits of gold, which melts at a much lower temperature, the smiths created an alloy that their tools could hammer, cast and form into ornaments.

The Manta culture, in the modern province of Manabi, flowered during the period of integration, and also produced objects of surpassing beauty in gold, silver, cotton textiles, pottery and stone. The great city of Manta housed more than 20,000 people, and by including the population of outlying villages, archaeologists have arrived at very large figures for the people who lived during the Manta culture. This culture produced the greatest mariners of pre-Colombian Ecuador, and there is evidence that the Manta people settled extensive coastal areas, and traded with the coastal peoples of western Mexico and central Peru.

Perhaps most intriguingly, a persistent theory among some archaeologists hypothesizes that Manteña mariners, along with pre-Colombian Peruvian sailors, discovered the Galápagos Islands. A quantity of ceramic shards, almost certainly of pre-Columbian vintage, have been found on three islands; the presence of cotton plants, domesticated on the continent, also indicates some sort of contact between the islands and the mainland. Whether the contacts were only very occasional, or even just accidental as some believe, whether the islands were used as a seasonal fishing outpost as Thor Heyerdahl and others favor, or whether the islands were truly settled by groups of Manteñas as only a few archaeologists assert, has yet to be positively established.

Left, Jama Coaque drinking cup. Right, figurine from the Bahia culture, 500 BC–AD 500.

The present nation of Ecuador was carved quite randomly out of a larger mass, its borders faintly drawn across swamps and lowlands, across mountains and through rainforests. These disparate zones were united only in name, taking a geographic term which, ironically, divides the world. Understandably, the sometimes desperate search for national unity has often fallen prey to older regional loyalties, which account for the uncoordinated development of the country.

The forces of historical change have frequently been imposed on Ecuador from beyond. Successive invaders – the Incas, the Spaniards and, more recently, bullying neighbors – have swept across the country in great waves of destruction, each seeking to remake the country in their own image. Their success is reflected in the varied ethnicity of the Ecuadorian people – 40 percent Indian, 40 percent *mestizo* (mixed European-Indian blood), and the remainder an assortment of full-blooded Europeans (*criollos*), and the descendents of black Caribs and Africans (*morenos*). Their legacy of brutal exploitation constitutes an ongoing struggle for modern Ecuadorians.

Sierra cultures: The land that is now roughly Ecuador was first brought under one rule when the Incas of Peru invaded in the middle of the 15th century. By this time, the dazzling coastal cultures of Manta and La Tolita on the Ecuadorian coast (see chapter *Lost Worlds*) had flowered and faded, while an increasingly powerful series of agricultural societies had divided the region's highlands amongst them.

The greatest of these cultures was the Cañaris, who inhabited the present day sites of Cuenca, Chordelag, Gualaceo and Cañar. They maintained a rigidly hierarchical society over a broad federation of villages, each with considerable independence. Only the Cañari elites were allowed to wear the fine, elaborate gold and silver produced by their metalsmiths. Among the Cañari artifacts, figures of jaguars, caymans and other jungle

Left, rural worker overlooking the Quito of the 1890s. **Right**, fanciful European depiction of the Inca Atahualpa.

animals predominate – showing their strong links with Amazonian groups.

Another advanced group were the Caras, forefathers of the modern Otavaleños. Arriving in Ecuador "by way of the sea", the Caras ascended the Río Esmeraldas during the tenth century and established themselves in the land of the Quitus. They worshipped the sun and believed the moon was inhabited by humans. They built an observatory to chart the solstices, and identified the equator as "the path of the sun". Their economy was

based on the spinning and weaving of sheep's wool, and a traveling class of merchants traded with tribes in the Oriente.

The Puruhás, fearsome and habitual warriors living around Ambato, were ruled by the Duchicela family, as the Caras were by the Shyri. In the 14th century, these two families intermarried to create the greater kingdom of Quitu. While little social or economic influence was exerted over the kingdom's lesser tribes, they nevertheless contributed manpower to the frequent bouts of war, particularly against the Cañaris of Cuenca region.

The Inca invasion: On to this landscape of tribal identity marched the Incas – literally,

"Children of the Sun" – who, in retrospect, were the short-lived precursors of the Spaniards. Although established in the Peruvian Andes from the 11th century, it was not until about 1460 that they set upon the Cañaris; their ultimate objective was the subjugation of Quitu. From this moment in history, Ecuador became brutally embroiled in imperial ambitions as armies dispatched from distant capitals turned the country into a battlefield.

The Cañaris fought valiantly against superior odds for several years before being subdued by the Inca Tupac-Yupanqui. His revenge decimated the indigenous male population: when the Spanish chronicler Cieza de León visited Cañari territory in 1547, he

icated to the service of the sun". At nearby Ingapirca, the best preserved pre-Hispanic site in Ecuador, the Incas built an imposing fortress that also served as temple, storehouse, and planetary observatory.

Inca conquest along the spine of the Andes continued inexorably. Quitu, which had fallen by 1492, became a garrison town on the empire's northern frontier and, like Tomebamba, the focus of ostentatious construction. The battles continued to rage, however: for 17 years the Caras resisted the Inca onslaught before Huanya-Capac, Tupac's son, captured their capital, Caranqui, and massacred thousands in retribution.

The Incas at war were a fearsome sight.

found 15 women to every man. Inca occupation was focused on the construction of a major city called Tomebamba on the site of present-day Cuenca. It was intended to rival the Inca capital of Cuzco, from whence stonemasons were summoned to build a massive Temple of the Sun and splendid palaces with walls of sculpted gold.

Tomebamba represented the flourish before the fall, for by the time Cieza arrived, it was already a ghost town. He found enormous warehouses fully stocked with grains, barracks for the imperial troops and houses formerly occupied by "more than two hundred virgins, who were very beautiful, ded-

Dressed in quilted armor and cane or woollen helmets, and armed with spears, *champis* (head-splitters), slingshots and shields, they attacked with a blood-curdling cry. Their vanquished foe had no recourse to an ancient form of the Geneva Convention: any prisoners taken in battle were transported to a sun temple and slaughtered. The heads of enemy chieftains became drinking cups; their bodies were stuffed and paraded through the streets; and their stomachs were turned into drums which were beaten at the next battle.

Imposing the new order: Inca colonization brought large numbers of loyal Quechua subjects from southern Peru to Ecuador, and many Cañaris and Caras were in turn shipped to Peru. The Incas introduced their impressive irrigation methods and some new crops – sweet potatoes, coca, and peanuts – as well as the llama, a sturdy beast of burden and excellent source of wool. The chewing of coca, previously unknown in highland Ecuador, quickly became a popular pastime. The Imperial Highway was extended to Quito, which – although 1,980 km (1,230 miles) from Cuzco – could be reached by a team of runners in just eight days. Loyalty to the Inca, with his mandate from the Sun, was exacted through the system of *mita* – imperial work or service – rather than taxation. As large areas came under centralized control

caught the amorous as well as the political eye of the Incas: Tupac-Yupanqui married a Cañari princess, and Huanya-Capac, in turn, the daughter of the Duchicela king of Quito. In this way, Ecuador played a crucial part in the collapse of the Inca empire, for Huanya-Capac, seeking to unite his expansive domain through marriage, in fact achieved just the opposite.

Huanya-Capac had been born and raised in Tomebamba; his favorite son, Atahualpa, was the offspring of the Duchicela marriage and heir to the kingdom of Quito. Atahualpa's half-brother, Huascar, was descended from Inca lineage on both sides, and thus the legitimate heir. In 1527, Huascar ascended

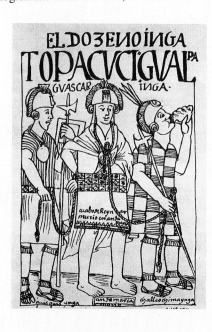

for the first time, a nascent sense of unity stirred; but it was an alien and oppressive regime, attracting little genuine loyalty.

The Ecuadorian Indians who suffered Inca domination were proud, handsome peoples. Cieza spoke of the Cañaris as "good-looking and well grown", and the native Quiteños as "more gentle and better disposed, and with fewer vices than any of those we have passed; and indeed than all Indians of Peru". They

Left, famous Inca masonry at Ingapirca ruins. Above left, Inca society boasted a well-ordered system of public works. Above right, the capture of Huascar during the Inca's bitter civil war.

the Cuzco throne, dividing the empire for the first time. Civil war soon broke out, over a province in central Ecuador, and continued for five years before Atahualpa defeated and imprisoned Huascar after a major battle near Ambato. (Some Ecuadorians interpret Atahualpa's victory in terms of Quiteño supremacy over the Incas, and consider this rivalry between Quito and Cuzco the source of the modern border dispute with Peru.)

Atahualpa, an able and intelligent leader, established the new capital of Cajamarca in northern Peru, indicating the importance of Ecuador to the empire. But the war had severely weakened both the infrastructure

INTO THE AMAZON

Once Quito had been settled, the *conquistadores* sought new adventures. Legends of *El Dorado* and *Canelos* (a Land of Cinnamon supposedly to the east), filled the mountain air. Francisco Pizarro appointed his brother, Gonzalo – "the best beloved of any man in Peru" – head of an expedition to find these rich and fabled destinations. On Christmas Day, 1539, the band departed Quito with 340 soldiers, 4,000 Indians, 150 horses, a flock of llamas, 4,000 swine, 900 dogs, and plentiful supplies.

Surviving an earthquake and an attack by hostile Indians, the expedition descended the Cordillera. At Sumaco on the Río Coca, they were joined by Francisco de Orellana, who had been called from his governorship of Guayaquil to be Gonzalo's lieutenant.

Hacking their way through the dense, swampy undergrowth along the riverbanks, the party encountered naked Indians; for their ignorance of *El Dorado*, Gonzalo had them burnt alive and torn to pieces by dogs.

Hampered by incessant heavy rain, and after a few months reduced to eating roots, berries, herbs, frogs, and snakes, they met more Indians who spoke of an inhabited city, supposedly rich in provisions and gold, just 10 days' tempting march away at the junction of the Coca and Napo rivers. A large raft was constructed, and 50 soldiers under de Orellana's command were dispatched to find the city and return post-haste with food: already 2,000 Indians and scores of Spaniards had starved to death.

Hearing nothing of the advance party after two months, Gonzalo trekked to the junction, but there was no city: the jungle Indians had lied to save their necks. In early June, 1542, the 80 surviving Spaniards from Pizarro's group staggered thankfully into Quito, "naked and barefooted".

By then, Francisco de Orellana was a continent away. The brigantine's provisions were exhausted when they reached the river junction: after three days, hunger was their constant companion.

Sailing back upstream against the current was impossible, and the difficulties of blazing a jungle trail could easily kill the weary men. Hearing the call of destiny and whispers of *El Dorado* across the wilderness, de Orellana sailed on.

For nine months the expedition drifted on the current, never knowing what lay around the next bend. Crude wooden crosses were erected as they progressed, purporting to claim the unconquerable lands in the king's name. They encountered many Indian tribes: some gave them food – turkeys, turtles, parrots and fruits – and ornaments of gold and silver; others attacked with spears and poisoned arrows, claiming many Spanish lives.

On one occasion, a reported 10,000 natives harrassed them from the shores and in canoes, but the Spaniards' arquebusses sent them in fearful flight.

De Orellana compiled a rudimentary dictionary during his leisure moments, and from a captive Indian woman he was able to learn of other Spaniards in the interior.

They heard frequent reports of a tribe they termed "Amazons", who lived in gold-plated houses. Near Obidos, the "Amazons" attacked – fearsome women, "very tall, robust, fair, with long hair twisted over their heads, skins round their loins, and bows and arrows in their hands". From this report, the great South American river and jungle area was given its name.

Finally, in a lowland area with many inhabited islands, de Orellana noticed signs of the ebb of the tide; and in August 1541, sailed into the open sea. For the first time, Europeans had traversed South America.

Today, if you want to emulate something of this experience but in rather more style and comfort, de Orellana has a namesake riverboat the *Flotel Orellana* – in style rather like something found on the Mississippi – which travels up and down the Amazon. Bookings can be made with Metropolitan Touring. ■

and the will of the Incas, and in a remarkable historical coincidence, it was only a matter of months before their death-knell sounded.

The bearded white strangers: Rarely have the pages of history been stalked by such a greedy, treacherous, bloodthirsty band of villains as the Spanish *conquistadores*. They hailed from the impoverished plains of Extremadura. With their homeland ravaged by 700 years of war with the Moors, the Spanish believed they had paid a heavy price for saving Christian Europe from Moslem domination. When news of the glittering Aztec treasury, snatched by Cortéz in 1521, sailed back to Spain, it fired the imaginations of the desperate farmers of Extremadura – and the

a year or so later. Near Tumbes, he found an Indian settlement whose inhabitants were similarly adorned, and so planned a full-scale invasion. Late in 1530, having traveled to Spain to secure the patronage of King Charles V and the title of Governor and Captain-General of Peru, Pizarro – this time with 180 men and 27 horses – landed in the Bay of San Mateo near Manabí.

For two years the *conquistadores* battled against the Indians – who were robbed, slaughtered, and recruited as guides – and against the treacherous terrain of mosquito-infested swamps and jungles, and frozen, cloud-buffeted mountain passes. Arriving exhausted in Cajamarca in November, 1532,

Church – and spawned dreams of other such empires in the New World.

The first *conquistadores* to set foot on Ecuadorian soil landed near Esmeraldas in September, 1526. They had been dispatched from Colombia by Francisco Pizarro to explore lands to the south. The party, led by Bartolomé Ruíz, discovered several villages of friendly natives wearing splendid objects of gold and silver, news of which prompted Pizarro himself, with just 13 men, to follow

Left, *conquistadores* abuse a press-ganged porter. **Above**, 16th-century depiction of the Spanish advance during the Conquest.

they formulated a plan to trap the Inca Atahualpa himself. At a pre-ordained meeting, the Inca and several thousand followers – many of whom were unarmed – entered the great square of Cajamarca. A Spanish priest outlined the tenets of Christianity to Atahualpa, calling upon him to embrace the faith and accept the sovereignty of Charles V. Predictably, Atahualpa refused, flinging the priest's Bible to the ground; Pizarro and his men rushed out from the surrounding buildings and set upon the astonished Incas. Of the Spaniards, only Pizarro himself was wounded when he seized Atahualpa, while the Incas were cut down in their hundreds.

The *conquistadores* had arrived, in their inimitable fashion. Atahualpa was imprisoned and a ransom demanded: a roomful of gold and silver weighing 24 tons was amassed, but the Inca was not freed. He was held for nine months, during which time he learnt Spanish and mastered the arts of writing, chess and cards. His authority was never questioned: female attendants dressed him in robes of vampire bat fur, fed him, and ceremoniously burnt everything he used. The Spaniards melted down the finely wrought treasures, and accused Atahualpa of treason. Curiously Pizarro baptized him "Fransisco", and then garotted him with an iron collar. An epic lament was composed by the Incas upon

gold was that they either ate precious metals, or else suffered from a disease cured only by gold. Their horses – to the Incas, strange and fearsome creatures – were "beasts who wear sandals of silver".

Conversely, the Spaniards perceived the natives as semi-naked barbarians who worshipped false gods, and were therefore good for nothing; Cieza's more positive remarks only illustrate his unique fair-mindedness. These perceptions – the Spanish intolerance, the Indian incomprehension – survive in diluted forms today, constituting Ecuador's fundamental social disunity.

While Pizarro continued southward towards Cuzco, his lieutenant, Sebastian de

Atahualpa's death: "Hail is falling/Lightning strikes/The sun is sinking/It has become forever night". To this day, Atahualpa is considered by many to have been the first great Ecuadorian.

Two worlds collide: To the Incas, the Spanish conquest was a cosmic mistake, an apocalyptic reversal of the natural order. In the eyes of a 16th-century native chronicler, Waman Puma, these strangers were "all enshrouded from head to foot, with their faces completely covered in wool... men who never sleep". The Incas had no money or concept of private wealth: the only possible explanation for the Spaniards' craving for

Benalcázar, was dispatched to Piura to ship the Inca booty to Panama. But trouble was brewing, for rumors of these treasures had traveled north, and Pedro de Alvarado set out from Guatemala to conquer Quito. Alvarado was an abomination even in this company: his actions against the Maya, whom he "burned for the sake of peace and welfare in this land", prompted Cortéz to call him a madman. With 500 men and 120 horses, he landed at Manta in early 1534, and during an epic trek similar to Pizarro's decimated the coastal Indians.

Hearing of this, Benalcázar quickly mounted his own expedition to capture Quito. Approaching Riobamba in May, he encountered a massive Quiteño army under the Inca general Quisquis. Fifty thousand Indians, the largest Inca force ever assembled, were deployed, hopelessly outnumbering the Spaniards. But under the cover of night, the latter detoured around Lake Colta and returned to the Imperial Highway north of Riobamba. The Indians, owing no loyalty to the Incas, mutinied and dispersed; the best opportunity to defeat the Spanish was lost. For his part, Alvarado was paid a handsome sum by Pizarro to abandon his Ecuadorian excursion and return quietly to Guatemala.

The circle of history was drawn. Benalcázar marched northward with thousands of Cañaris and Puruhás in his ranks, for both tribes sought revenge on the brutal Incas. Arriving in Quito in December, 1534, he found the city in ruins; Rumiñahui, the Inca general, had destroyed and evacuated it rather than lose it intact. Atop Cara and Inca rubble, with a mere 206 inhabitants, the Villa de San Francisco de Quito was founded on December 6; and Guayaquil the following year. Rumiñahui launched a counter-attack a month later, but was captured, and subsequently tortured and executed.

By 1549, the conquest was complete: a mere 2,000 Spaniards had subjugated an estimated 500,000 Indians. The number of casualties is impossible to ascertain, but approximately 20,000 Indian porters died in this 15-year period, while starvation, disease, war and suicide claimed many more. Chroniclers record that mothers even slaughtered their newborn babies to free them from the torments of the new age.

The Spanish yoke: With the restless natives quietened, the *conquistadores* fought each other for the prizes: not until 1554 did the Spanish Crown finally subdue them. In 1539, Pizarro appointed his brother Gonzalo governor of Quito, but when the first Viceroy to Peru passed through shortly thereafter, he found the colonists in revolt. Gonzalo fought off the Viceroy's forces in 1546, only to be deposed and executed by another official army two years later. During Gonzalo's governorship, an expedition was mounted to explore the lands east of Quito: under the

mesmerized, renegade leadership of Francisco de Orellana, the first transcontinental journey by Europeans was made.

When Cortéz cried, "I don't want land – give me gold!", he spoke for all *conquistadores*. But the immediately available treasures, however great, were soon exhausted and the area of occupation became one of production. The land and its inhabitants were quickly divided among the *conquistadores*, and the first settlers soon followed. Of the Quito region, in contrast to the damp, ghostly barrenness of Lima, Cieza wrote: "The country is very pleasant, and particularly resembles Spain in its pastures and climate". The "Avenue of the Volcanoes", the strip of land

between 1,500 and 3,000 meters (4,000 to 8,000 ft) high, and 40 to 60 km (25 to 40 miles) wide running the length of Ecuador between two towering rows of volcanoes, was ideal farmland. In addition, workshops were established to produce textiles, and slaves were brought from Africa to man the coastal cacao plantations. Ecuador escaped the murderous excesses of mining that befell Peru and Bolivia as the disappointed Spanish found few precious metals here.

Along with horses, pigs and cattle were introduced, and Ecuador nurtured the first crops of bananas and wheat in South America. Many Spaniards consorted with Indian

Opposite, colonial art in the Museo Guayasamín, Quito. **Right**, the *mestizo* chronicler Waman Puma portrays the corruption of the Spanish clergy.

women, and imported diseases such as smallpox, influenza, measles, cholera and syphilis swept through the population. But with much of the highlands and all of the Oriente so inaccessible, Spanish settlement – in comparison with other colonies like Mexico and Argentina – was relatively light. In this way, geography saved the Ecuadorian Indians from possible extermination (although with the current taming of the Oriente, deadly interracial contact continues).

Colonial administration was based on the twin pillars of the *encomienda* system and the Church. The former effected the transition from conquest to occupation. The *encomendero*, or landowner, was responsible for

Church, as dying *hacendados* donated their estates to secure passage to heaven. With an eye to survival, the Indian serfs tacitly accepted the Catholic faith, often embellishing it with their own ancient, animistic beliefs and ceremonies. Mere days after Benalcázar founded Quito, the cornerstone of South America's first major church, the San Francisco, was laid. Following the Franciscans came the Jesuits and the Dominicans, each enriching themselves at the Indians' expense while claiming a monopoly on salvation.

Methods of conversion were usually brutal: children aged four were separated from their families to receive the catechism; lapsing converts were imprisoned, publicly

the productivity of his plot and the religious conversion of his laborers. As they had done with the Incas, the Indians brought tribute, in the form of animals, vegetables and blankets, to their new masters; their labor was unrewarded, but withheld at their peril. For their own safety, *encomenderos* were forbidden to live on their estates; instead, they resided in well-guarded Spanish communities. It was a brutally efficient form of feudalism whereby the Spanish Crown not only pacified the *conquistadores* with a life of luxury, but also gained an empire with no risk or expense.

For centuries, the main landowner was the

flogged, and shaved of their hair. Some dissolute priests kept Indian women in their houses, and the *mestizo*, or mixed-blooded race, flourished. On the strength of such practices, Quito – the seat of a royal *audencia* from 1563 – grew into a religious and intellectual center during the 17th century as seminaries and universities were established.

Scientific curiosity: After centuries of piratic raids, in which Sir Francis Drake and William Dampier figured prominently, Ecuador hosted several pioneering scientific and geographic expeditions. The first of these was mounted by the French Academy of Sciences in 1735 to measure a degree of the meridian near the equator, and thus determined the circumference of the earth. Surveying with pendulums and plumb lines, Charles Marie de la Condamine and Pierre Bouguer fixed the global measurements on which our metric system is based. Less accurately, they declared Mt Chimborazo – Ecuador's highest peak at 6,310 meters (20,800 ft) – the highest in the world, a misconception that lasted 90 years. La Condamine also conducted the first scientific exploration of the Amazon, and mapped his journey from Quito to Cayenne.

The German explorer and scientist Alexander von Humboldt arrived in Ecuador in 1802. His discoveries, which laid the foundations for the sciences of physical geography and meteorology, made him – apart from Napoleon – the most famous man in Europe. He was the first to measure falling temperature against rising elevation; to chart isothermal lines; to explain the links between plant composition and physical conditions; and to measure the lessening of the earth's magnetic force from the poles to the equator. He coined the phrase "Avenue of the Volcanoes", and proved the connection between

the occurrence of volcanoes in linear groups, and subterranean fissures in igneous rock. His name has been given to the cold current of the South-East Pacific, and to a penguin.

The pre-eminent scientific visitor, however, was Charles Darwin, who studied the life forms of the Galápagos Islands for five weeks in 1835. Although he bypassed mainland Ecuador, it was while in the Galápagos (which had been annexed by Ecuador three years previously) that he made many of the observations upon which he based his theories of evolution and the mutability of species.

Push for independence: Meanwhile, from the the bleeding soul of the Spaniards' oppressive socioeconomic actions sprouted, in

reaction, violent popular uprisings and nascent cries of "Liberty!" As early as 1592, the lower clergy supported merchants and urban workers in the Alcabalas Revolution, protesting against increased taxes on food and fabrics. The authorities put an end to the agitation after 10 months by executing 24 conspirators and publicly displaying their heads in iron cages.

During the 18th century, the ideas of the European Enlightenment crept slowly towards Quito University. The works of Voltaire, Leibnitz, Descartes and Rousseau, and the revolutions in France and the United States gave intellectual succor to hesitant

Left, colonial depiction of weaving; a *criollo* noble. **Above**, monument to the meeting of Simón Bolívar and José de San Martín, Guayaquil.

colonial libertarians. In Quito, the physician-journalist Eugenio Espejo – born in 1747 of an Indian father and mulatto mother – emerged as leader of the anti-imperialists.

Although only recently accorded his rightful place alongside Atahualpa as a great Ecuadorian, Espejo was a pioneering, fearless humanist. He published books, both satiric and bitterly combative, on the subject of Spanish colonialism; and as founding editor of the liberal newspaper *Primicias de la Cultura de Quito*, was perhaps the first American journalist.

He was jailed several times, exiled to Bogotá for four years, and finally died impoverished, aged 48, in a damp Quito dungeon.

orders and attained greatness, and Pizarro answered to no-one – the ethos that these men bequeathed their progeny was devoid of ideas and morality. Through the age of *caudillos* in the 19th century, and of military dictators in the 20th, Ecuador has been viewed as a treasure, like Inca gold, conveniently there for the taking.

Ecuador's first step towards independence was also its first coup. In response to the fall of Spain to Napoleon in 1808, a new wave of repressive measures was enforced in the colonies, prompting members of the *criollo* oligarchy to seize power in Quito in August 1809, and imprison the President of the *Audencia*. Within a month, loyalist troops from

From his cell, he wrote to the President of the *Audencia*: "I have produced writings for the happiness of the country, as yet a barbarian one". His achievement is doubly remarkable given his lowly birth, and his name now graces the National Library and countless streets in Ecuador.

Power of the sword: As the Crown's grip on its colonies began to loosen, the ghost of the *conquistadores* stirred from its restless slumber. From the dawn of the Spanish era, money and muscle had meant power; laws, constitutions and governments were, and remain, subject to the greed of reckless individuals. Cortéz and de Orellana disobeyed

Bogotá and Lima had displaced and executed the usurpers, but the subsequent reprisals were so harsh that two years later a second rebellion broke out. This time, a constitution for an independent state was formulated, but the uprising remained confined to Quito, and so was likewise easily suppressed.

The continent was, however, moving inexorably towards liberation. With English support, Simon Bolívar – *El Libertador* – took on the Spanish loyalists in New Granada (Colombia) and his native Venezuela in 1818. In October, 1820, Guayaquil ousted local authorities and established a revolutionary junta; and following the Battle of

Pichincha in May, 1822, when forces led by Antonio José de Sucre resoundingly defeated the royalist army, Quito was liberated.

A few weeks later, Bolívar arrived in Quito, where he met the beautiful, illegitimate Ecuadorian *criolla* Manuela Sáenz. She became his jealous mistress, accompanying him from camp to battlefield to presidential palace, as much in love with the cause of liberation as with its manly embodiment. When Bolívar quit Bogotá in May 1830, bound for disillusioned exile, he left a bitter Manuela behind; upon his death seven months later, she tried to take her own life. She passed her final days selling sweets and tobacco in a small town in Peru.

moments – Bolívar's obstinacy sent an exasperated San Martín into European exile.

As Bolívar decreed, Gran Colombia was formed in 1823, incorporating Ecuador, Colombia and Venezuela. It lasted just seven years: in September, 1830, the 30 year-old military commander of Quito, General Juan José Flores – a Venezuelan who married into the Quito aristocracy – announced the creation of the Republic of Ecuador. The new nation's population stood at approximately 700,000 and its ill-defined borders were based on those of the colonial *Audencia*. That same year, Sucre – Bolívar's chosen successor – was assassinated en route from Bogotá to his home in Quito, prompting Bolívar to grieve,

Bolívar was the archetypal *criollo* – ambitious, paternalistic, impatient, never doubting his methods or goals. His brilliance sprang from the singular intensity of his vision, which brought liberation to a continent but failed to appreciate the dynamics of the new nations. His Argentinean counterpart, José de San Martín, was stoic, taciturn, and self-effacing – Bolívar's ideal complement. But when they had their only meeting, in Guayaquil in July, 1822 to plot the future of Peru and Gran Colombia – one of Ecuador's greatest

Left, workers on a banana plantation in the 1880s. **Above**, Quito street, around 1890.

"They have slain Abel". On the northern shores of the continent he had transformed, *El Libertador* died a broken man: overcome with frustration, he said of his life's work, "We have ploughed the sea".

False freedom: The inequalities of the colonial social structure were preserved with ruthless duplicity by the "new" Ecuadorian elite. While cries of "Patria" and "Freedom" echoed across the country, the poor remained enslaved in workshops, on *haciendas* and plantations. National power was up for grabs, and the struggle between the Conservatives of Quito and the Liberals of Guayaquil, which has characterized Ecuadorian politics, began immediately. Flores made a deal with the opposition Liberal leader, Vicente Roca-fuerte, to alternate the presidency, with Flores retaining military control. In 1843, however, he refused to step down from his second presidency; Rocafuerte was bribed into exile, and Flores held power for two more years before being toppled by the Liberals. His bizarre response was to organize a Spanish invasion of Ecuador, which was only aborted when Great Britain intervened at the request of other South American nations.

In the first of several periods of chronic political disorder in Ecuador, the next 15 years saw 11 governments and three constitutions come and go, and the economy stag-

ture him, clad in black, carrying a heavy wooden cross on his shoulders through the streets, followed by his entire cabinet.

Freedom of speech and press were non-existent, political opponents were imprisoned or exiled. But as the country's mind regressed, its body matured: hospitals, roads and railways were constructed; schools were opened to Indians and women for the first time; Guayaquil's port facilities were improved; and new crops enhanced agricultural productivity. From this important era emerged a spirit of national identity.

Moreno's critics were many, and trod a dangerous path: they remembered the fate of Colonel Francis Hall, an Englishman who

nate. Border disputes sprang up with both Peru and Colombia, with the mayor of Guayaquil actually ceding his city and southern Ecuador to Peru. This morass was tidied up by one of the strongmen of Ecuadorian history, Gabriel García Moreno.

Rising from humble origins to the rectorship of the University of Quito, Moreno was a many-faceted man. During his decade, the nation became a theocracy where only practicing Catholics were allowed to vote. He renamed the best regiments "Guardians of the Virgin" and "Soldiers of the Infant Jesus". He frequently indulged in acts of physical self-humiliation: sepia photographs cap-

had fought under Bolívar and later edited the liberal news-sheet, *El Quiteño Libre*. Annoyed by Hall's unbridled criticisms, President Flores had him shot and his body hung naked from a lamp-post. In the tradition of Espejo, a Quiteño journalist named Juan Montalvo railed against Moreno's tyrannical clericalism – becoming, in the process, one of Latin America's leading intellectuals. From his enforced exile in Colombia, he rejoiced upon hearing of Moreno's assassination in 1875: "My pen has killed him".

Travelers' views: In *Four Years Among Spanish-Americans*, Friedrich Hassaurek paints a comprehensive portrait of life in

Moreno's Ecuador. The US Minister-Resident in Ecuador from 1861 to 1866, Hassaurek found "convents instead of printing presses, military barracks instead of schoolhouses". Ecuadorians flocked to the church in their leisure time to "break the monotony of daily life". Traveling with complete safety on roads built, as the locals say, for birds and not men, he noticed the Indians doing "more work than all the other races together". He mourned the predominance of personalities over principles in political life, with the populace diverted from revolution by frequent bullfights.

English mountaineer Edward Whymper journeyed to Ecuador in 1879–80, where he

all work until *mañana* (tomorrow). A foreign businessman informed him: "I never consider a transaction terminated unless I give my customer a whipping". The Indians, living in abject misery, exhibited "hospitable instincts… and an extreme timidity, heightened by an all-pervading mistrust."

As the century turned, the liberal President Eloy Alfaro managed to improve the Indians' lot, modernize the legal code, and separate the Church and State before an incensed pro-clerical mob tore him to pieces. Along with assassination, nepotism and mindless populism have characterized the political landscape. José María Velasco Ibarra, who enjoyed five presidential terms be-

became the first man to conquer a host of peaks, including Chimborazo, Cotopaxi and Sangay. At Guayaquil, he found life "too easy for the lower orders", who "breakfast on chocolate, dine on bananas and coconut, and fall back at night on pineapples". Continuing to Quito by steamer and muletrain, he met the President, General Veintemilla, who rose and fell through coups, and had little respect for Moreno's clerical legacy. Whymper found the Ecuadorians, although polite, overwhelmed by ennui and leaving

Left, river boat in the Oriente, around 1900. **Above**, *indígenas* on hunger strike in the 1970s.

tween 1934 and 1961, was an unabashed crowd-pleaser, but an inept administrator. He was known as "The National Personification" for his ability to transcend regional barriers, and on one occasion cried, "Give me a balcony and I will be president again!"

War in the Amazon: One of Velasco's most popular and inflammatory whipping boys was the border dispute with Peru. Ecuador was originally more than double its present size, but Brazil, Colombia and Peru have each taken generously from its portion of Amazonia. In 1941, Peru snatched almost half of Ecuador's territory in an invasion that was largely uncontested as President Arroyo, fearing a coup, kept most of his troops in Quito. Much of El Oro, a region rich in gold, oil and coffee, was lost, though Ecuador has subsequently reneged on the Rio de Janeiro Protocol of 1942 that ratifies this. Several skirmishes have broken out since then, the most recent one (1995) developing into a rather more serious conflict that lasted 3 months, cost both sides several hundred casualties and had a damaging effect on the Ecuadorian economy. A ceasefire was finally held with Ecuador accepting the Rio Protocol. Further hostilities remain a constant possibility but International observers are helping to maintain a tenuous peace. This is Ecuador's main international dispute, and

massive oil deposits in the Oriente has – in addition to changing the face of that neglected region – permanently shifted Ecuador's economic emphasis away from agriculture. Oil is now the major industry, controlled by the state-run Petroecuador and several multinationals; in 1994 the value of oil exports was over a third of the nation's exports bringing in more than $1,000 million.

Democratic leaders: Ecuador was the first Latin American country to return to true democracy. In 1978, the army drew up a constitution – the latest in more than a dozen – which extended the vote to Ecuador's 750,000 illiterate adults. The center-left government of Jaime Roldós, elected the follow-

war is a constant, if unlikely, possibility.

The economy has expanded from its original bases of cacao and textiles to include coffee, Panama hats, shrimp farming, fresh flowers and particularly bananas. Under the iron fist of the Boston-based United Fruit Company, Ecuador became – and remains – the world's leading exporter of bananas. The accompanying ethos of rampant capitalism produced a crisis in the archaic *hacienda* system in the 1950s as, for the first time, money spread beyond the few hundred dominant *criollo* families. The long-overdue land reforms of 1964 further eroded traditional socio-economic ties, and the discovery of

ing year, launched massive literacy and housing programs. Emphasizing issues instead of personalities, the government increased workers' wages and encouraged the emergence of a politically articulate middle class, and of mass-based organizations such as peasant co-operatives and labor unions. An economic crisis loomed as oil prices dropped and payments on foreign debt fell due; for a while rumors of a military coup were rife.

In 1981, Roldós died in a plane crash, sending the nation into mourning. Vice-President Osvaldo Hurtado fulfilled his pledges to serve his full term, continue Roldós reforms, and maintain civil liberties – despite the added difficulty of the great *El Niño* floods of late 1982, which ruined banana and rice crops and destroyed roads and railways.

Leon Febres Cordero, a Conservative, won the 1984 elections. A Machiavellian figure who, despite leading the opposition during the military era, had several times tried to engineer his own presidential appointment, Febres oversaw sustained economic growth. His reputation suffered severely when, in 1987, he was kidnapped by troops loyal to a mutinous general. Febres quickly secured his release by granting the general an amnesty – hardly the action of a courageous leader. While four of his former ministers fled the country to avoid arrest, Febres faced charges

flation fell, the foreign debt was serviced regularly and foreign investors continued to be attracted, both under Borja and under his successor, Sixto Durán Bellén of the Christian Social Party, who was elected in 1992. Sixto has not been particularly popular as president, although the conflict over borders with Peru did yield a temporary surge in support. One unpopular policy was the introduction of the privatisation programme intended for telecommunictions, electricity and parts of Petroecuador. Congress, the majority opposition, stalled the programme.

Jaime Nebot of the Christian Social Party looks set to lead Ecuador through the late 1990s, though there is likely to be some

of misuse of public funds for a payment of US$150,000 to an Israeli counter-insurgency adviser, who supposedly helped dismantle the *Alfaro Vive Carajo*! (loosely, Alfaro Lives, Damn it!) guerrilla movement.

Elections in 1988 brought to power President Rodrigo Borja Cevallos, a Social Democrat from Quito. Like the Roldós-Hurtado administration, he set an honest, competent political course. Civil disturbances such as transport workers' strikes and student riots over price rises were handled leniently. In-

Left, political graffiti, Otavalo. **Above**, Rodrigo Borja, president from 1988 to 1992.

electoral competition from the independent Ricardo Noboa, a former CSP congressman for Guayaquil and also from General Jose Gallardo, who has been the defence minister. Both Noboa and Gallardo stress the alleviation of poverty.

Ecuador remains a peaceful haven in a troubled region, and its population of about 10 million – split evenly between the coast and the highlands – is not so unwieldy as to prohibit genuine improvements in living standards. Having suffered unscrupulous leadership and avoidable poverty for centuries, Ecuador could be approaching prosperous stability.

Gold has long been a theme of Ecuadorian myths. The lost city of El Dorado was once believed to exist in the country's Amazon basin, while rumors of Inca mines and buried treasure on the eastern slopes of the Andes have been passed down for generations. Little wonder, then, that when a new source of wealth was unearthed in the mysterious Oriente – petroleum oil – it was nicknamed *el oro negro* (black gold).

Oil has occupied a key place in recent Ecuadorian history: it has changed frontiers and caused governments to rise and fall; it has paved the roads, connected the regions, fueled urban growth and penetrated the Amazonian jungle. Since oil exports began in the early 1970s, they have come to provide half the country's foreign revenue and up to 50 percent of the state budget.

Early uses: Petroleum oil from surface deposits has actually been used in Ecuador for centuries. The native population used to dig pits that filled with oil within a few days, then evaporate it to make tar. It served them for caulking canoes, waterproofing arms and utensils, for torches and in medicine. Later, Spanish ships used to stop off for tarring at the Santa Elena Peninsula before starting the long trip home.

The first oil wells on the Peninsula began to operate in 1925 and still produce small amounts today. In the meantime, a great mystery was woven around the reality or fiction of huge oil deposits in the Oriente.

During the 1930s, oil companies began exploring in the Oriente but their findings were kept secret. Even if large reserves had been found, the region was as yet too inaccessible to justify the cost of production. These were years of fierce competition between European and American companies to gain concessions in reserve areas – with Royal Dutch Shell and Standard Oil of New Jersey making the most strident claims. In 1942, following an invasion by Peru, Ecuador was pressed into signing away two-fifths of its territory to its southern neighbor, Peru, though ever since it has questioned the legitimacy of this treaty. Almost three decades

later, Ecuadorian writer Jaime Galarza caused an uproar with his polemical book *El Festín del Petroleo* (The Oil Feast), in which he argued that the real motive for the war was rivalry between foreign oil companies for concessions in the Oriente.

Yet, in 1949, President Galo Plaza surprised the country with his declaration: "The Oriente is a myth." He denied the existence of oil and put paid, for a time, to the idea that the Oriente was to be the country's salvation.

It was only after a further two decades that significant oil finds were finally made public. But as the first pumps churned into action in the early 1970s, and as oil began to flow through the new trans-Ecuadorian pipeline that stretches up 4,100 meters (13,700 ft) over the Andes and down to the Port of Esmeraldas, a new myth was born: that of the superabundance of the Oriente oil fields. Experts spoke of reserves greater than those of Venezuela, even comparing them to those of the Middle East.

The following years were gradually to bring disillusionment, as many of the exploratory wells proved dry. Today, even though Ecuador is the second largest oil exporter of South America, it still produces less than 400,000 barrels a day, and present reserves will last only 10 to 15 years. All the same, for a poor country, even this small amount has made a big difference.

The oil explosion: The first shipment of oil that left Esmeraldas in August 1972 set off a virtual explosion of social and economic changes. Six months earlier, a military dictator with nationalist leanings had taken power and set about getting a better deal for the Ecuadorian government from the petroleum companies. At the same time, world oil prices rose dramatically. Public income quadrupled in the space of only three years. For the first time, the government could count on its own source of finance without bowing to the whims and dictates of the agricultural exporting oligarchy.

The military government built roads, constructed an oil refinery, provided credit for agriculture and acquired sophisticated equipment for the armed forces. It set up the state oil company, CEPE (now Petroecuador).

Left, oilman on a dusty road through the Oriente.

Meanwhile, thousands of new jobs were created in the public service, attracting people from the provinces to the capital and stimulating the growth of an urban middle class. The so-called *burocracia* grew from less than 100,000 employees in 1972 to almost half a million today.

Paved roads, cheap domestic gasoline and internal air travel began to draw the country together, increasing commercial exchange between regions and breaking the isolation of much of the Sierra. New areas of industry developed, albeit marginally, and oil revenue flowed into the building trade. At the same time, new social demands emerged, and the labor union movement gained force.

The lean years: But the fat years of the 1970s were followed by the lean years of the 1980s. First the foreign debt crisis hit, with Ecuador being stung by increasing interest rates on its many loans. Then oil prices bottomed out. Ironically, the oil bonanza had itself been one of the causes of Ecuador's heavy foreign debt: during the 1970s, readily available foreign credit had induced governments to accept large loans, confident in the power of oil money to repay them.

As the economy subsided into the vicious circle of inflation and recession, social problems multiplied. Even so, with oil dollars still trickling in and cheap domestic gaso-

line, the social impact of the debt crisis in Ecuador was less severe than in other Latin American countries. Then disaster struck. In March 1987, an earthquake on the eastern slopes of the Andes unleashed waves of earth and rock that swept away the oil pipe-line in a stretch of some 40 km (25 miles), cutting the artery of the nation's economy.

For most Ecuadorians, the immediate economic impact of this disaster completely overshadowed the grave ecological consequences. The country was in crisis, the northeast was cut off and few scientists or officials could reach the region to witness the damage to the environment, which only began to be partially understood months later. Millions of gallons of oil had been spilt in the forest, and tidal waves of mud and oil had washed down the rivers, destroying banks, riverside vegetation and wildlife, and leaving the rivers dead. No attempt was made to reduce the ecological damage.

Those who did witness the devastation were the local Indian population. For them it was the most dramatic incident in a long series which little by little had been contaminating the soil, lakes and rivers. Environmentalists estimate that at least 30 major oil spills have occurred along the pipe-line in the last 18 years, unleashing in all close to 17 million gallons of oil into the environment – more than was spilt off Alaska's shores in the *Exxon Valdez* tanker accident. Clean up work has been, at best, rudimentary.

With support from the environmental lobby, the Indians began to create awareness of the problem at home and abroad, putting pressure on the government and oil companies to clean up their act. As a result, the Ecuadorian Energy Ministry has adopted an environmental protection policy and, in 1990, the oil companies operating in Ecuador signed an agreement to adopt similar measures. But the oil industry's damage to the environment is not only due to spills. The oil companies build roads through the jungle, giving access to a flood of colonizers. These refugees from the coast and Sierra cut down trees to plant crops, displace the local Indian population and scare away the wildlife.

Attempt at protection: The most controversial area for oil production is the Yasuni National Park, which covers some 7,020 sq. km (2,700 sq. miles) in the north-east and has been declared a "biosphere reserve" by

UNESCO because of the amazing variety of wild-life to be found there (an incomplete study has identified 500 varieties of birds, 200 different animals and 473 kinds of fish, many of them exclusive to this area). Huaorani Indians inhabit the park.

Unfortunately, it is precisely in this park that recent oil prospecting has shown most promising results, opening new hopes for the economy, but provoking fierce opposition from Indians and environmentalists. Although a large area of the park was recently recognized by the government as Huaorani territory, the land titles do not include rights over the subsoil, which belongs to the state.

CONOCO, the oil company originally contracted to do most of the oil exploration in the park pulled out because of international pressure and sold its interest to MAXUS, a less visible Texas based company. Oil began flowing out of the project site in 1994. MAXUS has attempted to minimize the impact on the park by using innovative technologies such as drilling 10 wells from a single platform similar to offshore drilling methods. Most of the water extracted from the wells is reinjected, avoiding the previous practice of polluting the rivers with high levels of toxic heavy metals and hydrocarbons.

The biggest potential impact is the construction of a 120-km (75-mile) long all-weather access road. So far colonists have been kept out by guard stations set up by MAXUS and the Huaorani, preventing deforestation along the road. An attempt was also made to limit the area cleared but a combination of hilly terrain and heavy rains has resulted in large and frequent landslides which threaten to break the buried pipeline and have silted up many of the small streams.

Scientists working on an assessment of the project admit that actual impacts have been minimal compared to a similar oil road built to the west about 15 years ago, the Via Acua, where deforestation and oil spills have decimated the rainforest near the road. Still they fear impact from the 30-meter (98-ft) wide clearing may reach far into the forest. They are studying the effects of the noise and dust that keep birds and animals away, the influence on water quality and sedimentation of

the surface runoff, and changes in behavior of tree-dwelling animals that are blocked by a break in the forest canopy.

A great amount of money is being spent to study and correct environmental problems, but the oil is costing more to produce than it can be sold for on the international market. Environmentalists, ethnic organizations and a growing number of people in the highlands of Ecuador are arguing that oil exploration and production in the remote areas of Amazon does not make sense economically. The growing income from ecotourism and pharmaceutical products will soon outpace oil.

Others argue that initial infrastructure investments will make the project economical-

ly viable in the future and will set an interesting precedent which could be followed by oil companies working in other tropical rainforests. Unfortunately it is an experiment that will not have a result for tens of years.

Meanwhile, if Ecuador does not find new oil reserves within the next decade, it may cease to export "black gold" towards the beginning of the next century. And that means it must find alternative forms of development. One of these could be gold-mining: if it proves true, as many people believe, that Ecuador is "sitting on a gold-mine", it may yet become "the country of gold" once again. Or maybe that is just another legend.

Left, the petrol boom began an invasion of the Amazon in the 1970s. **Above**, knocking a highway through the jungle.

Like other Andean countries, Ecuadorian society reflects divisions that can be traced back to the Spanish Conquest of the early 16th century. But the country's people have been shaped as much by Ecuador's wild geography as its history: the racial makeup, temperament and outlook of Ecuadorians is radically different in the coast, Sierra and jungle. As the more fair-minded Ecuadorians say about the country's variety, "If Quito doesn't do it for you, then Guayaquil will." And if you still want something different, then try the Oriente frontier.

Until the discovery of oil two decades ago began an urban explosion, Ecuador was an almost completely rural society. To a large extent it still is: how its people behave and think is closely related to their relationship with the land, and even modern urban life conserves elements of traditional, rural customs. To understand the differences between Ecuador's three regions, one should first look to village life.

Images from the countryside: The typical *campesino* (peasant) of the Sierra works hard to obtain a meagre production from rocky, volcanic soil. Andean families live in contact with an abrupt environment, where bare mountains descend into shelving ravines and gentle valleys. The land is rarely flat, except on the valley bottom, which generally belongs to the rich landowners. So he must use ingenuity to terrace and cultivate the steep mountain sides on slopes with up to 60-degree angles where the topsoil is easily washed away by rain and, later, load the crops on his back to get them down to home or market. In the cool mountain air, the fierce heat of the midday sun is quickly lost in the shadow of the afternoon, so he rarely takes off his poncho which protects him from both the sun's rays and the cold.

In harmony with this environment and way of life, the typical *serrano* tends to be reserved, melancholic and contemplative.

He is tough, patient, frugal and resigned to the difficulties of life, but also mistrustful. And he is more submissive than his counterpart from the Costa. Yet at another level, his emotions are easily stirred and he can be elated and vivacious when his imagination is fired. Andean music, with its plaintive tones, melodic pipes and sorrowful, fatalistic lyrics, admirably expresses this temperament.

The peasant of the Costa lives in contact with the wild and abundant nature of the green lowlands, where the warm climate and

fertile soil make daily living easier. But life is also more uncertain because of the dangers of diseases, wild animals, floods and other hazards. Like his environment, the *costeño* tends to be more easygoing and exuberant than his cousin from the Sierra, but is also more uncouth and quick-tempered. He is careless about tomorrow and shows a casual disregard for the susceptibilities of others.

The Oriente is a case apart, as it has only begun to be colonized in recent years, and represents scarcely 2 percent of the population. The Indians there have lived for centuries in relative isolation and their way of being is very different from that of the Indi-

Preceding pages: impromptu concert at Otavalo market; light refreshment at Quito bullfight; steaming afternoon on the Amazon frontier. Left, marcher in the "Mama Negra" parade, Latacunga. Right, laundry in the Napo River.

ans of the Sierra who have suffered long years of discrimination. Lighthearted and self-confident, they are accustomed to a pleasant and generous natural environment and a free lifestyle. This situation has begun to change with the presence of timber and oil companies that are endangering their environment, as well as encroaching colonization that has brought about an accelerated process of assimilation of Indian people.

These natural differences between the regions have been accentuated by slow and hazardous transport and difficult communications. But within each region, society is broken up by the diverse racial and ethnic origins of its inhabitants and the resulting

or estate. These large properties were the main pole of production. Their owners were usually descendants of the Spanish *conquistadores* who controlled the country's economy and politics. The landowner would allow Indian families a small lot of land for their own subsistence in exchange for their labor on his land.

This form of dependence, akin to European feudalism, still exists in a few areas, though it was officially abolished in 1971.

Each estate would also maintain a local church to take care of the spiritual side of things, as well as keeping the Indians in line. And the more enlightened landowners would provide a minimum of social care.

racial mixes: mainly Indian, Spanish and *mestizo* (mixed race) in the Sierra; these plus Africans, half-castes and *sambos* (a cross of Indian and black) in the Costa.

Traditional Andean society: The rigid social order that reigned in the Sierra from colonial times until the land reform of 1964 is the basis from which modern society emerged and accounts for many of its present features. Cut off by the difficult mountain passes from the rest of the universe and under the strong influence of the Catholic Church, Andean society engendered a world of traditional values centred around the family.

The nucleus of rural life was the *hacienda*,

As for the *mestizos*, they were employed on the estates as managers, stewards or clerks. They were in charge of running the estate and, as many landowners preferred to live in the towns, they wielded great power over all those under their authority. Not surprisingly, the steward was generally hated by the Indians, and this fuelled racial animosity between Indians and *mestizos*.

Moreover, the typical Spanish settler in this part of America considered work degrading, whereas the Indian valued it and disapproved of laziness. This was a further element in racial tension, since the Spaniard expected the Indian to work all out for him, but at the same time despised him for doing so. A similar attitude is still present in much of the middle-class today (and notoriously so in the public service), which has coined the motto: *El vivo vive del tonto, y el tonto de su trabajo* ("The clever person lives off the fool, and the fool lives off his work").

The traditional social order of the Sierra began to disintegrate from the 1960s with the introduction of agrarian reform. In the face of rapid population growth and increasing unrest among the peasants, who were pressing for more land, the authorities passed legislation to break up the larger estates and *haciendas* and hand over uncultivated land to the peasants.

plantations or a piece of undeveloped land to till. Thus, in the space of a century, the inhabitants of the Costa passed from being a small fraction to slightly more than half the total population.

As for the *haciendas* of the Costa, their owners tended to be more business-minded and enterprising than their Sierra counterparts and they generally did not mind dirtying their hands alongside their wage-earning farmhands.

Rough living conditions in the frontier colonies meant that many of the traditional values and customs of the Sierra were abandoned, creating a more liberal and egalitarian society. Greater contact with the outside

Frontier settlements: While the Sierra has mainly produced food for local consumption, the Costa, with the advantage of its navigable rivers, sea-ports and extensive fertile plains, has been developed over the past 100 years for export crops. Cocoa, bananas and, more recently, cultivated shrimps have each had their boom period.

Landless peasants from the Sierra travelled to the coast in search of work on the

Left, Sierra *indígena* from Cañar; many descendants of African slaves populate the coast. Above, healer from Santo Domingo de los Colorados; schoolgirl from Quito.

world via the seaports and the arrival of foreigners accelerated the change.

Today the Ecuadorian Costa has a Caribbean flavour. In fact, Guayaquil has been referred to as "the last port of the Caribbean", even though it is in the wrong ocean. Ecuadorians claim to recognize what region a person is from by the way he or she walks: supple and with graceful ease in the Costa; plodding and sure-footed in the Sierra.

The urban explosion: In the 1970s, following the discovery of petroleum deposits in the Oriente, Ecuador began to export oil, which meant more jobs and the promise of new opportunities in the cities. At the same time, those peasants who had been unable to get land under the agrarian reform had to leave the *haciendas* and many sought work in the towns.

In just two decades, one quarter of Ecuador's population moved from the countryside to the towns, causing an urban explosion which the country was unprepared to meet. Housing, water supplies and electric power could not keep up with demand. Today Ecuador is short of an estimated one million homes needed to house its population. Half the existing homes lack running water and sewage and a third have no electricity.

With the foreign debt crisis of the 1980s, unemployment increased dramatically. This

new urban population had nowhere to turn, except to the streets to scrape together a living by the use of their wits. Vendors of trinkets, sweets, clothes or electrical goods of doubtful origin throng the streets of the city centers, competing for the attention of passers-by. The more enterprising ones announce their wares on the public buses. And on the street corners, five-year-olds sell newspapers, shine shoes or urge you to buy chewing-gum with a "go on, don't be mean", in the hopes of earning their daily meal.

Today, barely half the workforce has a steady full-time job, while 38 percent are in the informal sector of street-vendors and

self-employed craftsmen and 12 percent are unemployed. Unofficial sources put these figures even higher.

Meanwhile, the well-to-do can find all the comforts of modern life in high-rise apartment blocks, well protected by armed guards; Miami-style shopping precincts display a broad variety of mod-cons and the latest electronic inventions; and chauffeur-driven Mercedes Benzes wait at the doors of luxury restaurants.

These contrasts are an expression of the erratic modernization of Ecuador which has radically changed living and working conditions in scarcely two decades, without being able to answer the basic needs of its population. The most flagrant social contradictions are to be found in Guayaquil, center of the nation's wealth, which is surrounded by vast slum areas built on marshland, the scene of abject poverty and rampant delinquency.

Chronic poverty: It is sadly ironic that in Ecuador, a country rich in natural resources with its fertile valleys, abundant marine life, extensive forests and reserves of oil and gold, most people face a daily struggle to scrape together the bare necessities of existence. UNICEF estimates that about two thirds of Ecuadorian families live below the critical poverty line. Even so, compared to the level of poverty in neighboring Peru and Colombia, Ecuador does not come off so badly. The cost of living is relatively cheap and as Ecuador produces most of its own food, few families are unable to get at least one square meal a day and most do have a roof of some kind over their heads.

Hardship is not reserved to the towns. In the countryside, life is becoming increasingly difficult for the peasants. Those who became small landowners cannot keep up with production costs, which rise faster than the price they receive for their crops, and they can rarely get cheap credit or adequate technical help. And once the paternalistic relations of the *hacienda* disappeared, the lack of social services became acute.

Successive governments have implemented social welfare programs in health care, aid to small farmers, food distribution, cheap housing, child care, employment and other needs. But the needs are a bottomless pit and there are never enough resources. So these programs multiply during electoral campaigns, only to be abandoned later.

All the same, in spite of hardship, the Ecuadorian people are patient, peaceable and honest. The violence that has become typical in Colombia and Peru is practically unheard of here, and though the crisis has brought about a rise in delinquency and crime, the level of violent crime (with the possible exception of Guayaquil) is lower than in many of the industrialized world's big cities.

Indigenous groups: The visitor to Ecuador is readily seduced by the unique costumes and skilful handicraft of the Indians: the women's embroidered blouses, the ponchos, the woven belts; but behind this appearance, which the visitor may see simply as folklore,

(Indian and white) are social and cultural, rather than racial definitions. The term *mestizo* (mixed blood) is not used frequently, although it is probably the most accurate description of the actual genetic heritage of most Ecuadorians. About half the population of Ecuador can be considered self-identified as indigenous. Basically, a person is considered an *indígena* if he or she lives in an indigenous community, speaks Quichua (or another indigenous language) along with or instead of Spanish, and wears a particular kind of dress that identifies him or her as *indígena.*

Ethnicity in Ecuador is, to a certain degree, fluid and malleable. To some extent, partic-

is a whole culture, an identity and a long history of resistance to assimilation by colonial society.

There are 10 different native ethnic groups in Ecuador, each of which considers itself a distinct nationality, with its own language and culture. Together, they make up between a quarter and a third of the population. The most numerous are the Quichua Indians who live mainly in the Sierra and are related to the Quechuas of Peru and Bolivia.

In Ecuador, the terms *indígena* and *blanco*

Left, dressing up at Latacunga. Above, wealthy Quiteños enjoy a meal in the Hotel Colón.

ularly over a generation or two, people can change their ethnic identity. An indigenous family can move to Quito, for example, send their children to school dressed in modern, white-style clothing and these children will generally be considered white. But these same children can return to their parents' community, and identify themselves as *indígenas* should they so choose.

Some Ecuadorian indigenous groups have been residents of the land for centuries, while others are descendents of groups of people (called *mitmakuna*) who were moved around the Andes by the Incas. The Incas had two categories of *mitmakuna;* loyal Inca Quichua-speakers who were sent to a recently conquered area to serve as a teaching and garrison population, and people who were moved far from their homelands as a punishment for resistance to Inca rule. The *indígenas* of modern Ecuador include descendants of native Ecuadorians and of transferred populations.

Racism is deeply engrained in Ecuadorian society. Indians who become "white" by leaving aside their traditional dress, language and identity are often those who show the most virulently racist attitudes towards other Indians. "Stupid Indian" or "dirty Indian" are typical epithets towards these people, who for years were excluded from public

despite the odds, is witness to their endurance: their festivals, which they have superimposed on the Christian religion; their language, despite periods of prohibition; their form of dress, even though it entails discrimination.

Curiously, some of these manifestations of identity were originally signs of subjugation. For example, many of the typical costumes which today they wear with pride were in fact adaptations of Spanish-style costumes of the time of the conquest, which they were obliged to wear to identify which *hacienda* they were from.

A number of Quichua Indians escaped from the colonizers to the Oriente, where

education, while their cultural heritage and language were treated with disdain.

In this part of America the Indians were not exterminated by the conquistadors, as occurred in South American countries like Chile and Argentina. Instead, they were subdued and used as forced labor on the land that was once theirs. Since this time, many of them have defied attempts to integrate them into *mestizo* society, manifesting a tacit resistance to the ill-treatment and discrimination practised against them. There have even been occasional rebellions which were quickly put down.

The survival of Indian culture and identity,

they had to face hazardous acclimatization. Until about three decades ago, these Quichuas and the native Amazonian Indians lived in almost complete isolation from the rest of the world, apart from a few missions that were established there. But when oil companies began to build roads into the region, settlers followed, and the Indians they came into contact with were rapidly assimilated into modern society.

Recently, however, with international campaigning for protection of the Amazonian forest, Indian groups who are still seeking to preserve their environment and lifestyle have found a worldwide audience for their claims, which gives them greater leverage on governments and authorities.

In July 1990, CONAIE (the Confederation of Indian Nations of Ecuador) held a meeting in Quito with representatives of indigenous groups from throughout South, Central and North America. The meeting was called to organize and protest against celebrations in 1992 for the quincentenary of Columbus' discovery of America, which *indígenas* correctly maintain was neither a "discovery" (they were already there) nor an "encounter," but a conquest and a particularly brutal one at that. Their motto is "500 Years of Resistance and Survival" and indigenous people are pushing for land rights, economic

The north-western province of Esmeraldas is inhabited by black peasants who for centuries have cultivated land in the dense tropical forest that still covers much of the province. Historians believe a Spanish frigate loaded with slaves was shipwrecked off the northern coast towards the middle of the 17th century, and that the Africans spread across the province, and lived practically in isolation there for many years. The warm Chota Valley of the mountainous province of Imabura is also populated by black people, descendants of freed slaves who had been originally brought in to work on the sugarcane plantations.

In both areas there is a strong African

reform and recognition as separate nations within their larger nation states. Because of the incompleteness of the 1964 Agrarian Reform, which left many large landholdings virtually intact, a major rallying cry in Ecuador is "No more *haciendas*."

Afro-Ecuadorians: Much of the coastal population has varying degrees of curly hair and darkish skin, revealing their descent from the African slaves brought over in previous centuries. But in two areas, there is a predominantly black population.

Left, learning to use technical skills. **Above**, traditional woman selling roots for tea-making.

cultural heritage, which has mixed curiously with Indian culture. The black people of the Chota Valley, for example, play the plaintive Indian music of the Sierra on African-type instruments, while the Awa Indians north of Esmeraldas have adopted the *marimba*.

The "Turks": While numerous Ecuadorians have emigrated in this century, especially to the US, there has been limited immigration of other nationalities and most of these have blended with the local population. Apart from an influx of Colombians in the north, Guayaquil has been the main attraction, where groups like the Chinese stand out.

But the foreign ethnic group that has had

most impact in Ecuador are the so-called "Turks" – in reality Arabs, and particularly Lebanese. They arrived in Ecuador during the first part of this century, when the local population gave them this unlikely nickname. Dedicated to commerce, they and their descendants have accumulated considerable economic power and political influence, and it would be no surprise if a future President of the Republic were to have an Arab name.

Patterns of politics: After a decade of democracy, Ecuadorian politics are still marked by the heritage left by frequent military coups and the tradition of *caudillos*: leaders around whom the political parties revolve. Political

largest city, Guayaquil, pride themselves on their boisterous *macho* style, caustic language and free-handed use of fists and firearms; and they glibly claim that what is good for Guayaquil is good for Ecuador. This style is scarcely appreciated in the Sierra, more conservative in its customs, though more progressive, in recent years, in its politics. Quarrelling and fighting between regions and political groups thus absorb a large part of the political life and energy of the country and constitute an obstacle to progress.

The correlative of politics is the public service, which grew enormously under the oil boom, and is considered by many politicians as booty to be shared among their

rivalry between the regions remains strong and often takes precedence over the national interest.

In recent times, several parties with a more national outlook and modern structure have emerged. But, especially in Guayaquil with its large electorate of shanty-town dwellers and its endemic social problems, politics continues to show a regionalist bias and populist rhetoric. Thus, political style from one region to another is so different that it is difficult for a politician to be accepted in both Costa (or, more specifically, Guayaquil) and Sierra.

The populist *caudillos* of the country's

faithful followers. As in most of Latin America, corruption is engrained in the public system and is very hard to uproot, even by those governments that have the will to do so. And bureaucratic red tape is a cancer that inevitably inhibits the smooth running of the State.

Religious fervor: Since the arrival of the early missionaries, Ecuador has been under the strong influence of the Catholic Church. The word of the local priest or bishop still has great weight, especially in the rural areas of the Sierra. However, since the end of the last century, when the strongly anti-clerical liberal movement of the Costa took power,

State and Church have been separate. So in state schools, for example, the curriculum does not include religion.

The Catholic religion instilled fear of punishment for sins, and resignation to suffering, and these elements, combined with popular superstition, engendered a fatalistic mentality which discouraged enterprise and progress.

For the Indians, Christianity was in many ways foreign to their vision of life, so they adapted their own forms of religious expression to the Catholic festivals, with masks, disguises and dances, which have often lost their original meaning, but symbolize their spirituality. These occasions were also a rare option to work in favor of the poor. Some Catholic groups in Ecuador, as in other countries, have taken this attitude further and are promoting political organization among the rural and urban slum populations as a means of seeking solutions to their grave problems.

Meanwhile, Protestant groups are engaged in active evangelization, particularly among Indians. Their success is partly due to the funding they provide for development projects and infrastructure, but also to their way of encouraging people to work hard and better themselves, which has received a favourable echo in many communities. All the same, there can be no doubt that for several Protestant sects, the priority is to counteract

opportunity to break with the drudgery of daily life.

Catholic teaching, with its emphasis on moralism and dogma, on believing rather than doing, also clashed with the ethic principles of the Quichuas, whose motto *Ama shua, ama quilla, ama llula* ("Do not steal, do not be lazy, do not lie") is not just a phrase to be repeated but a rule for daily conduct.

In recent years, however, the Catholic Church in Latin America has reaffirmed its the organizational work of particular progressive sectors of the Catholic Church.

Community life: Indian culture puts great value on the community. For example, *indígenas* advocate communal ownership of land – a concept which has often come into conflict with Ecuadorian tenancy laws. Another facet of the community spirit is the *minga* – a collective work effort where everybody and his uncle joins in. The tradition was inherited from Inca times via the *hacienda* system but has been adopted by the population in general.

Ecuadorians are generally glad to share whatever they have with family and friends,

Left, *indígena* couple admire an amusement park in Riobamba. **Above**, Holy Week Passion Play, Otavalo.

whether there is abundance or scarcity. When the sheep is fat for killing, all are welcome. And when there is barely enough food or drink to go round, everyone shares what there is. The kind of individualism typical in northern countries, such as wanting to live alone, is considered a strange and antisocial aberration.

But this sense of community only operates within the immediate group of family and acquaintances. Outside, in the cement jungle of the cities, the rule is each one for himself.

The family unit: Middle-class families in Ecuador are typical of Latin countries: they value strong family ties and close supervision of the womenfolk. Marriage before 20 is

the norm, and children follow within the first year or two of married life. Young girls are transferred from the protection of their parents directly under the authority of their husband, but men tend to take their sexual freedom for granted.

Among the poorer urban classes, and especially in the Costa, family relations are often far more informal, and it is not unusual for a man to have several families with different women, to whom he goes in turn for food and bed, rarely contributing much to their upkeep. Young Indian couples often live together as a "trial marriage" before taking the vows. And in the Costa, a man is likely to kidnap the girl he is courting until her parents consent to marriage.

The status of women: Early marriage, numerous children and religious upbringing have taught Ecuadorian women to be self-sacrificing, long-suffering and resigned to their lot. All the same, in their role of service to the family, mothers are held in great respect, which means they have a degree of influence and authority.

Equality of the sexes is now accepted in principle and many women go out to work. Cheap domestic help makes this easier for middle-class mothers, but in practise they still dedicate their greatest energies to raising their family, a task in which most men are not willing to take an equal share.

Ecuadorian men, and especially *serranos*, pride themselves on their gallantry, but this is not inconsistent with the tradition of *machismo*, which, particularly in the Costa, is valued as a necessary attribute of manhood. Married women in the Costa are expected to be entirely at the service of their husbands. Maybe that is why many women prefer the freedom of an informal union, even though they cannot claim exclusivity.

A country in search of its identity: In the Latin American context, Ecuador is one of the smallest and least developed countries, and this is reflected in the lack of self-affirmation of its people. They are peaceable, polite, friendly, welcoming to strangers, but also denigrating of one another and concerned with appearances. And their internal differences have prevented them from asserting a national identity or establishing comprehensive development projects.

Ecuadorians hesitate to value what is their own: foreign products are often assumed to be better. Particularly among the younger generation, fashions, music and culture follow external models: American and Caribbean music, clothes "Made in USA", American TV programs, and so on.

Maybe that is why these people are so noncommittal: they will rarely say a direct "yes" or "no": only *está bien* (that's OK), *¿cómo no?* (why not?), *talvez* (maybe) or *ya veremos* (we'll see).

Left, German immigrant in the Galápagos Islands, with friend. **Right**, the allegorical figure "poorly educated" throws sweets during "Mama Negra" festivities, Latacunga.

Every nook and valley of the Ecuadorian highlands is populated by distinct indigenous groups, some descendants of original Ecuadorian tribes, others descendants of the Incas or of people brought in by the Incas. It's virtually impossible for a curious person to travel in Ecuador without wondering what kinds of lives indigenous people lead and what kinds of tales they tell. Any guide book that assures you "the people lead lives unchanged since Inca times" should be tossed right out of the window since indigenous Ecuadorians don't live in a static universe any more than we do.

Europeans and *indígenas* (the name most indigenous people prefer) have been in contact for nearly 500 years, and Europeans have influenced the lives of Ecuadorian *indígenas* in profound ways. Language, clothing, food, housing and religion all have a European imprint. The influence, of course, has also gone the other way. For example, more than half the food crops consumed in the world today were domesticated in the Americas before the arrival of Europeans. Most significant are corn (maize) and potatoes, which were the economic foundation of the Inca empire.

One of Ecuador's attractions for visitors is that indigenous people still retain a number of customs of pre-Hispanic origin (as well as many that are European). Although the various groups have unique subcultures they share a number of traits. Some might argue that a poor, evangelical Protestant family in Chimborazo which ekes out a living on half an acre of bad land has nothing in common with a wealthy, Catholic weaving family in Otavalo which has just finished the construction of a four-storey apartment building in town. Yet both families consider themselves *indígenas*, both wear a distinctive dress that identifies them as members of a particular ethnic group, and both families speak Quichua in their homes.

Highland tongues: To paraphrase Winston Churchill, the *indígenas* of Ecuador are separated by the barrier of a common language,

Preceding pages: market day, Zumbahua. **Left,** market stalls. **Right,** Easter procession in Cacha.

Quichua or Runa Shimi (The People's Tongue). Quichua is part of the Quechua language family. There are, for example, five different Quechua languages spoken today in Peru, and two or three different Quichua languages spoken in Ecuador. This means that *indígenas* from different regions of Ecuador don't necessarily understand each other's Quichua and sometimes have to converse in Spanish when they meet.

The origins of Quechua are unknown, but we know it was spoken around the time of

Christ by the Chinchay, a trading group on the coast of Peru. The Incas adopted Quechua from the Chinchay and spread it throughout the Andes as they expanded their empire in the 14th and 15th centuries. The Spanish spread Quichua as a *lingua franca*, a universal language they could use to Christianize the *indígenas*. The Quechua language family is growing; more people speak it now than in Inca times, including several million people in Ecuador. Today most *indígenas* are bilingual in Quichua and Spanish, but some older people and some remote communities speak Quichua only.

Quechua and Quichua were not written

languages when the Spanish arrived. People have devised various alphabets for these languages over the centuries and this accounts for inconsistencies in spelling. The Quichua word for baby, for example, can be spelled *wawa, guagua* or *huahua*.

Co-operative values: If there is a core value in indigenous society it is reciprocity, and naturally there are Quichua words which express this. One such word is *minga*, a collective work party, of which there are several kinds. In community *minga* the leaders organize an effort to repair the roads or clean the irrigation canals, and every family must furnish several workers. (If they fail to show up some communities levy a fine.)

Another kind of *minga* is private. A family needs to roof a house, so they invite the neighbours to a roofing *minga*, supplying copious quantities of food and *chicha* for the workers. Of course, people come because they know they'll need help themselves one day. In the same way, *compadres* (two couples who are ritual kin because one couple became godparents to the other couple's child) also know they can call upon each other for help – anything from a loan of money to working in the kitchen at a fiesta.

Before the Spanish conquest money did not exist in indigenous societies. Items were bartered or labor was traded. Under the Incas, people paid their taxes to the state in the form of labor (*mita*) or goods, and were taken care of by the state in return with food from state storehouses in times of famine. In many places, reciprocity still means the return of goods or services rather than money. For example, if you have a Polaroid camera, giving people photographs is much better than paying them to let you take their picture. (This works much better in homes or in private situations than in public places like markets where you're likely to draw a huge crowd.) In the same way, sharing food or gifts of food are culturally appropriate in most situations.

Sacred mountains: *Indígenas* throughout the Andes have worshipped mountains for millennia. In Ecuador mountains are seen as male or female individuals, inhabited by powerful spirits. Mountains are also believed to control the rain and therefore the fertility and well-being of the entire region. The highest peak in any area was considered to be a *waka* (*huaca*) or sacred spot by the Incas. The Spanish constructed Catholic shrines over Inca sacred places, which is why you will see so many isolated chapels on hilltops today in Ecuador.

Chimborazo, in the western cordillera of central Ecuador, is the highest mountain in the country, an enormous snowcap that looms over the province like a giant ice cube. Chimborazo is called Taita (Father) Chimborazo, while slightly to the north and in the eastern cordillera is Mama Tungurahua. Lesser peaks in the region are also seen as male and female pairs. Offerings (guinea pigs, *trago*, plants) are sometimes made to the mountains to propitiate them.

In Imbabura Province, Mama Cotacachi reigns to the west of Otavalo while Taita Imbabura dominates the east. When Cotacachi's peak is snowcapped the *indígenas* say it is because Taita Imbabura visited her during the night. Needless to say, this encounter resulted in a baby, Urcu (Mountain) Mojanda, which lies just to the south of Otavalo. The connection of mountains with fertility is obvious here, and many *indígenas* carry it even farther. When people who live on the flanks of Imbabura plant crops they first ask Taita Imbabura to give them an abundant harvest. And when it rains in the region people say that Taita Imbabura is pissing on the valley.

If the mountains send the rain, Mother Earth (Allpa Mama or Pacha Mama) feeds the people by producing crops. Like the mountains, Mother Earth should be thanked so it is customary to throw the last few drops of an alcoholic drink on the ground as an offering to her. The concept of reciprocity not only holds among humans, but carries over to relations between the human and natural world. If Mother Earth feeds us, she should also be fed and Mother Earth likes alcohol.

Shamanism and healing: Virtually every Ecuadorian community has a man or woman who knows the healing properties of various plants, or who can diagnose and cure by

number of reasons: it might be because they have intestinal parasites, or because they believe an envious neighbor has cast a spell on them *(envidia)* or because they are looking for success in love or business. In addition, many people in the highlands have combined the Quichua belief in an inner and outer body, which must be kept in balance, with the medieval Spanish belief in humoral medicine. This ancient tradition held that the body was composed of four humors: yellow bile, black bile, phlegm and blood, whose relationships determined a person's disposition and health.

Today people believe that such illnesses as infant diarrhoea occur because the baby has

correcting spiritual imbalances or undoing spells. Healers are known by various Spanish names: *curanderos* (curers), *brujos* (witches), or *hechiceros* (sorcerers, witches). In Quichua traditional healers are called *yachaj mamas* or *yachaj taitas* (knowledgable mothers or fathers). There are also midwives, called *parteras,* who specialize in pregnancy and childbirth.

The details of healing vary among the different ethnic groups, but in the Sierra a person might go to the local healers for a

Left, a smile in the Sierra. **Above**, family sifting grain in Guamote.

had a fright *(susto* or *espanto)* which caused his or her inner and outer bodies to become unbalanced. If the inner body actually flees, then death can result, so the *yachaj mama* (or *taita)* performs a ceremony called "calling the soul" to bring the baby's inner body back. Bodies can also become diseased because of bad air *(wayrashka* in Quichua), known as *mal aire* in Spanish. *Mal aire* gave us our word malaria, because people initially believed that the disease came from swamp vapors rather than from the bites of mosquitoes that lived in the swamps.

Many Sierra healers diagnose ailments by passing a guinea pig over the patient, killing it and afterwards examining its entrails, which supposedly indicate the patient's problem.

Calling the soul involves a cleaning, in which the patient's body is rubbed with a raw egg. The egg is shaken and the sounds it makes indicate that the bad air is being absorbed. After the cleaning a child is sent to hide the eggs in the fields behind the house. Calling the soul also includes prayers in Quichua to God the Father, Son and Holy Spirit, the Virgin Mary and the saints. The healer tells the patient's heart to rise up (that is come back), passes alcohol to all present and smokes cigarettes, blowing the smoke on the patient. Tobacco has long been used by indigenous Americans as a medicine and

pends on your belief system and what kind of results you expect. A positive attitude is tremendously important in healing. Western medical doctors say that 80 percent of all illnesses are self-healing – it's the other 20 percent that need medical intervention. If local healers have an 80 percent success rate, that looks impressive. Then, too, many western drugs (cocaine, curare, quinine) come from plants which local healers know well.

A calendar full of fiestas: What's life without a party once in a while to break the monotony of daily life? Pre-Hispanic community fiestas were organized around the agricultural and solar cycle. After the Spanish conquest, on the grounds that people were going to

in healing. There are many early Spanish accounts of its use among the Maya, and it is still used in healing and religious rituals throughout the Americas.

While most communities have their own healers, several areas are famous for their *curanderos*. People in the Sierra believe that the Shuar of the jungle have special healing powers, as do the Taschila *indígenas* of Santo Domingo de los Colorados on the western slopes of the Andes in Pichincha Province. The healers of Iluman, outside Otavalo, are also famous and people come from all over the highlands to be treated by them.

How effective are these healers? It de-

celebrate anyway so they might as well observe a Christian occasion, the church turned many traditional indigenous religious celebrations into Catholic feast days.

While a number of civic festivals are observed throughout the year in Ecuador, the most interesting fiestas by far are the traditional celebrations in the countryside. These mainly occur in the spring and especially the summer, after the harvest and during the dry season. Every community has its own ritual calendar, so you might by serendipity at any time of the year wander into a town in the middle of a fiesta in honour of their patron saint. Here, however, are a few of the major

Sierra fiestas that are well worth catching:

Carnival (February or March) during the week before Lent begins on Ash Wednesday. *Carnaval* is a transplant from Europe, and represents a last fling before the austerity of Lent. Carnival in Ecuador is not like Rio. In fact, in the Sierra the main activity is throwing water, and it is definitely Not Fun to be hit in the back with a water balloon or to have a bucket of water dumped on your head in a chilly mountain village.

Ambato, however, has outlawed water throwing and has a fiesta of fruit and flowers that includes street dances and folklore events. Hotels fill early, but Ambato is only an hour from Quito by bus so it's worth a day trip.

men dragging huge crosses, and penitents dressed in what looks like purple Ku Klux Klan outfits.

There are also impressive Good Friday processions with costumed penitents in such Chimborazo province towns as Yaruquies, Tixán, Chambo and Chunchi.

Corpus Christi, in honor of the Eucharist, is a moveable feast, held on the Thursday after Trinity Sunday. It usually falls in early to mid-June. Corpus Christi is a major fiesta in the central Sierra, especially in Cotopaxi and Tungurahua Provinces, but it is celebrated in many places including some communities in Chimborazo Province and in Saraguro, Loja Province.

Holy Week (*Semana Santa*, the week before Easter) begins with Palm Sunday (*Domingo de Ramos*). Throughout Ecuador people buy palm fronds in the market, weave them into different shapes and take them to church on Palm Sunday. On Maundy Thursday, families visit the cemetery and bring food and drink for the dead in an observance similar to that of the Day of the Dead.

In Quito on Good Friday there is an enormous, spectacular procession through the streets of the city, complete with flagellants,

Left, leading a llama from market. **Above**, All Saints' Day at a graveyard near Zumbahua.

Dancers with ornate headdresses and spectacularly embroidered costumes are now found only in such communities as Pujili, Cotopaxi and San Antonio de Pillaro, Tungurahua. In Salasaca, Tungurahua, Corpus is celebrated with music and dance. The *indígenas* wear plaster masks, ribbons and feathers on their hats and dance from Salasaca to the nearby town of Pelileo.

The winter solstice, Inti Raymi, on June 21, was once a major Inca festival. In the Cuzco area, far south of the equator, the winter solstice was the shortest day and longest night of the year. Closer to the equator, the differences in the length of the day and night are hardly dramatic, but astute indigenous astronomers still recognized them. Today, **Saint John the Baptist** (*San Juan Bautista*, June 24) is the major fiesta in the Otavalo valley and probably replaced an ancient, pre-Inca solstice festival.

Among the Otavaleños, San Juan is a male fiesta lasting the better part of a week. On the night of the 23rd, the male vespers (*la víspera*) dress up in costumes. The dancing begins after dark both in Otavalo and in the outlying towns. The variety and ingenuity of the costumes is a sight to see – Batman, Káliman, North American plains Indians with feathered headdresses, Mexicans with giant sombreros, women, soldiers. Some *indígenas*

hurt. The point of spilling blood seems to be a payment or sacrifice to Mother Earth after the corn harvest. Similar ritual battles (*tinku*) with rocks and fists still occur in the highlands of Peru and Bolivia.

Saints Peter and Paul (*San Pedro y San Pablo*, June 29) is another major fiesta in Imbabura Province, and in many places the San Juan and San Pedro y Pablo festivities run together. On the night of June 28th bonfires are lit in the streets throughout the province. This seems to be a combination of both indigenous and Spanish customs and young women who want to have children are supposed to leap over the fires.

San Pedro is especially important in Cota-

even parody *gringos* by wearing blonde wigs, down jackets, backpacks, blue jeans and running shoes.

The dancing goes on each night for a week, with groups of musicians and dancers moving from house to house and dancing (actually stomping) in a circle, with sudden reverses in direction that may represent the movement of the sun.

Also connected with San Juan is a ritual battle with rock throwing at the chapel of San Juan, which is located on the west side of the Pan-American highway from the town proper. Until the 1960s people were killed during the fights, and people still sometimes get

cachi, where there are also ritual fights, and in Cayambe. While San Juan is important to the Otavaleños, San Pedro is the big event for the other main ethnic group in Imbabura, the people who live on the east side of the mountain in such communities as Zuleta, Rinconada, La Esperanza and Angochagua.

Because San Pedro is the patron saint of the canton of Cayambe, hundreds of *indígenas* come into town and parade under the banners of their communities. The groups dance down the streets, around the main plaza and past a reviewing stand, where local officials award prizes to the best groups.

Among the dancers are men and women

carrying roosters in wooden cages or tied to poles. These are for a ceremony called the *entrega de gallos* (delivering of roosters). In the days of *wasipungo* (serfdom) the *indígenas* on the *haciendas* showed their loyalty to the *hacienda* owner by a ceremonial gift of roosters once a year at this time. It is still done on some *haciendas,* but the ceremony is also performed for the indigenous sponsor (*prioste*) of local fiestas.

San Juan and San Pedro are also major fiestas in southern Chimborazo Province. In Tixán, San Juan is celebrated more by the white population of the town, with the *indígenas* of the region beginning their celebration of San Pedro on June 28. San Juan is also

chapel was built on a mountain over what was undoubtedly a pre-conquest holy spot. The shrine is dedicated to the Virgen de la Fuente del Carmelo de Catequilla (the Virgin of the Fountain of Carmelo of Catequilla). *Indígenas* from throughout Chimborazo, in their finest traditional dress, visit the shrine and chapel on the 16th. There is also a small fair at the base of the springs where food, drink, candles and holy items are sold.

Saint James (*Santiago*, July 25) is the patron saint of Spain, and his image (on horseback with a raised sword, killing Moors) was carried into battle by the Spanish during their conquest of the Americas. The Spanish had firearms, which were unknown to *indí-*

celebrated in Achupallas, while San Pedro is the saint who is honored in Alausi.

The feast of the **Virgin of Carmen** (July 16) is a notably larger celebration in the southern provinces than in the north. There is a fair (*feria*) in front of the church of that name in downtown Cuenca. In Chimborazo this fiesta is celebrated in Pumallacta and in Chambo.

Chambo, located just outside Riobamba, is the site of a miraculous shrine and fountain, one of those instances where a Catholic

Left, off-loading logs. **Above**, fiesta of San Pedro celebrated in Cayambe.

genas, who associated Santiago with their powerful god of Thunder and Lightning (called Illapa by the Incas). This conflation was so blatant that for a time in the early colonial era *indígenas* were forbidden to name their children Santiago. Today Santiago is the patron of many communities and there are many fiestas in his honor.

The feast of the **Virgin of Mercy** (*La Virgen de la Merced*, September 24) is a major fiesta in Latacunga (Cotopaxi Province), where a local dark-skinned statue of the Virgin is known as *La Mama Negra*, the black mother. The unusual fiesta runs for two days beginning on the 23rd. La Merced is also celebrated in Columbe (Chimborazo Province).

All Saints' Day and Day of the Dead (*Todos Santos y Dia de Difuntos*, November 1 and 2). These two Catholic feast days are another example of indigenous and European religious syncretism – the blending of Andean and European traditions. In pre-conquest burials, food and drink were placed in graves to feed the dead in the next life. Some communities believe that the spirits of the dead return to earth for 24 hours and will be unhappy if they aren't remembered.

All over Ecuador, little humans and animals are baked from bread dough and taken to the cemeteries on November 2nd, where

Among the local Christmas customs is the *Pase del Niño* (the presentation of the Christ child). Families or villages which own statues of the baby Jesus carry the statues in a procession to the church, accompanied by musicians and by children dressed as Mary, Joseph, shepherds, angels, the Three Kings and other nativity figures. The statues are blessed during a special Mass and then taken back to the families' household creches.

The most famous *Pase del Niño* occurs in Cuenca, on the morning of December 24. The procession begins at the churches of San Sebastián and Corazón de Jesus and converges on the cathedral on the Plaza de Armas. Families from around the region

they are placed on the graves along with paper wreaths and other offerings of food and drink. In a nice local variation on the theme of waste not, want not, poor people come to the cemeteries and offer prayers at each grave site in return for some of the food.

Finally, there are many beautiful Christmas (**Navidad**, December 25) pageants and celebrations throughout Ecuador; it's a wonderful time of year to be traveling there. Christmas is a religious holiday, not a commercial one, and for the most part such European and North American customs as Christmas trees and the exchange of gifts are virtually unknown.

bring their children in, some dressed as *cholo* Cuencanos or as Ecuadorian *indígenas*, and mounted on horseback, their horses covered with food, liquor, sweets, fruits and other offerings. Other children participate on foot dressed as nativity figures or as gypsies, gauchos, moors, or shepherds, each group carrying its own statue of Jesus. Inside the cathedral the children are given *chicha* and bread, then the participants wind their way through the streets to celebrate Christmas in their own homes.

In Saraguro, Loja Province, each indigenous community outside of town owns an antique statue of the Christ child which is carried in a procession on Christmas Day from the main church in Saraguro to the home of the Christ child's "godparents," the *marcan taita* and *marcan mama*. The procession is led by violinists and drummers and accompanied by costumed dancers including devils, bears and little boys dressed up like *jivaros*, jungle savages, who guard the Christ child. At the *marcan taita*'s house the statue is placed on an altar decorated with flowers, greens and cloth, and the entire community assembles for an enormous Christmas meal and an afternoon of music and dancing by special groups.

The *Pase del Niño* is also celebrated in Pujilí and Tanicuchí, Cotopaxi Province,

thousands of onlookers, a couple of *gringos* in the crowd are no big deal.

If you are the only outsider at a small village event, then circumspection is the word. Put your camera away, watch the festivities, greet and talk to people, and then ask if you can photograph. *Indígenas* have been pushed around by white people for nearly 500 years and they're pushing back. The problem is less your presence than the arrogance of outsiders who assume that they can photograph anything, anywhere without asking permission. Remember, you're a guest, not Sebastián de Benalcázar.

Also, ritual drinking is customary at all fiestas and it is insulting to Ecuadorians if

and throughout Cañar Province. Other Christmas observances include the fiesta of the Holy Innocents *(Santos Inocentes)* on December 28, which is celebrated in Quito, and the feast of the Epiphany or Three Kings *(Tres Reyes* or *Reyes Magos)*, on January 6.

Fiesta etiquette: There are right and wrong ways to behave at fiestas and everyone will have a better time if you know how to act. Basically, you will be less conspicuous and find it easier to take photographs at the larger and more public fiestas. When there are

Left, spinning wool in Saraguro. **Above**, potato harvest on the slopes of Caihuairazo.

you refuse to drink when the *trago* bottle is passed around. Join the revellers in a cup or two and don't forget to throw the dregs on the ground as an offering to Pacha Mama. By late in the day fiesta participants are often hopelessly looped and your basic belligerent drunk, who seems to be a universal archetype, comes staggering out of the *chicherias* bent on blaming you for every injustice perpetrated since 1534.

One of the best ways to enjoy a fiesta is to arrive in the morning and leave by 2pm, before things get out of hand and before you've shared so many cups that you can't find your way back to the bus stop.

THE SOUNDS OF THE ANDES

What's a party without music? Making a joyous noise unto the Lord (or Mother Earth or someone) seems to be a universal human activity and the Ecuadorians are no exception. Two kinds of music are usually played at fiestas in Ecuador: traditional, pre-Conquest indigenous music and Spanish (or European) music. Naturally after almost 500 years there's been considerable blending.

You can hear traditional music groups (*grupos* or *conjuntos*) at many indigenous fiestas and at programs in folkmusic clubs (*peñas*). There are also local and national traditional music competitions, with an amazing variety of talent (or lack thereof). The competitions are usually free to the public and at that price it's hard to go wrong.

Ancient instruments: Pre-Hispanic vocal and instrumental music was based on a pentatonic (five-note) scale, which gives Andean music its haunting, melancholy sound. Pre-Hispanic instruments were of three basic varieties: wind (flutes, panpipes, conch shells), percussion (drums), and rattles and bells. Flute-like instruments used today include the *quena*, a notched bamboo which usually has six finger holes and a thumb hole and a smaller flute (*pingullu*), which has three or four holes. When condors were more plentiful in the Andes *quenas* were sometimes made from their leg bones. The pre-Hispanic flutes were always held vertically; flutes (*flautas*) which are held horizontally are modelled on the European instrument.

The panpipe (*rondador*) goes back at least 2,000 years. Its modern Spanish name comes from that of the night watchman in colonial Ecuador who played the instrument on his rounds. A typical *rondador* is made of varying lengths and widths of cane or bamboo tied together in one long row; the different lengths and diameters produce distinct tones. Recently, many Ecuadorian musicians have been using *zampoñas*, the panpipes typical of Peru and Bolivia. The *zampoña* is tuned differently than the *rondador* and usually has two rows of pipes lashed together, fac-

Preceding pages: *indígena* celebration. **Right, musicians at a fiesta near Otavalo.**

92

tors which musicians say make it easier to play. The large *zampoñas* have a deep, breathy sound like the wind off Chimborazo on a gentle day. There are many kinds and sizes of *zampoñas* with different names in Quechua and Aymara, but *zompoña* seems to be the Ecuadorian generic name for southern Andean panpipes.

The frequent use of Peruvian and Bolivian instruments by Ecuadorian musicians is indicative of the remarkable cross-fertilization that is occurring as Ecuadorians travel in Peru and Bolivia and southern Andean musicians (or their tape cassettes) come north. The musicians teach each other songs and trade instruments.

attached to a piece of cowhide and are worn over the shoulder by dancers at the fiestas of San Juan and San Pedro.

Spanish influences: Stringed instruments were introduced by the Spanish and were soon incorporated into the traditional repertoire. (After all, how many years does it take for something to become "traditional?" Nearly five centuries ought to qualify). These instruments include the guitar (*guitarra*), violin (*violín*), mandolin (*bandolín*), *charango* and Andean harp (*arpa criolla*). The *charango* originated in Bolivia and looks somewhat like a ukulele but has five pairs of strings and eight frets. Its body is sometimes made of wood, but is more often made from

When Los Kjarkas, one of Bolivia's premier folk music groups, toured Ecuador not long ago, they shared their venue with various local groups. Ecuadorian groups had already been playing Bolivian music, including songs learned from Los Kjarkas tapes, but chances are good that you'll hear even more Los Kjarkas songs if you go to Ecuadorian *peñas*.

Percussion instruments played today include large and small drums (*bombos*). Gourd rattles (*maracas*) are also played. Various bells (*campanas*) and rattles are still used, especially by dancers at fiestas. In Imbabura Province, for example, 10 or 12 cowbells are

an armadillo shell. The Andean harp is a homemade version of the European harp, beautiful to hear but difficult to make and transport, so that few musicians still use them.

After the Spanish introduced cattle into Ecuador, the *indígenas* made a unique instrument from cow horns called a *coroneta* or *bocina*. Between 16 and 20 horns are cleaned and joined and then the joints are bound. The tone of the *coroneta* depends on the number of horns used.

The accordion (*acordeón*) and harmonica (*rondín*) were probably introduced in the 19th century. The most recent addition is the portable, amplified Yamaha organ. Today, a mix of instruments is used to play both older and new kinds of music.

Generally, in Ecuador males play musical instruments and sing, while females are only vocalists. Some kinds of music, including the *wayñu* (or *wayno*) and the *yaraví*, were probably introduced by the Incas and are almost always sung in Quichua. But the most common is the *sanjuanito*, which qualifies as Ecuador's national dance music. *Sanjuanitos* can be both instrumental and vocal and are played by folk music groups and by modern bands at most fiestas.

If this sounds confusing, some examples might help clarify things. At a *peña* a typical group will be composed of young men playing all or a combination of the following instruments: guitar, mandolin, *charango*, violin, drum, *quena, pingullu, zampoña* and *rondador*. They will alternate purely instrumental music with songs with instrumental accompaniment. Many of the songs will be in Quichua and are considered traditional folk songs. Some instrumentals such as "El Condor Pasa" (The Condor Passes) are pan-Andean. Songs such as "Nuka en la Plaza Mi Chicha Vendiendo" (I, in the Plaza, Selling My Chicha) or "Rosa Maria" are pan-Ecuadorian; you will hear them everywhere. Other songs, such as "Antonio Mocho" or "Chimbaloma" are typical of Imbabura Province.

Festival music: Rather than variations on a theme, to North American and European ears much traditional fiesta music sounds like an obsession with one theme. The same refrain is repeated over and over, endlessly hypnotic and great to dance to. During San Juan, the musical groups literally dance all night (to *sanjuanitos* naturally), moving from house to house throughout the village.

Increasingly, traditional musical groups are being replaced by ones which use amplified instruments, especially for such occasions as weddings and other large parties. Into the house come the musicians in traditional dress, but instead of guitars and *quenas* they are carrying an electric sound system including microphones, amplifiers, speakers, maracas, and a Yamaha organ, which will prevent any sleep in the *barrio* for the next three days. (If you happen to be in the *barrio*, you might as well go to the party).

Such bands are hired for white and *mestizo*, as well as indigenous, events.

The musicians tune up and launch into "La Rasca Bonita", a *sanjuanito* with a catchy little tune and upbeat tempo that qualifies as Ecuador's national party melody. *La rasca bonita* (the pretty itch) is actually the name of a skin disease – we are definitely talking about a folk tradition here. The band alternates *sanjuanitos* with *cúmbias*, music of Afro-Caribbean origin from the coasts of Colombia and Ecuador. Everyone dances at these parties, from grandparents to toddlers. As the band launches into its fifth *sanjuanito* you can't help tapping your toes, grabbing a bottle of *trago* and wading in to join the fray.

A dance which is done less and less at parties and now seems to be performed mainly at folk music programs is the *cueca*. It's a Spanish dance derived from the *jota* and is danced by any number of couples holding handkerchiefs.

Buying recordings: Music stores throughout Ecuador sell traditional music on records and tape cassettes (no compact discs yet). Ask the store clerk for traditional music (*música tradicional*) and find out which Ecuadorian groups are popular. If you want Yamaha organ party music ask for *música nacional*, and if you want Afro-Caribbean music ask for coastal music (*música costeña*) or *cúmbias*.

Brass instruments are another European introduction. Ancient trumpets, trombones, clarinets, cymbals, French horns and tubas, many of them battered beyond repair and the possibility of producing a harmonious note, are hauled out of nooks and crannies. It is traditional for brass bands to play at small town fiestas and civic events, during which the musicians pass the *trago* bottle and are soon beyond repair themselves. In the ensuing musical interlude, volume and enthusiasm surpass musicianship.

Another venerable musical tradition is the weekend concert in the park. Many towns have municipal bands which assemble in the Plaza de Armas on Sunday mornings and rouse the populace from their torpor. Surely it is not the "Marine Corps Hymn" or "It's a Long Way to Tipperary" or the "Theme for Teenage Mutant Ninja Turtles" that you are hearing in the plaza in Songolquí, Ecuador? Who can tell? Who cares? As art it's debatable, but as entertainment it's unbeatable.

When Westerners think of indigenous Amazonian peoples, they conjure up strings of age-old stereotypes. The popular image is of naked men and women slipping through the jungle with Stone Age tools, isolated until recently from history and the outside world. According to this image, they have always hunted for their food rather than grown it, and often engaged in brutal wars, shrinking their enemies' heads and occasionally eating their flesh. They are also held to be ecological saints, protecting their delicate environment at all costs.

Not surprisingly, the image has little to do with reality – as anthropologists in the Ecuadorian Oriente are rapidly finding out.

Coping with change: Far from being unchanging, undeveloping societies – and thus somehow "idyllic" – all Amazonian peoples have their own histories, and very dynamic histories at that.

Because Amazonians did not possess writing systems, and even more importantly, because their rain forest home is particularly unconducive to preserving the remains of past civilizations, there is little data with which to reconstruct Amazonian history. However, archaeologists can now show that human beings have lived in the Amazon since at least 10,000 BC, and that major technological breakthroughs occurred in the Amazon basin.

Amazonians domesticated manioc around 8000 BC, and probably invented clay pottery around 4000 BC, before any other indigenous cultures in South America. Migrations, new languages and vast cultural and religious transformations characterize the history of the Amazon Basin. Archaeologists believe that cultural advances moved out of Amazonia into the Andes, not the reverse.

After the arrival of the Portuguese and Spanish *conquistadores*, Amazonian societies changed tremendously, whether they had direct contact with the invaders or not. Plagues of diseases to which indigenous peoples had no resistance moved in waves from the coast, over the Andes, into the rain

forest, decimating populations. Migrations of peoples away from regions conquered and colonized by the Spanish and Portuguese provoked chain reactions of indigenous peoples being forced off their original lands into unfamiliar territories.

New technologies reached the Amazon as well, again brought by intermediaries so that no direct contact occurred with Europeans. Steel tools and new foods (especially the banana, plantain and papaya, which originated in Southeast Asia) transformed life-

ways throughout the Amazon, traded from one people to the next throughout the jungle. In this way, the pressures created by the Spanish Conquest of Ecuador and Peru transformed Amazonia and pre-Conquest jungle lifestyle will remain forever a mystery.

A range of jungle groups: The Ecuadorian Amazon is small compared with the vast jungles of Brazil, but it is nevertheless an important, even crucial, part of the region. It is inhabited by six major ethnic groups (the term "tribe," which implies primitiveness, has been discarded). Largest are the Quichuas (60,000 people), followed by the Shuar (40,000), Achuar (5,000), Huaorani (3,000),

Left, Shuar woman in traditional dress. **Right**, at work in the Oriente.

Siona-Secoya (650) and the Cofan (600).

Although the popular Western image persists of Amazonians surviving by hunting wild game and gathering wild fruits, the truth is that most indigenous peoples get nearly all of their foodstuffs from cultivation. They either raise moderate-sized, temporary gardens (horticulture) or grow plants as crops, on a permanent basis and often on a larger scale (agriculture).

The Huaorani are the most nomadic of all of Ecuador's indigenous Amazonians. Because they customarily went about naked, and because they relied so much upon gathering and hunting wild foods, the Huaorani were originally called "Aucas," which means

"backwardness," but as the basic survival mechanisms of those forest cultures that endured the most intensive stresses.

The Amazonian Quichuas are closely related to the people of the same name who dominate the Andean highlands of Ecuador. Anthropologists surmise that Quichua-speakers migrated down into the rainforests after the Spanish conquered the highlands in the early 1500s. The most numerous of the indigenous Amazonians, the Quichuas are composed of two distinct ethnic groups, the Canelos and the Quijos. These peoples brought the knowledge of well-developed agricultural systems from the Andes to the jungle, although they had to learn how to grow very

savages in Quichua. The Huaorani have rejected this name, which they consider very derogatory.

During this century, the Huaorani have adopted horticulture, yet they remain the most nomadic and least interested in cultivation of the Ecuadorian Amazonians. It appears almost certain that the Huaorani, who are composed of a number of discrete groups (Guequetairi, Pijemoiri, Baihuairi, Huepeiri, etc) are an amalgamation of survivors from many different groups diminished by diseases, war and migrations. For this reason, anthropologists view the sparse material culture of the Huaorani, not as evidence of

different crops in their new home. Living in dispersed, permanent settlements on individually owned plots of land, Quichua men clear land, plant crops, and let the plots rest for three years after approximately five years of cultivation, while Quichua women maintain, weed, and harvest the crops.

In the northern Oriente: The small ethnic groups that live in the northern region of the Ecuadorian Amazon are the Cofan (who call themselves the A'I) and the Siona-Secoya, a combination of two once separate groups with very similar customs that unified when their numbers dwindled drastically earlier this century. These peoples practice what anthropologists call "slash and burn," a technique for creating small clearings in the forest which produce food for two or three years and then must be abandoned to replenish their fertility. The Siona-Secoya usually leave big trees standing, especially those that produce fruits, and they do not always burn off the vegetation they have cut, but allow it to rot and mulch the exposed earth.

These peoples are semi-nomadic, which is to say that they move about within defined territories, abandoning old plots for new ones located in richer hunting grounds. They most frequently locate their gardens close to their houses, but sometimes plant smaller, less complex gardens at some distance from

the tuber 12 or more months after planting it, and they simultaneously re-sow small tuber cuttings as they harvest. When manioc is mature, it can be left in the ground to continue growing without any risk of spoilage, which has obvious advantages in tropical Amazonia. The Shuar and Achuar may perhaps be described as semi-settled, rather than semi-nomadic.

In recent years, Shuar and Achuar men have started raising cattle in increasing numbers, converting jungle to pasture. This income-earning strategy is probably not sustainable considering the fragile soil and subsoil ecology of the jungle, yet the Shuar and Achuar are increasingly sophisticated in plan-

home. Siona-Secoya and Cofan farmers are women, and the profundity of their knowledge about soils and maintaining their fertility, about weather patterns, plant behavior and diseases, and crop associations (beans and corn, or corn and manioc, for example) is truly astounding.

The Shuar people of the southern region of Ecuadorian Amazonia, and their closely related cousins the Achuar, practice a horticultural system heavily dependent upon one crop plant – sweet manioc. Women harvest

Left, missionaries at work in the early 1900s.
Above, Cofan family in traditional dress.

ning their survival in the rainforest.

Movements through the forest: It is still true that hunting, gathering and fishing determine the movements and rhythms of life for indigenous peoples. Anthropologists once assumed that hunting is the most important of these activities, but the gathering of wild fruits, honey, nuts, roots, grubs and insects – a task performed exclusively by indigenous women – actually provides the largest part of the diet. (The origin of the "hunting" myth was undoubtedly due to the fact that the mostly male Western anthropologists talked almost exclusively to indigenous men, who naturally talked about their own activity.)

Another, more recent, myth held about indigenous Amazonians is that they never kill more than they need in the rainforest, revere the jungle's animals, and are attuned to the natural balances of their environment. There is some validity to this view. But much of it stems from industrial nations' recent awareness of how they have abused the planet's ecology, coupled with a romanticization of Amazonian life. It can plainly be seen that the indigenous people of the Oriente kill animals for food in whatever zone they happen to be in until those animals are scarce. Then they move on.

Yet the nomadic and semi-nomadic lifestyles of most indigenous Amazonians have

for similar reasons, and also prohibit the hunting of tree-sloths, black monkeys, opossums and weasels. The Siona-Secoya revere and fear the pink river dolphins, and never harm them. The Quichua honor the jungle puma, a very rare feline, and would never shoot one.

Crafts of the Oriente: For all groups except for the Huaorani (who wore nothing, even though men would use string to tie their penises up by the foreskin), a major craft was once the making of clothes. Shuar men and Achuar women spun homegrown cotton, wove it into cloth and dyed it with vegetable-based colorings. The men wore wrap-around kilts, tied in place by bark string, and the

prevented and continue to prevent the extermination of game animals upon which indigenous peoples depend. The horticultural peoples have always placed an overwhelming social emphasis upon having small families with no more than two children. Population stability unlocks the door to ecological stability. Amazonian belief-systems also encompass a number of iron-clad taboos against killing certain animals.

The Shuar and Achuar believe that deer, owls and rabbits are the temporarily visible embodiments of the "true soul" of dead human beings, and therefore do not hunt these animals. The Siona-Secoya do not eat deer

women fastened their dresses over their right shoulders, using a belt around their waists. The Siona-Secoya and Cofan men wove ultra-lightweight knee-length cotton smocks, called *cushmas*, which they dyed blue or red. The Quichuas adapted forms of clothing their highland cousins wore. All of these peoples now mostly wear trousers, shirts and blouses, dresses, skirts and shorts indistinguishable from other Ecuadorians.

Basket-weaving, a male craft, has survived much more intact. Plastics simply do not perform as well as baskets in the tropics because they are much heavier, induce food to rot, and are not nearly so versatile. The normal carrying basket of the Amazon is a plaited, openwork cylinder, no higher than a meter, tightly woven and very sturdy. The finest baskets are woven by the Shuar, for holding personal ornaments and other finery; it is lined with smooth banana leaves, and has an attached cover.

The tourist market has almost completely transformed another craft, pottery, which has always been the domain of women. Quichua women make clay vessels for household use, as well as sacred vessels with ritual character. These vessels are meticulously executed, elaborate, and eggshell thin, with geometric and zoomorphic shapes and motifs. Shuar women lavish intricate geometri-

power over their lives in the midst of ongoing cultural transition.

Most fantastic of all Amazonian arts are the feather and beadwork crowns, necklaces, earrings and other ornaments, which rely upon the plumage of toucans, parrots, macaws, hummingbirds and other magnificent birds. These stunningly beautiful works of art have always possessed enormous ritual and spiritual significance for Amazonian peoples, directly linked to their use in the *ayahuasca* ceremony. Today, tourist demand for such ornaments, considered souvenirs, is encouraging indigenous Amazonians to kill the most colorful, and usually the most endangered, birds at an accelerated rate.

cal adornments on the jars used to boil and serve the hallucinogenic beverage, *ayahuasca* (see below).

Tourist demand for Amazonian pottery has transformed its production into something resembling an assembly-line, where scores of duplicates are produced with patterns that have no significance. The income derived from the sale of ceramics is, relative to the overall monetary income of indigenous Amazonians, rather considerable, and has given indigenous women a degree of

Because the importation of products made from endangered species is prohibited by the United States, Australia, and Western Europe, tourists bringing their "trinkets" home inevitably lose them at the customs office, thereby making the death of these birds, and the devaluation of the traditions of Amazonian peoples, a tragic exercise in futility.

Amazonian shamans: One might say that it was in the realm of spiritual and mythical creativity that indigenous Amazonians made their greatest strides and their most momentous discoveries. Because the Amazonian storehouse of knowledge and wisdom has always been transmitted orally, a great deal

Left, Huaorani *indígenas* at a gathering. **Above**, thatch-covered huts in an Amazon village.

of the complexity has been lost. Indigenous spirituality has been mercilessly attacked by missionaries from a number of different Christian sects ever since the Spanish Conquest; in recent years Protestant groups, such as the Summer Institute of Linguistics, have worked to blot out the legacy of thousands of years, preventing the transmission of traditions from the old to the young. Nevertheless, the enduring center of that legacy, shamanism, continues to survive among each of the six principal peoples, albeit by evermore slender threads.

Shamans are the individuals who learn and preserve the oral histories, myths, legends and other belief systems of their peoples.

The tools that shamans use vary. Quichua shamans own magical stones, which act as their familiars. The Shuar and Achuar shamans utilize magical darts called *tsentsak*, to carry out both healing and hurting. But the most important tools that all the Amazonian shamans employ are hallucinogenic substances extracted from jungle plants. The vine known as *ayahuasca*, Quichua for "vine of the soul," is the hallucinogen par excellence of the Amazon.

Using drum rhythms and other musical patterns, vocal incantations, the light of fires, and the colors of feather ornaments and body paint, the shamans guide those who have drunk potions derived from *ayahuasca* to see

Amazonian shamans are usually men among the Siona-Secoya, Quichua and Cofan, but female shamans are not unknown in the Shuar and Achuar cultures. Many shamans devote their time to curing people of diseases through elaborate rituals. There are shamans who bewitch others, causing disease and misfortune to their enemies, or to the enemies of others who pay the shaman to carry out the bewitching ceremony. Shamans enact the ceremonies of initiation, the rites of passage of young men and women into adulthood. And, of course, shamans train others to be shamans, passing on the knowledge and the rituals.

visions based on the symbolism and mythology of their cultures. The jaguar, anaconda, and harpy eagle recur over and over again in *ayahuasca* visions. This very real and immediate communion with their ancestral past and the supernatural is a continuous source of social and cultural cohesion for indigenous Amazonians – it has nothing in common with the often self-destructive use of drugs encountered in Western cultures.

The power of the family unit: In indigenous Amazonian society the most important organizational unit is the extended family. The rules of kinship define an individual's rights of inheritance, who he or she should marry, and where the married couples should live.

The Huaorani, with their very loosely defined kinship rules that do not even define the authority of older people over younger, can be seen, again, as a society pared down to essentials in its struggle to survive. Cofan and Siona-Secoya men marry women allowed to them by a patrilineal system: couples live with the man's father's family, or in a house built close to the father's house, and they inherit property and privileges from the man's father.

Shuar men live close to their wives' families at first, before moving away to their own houses, but inherit through their fathers' line. Achuar men permanently reside near their wives' families, inherit through their mothers' lines, and marry women according to matrilineal relationships. The Quichua possess a patrilineal system, but one which is broader and more complex, defining a kinship group called the *ayllu*, several of which compose a community.

Amazonian cultures have no single leader or chief. Instead, leadership has always been provided in crises by shamans and war-captains. While the Quichua farmers probably did not wage raids and wars as much as they suffered from them, the other groups' lifeways were greatly defined by feuds, raids, and war. The Siona-Secoya, Cofan, and Huaorani raided to capture women and to avenge raids carried out against them, but never for territory. For the Shuar and Achuar, warfare symbolized the spiritual quest for power. Only by killing a designated enemy could a man gain the visionary magical soul called *arutam*, and thus possess the power to lead others.

The practice of severing an enemy's head, removing the skull, and shrinking the skin is the source of much fame for the Shuar and Achuar. As exotic and gruesome as this practice seems, and as perverse as it became earlier this century due to Westerners' fascination and their desire to purchase shrunken heads, the rituals associated with shrinking heads were an integral part of the shaman-leader complex that defined war and peace among these peoples. Far from shrinking heads, the Shuar and Achuar today have organized the most successful ethnic federation in the Amazon basin, a model for groups in Ecuador and other nations.

Twentieth-century politics: The recent discovery of oil deposits in the Ecuadorian Amazon has meant that air, water and the rainforest itself are at risk. All indigenous Amazonians have no choice but to change and organize in order to survive.

In the Federation of Shuar Centers, shamans today use their powers for less vengeful purposes, and are organized around health and community issues, working within the Federation. In addition to fighting for Shuar and Achuar land rights, the Federation is increasingly involved in the protection of the environment in the southern Amazon region. The Shuar Federation has also published scores of books about Shuar and Achuar oral traditions, making them far more accessible to future generations.

For the Quichuas, organizational models are available from their highland cousins, who have become intensely political. The Quichua regional federations have helped link indigenous Amazonians and the indigenous highlanders; as a result, an Amazonian and highlander confederation, CONFENIAE, has been formed at national level.

For the smaller peoples, the specter of demographic disappearance is real and terrifying. The Siona-Secoya community in the Cuyabeno Fauna Reserve recently aided in the clean-up of an oil-spill in several pristine lakes, demonstrating very clearly how much a part of the modern world indigenous Amazonians are, and how their knowledge and commitment is, and will be, essential to the rainforest's survival. Meanwhile, working through CONFENIAE, the Huaorani have struggled with the Ecuadorian government to gain title to at least part of their former range. In the territory they have regained, about 600,000 hectares (1½ million acres), they will theoretically have enough land to create a way of life that retains some hunting and gathering. Unfortunately, the Ecuadorian government maintains the right to explore for and exploit deposits of oil under Huaorani lands, almost completely undermining the Huaorani's victory.

The survival of indigenous Amazonians is still being determined moment by moment. It can only be hoped that indigenous peoples will themselves create the forms of survival that will bring them into the next century.

Left, Huaorani spokesman accepts land title agreement in 1990.

At first blush, Randy Borman looks like many other guides now catering to the boom in Amazon tourism. Ruddy-complexioned and powerfully built, Borman leads groups of Westerners down Ecuador's Aguarico River to spend a week or two at a small Indian village, Sabelo – home to a splinter group of Cofan Indians who have relocated eight hours downriver (by motorized dugout canoe) from their main community of Dureno in search of more abundant game.

Borman's tour operation would be a typical case of privileged *us* getting a good look at exotic *them* were it not for the fact that Borman, a North American in his thirties, considers himself to be a card-carrying member of *them*. Officially, he is the elected president of Sabelo; in an unofficial sense, he is the chief of the community.

A life among the Cofan: White men are rarely chosen to become Indian chiefs, but Randy Borman was, as the saying goes, uniquely qualified for the job. The son of American missionaries who spent their careers with the Cofan, Borman combines an intimate knowledge of Cofan culture and the jungle with a Western education and an analytical turn of mind. He is an unabashed romantic and a rationalist, a useful schizophrenia for a man who would be gringo chief.

It's the romantic that catches your attention first. "At Sabelo," Borman says, "there are enough daily experiences on the edge, enough necessary contrasts, to make it life with a capital L." Borman is fond of a good wrestle with a giant boa, he hunts wild pigs with a lance and gaffs 68-kg (150-lb) catfish with a fist-through-the-gills jab.

The rationalist in Borman is, in a way, tackling more dangerous game. The Cofan and their neighbors, the Siona-Secoya, are the two peoples indigenous to the Aguarico who are facing a kind of cultural extinction. Their combined populations number just over a thousand. In the last two decades, by contrast, the oil industry has paved the way for 10,000 *mestizo* colonists to settle in the Lago Agrio area alone.

With the numbers against him, Borman is trying to guide the Cofan through a potentially lethal stretch of modernity. "The Cofan

collected around me because I was doing what the old chiefs did," he explains, "protecting them from the outside forces and providing for them." If Borman fails in his chiefly mission, the Cofan can anticipate one of several disturbing fates. Like the Yagua tribe in Peru, they could adopt Spanish language and customs, saving their "native dances" for the tourist groups. Or worse, the Cofan could lose even that *ersatz* sense of themselves: the slums of Latin American cities are filled with deracinated Indians oc-

cupying the bottom rung of society.

Borman is playing for time, trying to cut a deal with Western progress. Since the West holds the strongest cards – science, tourism, industry – his strategy is to borrow a few.

Escape from the petrol boom: Persuaded that the Cofan's most deeply rooted values were being eroded by the oil operations near Dureno, Borman founded the village of Sabelo several years ago. The village's economy is based entirely on the American tour groups he brings down to observe the traditional hunting and fishing lifestyle he feels he's preserving there. He also hopes to set up the Cofan as "scientific sherpas" who will, for a price, assist Western scientists who wish to study the virgin rainforest. And there are other, more controversial, plans.

One of Borman's recent schemes is built around a $23,000 saw, recently arrived from Wood-Mizer Products of Indiana. A small sawmill operation supplements tourist income. "There's not going to be infinite elbow-room out here forever," he says. "We have to be sure we're jolly ready when the rainforest is gone."

Whatever the merits of any of his projects,

"He's our people, he speaks our language," Mauricio said. "We hope everything will work out well."

Childhood in the jungle: Randy's parents, Bub and Bobbie Borman, arrived as missionaries in Dureno in 1955, with the task of translating the Bible into Cofan. They raised their four children in the rainforest, but it was Randy, the eldest, who received the most significant Cofan immersion. He spent the first five years of his life in Dureno, for most of that time the only non-Cofan child in the

Borman is probably the only person in the world who could – or would – attempt them. Judging by the comments of Mauricio Mendua, a respected elder and one of the few Cofan who speaks passable Spanish, not even the Cofan are sure what is coming next. "We don't know what Randy is going to do," he says. "it's something we think about."

The Cofan live in a world that keeps shifting underneath them and they need to believe in Borman, albeit in their fatalistic way.

Left, Randy Borman guides a Wilderness Travel group through an Amazon tributary. **Above**, Cofan *indígena* girls.

community. His later childhood was spent 64 km (40 miles) away in the missionary community at Limon Cocha where he fell under the sway of visiting botanists and zoologists.

As an adolescent, Randy wasn't sure in which world he belonged. His Western mission friends, he says, "were getting interested in basketball or whatever. I became somewhat of a loner." Two years at two different colleges in the Midwest persuaded him that he would never be the American boy-next-door. He returned to the Cofan and by assisting the occasional gringo traveler, he slowly developed his own tourism business. By his third full year in Dureno, he was hiring villagers to help lead tours for Wilderness Travel of Berkeley, California.

While Randy's fledgling business was doing well, Dureno was not. Texaco's first well in the region began pumping oil in 1972. Since then, the oil town of Lago Agrio, a mere hour's bus ride from Dureno, has mushroomed into a rough-and-tumble regional center linking the Amazonian Oriente district to the world. Unfortunately for the Cofan, their hunting land on the Lago side of the Aguarico River was cut to ribbons by a 504-km (315-mile) oil pipeline.

That first year back in Dureno, Borman organized local efforts for the Cofan to win legal title to their land. Pressured by a coalition that included missionaries and American academic leaders, the Ecuadorian government did finally recognize 8,000 hectares (20,000 acres) on the Dureno side of the river as a Cofan *communa*. While *communa* status affords a somewhat porous protection, it did give the Cofan the confidence to fight back.

In the late 1980s, Texaco began work on a new service road to a projected series of wells on the Cofan side of the river. The Dureno leaders demanded, among other things, 25 million sucres (about $80,000) in compensation, which Texaco refused.

When the Texaco workers returned to the road site, they were greeted by rifle-bearing Cofans, who blocked work on the road for four months until Texaco withdrew its people. Although Borman was at Sabelo at the time of the original confrontation, he did several weeks' strike duty when he returned to Dureno. He and the Dureno leaders had earlier hit upon this strategy of assertive nonviolence. "We borrowed it from Gandhi," Borman says.

Invasion of the Sierra: Most observers feel the oil road won't be built – not by Texaco anyway, since the company's government-granted drilling rights expired in 1992. But even without additional wells, Borman believes, the damage has been done. While the Aguarico's oil-eating bacteria have apparently been able to handle the dumping and the spills (several per year), there is no such handy solution to the problem of the colonists. These Ecuadorians of modest means have used the oil company roads to gain access to the jungle, transforming it into a patchwork of little coffee farms.

"So many of the bases of culture in Dureno have been knocked away," Borman says. "The Cofan now support themselves by growing coffee for export, just like the colonists. The majority of kids there feel kind of directionless. They tend the coffee plants, play volleyball, party, and get drunk." He regards Sabelo as a way out of the abyss; for him, wandering around the jungle is moral regeneration itself. "Hunting and fishing," he says, "are just the most common points of contact with the jungle. The crux of the matter is freedom." Sabelo, by his standard, is one of the most free places on earth.

Oriente refuge: The village of Sabelo sits on a small island separated from the shore by a narrow channel where stingrays live. During flood season, the huts are up to their stilts in water. Five of these huts are inhabited by the Cofan, two by the visiting tour groups. You can walk from one end of the clearing to the other in less than a minute, though it would take about three hours to walk the perimeter of the densely wooded island. Downstream from the central clearing there are five more Cofan huts and a one-room schoolhouse. Borman has encouraged this untraditional sprawl to solidify the Cofan's claim to the land, which isn't yet recognized by the Ecuadorian government.

At Sabelo, you can't help but notice Borman's ingenuous brand of leadership at work. His village is, in effect, a company town. Wilderness Travel subcontracts Borman to lead approximately 12 jungle tours a year. He in turn has formed his own company with two Cofan partners to provide the Western tourists with the exotic jungle experience they desire.

"The tourism business is a wonderful way of robbing from the rich and giving to the poor," Borman continues expansively. He tries to emulate his mentor in these matters, Robin Hood, who he says "gave the people a feast, a hell of a show, before he asked for a fee."

In the ten years that he has been leading tours, Borman has learned that real life occasionally gets in the way of the show. In the first years, tourists would sometimes complain to him that Cofan guides were shooting at the same toucans and macaws they had traveled thousands of miles to see. "Now we discourage hunting the animals that are popular with tourists," he says. "There are a few guys hunting on the side, but no one has to see it."

There's no question but that Randy Borman has created an unusual place, a postmodern Indian village. Semioticians would have a ball with Sabelo, the traditional Cofan village that supports itself by looking like a traditional Cofan village. Borman is ready to answer the unspoken charge that he is selling culture, not preserving it. "A traveler will come back with a deeper appreciation of the jungle, but also of Mauricio, the Cofan man who showed it to him. At that point, the Cofan are not selling themselves, they are enhancing their integrity."

Domestic life: Talking with Borman in his

Precisely because his fate is so bound to the Cofan, Borman is willing to contemplate survival plans that offend many disinterested purists. For starters, he wants to build a small sawmill which would be run by Indians. Borman proposes to cut trees from the floodplains, the islands of silt that form and unform in the river.

"We could sell finished lumber to the internal Oriente market," he says, meaning the same colonists who are clearing the rainforest and building the coffee farms that have driven the Cofan downriver to Sabelo.

Some might also see a contradiction in the fact that Sabelo's current tourist economy is dependent on the motorboat and hence on

hut is not a meditative activity. His Cofan wife Amelia will usually be preparing something in incongruous aluminum pots. His young son Felipe will be rolling around on the plank floor, either playing with his plastic toys or disturbing the already-frazzled equanimity of the family cat. Sabelo may be a business and a cultural experiment for Borman but it is also home. He can't imagine wanting to wriggle out of his rural Indian life for a more comfortable, more sophisticated life back in the US. "This is my hometown," he says of Sabelo, "and these are my people."

Above, Borman oversees the making of a canoe.

oil, the scourge of Dureno. "I call it realism," Borman says. "Trying to keep the Indians in stasis as some kind of pristine showcase denies them their dignity." Of course, Sabelo is a showcase in its own right, but at least it's co-produced by the Cofan.

Borman believes the Sabelo enterprise offers one group of the Cofan a way to control the pace of change so that they don't lose their language and their sense of themselves as a people. "A language is a way of thinking about the world," he says. "Keeping that is half the battle. The other half is holding on to the jungle – and there we might win a few battles, if not the war."

ARTESANIAS

There is something awesome about the human propensity to make beautiful objects. Chimps might make tools, but only humans embellish them. Since time immemorial people in Ecuador have lavished attention on their homes, tools and clothing far beyond what mere function demands.

There are no words in the indigenous languages for art, nor is there a distinction between fine arts and crafts. Seduced by their beauty, we have included many traditional Ecuadorian *artesanías* in our own category of fine art, particularly textiles, ceramics, and metallurgy (jewelry). If you have the time, there's something particularly satisfying about buying things from the artisans themselves or shopping in the market, but *artesanías* from throughout the country make their way into Quito and to the famous market in Otavalo.

Woven textiles: Four or five thousand years ago, some genius in the northern Andes invented the stick loom, which is still in use and generally called the backstrap loom (local names include *awana, macana*, and *telar*). This loom, sophisticated in concept and simple in form, is made of sticks and poles, with one end fastened to a stationary object and the other to the weaver's back.

When the Incas made a census of their empire they counted humans first, camelids (fiber-producing plants) second and textiles third, before precious metals, gemstones, ceramics or food. The pre-Hispanic Andeans were textile-obsessed and the Spanish were stunned by the superb handwoven cloth made of cotton, plant and camelid fibers that they found in Inca storehouses. Ecuador's damper climate has not been as conducive as Peru's to the preservation of organic materials, but the few pre-Hispanic textile fragments that exist suggest a tradition as venerable and as exquisite as Peru's.

The Spanish introduced the treadle loom, spinning wheel, handcarders, wool and silk; later came electric looms and synthetic fib-

ers. But an amazing number of weavers still use the stick loom. Even in Otavalo, where most weaving is done on the treadle loom, some ponchos and virtually all belts are made on the backstrap loom. In Saraguro, blankets (*cobijas*), grain sacks (*costales*) and most items of traditional dress are handspun on simple spindles of the kind you see throughout the Sierra and handwoven on the stick loom. These pieces are difficult to come by, but some are sold in Quito stores. In Ecuador, by the way, men are the weavers,

although many women weave, too.

The Cuenca region is famous for its ikat textiles. Ikat (*amarrado* or *watado*) is actually a dyeing rather than weaving technique, where the warp threads are tied and dyed *before* the piece is woven. Pre-Hispanic ikat fragments have been found in Ecuador, so we know that ikat is ancient. The best-known ikat textiles are *paños*, indigo-dyed cotton shawls with elaborate macramé fringes, made in and around Gualaceo. A newer style has a black and red body with macraméd and embroidered fringe. While it takes hours to wrap the designs, dye and weave the shawl, it takes up to three months to knot the fringe.

Preceding pages: weavings made by Salasaca *indígenas*; hand-made belts at Otavalo market; weavers in Chimborazo province. Left, local ornaments. Right, leatherworker in Cotacachi.

Paños were traditionally worn by *chola* women, but young women aren't wearing them, so fine ones are becoming rare. If you want to see the older women in their finery, proud as queens, visit the Gualaceo Sunday market. The skilled dyers and weavers have switched to making ikat wool belts, scarves, and shawls without fringes, usually dyed black or brown over red, blue, green or purple. Some of these shawls are made into high-fashion clothing, available in Quito.

Ikat carrying-cloths called *macanas* are made around Salcedo and in Chimborazo Province. The Salcedo *macanas* are deep indigo blue like the Cuenca *paños*, but the designs are coarser and they have a short

fringe. *Macanas* are used throughout the sierra as carrying-cloths, to haul everything from the baby to large loads of firewood.

Ikat ponchos are made and worn in the Sierra from Cañar to Natabuela, north of Otavalo. The poncho is a post-conquest garment, an adaptation of the Inca tunic. Various kinds of plain ponchos are woven for daily wear, while the ikat ones are reserved for weddings and fiestas. Especially beautiful ikat ponchos are made in Cañar, Chordeleg, Cacha Obraje (outside Riobamba), and Paniquindra (outside Otavalo).

And while we're on the subject of ikat, let's not forget blankets (*cobijas*), those mundane, but necessary items. Like ponchos, ikat blankets are made in every highland province, but these are for daily or rather, nightly use. A good one of handspun wool, woven in two sections and sewn together weighs 4½ kg (10 lb) and will keep you warm in a tent on top of Chimborazo.

Belts (*chumbis*) are woven on the backstrap loom throughout the Sierra. Double-faced belts with motifs ranging from Inca pots to farm animals are woven from handspun wool or commercial cotton sewing thread in Cañar. These are among the finest belts made in Ecuador, rivaled only by those of Salasaca. Salasaca belts are still made of handspun wool and many are unique because they are dyed with cochineal, a natural dye made from crushed female insects which live on the Opuntia cactus. Running a close race are a number of double and single-faced belts with woven motifs made in Chimborazo and Bolívar Provinces, followed by belts made in Otavalo and Paniquindra in Imbabura Province.

Tapestries: In the late 1950s the Andean Mission embarked on one of those craft projects that usually die a slow and painful death. But this one was a resounding success. Weavers from Salasaca and Otavalo were taught how to make tapestries (*tapices*) on the treadle loom. This technique, in which the weft threads interlock, gives tapestries a painterly quality. Today the stores around the main plaza in Salasaca and half the Otavalo market are filled with tapestries, including wall hangings, handbags (*bolsas*) and pillow covers (*cojines*).

Handknit clothing: While Ecuadorian women have been knitting since the colonial era, a Peace Corps project in the 1960s got the modern industry off the ground. Today sweaters (*chompas*), vests (*chalecos*), and hats (*gorros*) of handspun wool are made in Cuenca and in northern Ecuador in Ibarra, Mira, San Gabriel, San Isidro and Atuntaqui. Exporters and Quito craft-store owners work with the knitters on exclusive designs. Some sweaters and vests are now being knitted in cotton. The highest quality sweaters are usually sold in Quito or abroad, although some fine ones do show up in the Otavalo market. Wherever you buy a sweater be sure to try it on. The knitter's concept of small, medium and large isn't necessarily the same as yours.

Embroidery: If you look carefully in the

Otavalo market you will see women from another ethnic group than the Otavaleños, wearing pleated skirts and blouses with extremely fine, intricate embroidery on the bodice and sleeves. The women come from communities on the south and eastern sides of Imbabura mountain such as Gonzales Suarez, Zuleta, La Esperanza, San Isidro de Cajas and Rinconada. You can buy these blouses in the Otavalo and Ibarra markets. In addition, the women embroider more commercial items such as dresses, napkins, towels and tablecloths.

Hats, baskets and bags: Once and for all, "Panama" hats aren't made in Panama; they're made in southern Ecuador, where

Sierra provinces of Cotopaxi, Tungurahua and Chimborazo. These unique bags, made by hand with a buttonhole stitch, are found nowhere else in the Andes. They have served as the traditional carry-all for *indígena* men and women, filled with burdens and tied over the shoulders. While originally meant for local use, *shigras* found ready acceptance in the tourist and ethnic arts markets and the best are true collectors' items.

Baskets (*canastas*) made from various plants including cane and totora reeds are made throughout Ecuador and found in every market. Giant ones with lids come from Cuenca, smaller ones from around Latacunga, mats (*esteras*) from the communities

they're called *sombreros de paja toquilla* after the palm fiber from which they're made. The hats have been woven in the southern Sierra and coast for more than a century, with the industry going through cycles of booms and busts. (See *The Panama Hat Trail,* page 131, for more on the industry). In the 1960s the Peace Corps introduced other items such as nativity sets and Christmas tree ornaments to tide the *paja* weavers through hard times.

Shigra means sack in Quichua. *Shigras* are made of *cabuya* (Agave) fiber in the central

Left, woodcarvers in San Antonio de Ibarra. Above, buses that look like fruit.

around Lago San Pablo and fine two-color baskets from the Oriente.

Leatherwork: Cotacachi is the main center for wallets, purses, knapsacks, and clothes made from leather (*cuero*). The main street of the town is lined with shops. Leather items can also be found in the Otavalo market and in the shops in Quito. While the leatherwork is quite good, be sure to check the quality of the zippers and clasps.

Jewelry: One look at the pre-Hispanic gold, silver and platinum objects in the Museo del Banco Central in Quito and you know the ancient Ecuadorians were master metalworkers. In indigenous communities jewelers make silver, nickel and brass shawl pins (*tupus*), with the finest coming from Saraguro. On a more contemporary note, gold and silver filigree jewelry is a specialty of Chordeleg, where jewelry stores (*joyerias*) line the road into town and the main plaza. The workmanship is excellent and the prices are reasonable.

In pre-Hispanic times the Ecuadorian seacoast was the source of the prized, coral-colored spondylus shell, traded throughout the Andes. Beads (*cuentas* or *wallkas*) are still an essential part of traditional women's dress. The preference for red or coral-colored beads goes back centuries, to the days when spondylus was queen.

Ceramics: Beyond a doubt the most beautiful ceramics in Ecuador – perhaps in the entire upper Amazon – are made by the Canelos Quichua *indígenas*, or Sacha Runa (jungle people), who occupy the territory between the Napo and Pastaza rivers in Ecuador's Oriente. Women make the vessels, mainly bowls and pots for household and ceremonial use, by hand coiling. The finest pieces have walls that are eggshell thin, with designs painted on them representing various aspects of Canelos Quichua life and mythology. In recent years some ceramics – also beautiful, for what counts is not the intended buyer but the craftwomanship –

have been made for the ethnic arts market.

There are several ceramic factories with showrooms in Cuenca, turning out handmade dinner sets and tiles. The Cuenca *barrio* of Corazón de Jesus, and the towns of San Miguel and Chórdeleg have also been traditional producers of pottery, which shows up for sale at the Cuenca market. These potters use the imported wheel, and in San Miguel and Chórdeleg you can see their wares drying in the shade outside their houses.

The Sierra around Latacunga and Saquisili is another pottery center, with enormous Inca-style amphoras (*tinajas* or *ollas*) for making *chicha* produced in the little town of Tejar. Pujili, noted for its Corpus Christi celebration, also has potters who make and paint figurines of birds, animals and fiesta scenes. In fact, many small towns throughout the Sierra have a potter who makes kitchenwares, sold in the local market.

Woodcarving: There are two main centers of woodcarving, the Canelos Quichua region and San Antonio de Ibarra north of Otavalo. Unlike pottery, Canelos Quichua woodcarvings of tropical birds and animals were made expressly for the ethnic arts market beginning in 1975. Most of the carvings are made from balsawood, which is painted and laquered. Some are works of art evincing an intimate knowledge of the forms and details of jungle fauna.

Woodcarvings in San Antonio de Ibarra run the gamut from elaborate furniture to nativity sets, boxes, wall plaques and statues of the Virgin, saints and beggars. Pieces range from elegant to kitsch, but there are some treasures and it's possible to watch the carvers at work in the backs of their shops, which line the main plaza in San Antonio.

Bread dough figures: Even before the arrival of the Spanish, people made offerings to the dead. The tradition continues in the Catholic feast of All Saints (*Todos Santos*) and Day of the Dead (*Dia de Difuntos*) on November 1 and 2, where humans and animals made of bread dough are placed on graves. Producing dough figures (*masapan*) for sale and export is a main industry in Calderon at the southern edge of Quito where the dough is dyed bright colors and shaped into nativity sets, Christmas tree ornaments and other figures.

Left, classic old man figure-carving. **Right**, tapestries hanging in Otavalo market.

THE WEAVERS OF OTAVALO

Most travelers' first encounter with the *indígenas* of Otavalo is in Quito, Guayaquil, Tulcán or maybe in Colombia, Spain or the United States, where they travel to sell their textiles. Who are these prosperous-looking men with the long braids, blue ponchos and spotless white pants? And the elegant women with long hair, gilded glass necklaces, red wrist wraps, embroidered blouses and dark body wraps? Why are people from Otavalo appearing all around the world?

The answer is an unprecedented crafts and tourist boom, which has its roots deep in the past, for the Otavaleños have taken a history of forced weaving in Spanish colonial sweatshops and made it the basis of their present success. The Otavaleños have entered the money economy while maintaining their ethnic identity, becoming the most prosperous indigenous group in Latin America. They've joined the modern world on their own terms, which itself is no small accomplishment.

Master weavers: The high, green Otavalo valley is nestled between two extinct volcanoes just 96 kilometers north of Quito. The ancestors of the Otavaleños have occupied the area for millennia and for as far back as anyone knows the people of the region were spinners, weavers and textile merchants. Shortly after Columbus landed on the island of Hispaniola in 1492 the Inca armies completed a long and savage war of conquest of the Otavalo region. The Incas built a few ceremonial centers, introduced the Quechua language (which the Spanish spread as a *lingua franca*) and collected textile tribute from the local people, but they had been in the area fewer than 40 years when their empire fell to Spain.

Because Ecuador lacks the mineral wealth of Peru and Bolivia, the Spanish set about exploiting Ecuador's human resources and their textile skills. Within a year of the conquest, grants (*encomiendas*) were given out to Spaniards which entitled them to the use of native workers in return for Christianizing them. By the mid-1550s an *obraje* (textile workshop) using forced indigenous labor was established in Otavalo. At its height the

Otavalo *obraje* had 500 workers, including boys as young as nine years old. *Obrajes* were established elsewhere in the region in such places as Peguche and Cotacachi with conditions so abusive that many workers committed suicide to escape.

While the Spanish were brutally exploiting the native population, they introduced the European technology which has formed the basis for the present prosperity: carders, spinning wheels and treadle looms. They also introduced sheep and the concept of production weaving – making cloth in huge quantities for commercial purposes, a legacy which the Otavaleños are putting to good use nowadays.

Between 1690 and 1720 the *encomiendas* were abolished by the Spanish Crown, but native land fell into white hands and many *indígenas* entered into a system of debt peonage (*wasipungo*) whereby they were virtual serfs on large estates (*haciendas*).

Many *haciendas* continued to operate weaving workshops and several of these were in operation in 1863 when Friedrich Hassaurek, the US President, Abraham Lincoln's ambassador to Ecuador, visited Otavalo. He described the *indígenas* as "industrious", and visited Cotacachi where he observed that in addition to various woollen goods 6,000 cotton ponchos were manufactured a month.

Growing fame: The modern industry got its start in 1917 when *indígenas* on the Hacienda Cusín were encouraged to make imitations of imported British tweeds (*casimires*). These proved successful in the national market and *casimir* weaving spread to other families and villages in the Otavalo valley. Unlike the trend towards centralization in many parts of the world, in Otavalo the textile industry decentralized and became a true cottage industry centered in the home. One reason is that many *indígenas* see themselves as farmers as much as weavers and arrange their weaving around the demands of the agricultural cycle.

In 1964 the Law of Agrarian Reform outlawed the debt peonage of *wasipungo* and other forms of debt servitude. All *wasipungeros* were to be granted immediate title to their plots with a minimum of 5 hectares (12 acres) of productive land per family. Although the land redistribution was often circumvented, *indígenas* were free to weave at home or to hire themselves out to other *indígenas*. The energy unleashed was awesome; many of the most prosperous contemporary weaving families are descendants of *wasipungeros*.

The Agrarian Reform coincided with an increase in tourism to the region. In 1966 there was one crafts store in Otavalo. By 1990 there were about 80, most of them *indígena* owned and operated. *Indígenas* in Otavalo also own restaurants, apartment buildings, hotels, *peñas* (folkmusic clubs),

such as the sweater knitters of Mira, Ibarra and San Gabriel and the felt hat makers of Iluman.

Modern industry: Counting the children's help, about 85 percent of the estimated 45,000 Otavaleños in the valley are involved in the textile industry either full or part time as spinners, weavers, knitters, finishers, wholesalers or retailers, including store owners, market vendors and traveling merchants. Almost all families have at least one spinning wheel or loom in the house. Involvement ranges from widows who spin 2 kg (5 lb) of wool yarn a week, to families weaving a few ponchos a month on the backstrap loom, to the Tejidos Rumiñahui in Otavalo,

and a travel agency which offers tours in English and Spanish of the local weaving villages (contact Zulay Saravino at Diceny Viajas by the Original Zulaytour on Calle Sucre near the corner of Colón).

It's a mistake, however, to think that the textile industry is mainly dependent on tourism. It's a rare Ecuadorian who doesn't own something from Otavalo and most textiles are sold to other South Americans. There is also a substantial export business to North America, Europe and Japan which brings several million dollars a year into the region. Textile production has expanded far beyond the Otavaleños to white and *mestizo* families

which produces up to 300 ponchos a day on electric looms.

Each weaving and merchant family seeks an economic niche to occupy and the marketing acumen they evince is impressive. One family in Quinchuquí makes several hundred acrylic ponchos each month, which are exported to Venezuela. A family in Iluman produces acrylic dresses and shawls which they market in Guayaquil. A family in Peguche weaves wool scarves, ponchos and capes which they sell to a North American exporter. Another family in Peguche weaves high-quality *tapices* (tapestries) which they sell to the major folklore stores in Quito, to visitors to their home and at their kiosk in the Otavalo market.

Families around Lago San Pablo weave *esteras* (mats) made from totora reeds, while families around Cotacachi make *alpargatas* (sandals) which are sold to other Otavaleños.

You can visit these artisan families by taking a taxi or local bus to Peguche, Iluman, Quinchuqui, Agato or Cotacachi (all located within a few miles of Otavalo) and stopping at any house/weaving workshop/store with a sign advertising textiles for sale.

While people are usually quite friendly, be sure to ask permission to take photographs and don't wander uninvited into the living quarters.

custom of wearing long hair and the use of *alpargatas* are pre-Hispanic.

The Otavaleños' economic success has also resulted in their ability to buy back land in the valley, to travel abroad, to own such consumer goods as watches, kitchen appliances, televisions, cars and trucks, and to educate their children. Young people are flocking to schools including *colegios* (high schools) and some are attending universities in Ecuador and other countries.

Although some older *indígenas* and residents of remote communities are monolingual Quichua speakers, most *indígenas* are bilingual in Quichua and Spanish and a few will surprise you by speaking fluent English,

Keeping ancient traditions: Increased prosperity has not meant the abandonment of traditional dress, but the use of more luxurious fabrics. The women's skirt wraps *(anakus)* and shoulder wraps *(fachalinas)* were traditionally made of handspun wool or cotton; today wealthy women wear velvet. The women's dress, incidentally, is one of the closest in form to Inca women's costume worn anywhere in the Andes today. The men's dress is less conservative; a mixture of colonial and modern elements, although the

Left, traditionally dressed Otavaleñas selling fine rugs. **Above**, weaving in a nearby village.

French, German or Portuguese.

The Saturday Otavalo Market *(la féria)* is the high point of the week, not only for the hundreds of travelers who come from around the world (including many Colombians and Ecuadorians), but also for the thousands of *indígenas* who come to buy, sell and socialize. The market takes place in three main plazas and the surrounding streets.

Around the Poncho Plaza you'll find an amazing and comprehensive variety of crafts and textiles from throughout Ecuador. For more detailed information on the Saturday market, see also pages 186–187 of the *Going North* chapter.

The name Oswaldo Guayasamín is practically synonymous with modern art in Ecuador. But there are a number of other nationally and internationally known 20th-century artists, such as Carrasco, Camilo Egas, Olga Fisch, Ramiro Jácome, Eduardo Kingman and Manuel Rendon.

In painting, the first three decades of this century saw a continuation of 19th-century formalism, and the rise of a school called *"indígenismo"* (indigenism). Because Ecuadorian artists have not been isolated from currents in the international art world and many have studied or traveled in Europe and North America, the unifying factor of the indigenist school has been subject matter (Ecuador's exploited indigenous population) rather than style. Indigenist paintings are in styles ranging from realist (or figurative) to impressionist, cubist and surrealist.

Inspired by a Sierra life: Eduardo Kingman is perhaps the prototypical indigenist. Since the 1930s he has painted murals and canvasses and illustrated books, exploring social themes and the use of color. *Jugeteria* (Toy Store), an oil painted in 1985, shows the back of a young, barefoot *indígena* girl peering into the window of a brightly lit toy store. The toys are rendered in cheerful primary colors while the girl outside in the shadows, the picture of longing, is painted in somber burgundy, black and blue.

Such Kingman oil paintings as *Mujeres con santo* (Women with saint), *El maizal* (The maize grower) and *La sed* (Thirst) exhibit many of the characteristics of his work including the indigenist subject matter and highly stylized, semi-abstract human figures with heavy facial features, and huge, distorted hands. These paintings convey powerful images of oppression, sorrow and suffering, but the people portrayed in them are generic Indians rather than individuals.

Camilo Egas, another indigenist painter, lived in France for long periods of time and moved through a range of styles until his death in 1961. *Desolación* (Desolation) paint-

ed in 1949, looks like Salvador Dalí gone south, a surrealist work with a walking eyeball and distorted women supine on a brown, barren landscape.

Then, in a surprising switch, Egas produced the most beautiful of all the indigenist works with a series of realist paintings in the 1950s. In *Indios* (Indians), three long-haired men lean diagonally into the picture, using ropes to haul an unseen burden. The painting is done in a few bright, clear colors: blue sky, black hair, brown skin, red, white and yellow clothing. Neither the bodies nor the features of the men are abstracted or distorted and the impression conveyed is one of dignity and strength rather than misery. *El Indio Mariano* is a beautiful profile portrait in the same idiom.

Finally, in another stylistic switch in the late 1950s and early 1960s, Egas painted a series of abstract expressionist oils in blues and grays. There is less to say about these paintings as uniquely Ecuadorian art, since abstract expressionism is not so much about any particular subject matter or theme as it is about painting itself, about color and form on the surface of the canvas.

Manuel Rendón was a prolific painter who produced a remarkably diverse body of work. Artistic talent ran in the family; the paintings of his paternal grandmother, Delfina Pérez, were included in the 1900 Paris Exposition. Rendon spent his youth in Paris, where his father was the Ecuadorian ambassador, and he was greatly influenced by the modern art movement in France.

Rendon is considered one of the indigenist artists, but he is equally well known for cubist-style paintings of men and women in the 1920s and for a series on the *Sagrada Familia* (Holy Family) in the 1940s. But he also painted pointillist figurative and abstract works, and did many sketches in pencil and pen and ink. No matter what the medium, he has shown a continuing fascination with line.

Ecuadorian maestro: Oswaldo Guayasamín is the best known of the generation of artists who came of age in the 1930s and 1940s. His father was an *indígena* and Guayasamín has consistently and proudly emphasized his in-

Preceding pages: political mural in Latacunga. Left, Oswaldo Guayasamín, Ecuador's most famous painter, in his studio.

Art 127

digenous heritage. Few people are neutral about Guayasamín's work with its message of social protest. His admirers see him as a gifted artistic visionary and social critic, while his detractors see him as a third rate Picasso imitator whose innumerable paintings of *indígenas* with coarse features and gnarled hands have become parodies of the genre (visit the Museo Guayasamín in Quito and see for yourself).

Anyone familiar with the graphic paintings and statues of bloody, agonized Christs in Spanish colonial churches can trace this theme of suffering in Guayasamín's work, although his figures are secular rather than religious. One of his early works, the 1942

of the Ecuadorian Congress in Quito, in which 23 panels convey episodes from Ecuador's history. As usual, Guayasamín produced anything but a romanticized picture. Nineteen of the panels are in color; four are in black and white. The latter depict the first Ecuadorian president to enslave the *indígenas*, Ecuador's civilian and military dictators, and a skeletal face wearing a Nazi helmet emblazoned with the letters "CIA".

While Ecuadorians took the mural in their stride, the United States was outraged. The US ambassador called for the letters to be painted out and various US Congressmen discussed cutting off economic aid to Ecuador – exactly the kind of bullying that Gua-

painting *Los trabajadores* (the workers) is realistic in a manner similar to that of the Mexican muralist José Clemente Orozco. The similarity is more than coincidental as Guayasamín had met and worked with Orozco in Mexico.

Guayasamín went on to develop a style influenced by cubism with its chopped up and oddly reassembled images, notably in his series of monumental paintings *La Edad de la Ira* (The Age of Anger), *Los torturados* (The tortured) and *Cabezas* (Heads).

In 1988 Guayasamín continued his tradition of making visual political statements with his enormous mural in the meeting hall

yasamín was protesting against (the panel has remained unchanged).

German immigrants: Olga Fisch is internationally known for her work as an artist and designer, for her collection of Ecuadorian folk art and textiles and for her promotion of Ecuadorian *artesanías*. She arrived in Ecuador 50 years ago as a refugee from Hitler and brought with her a strong background in the visual arts from her studies at the Academy of Art in Düsseldorf, Germany.

Fisch was among the first to recognize the value of Ecuadorian *artesanías* as art and the design potential of traditional motifs. A talented painter, Fisch is known for her work in textile design, especially rugs and tapestries, based on her interpretations of pottery, embroidery and weaving motifs. She also designed clothing and jewelry, available at her two stores in Quito (see the listing of *artesanías* stores in the *Travel Tips* section).

The younger generation of painters has moved away from *indígenismo* to more personal, idiosyncratic themes and subject matter. Ramiro Jácome of Quito was part of the neo-figurative movement in the 1970s, that is, a movement that painted works with recognizable figures in them. In the early-1980s he painted a series of abstract oils, characterized by deep, rich colors. Later in the 1980s he returned to figurative works.

the upper left, rendered in swirling lines of black and white. The painting very effectively conveys the feeling of desperation familiar to anyone who has ever tried to catch a taxi in Quito in the rain.

Where to find modern art: The Casa de la Cultura in Quito, on Avenidas Patria and 12 de Octubre across from the US Embassy, has a gallery with a good collection of modern Ecuadorian art. In addition, the lawn outside contains a number of representative 20th-century sculptures.

There are two interesting museums in Quito devoted solely to the work of Camilo Egas and Oswaldo Guayasamín, respectively. The Museo y Taller Guayasamín is located at 543

In *Barrio* (Neighborhood) painted in 1989, three semi-abstract people are delineated by swift, black, brushstrokes. They lean against store fronts in what looks like a seedy downtown neighborhood and the use of yellows and reds contributes to a carnival-like atmosphere. Jácome's 1990 oil *A la cola* (To the end of the line) depicts a slashing rainstorm in which three bright-yellow taxis outlined in black divide the canvas diagonally. They are balanced by a mass of frantic people in

Calle Bosmediano in north Quito (Tel: 242 779). The Museo Camilo Egas is located at 1302 Calle Venezuela near the corner of Esmeraldas in downtown Quito (Tel: 514 511).

If you want to buy as well as look, on weekends artists display and sell their work in the Parque El Ejido in Quito, on Avenida Patria a few blocks west of the Casa de la Cultura. Art-Forum, on Calle Juan Leon Mera 870, just across from Libri Mundi Bookstore, has changing shows of major modern artists, with a very pleasant outdoor café where you can ponder what you've seen over a glass of something cold.

Left, example of the indigenist painting style, by Eduardo Kingman. **Above**, recent canvases by Jaime Romero (left) and Washingon Iza (right).

Although you wouldn't guess from the name, Ecuador's most famous export is the Panama hat. The confusion over its origin must be blamed on North Americans. In the 1850s, a group of vagabond gold miners returned from California to New York via central America and were asked where they had bought their unusual straw hats. "In Panama", came the misleading reply. Fifty years on, workers on the Panama Canal found the light, wide-brimmed hats ideal protection against the tropical sun. Nobody cared where they were actually *made*, and the misnomer was popularly verified.

Obscurity of another kind has plagued the Panama hat industry itself, where unbridled capitalism feeds on socio-economic inequality. The hat weavers, mostly uneducated women with families in need of a supplementary income, spend painstaking hours intricately interlacing the fine straw threads. In a complex production process, they contribute by far the most work, but receive in payment a mere fraction of the hat's value. Bound by the horizons of their villages, they cannot imagine the prices their hats will fetch in a US showroom; they constitute the bottom rung in a twisting, international trade route, unaware of their exploitation.

Colonial origins: Exactly who were the first weavers of straw hats in Ecuador remains a mystery. The Spanish *conquistadores* noticed the indigenous inhabitants of Manabí Province (where the top quality Panamas, *superfinos*, are still made) wearing straw hats shaped like vampire-bat wings. They adapted them and called them *toquillas*, from the Spanish *toca*, or "headdress". The first Spanish weaver, one Francisco Delgado, was among a group of Manabí craftsmen sent to teach their skills in Guayaquil and Peru in the 17th century. As the first few specimens filtered through to the US in the late 18th century, it was believed that they were the hat-shaped fruit – which whitened when ripe – of the *paja toquilla* tree.

In the 1830s, the exporting of *toquilla* straw was banned temporarily by the fledgling Ecuadorian government in response to

lobbying by weavers: there were attempts to grow it in Japan and Formosa (Taiwan), but – luckily for Ecuador – the climate proved unsuitable. It was to escape confiscation by a military extortionist in Manabí in 1834 that large numbers of hats first left Ecuador, being smuggled to Peru and Colombia. The following year, the *toquilla* was introduced to Cuenca, where it was hoped that the hat industry would alleviate biting poverty. A school and industry were established, and the locals were obliged, on pain of imprisonment, to learn the craft.

In 1849, Ecuador exported 220,000 Panamas; Manuel Alfaro, father of the future president Eloy Alfaro, is considered the first major exporter. At the World Exposition in Paris in 1855, the hats caused a sensation: King Napoleon III commandeered the prize specimen and was henceforth rarely seen without it. As illustrated by Renoir's paintings, the hat became a tasteful, debonair item of contemporary fashion.

In its homeland, however, the Panama hat identified its wearer as a manual laborer or a *campesino*, and so was eschewed by the sophisticated. It was nonetheless worn in some suprising circumstances: early this century, alligator-hide hunters would dive into the Río Guayas, naked but for a Panama. When the beast approached, the hunter would swim underwater, leaving the hat afloat for the alligator to munch on while he plunged his knife into its soft belly.

The choice of soldiers and gangsters: It was the Spanish-American War of 1898 that finally cracked the US market for Panama hats: 50,000 were issued to soldiers bound for tropical battlefields in the Caribbean and the Philippines. For the next 50 years, the industry thrived on the strength of an American infatuation: the gangsters of the 1920s preferred the wide-brim style, which is still called *El Capone* by the Manabí manufacturers. Through the 1930s and 1940s, Panamas formed an indispensable part of summer fashion, and were the hallmark of confidence and achievement.

Every US president since Grover Cleveland in the 1880s has been given a *superfino* by the Ecuadorian government: Teddy Roosevelt and Herbert Hoover were the keenest *aficionados*, along with the English monarchs Edward VII and George V. Ever a mirror of popular taste, Hollywood embraced the Panama hat: Sydney Greenstreet and Charlie Chan made it their trademark, and the screen's private eyes were soon considered rank charlatans without one. The writings of Mark Twain and Graham Greene celebrated its exotic flavor; Albert Schweitzer and, more recently, the novelist Tom Wolfe have sustained its notoriety.

The industry peaked in 1946 when 5 million hats were exported, constituting 20 percent of Ecuador's annual export earnings. At that time, half the population of Azuay Prov-

ince, which includes Cuenca, was involved in the hat-manufacturing process. But the identity crisis continued: when Ecuadorian consuls began adhering stickers saying "Panama Hats are Made in Ecuador" to all official correspondence, Californians responded: "I see they are now making Panama hats in Ecuador".

Source of the hat's straw: The Panama hat production trail begins in the low hills west of Guayaquil, a region cooled by the sea breezes of the Humboldt Current, and where rainfall is plentiful but not excessive. Although found from Bolivia to Panama, it is here, in these conditions, that *Carludovica*

palmata – named after King Carlos and his wife Luisa by two Spanish botanists in the late 18th century – thrives.

The plant, which takes three years to mature, still grows wild, but is more commonly cultivated in fields divided according to the families' seniority in the trade. Slender green stalks rising to between 3 and 6 meters (10 to 20 ft) high are topped by thin leaves; inside the stalk, new shoots contain dozens of very fine fronds about a meter long. It is these fronds, a few millimeters wide, that are woven; but first they must be boiled in water for an hour, sun-dried for a day, then boiled and dried again to ensure maximum strength.

The fronds are packed into large sacks called *bultos*, each holding about 3,000 pieces and weighing 20 kg (45 lb), and taken by truck to the weaving villages – a journey formerly made by mule-train. In these villages – Montecristi and Jipijapa in Manabí; Azogues, Biblián and Sígsig in Azuay – the weavers, often wearing Panamas themselves, buy as much straw as they can afford in special markets, and go home to work.

The finest weaving is done by the light of the moon or on overcast days, as direct sunlight makes the *toquilla* too brittle, and sweating hands produce loose weaves. Women and children are the best artisans, their delicate fingers being more suitable for threading the pliable straw, which is moistened with water during weaving. A *superfino* – tightly woven with the thinnest, lightest straw – requires up to three months' work, whereupon it will, overturned, hold water as surely as a glass, and will fold up to fit in a top pocket without creasing.

Finest of the fine: Montecristi is to Panama hats what Lourdes is to miracles: for 150 years the best *superfinos* have been woven in this peaceful, nondescript town. It is here that tourists come to buy direct from the weavers' hands, thereby circumventing the astonishingly demarcated process most hats undergo to become retail items.

This process extends from the weaver to the *comisionista* or middleman, who buys the hats only to sell them to the factory. Before reaching the *comisionista*, though, the weaver may be intercepted by the *perro* (literally, 'dog'), who serves the same unnecessary function. Once in the factory – usually run by the exporter – the loose ends around the hats' brims are trimmed. Each hat is then bleached in sodium sulphate and peroxide for three days; the brim is hand-ironed into shape and then softened with a mallet. The force of the pounding is carefully measured: too hard, and the straw will break; too soft, and it will have no effect. The hat is then rolled into a cone and wrapped in paper in a balsawood box, ready for exporting.

The main export center, and site of most of the factories, is Cuenca, Ecuador's third largest city. The route that gave the hat its popular name, via steamer from Guayaquil to Panama and then on to various points north, has been superceded by Ecuatoriana Airline's flights to New York and Los Angeles – a good reason to rectify the misnomer.

leaving the US plant it's worth $20; and its final average retail price is $25.

These figures can vary significantly: a *superfino* that took eight months to weave once sold for $300; another fetched a phenomenal $750. But while retail prices skyrocket, weavers' wages have barely risen in the past 25 years.

A waning industry: Whereas every household in Montecristi once produced top quality Panamas, now a mere handful of families in all of Manabí maintain the highest standards. Many have gone into more profitable occupations like farming and ranching, or taken to weaving *toquilla* baskets, bags and plant-holders, which require much less time.

Uneven profits: In monetary terms, the Panama hat trail resembles a river: the further one is from the source, the larger the flow. On a day at the market, a straw seller will earn $5–$10. A weaver will make $1–$2 profit per hat (a hat takes about 4 hours to make), more for better-quality styles. A *comisionista* earns 15–20 percent, selling it at $3 apiece. After factory processing a hat is worth 50 percent more, thus $4.50; when it reaches the US plant it is worth $10. Upon

Left, Panama hats in various stages of completion. **Above,** a dealer displays a *superfino* in his Cuenca store.

The international demand has fallen steadily since the late 1940s. China and Taiwan now produce cheaper, imitation paper hats that resemble the genuine item.

Exports to other South American countries rose during the 1970s, partially alleviating the problem. But the future looks bleak. Señor Carlos Barberán, owner of the premier Panama hat shop in Guayaquil – and perhaps the world – believes that the weaving of Montecristi *superfinos* will, in the next 20 years, grind to a halt. Hopefully, for the sake of the weavers and Ecuadorian pride, he is over-pessimistic; but the heyday of the hat is undeniably gone – probably forever.

Outdoor enthusiasts of all types have discovered that the diverse topography of Ecuador provides an ideal environment for so-called "adventure travel". The country's diminutive size makes getting around a logistical dream: nothing is too far away from anything else, and roads to almost everywhere eliminate the struggle to get off the beaten track.

Yet, for so small a country, Ecuador boasts an amazing assortment of terrain, while the climate is favorable for almost year-round excursions. Except for February and March, when it seems to be raining everywhere, good weather conditions can be found in one region or another throughout the year.

Trekking in the Sierra: Trekking is one of the most popular adventure activities and there is no lack of out-of-the-way places in the Andes to explore. A number of national parks, some newly established, offer uninhabited areas for days of wandering; while the populated highlands of the Sierra are dotted with many small villages whose inhabitants are always bemused to meet a back-packing gringo, or foreigner, and offer a shy but friendly welcome.

When planning an outdoor adventure, one of the best places to start is the South American Explorers' Club in Quito. This nonprofit organization functions primarily as an information network for travelers. The staff offer useful advice and up-to-date information on trails and weather conditions, and a stock of guidebooks and maps are available. The Club is located at Toledo 1254 in the La Floresta section of Quito (Tel: 566 076).

One of the most popular treks in Ecuador is the easy three-day hike to the ruins of Ingapirca, the finest example of Inca stonework in the country. Though a poor relation to its spectacular cousin in the Sacred Valley of Peru, this trek is nevertheless a worthwhile endeavor for walking enthusiasts.

The trek begins in the charming village of Achupallus north of Cuenca 15 km (9 miles) off the Pan-American highway. A dirt track eventually gives way to a cobbled footpath leading to a pass. You must squeeze through a small cave to get to the other side. After a brief descent, the trail climbs again and traverses a mountain slope above the green valley of the Cadrul River. The sparkling waters of the high mountain lake Laguna Las Tres Cruces is an excellent site for the first night's camp.

After about a half-day walk on the second day – crossing rocky ridges and skirting boggy valleys – the trail drops below the peak of Quilloloma. The remains of the old Inca road appear in the valley below. There is an excellent place to camp near Laguna Culebrillas and some minor Inca ruins aptly named Paredones (ruined walls) for the surviving crude stonework. A final three to four-hour hike on the third day follows the grassy Inca road to the ruins of Ingapirca (For more on Ingapirca, see pages 221–223 of the *Southern Sierra* chapter).

Trekking in National Parks: Several national parks within the highland region of Ecuador are especially popular with trekkers because of the ease of accessibility, established trail systems and marvelous scenery. In most cases, day hikes easily supplant longer treks for those who prefer to see the sights with a lighter load. Facilities within the parks are at a minimum, if they exist at all, but that's merely another part of traveling in a developing country.

A park entrance fee is usually charged – normally about US$8. In some cases, permission from the local INEFAN office must be obtained in advance. It is a good idea to buy the appropriate topographical maps at the IGM (Military Geographical Institute) before leaving Quito.

Cotopaxi National Park not only attracts climbers who come to scale the Cotopaxi volcano, but its wide open *páramo* is ideal for cross-country treks. The lower slope of Cotopaxi is called the Arenal – a word coming from the Spanish *arena* meaning sand. Actually the slopes are covered by pumice from recent volcanic eruptions.

A four-day trek across Cotopaxi National Park includes camping one night below the peaks of Carachaloma and Ruminahui near Laguna Limpiopungo, home to an assortment of birds such as the Andean gull, American coot and Andean lapwing. The trek circles the perfectly cone-shaped Cotopaxi and the huge Andean condor is sometimes spotted gliding high above.

Las Cajas National Recreation Area lies about 32 kms (20 miles) west of Cuenca. Its 30,000 hectares (74,000 acres) offers hikers an incredible variety of landscapes. The region is dotted with over 250 lakes varying widely in size and color. Fishing for trout is not only permitted, but encouraged.

The terrain of this recreation area varies from the moonscape appearance of granite rock outcrops barely penetrable cloud forest where mountain toucans and tropical woodpeckers make their home. Except for day

Longer treks are possible with planning, good maps and patience for hacking your way through dense cloud forest. This area is not frequently visited and so the intrepid trekker can take advantage of a pristine area unspoiled by flocks of visitors.

Mountaineering: The Andean mountain range in Ecuador comprises one of the largest concentrations of volcanoes in the world. These peaks dot the countryside at seemingly regular intervals and give a different appearance to the more fully-formed mountainous regions, such as the section of Andes which runs through Peru and Bolivia. This scattering of mountains means that most of the major peaks can be easily reached, but

hikes around the ranger station, most of the area is totally without marked trails, yet a cross-country trek of several days is quite feasible here.

Podocarpus National Park is located south of Loja and was recently added to the national park system in Ecuador (permits to enter the park can be obtained at INEFAN office on Calle Azuay between Valdiviseo and Olmedo). The area is largely cloud forest and is home to the reticent spectacle bear, the flamboyant Andean Cock of the Rock and the mountain tanager. A trail system has been established which includes several day hikes from the park headquarters.

also that Ecuador lacks the awe-inspiring vistas produced by a tightly formed mountain range. Still, the view that a solitary volcano cuts on the horizon is, to say the least, impressive.

Climbing in Ecuador is especially good for many reasons. It is possible to gain valuable high altitude experience on mountaineering routes that require little preparation. With proper acclimatization, most summits can be conquered in a weekend. Huts, or *refugios*, have been constructed on many of the higher and more popular climbs.

Some of the huts are equipped with bunks (bring a sleeping bag), a communal kitchen with gas stove, tables for dining and a hut guardian who knows the present conditions and route descriptions.

Good climbing weather is possible almost year-round, but normally the best months are June through September and during a short dry spell in December and January. Being a tropical mountain range at the equator, the Andes in Ecuador generate unusual weather conditions. One part of the Cordillera, or range, may be inundated with rain, while the next section to the south will have clear skies and perfect conditions for climbing. This, at least, makes for plenty of options.

Proper equipment is essential for safe climbing, regardless of how straightforward

cloudy conditions will often obscure the descent. In addition, a good headlamp with spare batteries is essential since all climbing begins in the early hours of the morning. All mountaineering gear can be hired in Quito, but, as with the trekking equipment, quality can vary.

For the stay at the *refugio*, usually only a sleeping bag is necessary, but during the weekends the huts can get crowded and the communal kitchen over-used. Bringing your own stove during peak climbing periods may be a good idea. Water is available at the *refugios*, but must be treated with purification tablets or boiled before drinking.

High altitude acclimatization is an impor-

most mountaineering routes may appear. Any climbs which involve ice or glacier travel are considered to be technical and require special equipment and knowledge of its use. Crampons, ice axe and rope are necessary along with the complement of warm clothing which is demanded by high altitude mountain conditions.

A rucksack with plenty of water, food and extra warm clothing is essential for the summit attempt. Flag markers, or wands, are used during the ascent for route-finding as

Left, steaming crater of Guagua Pichincha. **Above**, evening sun on the north face of Chimborazo.

tant factor when mountaineering in Ecuador. Many climbs are of such short duration that the need for proper acclimatization is often underestimated, but with major peaks above 5,700 meters (18,000 ft), this is something that should not be overlooked. The best way to accustom the system to altitude is to stay in a city or town relatively high, and take a few day hikes to higher elevations. Quito is a good choice and there are several strenuous hikes that can help the climber get in shape. At 4,700 meters (14,000 ft), Rucu Pichincha volcano overlooking Quito is an ideal climb to start with, before graduating on to harder, more distant peaks.

Mountain guides are available for climbers with little or no experience, but caution in selecting the proper guide is strongly recommended. There are many locals who claim the title after only a minimum of direct experience, and the result is potentially dangerous. A decent guide charges a decent price – remember that if you make a cheap arrangement, you will probably get exactly what you pay for. It is best to go with an adventure outfitter or agency that specializes in mountain excursions. Another option is to look for a well-publicized guide who has worked in the mountains for years and has clearly established a reputation for safety and expertise. Many of the climbing shops or

the South American Explorers' Club in Quito can recommend someone.

Easier climbs: For would-be climbers with no experience but plenty of enthusiasm, there are a few Ecuadorian volcanoes. The most popular of these is Tungurahua, towering over the town of Baños at 5,016 meters (16,457 ft). With a small glacier at the top, this straightforward climb can be done almost year-round, though it's a rare day when the weather is completely clear up here. Because it is located on the Oriente side of the Cordillera, clouds continually rising from the rainforest normally keep the summit well hidden.

With proper equipment – sturdy hiking boots, possibly crampons, and ice axe – Tungurahua can be climbed in a two days. Technically it is considered easy, but quite demanding physically. A taxi from Baños is the most convenient form of transport to the ranger station, which is the take-off point for the four-hour climb up to the well-placed mountain hut.

For many the most beautiful part of the entire climb is the trail to the *refugio* winds through dense, vegetation, wild orchids blooming in season. After a night spent in the hut, climbers begin the ascent in the early morning hours in order to finish the snow traverse before the sun has softened it to make going heavy.

Several hours of scrambling over pumice scree slope brings you to the snowline. From here, it is only another hour across the snow to the highest point. Views from the summit are some of the best – especially since the clouds lift so rarely. It is a special day when you can look down from the summit over the cloud forest to the line of volcanoes forming the backbone of the Ecuadorian Andes.

Cotopaxi and Chimborazo: For climbers with greater technical experience, the volcanoes of Cotopaxi at 5,897 meters (19,348 ft) and Chimborazo, at 6,310 meters (20,703 ft) the highest peak in Ecuador, are the main mountaineering attractions. On weekends during the peak climbing season, the *refugios* are completely packed with bustling climbers preparing for the rigors ahead.

Each of these mountains are climbed similarly – departing around midnight and requiring eight to 10 hours for the round trip. Often large numbers of climbers will set out at the same time, and the flickering eerie light from their headlamps on snow is all that is visible as they ascend in the early morning darkness.

Cotopaxi is more beautiful – with gentle, curving snow slopes and the massive rock wall of Yanasacha just below the summit. It's a pleasurable ascent as the dawn rays of the sun catch the crystilline snow and set the whole glacier sparkling. The summit crater seems perfectly formed against the deep blue Andean sky.

Chimborazo, but holds the attraction of being Ecuador's highest peak. After several hours of negotiating one steep slope after another, the process becomes something of a slog and one begins to wonder if the summit will ever appear.

This anxiety only intensifies as the lower summit of Ventimilla is reached and it becomes obvious that the highest point is still far distant. In the end, the persistent achieve their goal, the final summit views are well worth the effort.

White-water rafting: The attraction of running untamed rivers draws world class rafters and kayakers to Ecuador. But those with little or no experience can safely enjoy the thrill of white-water with the growing number of adventure travel companies operating out of Quito and Baños. The climate and water are warm so it is possible to wear only a

off the west side of the Sierra are high from February to May, good water can usually be found year round.

The most accessible and most commonly run rivers by commercial companies are the Toachi and the Blanco. The Toachi flows west from cloud forest to tropical rain forest on the coast, passing through great biodiversity on the way. Virgin forested canyons are interpersed with small farming villages, and abundant wildlife completes the tropical picture. Numerous species of colourful birds such as toucans and macaws and sometimes even the southern river otter can be seen.

Rafting trips start near Santo Domingo de los Colorados, navigating 20km of Class III

minimum of clothes – shorts, T-shirt and tennis shoes – unless the bugs are bad. Then insect repellent, long sleeved shirt and trousers are necessary for protection from irritating bites.

Many of Ecuador's rivers can be run year round, while some of the more technically difficult ones are possible only during certain seasons. Since the rivers flowing off the east side of the Sierra into the Oriente are high from June to August and rivers flowing

Left, rafters tackling the white water on one of Ecuador's mountain rivers. **Above**, trekker on the "Inca Trail."

rapids. Other popular class III–IV rafting trips start at the confluence of the Toachi with the Blanco, another river that transcends the Western Andean slopes to tropical rainforest.

A two-day river trip on the Puyango in southern Ecuador is one of the best in the country. The range in white-water rapids – Class II to IV – adds to what is a marvelously scenic trip.

The put-in is at either Porto Vela or Zaruma. The latter is a mining town from the last century, mostly abandoned, but retaining the picturesque charm of colonial times. During the first day the vegetation is dry. Several pools and rapids remind you that this is more than a simple float trip.

The second day the river quickly enters a canyon, where the vegetation is a mixture of tropical and desert plants. Here hundreds of iguanas sunbathe on the rocks, waterfalls cascade down the canyon walls and in one place a tributary of clear water offers a spot for a leisurely swim.

As the canyon opens the remains of petrified forest can be seen on the far shore where gold miners are shifting through the sands. Eventually the canyon opens further to agriculture and cattle farming where *campesinos* watch crazy *gringos* float by.

For the experienced rafter and kayaker

Mountain biking: The best way to get off the beaten track is on a mountain bike exploring the extensive dirt and cobble roads that pass through villages rarely visited by tourists. The high elevation, hilly terrain, and poor road conditions of the Sierra are challenging, but views and colorful local indigenous people around every curve make cycling worth the effort.

If you stay off the main paved roads such as the Pan American Highway (Ecuadorians are known for their unsafe driving), the unpaved routes chosen on a good topographic map will usually offer solitude and pleasant surprises.

A good place to get acclimatized to the

Ecuador has many challenging class IV and V rivers.

One of the biggest is the Quijos, but beware of San Rafael falls (152 metres/500 ft high). The approach to the falls is not obvious and two kayakers made the (unfortunately fatal) mistake of missing the egress. Huge boulders litter the river and tropical vegetation competes with small beaches – good for a quick rest – for limited space.

The combination of the spectacular scenery and the strong feeling of isolation make the Quijos all the more exciting. The best time to attempt such a trip is between December and mid-February.

elevation is the market town Otavalo. Using this as a base for exploration, day trips can be made to the surrounding small villages known for their *artesania* (arts and crafts). Several outfitters in town will rent bikes for the day and give advice about good routes.

A more ambitious ride takes you up a paved road to the Laguna de Cuicocha, a spectacular collapsed volcanic caldera which is now filled by a lake. If it is a hot day, you can wash off the sweat produced from the 600-meter (2,000 ft) climb in the cool waters of the lake. A labyrinth of unpaved roads leads back to Otavalo.

Don't worry if you get lost, there are plenty

of *tiendas* (corner stores) to a buy a soft drink and local *campesinos* can point you in the right direction.

Ecuador offers such a diversity of geographic zones in a small area, that a cyclist can cross over the crest of the Andes and descend into the humid forests of the Oriente within a day.

A popular day trip is a mostly downhill ride from Baños to the jungle town of Puyo. Bikes of dubious quality can be rented in Banos. Since you are coasting most of time it does not matter. You follow the cliff-hugging road along the gorge of the Pastaza River passing several inspiring waterfalls. In the town of Rio Verde (Green River) bikes

may be left with a local shopkeeper while you visit the falls. Buses pass every half hour and whether you make it to Puyo or not, you can heave your bike and self on top thus avoiding the long climb back to Baños.

A popular three- to five-day ride takes you past the Laguna de Quilatoa. A long climb from the Pan American Highway to the indigenous village of Zumbagua (can be avoided by taking a bus) is rewarded by views of an incredible volcanic landscape decorated by wheat fields in different stages of growth

Left, taking a break in the *páramo*. **Above**, "who goes there?" Llamas in Cotopaxi park.

from deep greens and golden yellows to the dark brown earth ready for planting. A dirt track leads to the edge of Laguna de Quilatoa, an incredible volcanic crater lake. After a cold night on the rim of the crater, the next day you wind along the edge of deeply eroded pumice plain to the town of Siglos where a bus can be taken back to Quito.

Although several excellent mountain bike stores have recently opened in Quito, renting bikes of high quality – necessary for longer trips – is difficult. It is best to bring your own. Most airlines will allow you to check your bike on international flights as long as it is boxed. Once in the country, getting to your starting point is made easy by buses with topracks that go almost everywhere. Just make sure someone's harvest of potatoes does not end up on top of your bike wheel during the loading.

Paragliding: Imagine taking off from the slopes of Mount Pichincha in a paraglider and soaring over the city of Quito to land in the northern hemisphere on the other side of the equator. A small group of devoted and well-trained enthusiasts can be seen on weekends doing just this, the only place in the world where it is allowed to paraglide over a major city. Strict respect for local air traffic control authorities has prevented accidents.

The topography of Ecuador is well-suited for paragliding in both the Sierra and on the coast. One popular launch site is at the refuge (4,206 metres/13,800 ft) on Mount Cotopaxi where you can ride thermals to the top of the highest volcano in the world. Best time of year to fly is December. Equally exciting is a flight from La Crucita on the coast catching winds off the ocean following a ridgeline 9.7 km (6 miles) long and staying airborn for three to five hours. This spot has been compared to Torres Pines in California. Best times to fly are August through September.

A paragliding school was established in Quito in 1989 (Pichincha C & C) with an excellent safety record. They have trained hundreds of pilots from Ecuador and abroad. Classes are held on weekends over three months or during an intensive two-week period, during which time lessons are given on aerodynamic theory, flying techniques, and meteorology. After approximately 70 practice flights, graduation is the jump off Mount Pichincha, 1,000 meters (3,400 ft) above Quito.

CUISINE

You really can't talk about Ecuadorian cuisine in the singular, because there are several cuisines corresponding to the geographical regions of the country: coast, Sierra and Oriente (Amazon jungle). And then there are "high" and "low" cuisines: what you'll find in good restaurants is quite different to what most people in the countryside *(campo)* eat and what you'll find in market booths and in little cafés throughout the country.

Bananas, however, are ubiquitous. In fact, Ecuador was the original banana republic. For many years bananas were its main export and the country is still the world's largest exporter of them. Not surprisingly, a number of varieties are grown on the coast and in the Oriente, from tiny finger bananas *(oritas)* to large, green cooking plantains *(plátanos* or *verdes)*. The yellow eating bananas of the kind you are accustomed to are called *guineos* in Ecuador. Short, fat red bananas called *magueños* are also good to eat. Bananas and plantains are trucked up to every highland town and market so you'll have no trouble finding them.

Staple foods: Rice *(arroz)* while not an indigenous food, is also ubiquitous although sometimes potatoes *(papas)* will substitute for rice in the highlands. You can count on one or the other to come with every meal. And sometimes, for a complete carbohydrate overload, noodles *(fideos)*, potatoes, rice, *yucca* (a white starchy tuber), and *plátanos*, or four of the five, will be served and that's the meal. This is, needless to say, poor people's food and a partial explanation of why many Ecuadorians are short in stature: besides a genetic component, they don't consume much protein.

Ecuador is overflowing with fruit of all kinds, from enormous *papayas* to more mysterious and less familiar treats like passion fruit *(aya-tacso, maracuyá* and *granadilla* are just a few kinds to try). Then there are sweet custard apples *(chirimoyas)* and tart tamarinds *(tamarindos)*, melons *(melones)* of all kinds, *mangos*, pineapples *(piñas)*, oranges *(naranjas)* and tangerines *(manderinas)*, avocados *(paltas)* and lots more.

Left, fresh lobster dinner.

The *naranjilla*, a tiny fruit that looks like a fuzzy, orange-to-greenish crab apple, makes a tasty drink that is often served instead of orange juice in the morning. Don't be put off by the strange green color; the juice is *sabroso* (delicious).

Just to confuse you, lemons are called *limas* and limes are called *limones*, the opposite of what you'd expect. If you're uncertain about how to eat a fruit, try it as a juice *(jugo)*. You can ask for juice without water *(sin agua)* and without sugar *(sin azúcar)*.

For a really great eating adventure, go to the market right after your arrival in Ecuador. Don't be intimated by the strange-looking array. Instead, buy every fruit you've never eaten (much less seen) before. Then go back to your hotel or pension and ask the owner to tell you the names of the fruits and how to eat them and invite the owner to share them with you. You'll discover some favorite fruits which you can enjoy for the rest of your trip.

Pacific flavors: Cuisine, however, means a style of cooking, so how do Ecuadorians combine their abundant raw ingredients? Many of the coastal dishes are typical of the entire Pacific coast from Chile to Mexico. They include *ceviche*, which is fish *(pescados)* or seafood *(mariscos)* marinated in lemons or limes, onions and chili peppers. There's *ceviche* made of shrimp *(camarones* or *langostinos)*, lobster *(langosta)*, sea bass *(corvina)*, crab *(cangrejos* or *jaibas)*, oysters *(ostiones)* and mixed *(mixto)*. Don't get *ceviche* mixed up with *escabeche*, which means pickled.

Ecuador's superb *corvina* is served a number of ways, including fried *(frito)*, breaded and fried *(apanada)* and filleted *(a la plancha)*. Try any sea fish cooked in *agua de coco* (coconut milk). Besides the varieties already mentioned there are clams *(almejas* or *conchas)*, grouper *(cherna)*, mackerel *(sierra)*, marlin *(picudo)*, snapper *(pargo)*, tuna *(atún)*, and squid *(calamares)*. The *dorado*, or dolphinfish *(Coryphaena hippurus)*, which is not a mammal like the true dolphin, is also popularly eaten.

A thoughtful Ecuadorian custom for regulating the spiciness or hotness of food is to serve hot sauce *(salsa picant)* made from chili peppers *(ají)* in a little side dish so that you can add as much or as little as you like.

Coastal and Oriente foods are similar because of these regions' low elevation and tropical climate, although there is more game hunting in the jungle (everything from monkeys to tapir and *paca*, a large rodent) and river fish instead of seafood. In both places you'll find lots of *plátanos, yucca,* rice and fried fish. There are several dishes unique to the Oriente, however. One is *piranha* fish. That's right, the famous carnivorous fish is itself good eating. The Oriente rivers also have lots of catfish *(challua* or *bagre)*, which people make into a stew with plantains, chili peppers and *cilantro.*

For a jungle salad, try *palmitos* (palm hearts) or chonta palm fruits *(frutas de chonta)*, both considered delicacies. *Chucula* is a tasty drink made of boiled and mashed plantains, which resembles a banana milkshake. Another jungle speciality is *chicha* (or *aswa*), a fermented beer made from *yucca*, which is also known as manioc *(mucuna)*. In order to make the *chicha* ferment, women chew the manioc, spit it into a large jar and add water. Enzymes in the saliva cause the fermentation. While this generally strikes foreigners as gross, consider that we sometimes exchange saliva when we kiss.

Generally, *aswa* will only be offered to you in people's homes, so if you find the thought of it unpalatable you needn't worry about encountering the drink in the course of ordinary travel. In restaurants you can order beer or soft drinks. Note however that *chicha* in the highlands is *not* made by mastication; instead yeast and sugar are added to make it ferment.

Sierra cuisine: And now, as we climb to the highlands, a word about the tuber, that traditional mainstay of indigenous life in the Andes. Believe me, there are a lot of tubers in the Andes, beginning with dozens of varieties of potatoes. The potato was domesticated around Lake Titicaca, the region which still has the most varieties – some of which are so specialized they only grow at altitudes above 2,400 meters (8,000 ft). Potatoes *(papas)* are served with every meal, usually boiled, but sometimes cut up into thick soups. If you don't like potatoes you're in for trouble in Ecuador. Today, as in Inca times, everyone plants and eats potatoes, the food of the common people. The great Inca terraces were reserved for corn, which was usually made into *chicha.*

Besides regular white potatoes in many

sizes and varieties, you will come across the sweet potato (*camote*) as well as *oca*, which looks like a long, skinny, lumpy potato. One Ecuadorian potato specialty is *llapingachos*, potato pancakes made with mashed potatoes, cheese and onions. A better lunch cannot be had.

Soups are the essence of Sierra meals. Before the Spanish conquest *indígenas* did not have ovens for baking, which meant that most food was boiled, a cuisine which survives today. Soup is called *caldo, sopa, chupe* or *locra*. Generally, a *sopa* or a *caldo* is a thin soup with potatoes and various UFOs – unidentified floating objects of the faunal variety. A *locro* or *chupe* is a thick, creamy soup.

(the week before Easter). You name it and *fanesca* has it: fish, eggs (*huevos*), cheese (*queso*), corn and every imaginable grain and vegetable and no meat. *Mazamorra* is a thick soup with a ground corn base and cabbage, potatoes (of course), onions and spices. *Sancocho* is a stew made with *plátanos* and corn. Most soups and stews are liberally seasoned with *cilantro* (coriander) and many are given a yellow or orange color by *achiote* seeds.

Corn (*maíz* or *sara*) is another staple, especially in the Sierra. Unlike Mexico and Central America, corn in the Andes is not ground and made into tortillas. In northern Ecuador corn is most commonly served on the cob

Sopa seca or just plain *seco* (which means dry) is more of a stew than a soup, with meat and vegetables added according to the budget and whim of the cook.

One of the most common *locros* is *yaguar locro* (blood soup), a favorite in the countryside. *Yaguar locro* contains the heart, liver, and other internal organs (which is to say tripe, or *mondongo*) of a cow (*vaca* or *res*), pig (*chancho*) or sheep (*borrego*), and is sprinkled on top with blood sausage or the animal's dried blood. *Fanesca* is an incredibly rich soup served only during Holy Week

(*choclo*). Ecuadorian corn has enormous, sweet kernels arranged irregularly, and it's the best corn-on-the-cob imaginable. In the north corn is also served as parched kernels (*kamcha*) or as popcorn (*cangil*). In southern Ecuador corn is commonly served as boiled kernels (*muti* or *mote*).

Humitas are corn tamales: cornmeal seasoned and steamed in the leaf. Don't eat the leaf – unwrap it and eat what's inside. *Tostadas de maíz* are corn pancakes; they make a good breakfast or snack.

Miracle grain: Other gains grown locally include *quinua*, wheat (*trigo*) and barley (*cebada*). *Quinua*, like the potato, is native to

Above, *anticuchos* ready for the grill.

the Andes. This tiny, round grain is an amazingly nutritious food, consisting of 15 percent complete protein, 55 percent carbohydrates and only 4 percent fat. The Incas regarded *quinua* as sacred and it was their second most important food crop. *Quinua* is usually served in soup, but it can also be eaten as a side dish like rice.

Most barley is ground up and used in soup, but wheat flour is used to make a variety of good breads and rolls *(pan, pancitos* and *empanadas,* which are baked pastries filled with cheese or meat). Around Latacunga you'll hear women calling *iallullas, allullas!* (pronounced azhúzhas). These are homemade rolls, good hot but hard when cold.

has – guinea pigs running around the kitchen. They live in broken crockery under a bench or counter along one wall and are fed on greens and food scraps. *Cuy* is only eaten on special occasions, when one of the furry creatures is scooped up, killed, gutted, cleaned, rubbed with lard and spices, put on a spit and roasted in the fire or baked in the oven. You may find this shocking, but you should emancipate yourself from European cultural prejudices and try *cuy.* There's not much meat, but what there is is delicious, and as the Ecuadorians put it, what else are *cuy* good for?

All right, back to that steak *(lomo* or *bifstec)* or chop *(chuleta). Parrilladas* are steak

Besides the usual vegetables, Ecuador has some surprises. What we call lima beans (as in lime-a) are actually Lima beans (as in Lima, Peru) because they were domesticated in the Andes, where they're called *habas.* After the *haba* harvest these huge fresh beans are boiled and served hot, dipped in salty *campo* cheese.

In search of meat dishes: About now you're probably wondering about the possibility of getting a good steak. Are you willing to settle for something smaller than a sirloin? A lot smaller? Try guinea pig *(cuy).* Until the arrival of Europeans, *cuy* was the main source of meat in the Andes. Every family had – and

houses or grills, where the meat is sometimes charcoal-grilled right at your table. *A la parrilla* means grilled and *churrasco* or *lomo montado* is meat (usually beef) topped with fried eggs. You can also order veal *(ternera),* lamb *(cordero)* or pork *(puerco* or *chanco; kuchi* in Quichua). *Lechón* is suckling pig. *Salchicha* is sausage in general, while *chorizo* refers to pork sausage. Bacon is *tocino,* ham is *jamón.*

Speaking of pork, this European introduction has become firmly entrenched in Ecuador's culinary repertoire. *Asado,* which means roasted, always refers to whole roasted pig in Ecuador, unless otherwise modified. Every food market has at least one vendor and sometimes a whole row selling *asado*. *Fritada* (fried pork) is also ubiquitous. *Fritada* is cooked in large copper and brass *pailas* (wok-like pans), visible in the market or in the doorways of small restaurants throughout the country. *Chicharrón* is fried pork skin, crispy and good.

The Quechua language has contributed one word to English: jerky from *charqui*, meaning dried meat. *Charqui* is more common in Peru and Bolivia, but you might encounter dried mutton.

Other sources of dietary protein include chicken *(pollo)* or hen *(gallina)* and eggs served in the usual ways, pasteurized cow's milk *(leche)*, sold in liter-sized plastic bags, and excellent cheese *(queso)*. Duck *(pato)* and turkey *(pavo)* are, alas, uncommon. The quality of Ecuadorian cheese has soared in recent years with the arrival of Swiss and Italian immigrants who have introduced European varieties. As for fish in the Sierra, many streams and lakes have been stocked with tasty, if bony, trout *(trucha)*.

Choosing drinks: In terms of beverages *(bebidas)*, Ecuadorian wine *(vino)* is highly unlikely to win international awards although occasional bottles surprise; the excellent Argentinian and Chilean wines are expensive. You're better off with beer *(cervesa)*, soft drinks *(gaseosas)* or mineral water *(agua mineral*, with Güitig – pronounced *wee-tig* – the most common brand). There is also tea *(te)*, herb tea *(agua aromática)* hot chocolate *(chocolate caliente)* and coffee *(café)*.

As with wine, Ecuadorians seem unclear on the concept when it comes to making coffee. Unmindful of the aphorism that "coffee boiled is coffee spoiled", they usually boil coffee until it becomes a sludge *(esencia)*, which is set on the table in a small carafe. *Esencia* looks just like soy sauce and is cause for some interesting culinary confusion in Chinese restaurants *(chifas)*. When you want hot coffee, the *esencia* is poured in your cup and hot water or milk is added. Sometimes instant coffee substitutes for *esencia*; the taste, unfortunately, is the same. Black coffee is *tinto*, coffee with milk is *café con leche* and coffee with hot water and milk is *pintado* (which literally means "painted").

Left, *ceviche*, popular on the coast. **Right**, barbecued *platano*.

Api is a hot drink made from ground corn, and it is sometimes so thick it might also be considered a *locro. Chicha morada* is a sweet, non-alcoholic drink. When it comes to liquor, the concept is very clear indeed: the production of the most potent possible intoxicant with the highest imaginable octane rating; a distilled sugar cane liquor known as *trago*, which burns with a clear blue flame. Local brands include Cristal and Sinchi Shungu (Strong Heart), as well as nameless varieties produced illegally in the *campo*.

Hervidas are hot drinks served at every fiesta, consisting of *trago* mixed with honey and *naranjilla* or blackberry juice; *guayusas* are *trago* mixed with sugar and hot *guayusa*

tea, while *canelazos* are *trigo* spiced with cinnamon, sugar and lime. These drinks tend to sneak up on you like Jack the Ripper.

Quito has several restaurants which specialize in gourmet versions of typical dishes, and are accordingly busy at weekends. The best of these include *La Choza*, located on Avenida 12 de Octubre just south of Colón; *La Ronda*, located in the new town at 400 Belo Horizonte off Almagro; and *Taberna Quiteña* with two sites, on Avenida Amazonas south of Colón, and on Manabí off Vargas in the old city.

As they say in Ecuador, *¡Buen provecho!* (Enjoy your meal!).

Ecuador is the smallest of South America's Andean republics and without doubt the easiest to explore.

The capital city, Quito, is the perfect base for travelers – and, for most, their point of arrival. Located only 24 km (15 miles) south of the Equator, Quito's Andean setting ensures that it has a pleasant, spring-like climate all year round. Unlike other Latin American capitals, Quito has not been swamped by a population explosion: its elegant colonial heart is preserved in the 18th century, while the modern "new town" offers every comfort from the 20th.

The Andean highlands remain Ecuador's heartland. The classic excursion from Quito, and one of the country's most famous attractions, is a short hop north for the Saturday handicraft market in Otavalo. Then, stretching south of Quito, is the lush mountain valley that the German scientist Alexander von Humboldt dubbed "the Avenue of the Volcanoes." The city of Cuenca, considered Ecuador's most beautiful colonial relic, marks the beginning of the Southern Sierra – a remote and traditional region that boasts some of Ecuador's most unusual *indígena* communities and the country's only Inca ruins.

But Ecuador offers much more than Sierra cultures and the spectacle of ice on the equator. Just 20 minutes' flight west of Quito is the Pacific coast. Moving to a more languid rhythm of life than the highlands, the Costa is washed by warm sea currents from the northern Pacific – making the coastline lusher and swimming more pleasant than at the icy beaches of Peru and Chile. Comfortable resorts are dotted along both Ecuador's north and south coasts, which travelers often try to reach directly rather than pass through the tropical city of Guayaquil, Ecuador's chaotic and rarely attractive commercial heart.

Twenty minutes by air east of Quito is the Oriente region, the most accessible section of the Amazon basin in South America. Jungle lodges, floating hotels and canoe trips explore the farthest reaches of this endangered region which, paradoxically, is fast becoming the continent's greatest travel attraction.

Finally, the Galápagos archipelago is in a class of its own. Easily reached on tours or independently by three-hour flights from Quito, this naturalists' paradise alone can justify the journey to Ecuador. A several-day-long cruise – either in a luxury liner or small chartered boat – is an expensive treat, but remains one of the world's great travel experiences.

Preceding pages: old-style locomotion across the tropical lowlands; view from the summit of Mount Cotopaxi; a Quito mural; the colonial splendor of Cuenca. **Left**, Mount Sangay erupting.

Rada de Tumaco

Co. Manglares

Tumaco

B.de Ancón
de Sardinas

Mira

Nev. de Cumbal
▲
4764

La Tola

San
Lorenzo

Esmeraldas

PERU

Ens.de
Mompiche

Muisne

Esmeraldas

Rosa
Zárate

Cotocachi

Ibarra

Tulcan

Cojimíes

Pedernales

Maldonado

Otavalo
Cayambe

Vol.Cayambe
▲
5790

Equator 0°

Jama

El Carmen

Santo
Domingo

✈ Quito

C.Pasado

Baeza

Bahía de Caráquez

Chone

Iliniza
▲
5263

Machachi

Manta

Velasco
Ibarra

Quevedo

Saquisilí

Cotopaxi
▲
5897

Tena   Misa

C.San Mateo

Montecristi

Portoviejo

Latacunga

Jipijapa

ECUADOR

Ambato

Baños

Puyo

Chimborazo
▲
6310

Guaranda

Canelos

THE (

Pacific

Pta-Bálsano

Riobamba

Babahoyo

Sangay
▲
5230

Bahía de
Sta.Elena

Manglaralto

Guayaquil ✈

Milagro

Ayapungo
▲
4699

Macas

Ocean

La Puntilla

Salinas

Sta. Elena

*Golfo
de
Guayaquil*

Playas

Posorja   Puna

I. PUNA

Balao

Naranjal

Cañar

Cuenca

Azogues

Gral L. Plaza
Gutíerrez (Limón)

Minas
▲
4096

Gualaceo

Sígsig

Guayas

Machala

Gualaquiza

Morona

Pasaje

Tumbes

Arenillas

Zaruma

Los Encuentros

Pto. Baga

Máncora

Catacocha

Macará

Vilcabamba

Loja

Zamora

Talara

El
Chorro

Sullana

Paita

Piura

Canchaque

Bravo
▲
3923

*Bahía
de
Sechura*

Bayovar

Chamaya

Florida

Olmos

Ecuador

120 km / 75 miles

Vol. Cutanga
▲ 4300

Florencia

El Doncello

L.Chaira

Buenos
Aires

Vaupes

Miraflores

Mocoa

Valparaíso

Panamá

La Cocha

San Luis

Guayas

COLOMBIA

SA. DE CHIRIBIQUETE

Puerto Asis

Guamués

Pto.Cuba

Pto.Yavilla

Lago
Agrio

Equator 0°

ESCARPE DE ARARACUARA

Pto. Perú

Pto. Leguizamo

Yan

Aguarico

Monos

Araracuara

Coca (Pto. Francisco
de Orellana)

Nuevo
Rocafuerte

Morelia

ECUADOR

Tamboryacu

Yabuyanos

Putumayo

Curaray *Curaray*

Puesto
Arturo

ITE

I. PINTA
(ABINGDON I.)

I. MARCHENA
(I. BINDLOE)

I. GENOVESA
(TOWER I.)

Flor de
Agosto

Pucaurco

astaza

ROCA
REDONDA

ISLAS GALAPAGOS
(ARCHIPIÉLAGO DE COLON)

Equator

Vol. Wolf
▲ 1646

I. SAN SALVADOR
(JAMES I.)

Vidal

Napo

ISLA FERNANDINA
(NARBOROUGH I.) *

ISLA ISABELA
(ALBEMARLE I.)

I. SANTA CRUZ
(INDEFATIGABLE I.)

Cerro Azul
▲ 1689

Villamil

Puerto
Ayora

Baquerizo
Moreno

(CHATAM I.)

Francisco
de Orellana

Pebas

Galapagos Archipiélago

I. ESPAÑOLA
(HOOD I.)

Iquitos

Amazonas

120 km / 75 miles

I. SANTA MARIA
(CHARLES I.)

Tbo. Tello

Desengaño

Disputed Area

Sta. Ana

Curuca

Pto.
América

Marañón

Sta. Teresa

PERU

Requena

Colonia Angamos

Cahuapanas

Huallaga

Canal de Pumahua

Flor de Punga

Sta. Isabel

Yurimaguas

Sta. Elena

Moyobamba

161

QUITO

Surrounded by snow-capped volcanoes but only 24 km (15 miles) from the Equator, Quito is a strange and beautiful city with a spring-like climate all year round. Although an important Indian city in Inca and pre-Inca times, its indigenous buildings have been erased and today it is divided between the colonial architecture and sculpture of its Spanish conquest days and the clean lines of its modern section. This combination of superb well-preserved colonial churches and convents and shining glass and sleek contemporary architecture makes Quito one of the most beautiful cities in the whole of Latin America.

Nestled at the foot of 4,790-meter (17,716-ft) high **Rucu Pichincha**, Ecuador's capital owes its name to the Quitua Indians. When the Inca empire spread as far as Ecuador under the leadership of Huayna Capac, the Indians living in what is now Quito put up impressive resitance to the invaders from Cuzco. But, in the end, Huayna Capac not only added the area to the empire but he married a beautiful princess from the conquered tribe and set up the Incas' northern capital in Quito. A road was built to link Cuzco with Quito, from which Huayna Capac preferred to rule.

His decision to divide the Inca kingdom into northern and southern regions – and his fathering of sons in both – were key factors in the downfall of the empire. When Huayna Capac died, his legitimate heir in Cuzco, Huascar, claimed the throne at the same time as the leader's illegitimate (but some say favorite) son, Atahualpa, declared himself Inca in Quito. The rights to the throne were clouded, too, by the Inca line of succession – which was not based solely on birth order. In many instances, the first son of an Inca was passed over for younger siblings who showed greater leadership skills, wisdom and courage. And, in the case of Huascar and Atahualpa, their subjects at either end of the kingdom supported the local son.

A razed city: A year after Francisco Pizarro had Atahualpa executed on the main plaza of Cajamarca, now in northern Peru, Sebastian de Benalcázar, accompanied by conquistador Diego de Almagro, arrived to claim Quito for the Spanish crown. They skirmished with Atahualpa's general, Rumiñahui (Face of Stone), and when it became clear he would be overcome, he angrily set the Inca palace on fire. The flames spread and the city the Spanish finally claimed was razed. (Rumiñahui, meanwhile, was captured and executed.) For that reason Quito has no Inca structures; all that remained of those magnificent buildings perched on the city's beautiful high plain were massive rock foundations. On those bases, the Spanish conquerors built churches, convents and palaces in the exuberant style of the Latin American baroque.

By the end of the 16th century, the new colonial city's population reached 1,500 and it was declared the seat of the royal *audiencia*, a legal subdivision of the New World colony. Its proliferation of churches, convents and monasteries

Preceding pages: Quito and Cotopaxi seen from Pichincha. **Left,** statue of the Virgin of Quito. **Right,** Quiteña.

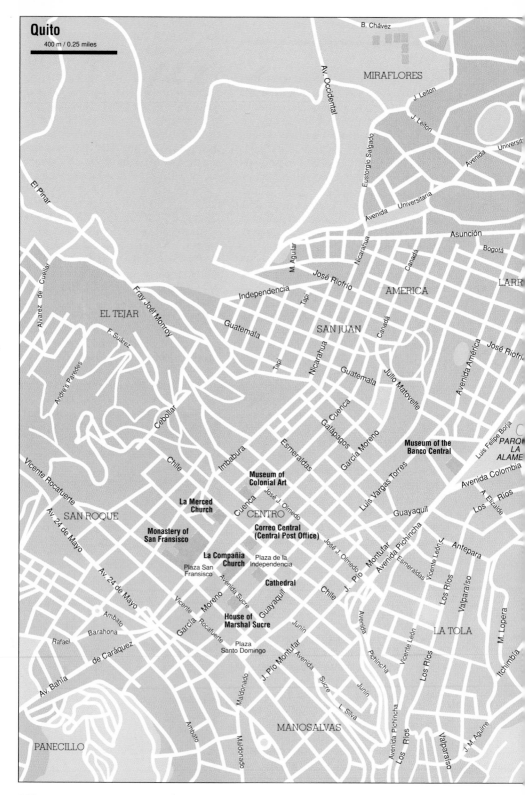

Quito

400 m / 0.25 miles

MIRAFLORES

B. Chávez

J. Leiton

J. Leiton

Av. Occidental

Universit

Avenida

Eustorgio Salgado

Asunción

Bogotá

M. Aguilar

Nicarahua

José Riofrío

Canadá

AMERICA

LARR

Avenida Universitaria

Independencia

Tapi

SAN JUAN

Canadá

José Riofrí

EL TEJAR

Guatemala

Nicarahua

Guatemala

Avenida América

F. Suárez

Tapi

Julio Matovelle

Fray Joél Monroy

Andrés Paredes

Cebollar

Cuenca

Galápagos

García Moreno

Museum of the
Banco Central

Luis Felipe Borja

PARQ
LA
ALAME

Esmeraldas

Imbabura

Luís Vargas Torres

Avenida Colombia

Chile

Museum of
Colonial Art

Cuenca

José J. Olmedo

Avenida

A. Elizalde

Los Ríos

La Merced
Church

CENTRO

Guayaquil

Antepara

Vicente Rocafuerte

SAN ROQUE

Correo Central
(Central Post Office)

Avenida Pichincha

Vicente León J.

Los Ríos

Av. 24 de Mayo

Monastery of
San Fransisco

José J. Olmedo

J. Pío Montúfar

Avenida Pichincha

Avenida Esmeraldas

Valparaíso

M. Lopera

Av. 24 de Mayo

La Compañia
Church

Plaza de la
Independencia

Chile

Plaza San
Fransisco

Avenida Sucre

Cathedral

García Moreno

Vicente León

Los Ríos

Ambato

Vicente Rocafuerte

House of
Marshal Sucre

Guayaquil

Junín

LA TOLA

Itchimbía

Barahona

Rafael

de Caráquez

Plaza
Santo Domingo

Avenida

Avenida

Pichincha

Los Ríos

J. Pío Montúfar

Sucre

Junín

Av. Bahía

Maldonado

L. Silva

Valparaíso

J. M. Aguirre

Ambato

MANOSALVAS

Avenida Pichincha

Los Ríos

PANECILLO

Maldonado

El Pinar

Álvarez de Cuellar

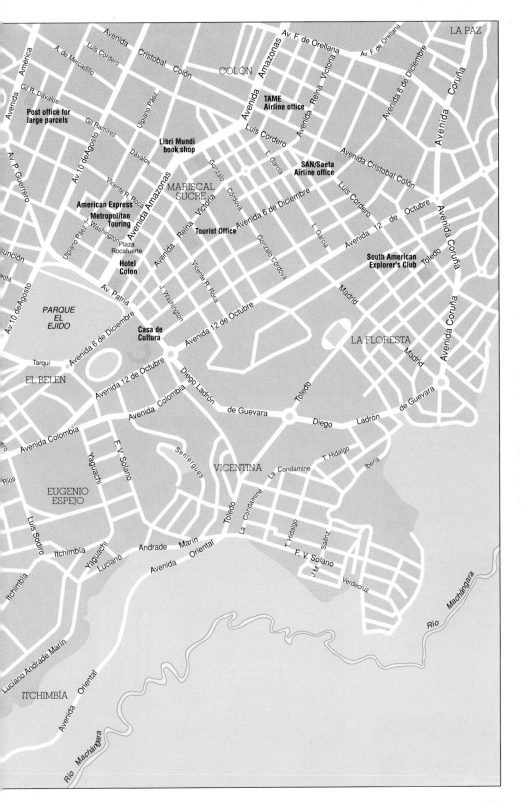

won Quito the nickname "The Cloister of America" and, in 1978, those very same colonial buildings prompted the United Nations to declare the city a World Cultural Heritage Site.

In early colonial Quito, changes came slowly but steadily as wheat farming was introduced, the Indians were converted to Christianity and colonial rule and laws replaced the Indian culture. In the centuries that followed, Quito became a center for art and sculpture in the New World, with the so-called School of Quito producing an art form characterized by violent Christian themes, such as saints drawing their last breath in horrifying and bloody scenes of martyrdom, and by the dark colors and gold brushings found in the similar School of Cuzco art in Peru.

The growth and development of Quito was not problem free. Quito had a bloody rebellion against a royal sales tax in 1592 and, in 1765, over the rumor that government-dispensed rum was poisoned to eliminate the poorer classes. But the biggest insurrection occurred when the winds of independence spreading across the continent reached this provincial city. In August of 1809 the first sparks of revolution flew in Quito and, on May 24, 1822, the city fell into the hands of the independence troops after a bloody battle in the foothills of Pichincha shadowing the city. (May 24, is now a national holiday.) For eight years Ecuador was part of a Gran Colombia – many countries united under a single government – but, in 1830, separated itself, against the wishes of Bolívar, to become independent under the presidency of Juan Flores.

Colonial buildings, modern problems: Although Quito's **old town** – called the *casco colonial* – with its churches, convents and white-washed houses with red tile roofs has not changed much physically since colonial times, social upheavals have been frequent. Despite its narrow cobblestone streets, traffic is thick and annoying during the day. And behind the doors of the mansions that once housed the city's richest residents in the oldest part of Quito are now the **The house of Marschal Sucre, now a museum.**

divided-up homes of the poor. In some of the most striking sections of the old city, such as **La Ronda** with its bright white buildings trimmed with blue window frames and doors and touched by pots of red geraniums, a daytime walk is a stroll into the past. But a saunter down the same street after dark is a near guarantee of robbery or assault, born of the poverty suffered by some residents.

Quito today extends far beyond the old town's borders, even spreading up the slopes of Pichincha on the west side. On the eastern side of the city is the **Los Chillos** valley, which has experienced considerable urban development in recent years due to a new highway connecting it with the city. In northern Quito, huge business centers have sprung up complete with banks, shopping arcades, embassies and government buildings. This part of Quito is also where upper class residential areas are concentrated. The poor share the city's south side with factories and heavy industry stretched along the Pan-American highway, known locally as the Pana.

Left, streets in the old town. Right, enjoying the sun in the Plaza de la Independencia.

Although the city's rapid growth – including a three-fold swell in inhabitants from 1950 to 1974 when the population reached 600,000 – has brought serious problems including street crime, marginal housing, pollution and a lack of basic services, Quito is still one of the few Latin American capitals where living conditions remain very good for the wealthy and supportable for the working class (although there has been a disturbing increase in the number of beggars in the plazas).

Quito from above: Three spots offer fine panoramic views of Quito and its surrounding volcanoes. **Cerro Panecillo** (little broad loaf), a hill dominating the old city and topped by a statue of the Virgin of the Americas with an observation deck, lures those who want to survey the basin in which Quito sits. A series of steps and paths from Calle Garcia Moreno and Ambato enable visitors to walk up the hill but assaults are frequent and visitors are strongly advised to ascend Panecillo only by taxi. There is a restaurant on this hill, which

was an Inca site for sun worship. The best times for taking photos from here are early morning and late afternoon.

An even more splendid view is available from the **Cima de la Libertad** – the liberty summit. Founded on the site of the 1822 Battle of Pichincha, this spot has a **museum** built by the Ministry of Defense and dedicated to the independence era in Quito. The museum exhibits flags, weapons, a model of this pivotal battle and a sarcophagus containing the remains of its heroes. Their tomb is dramatically guarded by an eternally-burning flame.

Also overwhelming is the view from **Cruz Loma**, one of the two antenna-topped peaks overlooking Quito on the eastern slope of **Rucu Pichincha**. On a clear day, the view extends about 50 km (30 miles) down the central valley and to the east. There are no roads up to Rucu Pichincha, but there are trails from the west side of the city to the summit. Assaults are common on the way up to Rucu, so it is essential you go in a group. For Guagua Pichincha, take a taxi up to the village of **LLoa** and then hike the six hours to the refugio just below the crater rim, or organise a trip with a travel agency who will provide 4WD transport and take you as far as the refuge.

Strolling through the past: Walking around the hilly, narrow streets is the best way to see old Quito, the heart of which is the **Plaza de la Independencia** dominated by the **Metropolitan Cathedral**. Also known as Plaza Grande, this palm-shaded square's other sides are flanked by the Presidential Palace, Archbishop's Palace and the disappointingly modern City Administration Building which was erected in 1978 to replace a colonial structure that was beyond rescue. At the center of the plaza is the city's bronze and marble Liberty monument.

The cathedral is easy to find because, joining the Amazon fervor of the rest of this country (which no longer contains portions of the Amazon River), the church has written on its facade *Es Gloria de Quito el Descubrimiento del Rio Amazonas* (Quito's Glory is the Discov-

Consulting guide books on the steps of the cathedral.

ery of the Amazon River.) The cathedral is believed to have existed first as a wood and adobe structure before the official church was built on the site in 1565. Earthquake damage has forced restoration on three occasions, including after the 1987 tremors that damaged many of the city's colonial buildings. The cathedral is filled with paintings and artwork from the hands of some of Ecuador's finest early artists. Among these is the famous *Descent from the Cross* by Indian artist Caspicara.

One of the side altars contains the remains of Venezuelan Antonio José de Sucre, leader of the liberation army that annihilated the royalists in the Battle of Pichincha; in his honor Ecuador's money is called the *sucre*. Left of the main altar is a statue of Ecuador's first chief executive and behind the altar is a plaque showing where President Gabriel García Moreno died on August 6, 1875 from gunshot wounds he received while returning to the Presidential Palace after mass. He was carried back across the street to the church but attempts to save

his life were futile. And this was not the only murder committed within the sanctuary of the cathedral. In 1917 a bishop of Quito died during mass when he drank poisoned altar wine. (Tourists are welcome to wander around the church but are asked not to do so during mass.)

The **Administration Building** is worth visiting to see the huge brightly-colored *naif* murals of Quito life, but you'll have to get past the plethora of children seeking to shine your shoes in order to do so. Around the corner from the cathedral on Calle García Moreno is **El Sagrario**, built over five decades as the cathedral's main chapel but now used as a separate church. This building is under restoration and allows visitors a peek at the painstaking work needed to save these centuries-old colonial buildings. Among the rescued works are frescoes by Francisco de Alban painted in the church's cupola.

Roller-coaster politics: On the northwest side of the plaza is the **Government Palace**, also known as the Presidential Palace (Palacio Presidencial)

Posing for a picture in the Old Town.

with Ecuador's flag atop it and guards in 19th-century uniform flanking its entrance. The guards' red, blue and gold uniforms from another era contrast with the automatic rifles they carry and used during a 1976 coup attempt. In fact, this building has seen much activity, especially in the early days of the republic. From 1901 to 1948 alone, Ecuador had 39 governments and four constitutions! (And at one point there were four presidents in a span of 26 days.) At the Government Palace, sightseeing is usually limited to the courtyard with its fountain and columns (the iron balconies were a gift from the French government) and Oswaldo Guayasamín's famous mosaic mural depicting explorer Francisco Orellana's jungle voyage to the Amazon. It was Orellana's journey, which began in Ecuador and culminated in Orellana's naming of the Amazon River near what is now Iquitos, Peru, that led Ecuador to declare itself "The Amazon Nation."

The palace, nearly 400 years old, is an unusual mix of the formal and informal and must be one of the world's few presidential offices where the street-level floor has been converted into small shops that sell souvenirs, including Panama hats, postcards and handicrafts.

Half a block from the plaza, at Espejo 1147, is the **Alberto Mena Camaño Municipal Museum of Art and History** in an early Jesuit house that later served as barracks for the royal Spanish troops in Quito. The stone column in the patio was the pillory and where prisoners were executed. The museum contains ecclesiastical art from the 16th and 17th centuries as well as a handful of works from the 1800s. Underneath is the dungeon where 36 revolutionaries of the 1890 uprising were imprisoned for nine months before they were executed. Wax figures in the museum graphically illustrate their deaths.

The museum was believed to have been built by Jesuit Friar Marcos Guerra, also credited with other buildings around the city until he and the other Jesuits were forced out of Quito in 1767 under a decree issued by King Carlos

Master cabinet-maker Carlos Carillo.

III. What had been the San Luis Seminary was then expropriated for government use.

From Plaza Independencia, two main streets – Carrera Venezuela and García Moreno – lead to the Avenida 24 de Mayo, crested by a new concrete building used as a market hall since street markets were officially abolished in 1981. Despite this ban, lively street trading still goes on at daily markets from Sucre down to 24 de Mayo and from the San Francisco church west past Cuenca street in what is the most indigenous section of the city. Peek into the buildings on the way by. Many are colonial structures that now anachronistically house auto supply shops and five-and-dime stores.

Roaming La Ronda: At Calle Juan de Dios Morales, one finds **La Ronda**, the neighborhood offering the most romantic slice of colonial Quito. Narrow streets of polished cobblestone are bordered on both sides by beautiful old houses with Spanish balconies. This graceful maze of passages and stairways runs from Carrera Venezuela to Calle Maldonado under two bridges. Its name comes from the guitar serenades – or *rondas* – that drew crowds here during colonial days and the musical history of this neighborhood is not forgotten. At intervals along the way are tile portraits of famous Ecuadorian musicians and composers. Unfortunately this area is not as safe as it once was. Tourist thefts at night are a particular problem.

Three blocks from La Ronda is the wide **Plaza San Francisco**, named for its church and convent honoring Quito's patron saint. Flemish missionary Fray Jodoco Ricke directed construction of the church and monastery on the site of the Inca palace only 50 days after the city's 1534 founding – making this the continent's oldest church. Ricke, who also introduced wheat to Ecuador by planting the first seeds in this plaza, is honored in the statue in front of the church. The San Francisco religious complex with its 104 Doric columns is the largest structure in colonial Quito, comparable in size to Spain's El Esco-

Good Friday procession through Quito.

rial and with a sumptuous Spanish baroque interior. But the Indian heritage of Quito sneaks into this Christian enclave; the church ceiling is decorated with images of the sun, the Inca divinity. Its main altar is spectacularly carved and the side aisles are banked by paintings by School of Quito masters, including the *Virgen Imaculada de Quito* by Bernardo de Legarda. This is reportedly the only winged image of the Virgin Mary found in either Europe or in the Americas.

The complex's finest artwork, including paintings, sculptures and furniture from the 16th century, is found in the **Franciscan Museum** to the right of the main entrance to the church. Actually located in the monastery, this building originally served as an art school. Note the details of the intricately wrought furniture; some pieces have literally thousands of mother-of-pearl mosaics in their construction.

To one side of the San Francisco atrium is the **Cantuña Chapel**, which legend says was built by the Indian Cantuña financed by treasures from the Inca empire. (Cantuña's remains lie in the San Francisco church.) The chapel has a magnificent carved altar – the work of Bernardo de Legarda – and its walls display finely carved wood.

America's most beautiful church: The magnificence of the San Francisco complex is overshadowed by an even more impressive house of worship – **La Compañía** two blocks away on Calle Benalcázar at García Moreno. This Jesuit church took 163 years to finish and is the most ornate in the country; some say it is the most splendid in Latin America. Richly intricate both inside and out, it is a masterpiece of baroque and Quiteño colonial art. Its altars are covered in gold leaf and the fine paintings on its vaulted ceiling have won it the nickname "Quito's Sistine Chapel." The pulpit and confessionals are of delicately carved wood and the walls are covered with School of Quito murals, including the painting of the *Last Judgment* at the entrance to La Compañía. The designs on the columns inside the church clearly show a Moorish influence and the columns themselves are said to be copies of those by Bernini in the Vatican; they are reproduced in the main altar.

Even with this, the church's most precious treasures, including an emerald and gold-laden painting of the Virgen Dolorosa are kept in the country's Central Bank vaults and taken out only for special religious festivals. Last time it was assessed, the painting was valued at more than $10 million. And the church's original holdings were far, far richer than what exist now. In 1767 when a decree banned the Jesuits from Spanish domains, the treasures in La Compañía were put into 36 boxes and shipped to Spain to pay war debts. What remained – mostly silver – was put up for sale but the devout Quiteños refused to buy it, saying that the items in question belonged to God.

At the foot of the altar in La Compañía are the remains of Quito's saint, Mariana de Jesus. In 1645, measles and diphtheria epidemics and an earthquake killed 14,000 people in Quito, prompt-

Triplets in the Plaza San Francisco.

174

ing a frantic attempt to break the city's bad luck streak. It was then that 26-year-old Mariana de Jesus stepped in. The orphaned daughter of an aristocratic family, she had already given all her wealth to the poor and was said to have miraculously healed the sick. Now she offered her own life to God if the rest of the city could be saved. As the story goes, she fell ill immediately after the public offer of self-sacrifice and, with her death, the plagues on the city ended. Just before she died, doctors bled her – as was the custom – and threw the blood into the garden of her home. It was said that a lily grew where the blood touched the earth and, for that reason, when the Pope canonized her, he called Mariana the "Lily of Quito."

Not far away is another of Quito's more than seven dozen churches, **La Merced** on Cuenca street at Chile. Its monastery contains the city's oldest clock, built in 1817 in London. Other non-religious features of this complex include the statue of Neptune on the fountain in the cloister's main patio,

considered one of Quito's most beautiful patios. (Visits to the cloister must be arranged in advance at the convent.)

The castle-like La Merced was one of the last churches built during Quito's colonial period – constructed from 1700 to 1734 – and it boasts the old city's tallest tower (47 meters/154 ft) and largest bell. Its walls are pink and white reliefs displaying more than three dozen gilt-framed School of Quito paintings, among them several with unusual scenes of erupting volcanoes and ash-covered Quito. Bernardo de Legarda carved the main altarpiece in this serenely beautiful church.

From here, the **National Museum of Colonial Art** is just a block away at Cuenca and Mejia in a beautiful 17th-century colonial house. The home of the Marquis of Vallacis now displays selected artwork from the School of Quito. Among its paintings, sculptures and crafts are works by Samaniego, Legarda and Caspicara.

Back to Plaza San Francisco and southeast along Calle Sucre is the **Casa de**

Sucre Historical Museum with its collection of weapons, clothing, furniture and documents from the Independence era. National hero Mariscal Antonio José de Sucre lived in this home.

A statue of Sucre, pointing toward Pichincha where he led independence troops to victory, is two blocks away at Bolívar and Guayaquil on busy Plaza Santo Domingo. Also here is the **Santo Domingo church**, especially attractive in the evening when its domes are lit against the dark sky, although the interior of the church has not been as well preserved as others in the city.

Santo Domingo is known for its fine religious sculptures, especially those of the Virgen del Rosario, donated by Spanish King Charles V. The **Dominican Museum "Fray Pedro Bedón"** also has an impressive collection of art (the friar himself was a painter). The museum is home to the astonishing silver throne used to carry the Virgen del Rosario during religious processions. A street off the plaza features arches that join houses together above eye level.

Quito's gold convent: Northward, passing the **Santa Catalina church** and the pretty **Plazoleta Andrade Marin**, at Mejía and Flores streets is the **San Agustín Monastery** where Ecuador's first Act of Independence was signed on August 10, 1809. Inside its flower-filled patio, robed monks pace, praying against a backdrop of oil paintings by Miguel de Santiago, who spent most of his life in the monastery illustrating the life of St Augustine. The third floor of one wing of the cloister, which is open to the public, houses restoration workshops of the Cultural Heritage Institute. The interior of the San Agustín church is an intriguing mixture of Gothic and arabesque styles and the complex was once dubbed the "Gold Convent" by Quiteños for its rich decor.

The room where the independence document was signed is called the "Sala Capitular" and contains a portable altar in 18th-century baroque style attributed to the Indian artist Pampite. In San Agustín catacomb are the remains of the independence leaders killed by the Span-

Skyscrapers over El Ejido Park in the new town.

ish loyalists a year after they joined the revolution.

Walking down Calle Flores you find the **Teatro Nacional Sucre**, the city's most beautiful theater and the frequent setting for concerts and plays. The National Symphony Orchestra performs here regularly. Two blocks to the north is the **Museo Camilo Egas** opened by the Banco Central to honor one of Ecuador's best known contemporary artists. Egas died in 1962 at the age of 73 but his art remains timeless. The museum has an extra attraction for it is located in a graceful colonial mansion.

Where old meets new: From here, Calle Guayaquil, with its 19th-century buildings, leads toward the area where the past is left behind. **San Blas Monastery**, in fact, is one of the last colonial complexes before the specter of modern Quito lying ahead at the point where old meets new. The landmark at this spot is the long, triangular **Parque de la Alameda** with an impressive monument of Liberation leader Simon Bolívar. The park has a number of other busts and

statues to famous Latin Americans, among them Manuelita Saenz – the Quito-born woman who was Bolívar's companion throughout the revolution.

It was 1598 when Spanish officials in Quito obtained permission to build the Alameda, an area for strolling, brightened by gardens, flowers and shade trees. The consensus was to place this park at the juncture of a natural lagoon – nowadays used by canoeists. At the center of the park is South America's oldest observatory, the **Observatorio Astronomico** started in 1864 and completed 23 years later. It is used by meteorologists and astronomers and is open to visitors on Saturday mornings. There is a French monument here honoring the European mission that traveled to Ecuador in 1736 to measure the arc of the equatorial line in order to work out the circumference of the earth.

Small **El Belén church** on the park's north side is often painted by Quito artists. It marks the site where the first mass in Quito was said after the city's founding by the Spanish. Simple and

The Casa de la Cultura Ecuatoriana.

graceful, this church's lone nave contains a magnificent Christ believed to be the work of Indian artist Caspicara.

Two blocks up Avenida 6 de Diciembre and right on Montalvo is the **Palacio Legislativo**, a new government building with the history of Eucador immortalized in carved stone. Following the east side of the park – El Ejido – to Avenida Paz y Miño, visitors can see the hilltop home of the Geographical Military Institute's planetarium, distinguishable by its white dome. Shows take place daily.

Parque El Ejido is a favorite spot – especially on weekends – for shy Otavalo Indians, picnickers, soccer players, couples out for a stroll, energetic children and street vendors seeking the park's shady trees as respite from the warm sun. Here women carry huge trays of food on their heads, offering for sale *fritada, papas y mote*, portions of grilled meat, potatoes and corn.

Banks, boutiques and bargains: At the north end of El Ejido, from Avenidas Patria to Colón, lies Quito's modern tourist and business area with hotels, offices, banks and restaurants. **Avenida Amazonas** is home to travel agencies, art galleries, money exchangers, outdoor cafés and the doubledecker airport buses. This is the best spot for strolling and shopping, with stops for cool drinks or snacks at the many restaurants and pastry shops along the route. Shopping bargains range from well-made handicrafts to clothing in boutiques carrying the latest fashions. In the **Colón Internacional Hotel** at the south end of the street is a shopping gallery with one of the city's top bookstores carrying English-language titles and maps.

The Casa de la Cultura, a large circular glass building, is located on the northeast edge of the park. The building houses the **National Museum of the Banco Central** inaugurated in June 1995. This unique presentation of Ecuadorian history through art should not be missed. The museum actually includes five connected salons: archaeology, gold, colonial art, Republican art and modern art. As you walk through the collections

The Museo Guayasamín.

in chronological order you will gain a sense of Ecuador's proud history as seen through the eyes of its artists. Each of the pre-Colombian cultures is represented by artifacts – including pottery, tools, jewelry – and well constructed diaramas. A separate gold room is highlighted by a ceremonial mask made of gold and silver. The transition to the colonial collection is marked by a gold sun, the god of the Incas, and a silver cross inlaid with precious stone, an early piece by the conquering Spanish. It contains pieces from the famous Quito School, including one of two known sculptures of the Virgin Mary pregnant.

The Republican collection has wonderful paintings of mountain and jungle landscapes as well as themes of national identity and social change. The indigenous people's struggle for freedom is forcefully presented in the paintings of Kingman in the modern collection. Another salon is reserved for presentations that are rotated every month.

Written explanations throughout the museum are in Spanish and English and guided tours are available in Spanish, English, German and French. The museum is open Tuesday through Sunday.

Next door is the **Museum of the Casa de la Cultura Ecuatoriana**, a less comprehensive collection of art from the Republican period to modern times. A separate room of the museum displays musical instruments, many of them several centuries old from all over the world. There is also a display of traditional dress from various indigenous cultures. A movie theater and concert hall are also housed in the Casa de la Cultura.

Just two blocks away, another fine museum with archaeological artifacts is run by the Universidad Catolica on Avenida 12 de Octubre. The **Museo Jíjón y Camaño** contains the private collection donated by the family of Jacinto Jíjón y Camaño after the aristocratic archaeologist died.

It was this man's work that provided the base for the modern-day theories on how pre-Hispanic Indians lived in Ecuador; his books on the subject are valuable rarities. The collection includes *aribalos*, the graceful fluted-mouth jars

with pointed bottoms that are synonymous with pre-Inca cultures in the Andes, as well as an assortment of religious idols, masks, weapons and shell and bone works. The museum also houses a small collection of the School of Quito colonial art.

Tracing the conquistadors' path: If you continue down tree-lined 12 de Octubre for another mile and a half (2 km) past the **Shuar Museum** and Hotel Quito onto a narrow cobblestone road, you'll come to the village of Guápulo on the outskirts of the city. (This route traces the mountain pass Francisco de Orellana followed on his journey to discover the Amazon River.) The Museo Shuar, run by the Salesian Mission, has artifacts from Amazon Indian tribes and cultural publications. The hotel, meanwhile, is surrounded by trendy restaurants, pubs and cafés.

Just over the ridge and down the hill from the hotel is **Guápulo** with its village sanctuary containing work by some of the country's best known 17th-century artists – and understandably so, for

Standing to attention at the Presidential Palace.

this was the founding spot for the School of Quito. This 17th-century church and former convent (now a private university), built by Indian slaves and dedicated to Our Lady of Guadalupe, has a pulpit by Indian sculptor Juan Menacho and is easily one of the most beautiful in the Americas. It is unquestionably the loveliest in Quito. Look carefully and you will see how Christian and Indian images are intertwined in the carving.

Perhaps the most intriguing colonial art collection in this city known for such paintings and sculptures is found at the **Guayasamín Museum**, actually one of the city's most beautiful modern houses perched on a hillside overlooking Quito. Set up by artist Oswaldo Guayasamín, the complex is divided into three: a colonial art gallery (Guayasamín's own collection), the artist's gallery for displaying and selling his work and a studio for him and his students.

Provocative and political, Guayasamín's art has made him perhaps the country's best-known and the gallery of his works should not be missed. Born of an Indian father and *mestizo* mother, his work delves heavily into themes connected with his mixed culture and this museum complex represents 30 years of planning. Sculptures are displayed in the flower-splashed tile roof. Although the house and museum are a bit hard to find, at José Bosmediano 543 in the Bella Vista neighborhood, any cab driver knows where it is. And afterwards, visitors can stroll through the eucalyptus forests in the **Parque Metropolitano** with views of Quito and the nearby peaks of Cotopaxi and Cayambe.

Located in the north, more affluent section of the city, is the large **Parque Carolina**. The playing fields on weekends are crowded with picnickers, soccer and volleyball players and runners. During part of the year Sunday outdoor concerts are offered by the National Symphony Orchestra. The Museum of Natural History is located on the south end of the park with a small collection of endemic species. Nearby a game of outdoor lifesized chess can be enjoyed at the **Cafe Ajedrez** (Chess Cafe).

Blood sports on the Quito Day celebrations.

THE MIDDLE OF THE WORLD

Monuments to mark the Equator can be found throughout South America, South-East Asia and Africa, but none are so accessible or boast the same historical significance as the site near San Antonio de Pichincha, only 24 km (15 miles) north of Quito.

Placed precisely at latitude 0, the monument known simply as La Mitad del Mundo (the Middle of the World) can be reached in a half-hour bus or car ride from the capital city. It was here, amongst some of Ecuador's finest mountain scenery, that an 18th-century French expedition made the first scientific measurements of the Equator. And although the monument – a 30-meter (90-ft) high block of stone topped by a huge metal globe of the earth – is sadly lacking in aesthetic appeal, it exerts an almost irresistible attraction for foreign visitors.

The imaginary 38,600-km (24,000-mile) Equatorial line around the world has here been turned into a tangible 10 cm (4 inch) wide strip of white pebbles set into the ground. Every day, thousands flock to have their photographs taken while straddling the Equator, with one leg in either of the world's hemispheres. Some spend half an hour leaping from one side to the other, so they can tell their friends they have crossed the Equator a thousand times. Should the whim take you, this is the spot to shake hands across the Equator, kiss across the Equator, play frisbee across the Equator or even arm wrestle across the Equator.

A particularly popular time to visit is at noon on the vernal and summer equinoxes (usually March 21 and September 22 respectively), when the sun shines directly overhead on the Equator. At that moment, neither the monument nor visitors cast a shadow – providing for even more unusual photo opportunities.

The site was not always the scene of such frivolous pursuits. In 1736, a famous scientific expedition – led by the French aristocrat and friend of Voltaire, Charles Marie de la Condamine – used this spot to first measure the length of a latitude. Commissioned by the French Academy of Sciences, the expedition's primary aim was to test Newton's theory that the earth bulged at the Equator. In the process, it determined the line's exact location and the unit of measurement that resulted in the metric system.

To mark the 200th anniversary of the expedition, which lasted for eight years, the Ecuadorian government erected a small monument on the site in 1936. It was replaced by the much larger present construction in 1986, including an impressive promenade lined with busts of the 13 members of La Condamine's expedition – nine of whom were Frenchmen, two Spaniards (possibly appointed to keep an eye on the Frenchmen for the Spanish crown) and two Ecuadorians.

One of the Ecuadorians, Pedro Vicente Maldonado, also accompanied La Condamine on a trek across the Andes and a grueling raft journey down the Amazon once the expedition was over in 1743. They were the first trained scientists to make the journey, and their map of the Amazon River remained almost unchanged until the 20th century.

The clumsy looking monument that marks the Equator today has nine levels that can be visited. First take the elevator up to the observation deck, which, on a clear day, offers spectacular views of the surrounding Andes, including extinct volcano Cayambe. From there, you can walk down a stairway to the other levels, which all have different displays on Ecuador's Indian tribes. Along the way are several souvenir shops, although their opening hours are erratic. Plans for a hotel, restaurant and shopping center at the site have been shelved.

After exploring the monument, there are several walks that can be made into the lush surrounding countryside. Only 2 km (1 mile) down the paved road towards the village of Calacali is a lookout over Pululahua volcanic crater – at 4 km (2½ miles) wide, the biggest in South America. The view into the Andean valleys beyond is also magnificent.

Alternatively, the Mitad del Mundo monument is within easy striking distance of the village of Calderon and the San Pablo Lake, which can easily be included on a relaxing one-day excursion from Quito. ∎

The Province of **Imbabura**, just a short step north of Quito, is one of Ecuador's most popular destinations. Its numerous Andean volcanoes, lakes and valleys combine to make a landscape of extraordinary beauty, while the variety of local indigenous groups makes the northern Sierra one of the most culturally vibrant regions in the country. Even more beguiling for many travelers is that Imbabura province is a rich source of handicrafts: it is home to the woodcarvers of San Antonio, the leatherworkers of Cotacachi and – most famously – the weavers of Otavalo.

Beyond the capital: Leaving Quito behind, most visitors take the shortest route to Imbabura: some 100 km (60 miles) along the paved Pan-American highway passing straight through the barren landscape of northern Pichincha. But for those who have time to explore, there are a number of ways of reaching the province and several places worth visiting on the way.

The main road passes through **Guayllabamba**. Surrounded by dry rocky hills, sparsely covered with tufts of grass, the Guayllabamba valley is warm and fertile, famous for its orchards and local fruit, such as the *chirimoya* (custard apple) – now grown in many countries – and the local variety of avocado pears, which are small, roundish and black-skinned. Visitors are pressed to buy the produce, and the local women compete by offering a *yapa* (one extra for the same price). Another specialty is the tasty *locro de cueros* (potato soup with pork rind) with avocados on the side.

Two roads lead out of Guayllabamba towards Cayambe: the left-hand one, via **Tabacundo**, follows a deep ravine, with curious rock formations. After crossing the Guayllabamba River it is possible to make a detour along the river-side down to the tranquil villages of **Puellaro** and **Perucho**, where oranges grow, and little seems to have changed in the space of several decades.

Another option is a visit to the archae-ological site of **Cochasqui**, on the southern slopes of **Mount Mojanda**, a short distance from Tabacundo. Some 15 flat-topped pyramids and 30 mounds are believed to have been built by Caranqui Indians around the 13th century, although some date as far back as AD 900. With the choice of a short or extended guided tour from the resident guardian, visitors can discover the world of religious and funeral practices, living styles and even astrological discoveries of the inhabitants of that era.

An alternative route from Quito to Cayambe, via the Tumbaco valley, passes through the sanctuary of **El Quinche**, a point of attraction for pilgrims from the whole of the northern Sierra. The Virgin of El Quinche is renowned for her miracles, and is a favorite among drivers and transport workers. The walls of the church, covered in gold-leaf, are hung with paintings of miracles performed during the last four centuries to the present day, each with its explanatory inscription. Devout Catholics from Quito go to ask for the Virgin's blessing

Preceding pages: Otavaleña displays rich tapestries. **Left,** headgear of Otavalo women. **Right,** Saturday market in Otavalo.

whenever they undertake some new venture, buy a car or build a house.

The small town of **Cayambe**, under the perpetual vigilance of the mountain of the same name located on the Equator, is worth a stop-over to try its famous local cheese, especially *queso de hoja*, and the *biscochos*, a savory shortbread.

A few miles outside Cayambe is the **Hosteria Guachala,** an old hacienda dating back to 1580, recently rennovated and converted into a hotel in 1993. Set in attractive grounds with plenty of opportunities nearby for horse-back riding, it is easy to conjure up the rich history that its owner, Diego Boniface, is more than willing to reveal to you.

Continuing north, a turn in the main road unexpectedly brings into view the **San Pablo Lake** and, towering behind it, **Mt Imbabura**, with its concave slopes covered in minute fields. Opposite, though often enveloped in clouds, is its sister mountain, **Cotacachi**, and on the flat valley floor between the two, known as "the valley of the dawn", lies the town of Otavalo.

Ecuador's greatest market: At dawn on Saturday mornings, the market square (called the "Poncho Plaza") in **Otavalo** gets busy as the stall-holders set up their display. Small handicraft workers from the outlying districts come to negotiate their wares with traders before the tourists arrive. By 9am the square is a feast of colors and textures: rolls of cloth, thick blankets for the cold mountain nights, woollen tapestry wall-hangings with pictures of mountains and llamas, embroidered blouses and dresses, chunky hand-knitted sweaters, long patterned belts or *fajas* such as the Indian women wind round their waists and *cintas*, tapes they use to bind their long hair. It is impossible to take it all in: the square is a maze of stands and narrow alleys with just enough room to pass.

Tourists making day-trips from Quito arrive by bus at around 10am, and the haggling begins. The Otavalo Indians are experienced in business, can size up their customer, and know just how far to lower their price. Several of them even speak English. Despite the crowds, the

Last light over Mojanda Lagoon near Tabacundo.

atmosphere is calm and relaxed – muffled, perhaps, by the walls of cloth.

Most of the handicrafts are tailored to foreign tastes, although some of the Otavaleño designs are reworkings of traditional motifs. The style of clothing sold to the public is adjusted each year according to fashion and demand; whereas the intricate hand embroidery of the Indian women's blouses is sold on Calle Jaramillo. Moreover, many high-quality handicrafts are often sold in Quito or abroad, and never appear at all at the Otavalo market. All the same, there is plenty to choose from, the Otavaleño work is always attractive and usually well made (though finishings are sometimes careless), and at prices that seem a dream to most foreigners.

Saturday is also market day for the local population. At the north end of the Poncho Plaza is hot prepared food and a corner market for such animals as *cuys* and rabbits. The market plaza for the larger animals – horses, cows, pigs, sheep and goats – is at the western edge of town. Just follow the unmistakeable evidence left by these animals along Calle Morales and across the Pan-American highway.

In parts of the Poncho Plaza and along Calle Jaramillo vendors sell every item of Otavaleño traditional dress as well as fleece, yarn, loom parts, aniline dyes and carders. Vendors also sell clothing worn by other indigenous groups in Imbabura Province and by *mestizos* and whites. This is the hardware and household goods section.

Calle Jaramillo runs south into the permanent food market, which overflows on Saturdays with a mind-boggling array of vendors and food. You'll find every kind of fruit, vegetable, grain and meat imaginable as well as some you'd rather not imagine, much less eat. Don't become so engrossed in your shopping spree in the Poncho Plaza that you miss the food market because if weaving represents one means of subsistence, agriculture represents the other.

Outside the town: While day tours to Otavalo from Quito are popular, many independent travelers arrive on the Fri-

Young Otavaleñas with chickens.

day night before the market and stay for the weekend to explore the lush surrounding countryside. Probably the best base for doing this is from the most unusual hotel in the Otavalo region and a well-known tourist attraction in itself: the **Hostería Cusín**. Located several kilometers out of town, the Hostería was once the main *hacienda* of the area. The new British-born owner has restored the building to its former splendor: the rooms are crowded with antique Spanish religious paintings, wooden armchairs and candelabras, while the grounds are divided up into elegant gardens with ponds and banks of glorious flowers.

A night at the Hostería is cheap, and the price includes three meals from one of the best kitchens in Ecuador – creating *haute cuisine* versions of the local specialties. You can also drop in for lunch or dinner, or just look in as part of a taxi-tour around the area.

Another worthwhile excursion is the walk around the enchanting **Mojanda lakes**, south of Otavalo. A dirt road leads up to the six lakes, divided by hills, habitat of wild rabbits. There are refuges on most of the lakes, where a fireplace cheers up the icy nights. Many Ecuadorians go fishing there, but they have to take their own boat.

The crystal-clear **San Pablo Lake** is the most easily accessible. On its shores there are several hostels where you can hire boats and horses. A walk around the lake shore is delightful and, for those who get tired on the way, there is a regular bus route. It is also a favorite place for water sports, and during the September festivals there is an annual race across its width – though it takes courage to plunge into the icy waters.

Artists at work: The villages close to Otavalo provide a chance to see another aspect of the handicraft trade: the craftsmen themselves at work. For example, in nearby **Carabuela**, they make scarves, woollen gloves, ponchos and *fajas*. Some still use the pre-hispanic loom. There are also craftsmen who specialize in making Andean harps.

The village of **Peguche** too has its

The colonial Hostería Cusín near Otavalo, now a hotel.

weavers, and is worth a stop-off to see its impressive waterfall. This is the home of several Indian musical groups – amongst them is *Ñanda Mañachi*, an ensemble that has become famous in Europe and North America for its haunting Andean tunes.

Another nearby village of artisans is **Iluman**, whose inhabitants make double-sided ponchos, felt hats and tapestries. But Iluman is also famous for its traditional healers or *curanderos*, who use guinea pigs, candles and ritual stones, as well as herbs and alcohol, to diagnose sicknesses and chase away evil spirits or negative energy.

The best-known shaman of the region is the legendary "Taita Marcos", who lives in **San Juan de la Calera** near Cotacachi. His house is worth a visit: he uses an altar built with thousands of bottles donated by grateful patients from all over the world, and adorned with pictures of saints.

Master leatherworkers: A short drive from Otavalo is the village of **Cotacachi**, Ecuador's center for leatherwork.

Mostly made of tough cowhide, the leather goods have increased in variety and quality in recent years, and there is an excellent choice of jackets, skirts and boots, as well as briefcases, handbags and travel bags, riding equipment, and a whole range of trinkets and keyrings, purses and wallets.

It is worth tasting the typical dish of Cotacachi: *carne colorada*, made of sundried and fried pork or beef, colored with *achiote* (a red seed), and served with avocados, jacket potatoes, a cheese, onion and egg sauce, and different kinds of corn. The restaurant El Meson de la Rosas is reputed to be the original inventor of this dish.

Further north: The highway northwards from Otavalo curves around Mt Imbabura and descends towards Ibarra, passing through **Atuntaqui**, which is reputed to have the best *fritada* (deep fried pork) of the whole region.

Shortly before entering Ibarra, a right-hand turn leads into the village of **San Antonio**, where the specialty is woodcarving. The visitor can see both the

Otavaleñas.

craftsmen in their workshops and the finished articles on sale. They make everything from sculptured furniture to chessmen, lamps or mirror frames; but the most typical examples of their work are the ornamental carved figures of people and animals, in any size from 7.5 cm (3 inches) to 1.2 meters (4 ft) tall.

A shorter, much slower, but very attractive route to Ibarra is along the old Pan-American highway from Cayambe, heading around the far side of Mt Imbabura via the villages of **Olmedo** and **Zuleta**. This narrow cobbled road, full of pot-holes, winds through several of the region's oldest *haciendas*: along the way, it presents an image of the traditional rural structure of Ecuador, mixed with modern farming techniques. The *hacienda* of Zuleta, famous for its embroiderers, has several handicraft shops.

The white city: The provincial town of **Ibarra** itself is quite large and enjoys one of the best climates of the Sierra – neither too hot, nor too cold – due to its moderate altitude of 2,225 meters (around 7,000 ft).

Despite severe damage and destruction in at least two earthquakes, Ibarra has retained a colonial style. Its streets are cobbled, and the town's low red-roofed buildings all have white-painted walls, which has earned Ibarra the nickname of "the white city". The population is an interesting cultural mix of Indians, blacks and *mestizos*.

Typical foods include *arrope de mora* (blackberry syrup) and *nogadas* (a sweet made with walnuts). And the original *helados de paila* (water ices) can be found at the Rosalia Suarez ice-cream parlor. These ices are made by continuously beating fruit juice in a copper *paila* or round-bottomed pan, while it sits on a pile of ice.

Close to Ibarra is **Yaguarcocha Lake**. Its name means "blood lake" in Quichua, because in the 15th century the tough inhabitants of this region held out against the Inca invaders for some 16 years, until they were finally defeated and massacred on the lake shore. Today Yaguarcocha Lake is sometimes used for sailing, but is mainly known for the

Left, antiques for sale at Otavalo market. **Right**, early-morning bargain on a cow.

motor-racing track that surrounds it. Car races take place on this circuit during the September festival celebrations.

On the other side of the mountain descends the warm **Chota Valley**, the lowest point in the northern Sierra, where sugar-cane, vines and tropical fruits grow. There are several thermal springs in this valley, such as **Chachimbiro**, though the road is somewhat arduous.

The Chota Valley is the only zone of the Sierra with a predominantly black population. Today peaceable farmers, the older members still tell tales of their ancestors who fought against slavery on the plantations of Colombia.

In the village of **Chota**, a concert hall regularly presents the *bomba negra* music of the local black population, which is a mixture of Indian music of the Sierra and African-type instruments and rhythms. One of the typical "instruments" involves blowing tunes on a leaf held between the hands.

On the Colombian border: The highway north from the Chota Valley climbs steeply with twists and turns into the Province of **Carchi**, over the high pass of **El Angel**, and down to the frontier town of **Tulcán**. This is rich agricultural country, which produces dozens of varieties of potatoes. It also has a reputation for its thriving trade in contraband goods with Colombia.

Carchi is the only province of the Sierra that has practically no Indian population. Unfortunately for the amiable inhabitants of this province – familiarly known in other parts of Ecuador as *Pastusos* – they have earned a reputation as the simpletons of the country and are the butt of endless jokes.

Carchi has its own sanctuary: the **Grotto of La Paz**, close to the village of **San Gabriel**, where pilgrims go to see the statue of the Virgin sheltered in a natural cave. In Tulcán, the main attraction is the cemetery garden, where huge clipped cypress hedges represent the shapes of animals, houses and geometric figures. It is quite a bizarre and impressive sight, and well worth a visit if you are overnighting here on your way to Colombia.

Woodcarver at San Antonio de Ibarra.

THE AVENUE OF THE VOLCANOES

The Andes are often thought of as the spine of Ecuador, but a ladder is a better analogy. Think of the Eastern and Western Cordilleras as the sides of the ladder, with the lower east-west connecting mountains (called *nudos* or knots) as the rungs. Between each rung is an intermontane valley at about 2,300 to 3,000 meters (7,000 to 9,000 ft) in elevation, with fertile volcanic soil.

The valleys are heavily settled and farmed today and were the territory of different ethnic groups in pre-Inca times. Both the Pan-American highway and the railroad run north-south between the Cordilleras, bobbing up and down over the *nudos* past fields, farms and startled cows beneath a range of dormant and active volcanoes, most of which have permanent snowcaps.

In 1802 the German explorer Alexander von Humboldt, in a fit of inspiration, named this route the "Avenue of the Volcanoes". Ecuador's position on the Equator means that you can travel through the Avenue of the Volcanoes past orchids and palm trees, with tundra vegetation, glaciers and snow visible in the mountains above. By leaving the valley and hiking or climbing up, you can pass through all the earth's ecological zones from sub-tropical to arctic.

A unique way of traveling through the Avenue is by train. The local train now runs on Saturdays from Quito to Riobamba, returning on Sundays. Foreigners are charged $20. Tickets need to be purchased the day before departure.

This may not be the quickest and most dependable way of going, but it does allow you to get an intimate look at life along the tracks, traveling through people's backyards so to speak, rather than down the prosaic main road. Metropolitan Touring runs an *autoferro* service, three times a week, from Quito to Riobamba that is more reliable and comfortable but considerably more expensive. If you just want a taste of the Avenue of the Volcanoes, try the Sunday excursion by train as far as Cotopaxi National Park.

The road south: Leaving Quito by car or bus for the south can seem to take forever. The streets leading to the Pan American Highway are jammed most hours of the day, but rest assured that everyone eventually escapes. At the southern edge of the city, a turnoff to the east leads a few kilometers to **Sangolquí**, which has a Sunday market at which *shigras* (net bags) and baskets are sold. South of Songolquí is the **Valle de los Chillos**, still a rural area, but fast on its way to becoming a residential suburb of Quito. The road through the Valle connects up with the main highway about 8 km (5 miles) farther south.

Heading south on the Pana (as the highway is called), the traffic eases a bit as you wind down off the Quito plateau and into the first intermontane valley. Way off to the east the snowy peak of **Mount Antisana** (5,704 meters, 18,717 ft) is visible from time to time.

About 45 minutes out of Quito, on the slopes of an extinct volcano to the east,

Preceding pages: Cotopaxi crater. Left, the Basilica at Baños against an Andean hillside. Right, man from the bleak *páramo*.

is the **Pasochoa Nature Reserve,** which is run by Ecuador's conservation organization, Fundación Natura, an affiliate of the Worldwide Fund for Nature. Fundación Natura has initiated an educational program which brings Quito schoolchildren to Pasochoa to teach them about the natural beauty and ecology of their country.

Looming over the region is **Mount Cotopaxi** (5,897 meters, 19,347 ft), Ecuador's second highest peak and one of the world's highest active volcanoes. On a clear day you can see its perfect, snowcapped cone from north of Quito. Cotopaxi elicits sighs of awe and appreciation from Japanese visitors because of its resemblance to Fujiyama. In the Western Cordillera, almost directly across from Cotopaxi is **Mount Illiniza** (5,263 meters, 17,277 ft) – or the Illinizas as they are called, for there are actually two peaks. The lower, northern peak makes a good climb for non-technical climbers and hikers.

Thirty-five kilometers (21 miles) beyond Machachi, as you climb toward the first pass, you leave Pichincha and enter Cotopaxi Province. Just over the pass on the east side of the Pana is the entrance to **Cotopaxi National Park**. Both sides of the highway are covered by a dense forest of Monterrey pines, many of them dying from a fungus disease. The pines are not a native species; they were introduced to Ecuador from California for a forestry project and they are a textbook example of the dangers of monoculture. The pines have crowded out indigenous vegetation and the fungus has spread quickly from one tree to the next. Deer, however, have made a comeback in the woods and with them the endangered Andean puma. Visitors to the Park must register when entering and leaving.

At the southern edge of the Park is San Agustín Hill, and **Hacienda San Agustín de Callo**, one of two *haciendas* in the area owned by the Plaza family. A member of this family, Galo Plaza Lasso, was President of Ecuador.

Farming heartland: As everywhere in Latin America, the prime agricultural

Dancing partners at a highland fiesta.

land in the valley was taken from the indigenous population soon after the Spanish conquest and turned into large, Spanish-owned estates, many of which still include vast landholdings despite the agrarian reform of 1964. The *indígenas* were forced into the mountains, where they remain to this day. At Km. 68 from Quito, on the east side of the highway, is the entrance to **Tambo Mulaló**, another *hacienda* which has been converted to tourist use, offering excellent typical food *(comida criolla)*. A *tambo* in Inca times was a way station or inn for travelers. During the colonial era, Tambo Mulaló was a retreat for Jesuits, then a *tambo* for travelers on the road to Quito. It is now a dairy farm with a small bullring and horseback riding.

A hop down the road is the tiny town of **Lasso** and the turn off to the west for the **Hosteria La Ciénega**. Now a hotel, its main house – a stone mansion with huge windows, stone-cobbled patios and Moorish-style fountains – was built in the mid-1600s for the Marquis de Maenza and was occupied by his family for

more than 300 years. Von Humboldt stayed at La Ciénega in 1802 when he surveyed Cotopaxi. The de Maenza-Lasso family also plotted Ecuador's independence from Spain at this site in the 1800s. The colonial chapel has a bell which is still rung on Sunday mornings and which was installed in 1768 in thanksgiving when Cotopaxi ended 20 years of devastating eruptions.

In 1982 La Ciénega was converted into an inn, complete with the original furniture, tapestries and paintings in the main living and sitting rooms. Besides excellent birdwatching in the gardens you can ride horseback and use the inn for day trips to Cotopaxi Park. Reservations should be made in Quito through Metropolitan Touring, which handles La Ciénega's bookings, although you can drop by any time for a meal.

The little towns in the valley, and the larger city of **Latacunga** (population 40,000), are interesting primarily for their fiestas and market days. Latacunga (90 km, 54 miles from Quito) is somnolent and pleasant, with a number

Horseman on the wind-swept Sierra.

of buildings constructed from local gray volcanic rock. It was founded in 1534 on the site of an Inca urban center and fortress. The town has busy Saturday and Tuesday markets, where some crafts are sold, especially *shigras,* baskets and ponchos. On clear days, if you aren't tired of mountains, there are views of Cotopaxi, Tungurahua and others.

Latacunga's town hall *(municipio)* and cathedral front are on the main plaza, the Parque Vicente León, which has topiary and a well-maintained garden. Behind the cathedral is a converted colonial building housing an arcade with shops, offices and an art gallery. Five blocks west down Calle Maldonado at Calle Vela there is a small ethnographic museum in the Molinos (Mills) de Montserrat which is operated by the Casa de la Cultura Ecuatoriana. The museum is open from 9am to noon and from 2pm to 5pm Tuesday through Friday. After that, it's easy to get the small town blues, but Latacunga makes a good base for side trips to other parts of Cotopaxi Province.

Market town: A few kilometers northwest of Latacunga, **Saquisilí** comes out of its torpor on Thursday market day and buses run regularly between the two towns. Naturally there are the ubiquitous Otavaleño *indígenas,* but there's lots of other activity and some local crafts for sale. The Saquisilí market is an economic hub for the surrounding region and various indigenous ethnic groups pour in from the surrounding countryside. While commercial clothes appear to dominate the market, sharp eyes will readily spot many local crafts including *shigras,* baskets, belts, ponchos, handspun and handwoven wool shawls, embroidered blouses and handmade hats.

Cotton is trucked up from the coast, sold at the Saquisilí market, handspun by local people and then sold to weavers who make it into (of all things!) dishrags and mop covers sold at the SuperMaxi stores in Ecuadorian cities.

The market is decidedly a local, rather than tourist, affair and a favorite of many travelers for that reason.

Chicken transport, economy class.

Northwest of Saquisilí, between Toacazo and San Juan de Pastocalle, are the ruins of **Pachuzala**, located on the property of the Hacienda Pachuzala, but open to visitors. The Pachuzala ruins, of which several stone chambers remain, were probably constructed by the pre-Inca inhabitants, the Panzaleo, and rebuilt in Inca times. To say anything more is to indulge in speculation.

The **Hacienda Tilipulo**, a superb example of colonial architecture, is located off the road to Pujilí. The best way to get there is to rent a cab in Latacunga. Before you hop in the cab, though, obtain a permit from the Latacunga town hall. Tilipulo was built from local volcanic stone in 1720 as a Jesuit monastery and textile sweatshop *(obraje),* which used local Indian labor. After the expulsion of the Jesuits from South America in 1767, Tilipulo became a private *hacienda*. The grounds include the main building, the ruins of the *obraje,* the chapel, a large kitchen and a patio with a sun dial. Tilipulo was acquired by the municipality of Latacunga in 1979

with the intention of preserving the site and eventually turning it into a museum.

Back in Latacunga, the Pan-American highway continues south, deep into the central Sierra. About 11.5 km (7 miles) outside of Latacunga on the right side of the highway is the **Hostería Rumipamba de las Rosas**, yet another converted *hacienda*. Rumipamba makes an excellent stopping place for meals, with the best food in the region. They have an especially good Sunday buffet, with folk musicians playing traditional music. It's also a good place to stay if you don't want to be in Latacunga, with comfortable rooms furnished with antiques. The grounds hold a swimming pool, garden, playground for children, and a small zoo, with sad-looking animals from the Oriente. It's best to book rooms ahead from Quito. (Tel: 551 635 or 233 715.)

Shortly after the village of **Negische** you cross the provincial boundary and enter Tungurahua Province named, like most of the highland provinces, after the area's dominant volcano. The region is

known for its relatively mild climate and production of vegetables, grain and fruit, including peaches, apricots, apples, pears, and strawberries, and you will encounter roadside vendors along the highway on both sides of Ambato.

Provincial center: At 128 km (80 miles) from Quito, **Ambato** is the capital of Tungurahua Province. Arriving in the city brings you abruptly face to face with the 20th century. Ambato was almost totally destroyed by an earthquake in 1949 and then rebuilt, so virtually nothing of colonial (or even early 20th-century) Ambato remains. With a population of about 120,000, the city is the fourth largest in Ecuador, after Guayaquil, Quito and Cuenca.

Industries include some textiles (especially rug weaving), leather goods, food processing and distilling, but the most interesting aspect of the city is its enormous Monday market, the largest in Ecuador. Thousands of *indígenas* and country people come into town for the different activities, which take place in various parts of the city. Several plazas contain nothing but produce vendors, while the streets are lined with kiosks selling goods of all kinds. The entire center of the city turns into a giant, outdoor department and hardware store. To reach the textiles, dyes, and crafts (ponchos, ikat blankets and shawls, *shigras,* belts, beads, hats, embroidered blouses) follow either Calle Bolívar or Cevallos about 10 blocks north from the center of town to the area around Calle Abdón Calderón.

After the market is a good time to visit Ambato's two central plazas. The main plaza, the **Parque Montalvo**, is named after the writer Juan Montalvo (1833–99), and has an imposing statue of him. Montalvo's nearby house, at Calles Bolívar and Montalvo, is open to the public. On the north side of the Parque Montalvo is Ambato's modern **cathedral**, with some fine stained-glass windows. Opposite, on the south side is the the post office. The **Parque Cevallos**, a few blocks to the northwest, is green and tree-lined, and is a good place from which to people-watch.

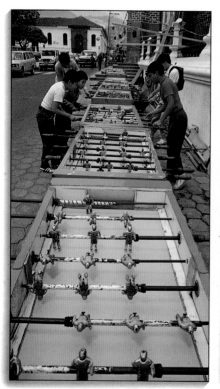

The Ambato River flows through a gorge to the west of the center of town. A walk south along the river leads to the suburb of Miraflores. There are several fine old *quintas* (country homes) along Avenida Los Capulíes in Miraflores, which have gardens open to the public.

In good weather you can see **Mount Tungurahua** (5,016 meters, 16,457 ft) directly east of Ambato. This rambunctious volcano has erupted several times in the past 300 years, wreaking havoc on the nearby towns. A paved road leads out of Ambato to the east, past Tungurahua and down into the Oriente, forming one of the main east-west links between jungle and Sierra.

About 14 km (8 miles) east of Ambato is **Salasaca**, the home of a small, beleaguered indigenous group, which is struggling to hold on to its land and maintain its customs in the face of enormous pressure from whites in the surrounding communities.

Salasaca legends say they were *mitmakuna,* moved from Bolivia to Ecuador by the Incas as punishment for a revolt. So far no one has found written evidence in the archives to document this claim, but it may be true. For one thing, the Salasaca's loom terms are different from those of other *indígenas* in Tungurahua Province and are similar to those found in colonial Cuzco Quechua dictionaries.

Salasaca men wear black and white ponchos and handmade white felt hats with broad, upturned brims at the front and back. Unique to Salasaca are the men's purple or deep-red scarves dyed with cochineal, a natural dye that comes from the female insects that live on the Opuntia (prickly pear) cactus. Salasaca women wear the same hats as the men, brown or black *anakus,* cochineal-dyed shoulder wraps, handwoven belts with intricate motifs, and necklaces of red and Venetian glass beads.

A few kilometers past Salasaca is **Pelileo**, a small town which has been leveled by earthquakes four times in the past 300 years (this is not the best place in Ecuador to buy property). Artisans in the *barrio* (neighborhood) of Pomatúg

Salasaca *indígenas* returning from market.

on the north side of the highway specialize in hand felting the different kinds of white hats worn by indigenous groups in the central sierra. Pelileo has a small Saturday market, which is attended by many *indígenas* from Salasaca.

Sub-tropical climate: Beyond Pelileo the highway drops 850 meters (2,780 ft) to Baños in only 24 km (15 miles), following various tributaries and then the Pastaza River itself in its headlong rush to the Amazon basin. The region produces sugar cane for distilled alcohol, and many kinds of fruits and vegetables.

Baños, with a population of only about 15,000, probably has more hotels per acre than any other community in Ecuador. The main attraction, of course, is the thermal hot springs bubbling out of the side of the wild and unruly **volcano Tungurahua**, which broods above the town. There are several public hot baths as well as private ones connected with the various hotels. The Piscina El Salado baths, with pools of varying temperatures, are half a kilometer back up the

road to Ambato, and are often less crowded than are the baths in town.

The gentle, sub-tropical climate and vegetation around Baños (altitude 1,800 meters, 5,886 ft) is another draw, especially after the chill of the highlands. The region is a hiker's Garden of Eden; you can also rent horses by the hour or day. It is possible to walk up the slopes of Tungurahua along many different trails leading out of town, or head for the Pastaza river gorge where there are dozens of waterfalls, some on the Pastaza, others cascading off the side of Tungurahua into the Pastaza's tributary creeks and rivers. If you follow the main highway east toward Puyo and the Oriente you will come to the spectacular falls of **Agoyán**, about 10 km (6 miles) from Baños. Many varieties of orchids grow along the road, and the area is also excellent for birdwatching.

If travelers come for the hot springs and hiking, thousands of Ecuadorians come to pay homage to the Virgin of Baños, known as *Nuestra Señora del Agua Santo* (Our Lady of the Holy Water), whose statue is housed in the basilica in the center of town. The Virgin is credited with many miracles, including stopping an eruption of Tungurahua, delivering people from certain death in a fire in Guayaquil, and saving the lives of travelers involved in such horrendous accidents as a plunge into the Pastaza River when a bridge collapsed. The walls of the basilica are hung with paintings depicting these events, with captions that describe the date and place. One visit to the church and you'll want a small holy card of the Virgin of Baños to carry with you on your next bus ride because, judging from the miracles, if anyone can prevent a wreck it's Nuestra Señora.

The basilica grounds has a small museum with moldering stuffed tropical birds and the Virgin's changes of clothing, and a tiny zoo with mouldering live tropical birds, tapirs and a few snakes and tortoises. Around the church are the usual Otavaleño *indígenas* selling their textiles, kiosks with baskets from the Oriente, and women pulling and selling homemade taffy.

Thermal baths beneath a waterfall in Baños.

202

Adventurous detours: While most travelers head east from Ambato, there is some gorgeous country to the northeast, in the Llanganates spur of the Eastern Cordillera; and also to the west, the territory of the Chibuleo *indígenas*.

The **Llanganates mountains** appeal to the Indiana Jones in all of us because of various legends of lost Inca treasure. These legends have about the same veracity as the sightings of Elvis Presley in supermarkets in the United States but, then again, life without legends would be an impoverished affair. So put on your slouch hat, pick up your bullwhip and head into an incredibly remote part of the Sierra.

The Llanganates are perpetually wrapped in fog and covered with virtually impenetrable cloud forest vegetation. When Atahualpa was captured by Pizarro in Cajamarca, Peru, (so the story goes), the Inca's ransom in gold that was on its way to Cajamarca was diverted to the Llanganatis after the *indígenas* learned of Atahualpa's death. (Never mind that this same story is told all over the Andes. You can still go ahead and pay a lot of money for a photocopied map of the treasure's location and mount your expedition.) From Ambato catch a bus or truck 20 km (12 miles) northeast to the small town of **Pillaro**.

The trip to the west of Ambato is a little easier; a paved road circles around **Mount Carihuairazo** (5,020 meters, 5,886 ft) and **Mount Chimborazo** (6,310 meters, 20,571 ft) and heads for Guaranda and the coast. *Rasu*, Hispanicized as *razo*, means "snowcap" in Ecuadorian Quichua. Chimborazo, of course, is the highest peak in Ecuador and it looms over Chimborazo, Bolívar and southern Tungurahua Provinces like a giant ice cube, dominating the landscape.

If Ireland is the emerald isle, then the Western Cordillera outside of Ambato deserves to be called the land of emerald mountains. Every inch of the vertical hillsides are farmed by the Chibuleo *indígenas,* turning the land into a patchwork quilt composed of every imaginable shade of green. Every so often, either Carihairazo or Chimborazo pokes

Hotels, bars and Coca-Cola on the main street of Baños.

its snowy head out above the clouds. The road climbs to the *páramo* above 4,000 meters (13,000 ft), with some superb views of Chimborazo, then drops again to Guaranda, which is 85 km (53 miles) from Ambato. Midway through the journey you enter Bolívar Province.

Art and fireworks: The capital of Bolívar Province, **Guaranda** (2,668 meters, 8,724 ft) is a small, quiet town of 14,000, that comes alive on Saturday with the weekly market. It is set among seven hills, which has led its citizens to make comparisons to Rome, but that's definitely stretching a point. One of the hills, Cruz Loma (Cross Hill) has a giant statue of an indigenous chief, a *mirador* (lookout) and a small, circular museum with both pre-Hispanic and colonial artifacts. There are three other small museums in the town with mixed collections including colonial art and ethnographic material: the **Museo Municipal**, the **Museo de la Casa de la Cultura Ecuatoriana**, and **Museo del Colegio Pedro Carbo**. The **Parque Central** has a monument to the liberator, Simón

Bolívar (from whom the province took its name), which was a gift from the government of Venezuela.

Guaranda is the market center for the **Chimbo Valley**, a rich agricultural region that produces wheat and corn (*maiz*). A 16-km (10-mile) ride through the valley south from Guaranda takes you to **San José de Chimbo**, an ancient town with colonial architecture and two thriving craft centers. The *barrio* of Ayurco specializes in fine guitars, handmade from high-quality wood grown in the province, while the *barrio* of Tambán specializes in hunting guns and fireworks.

But these aren't just any old fireworks. Bamboo frames (*castillos,* or castles) are fabricated in the shape of giant birds, huge towers or enormous animals, with fireworks attached. They are set off to striking effect at fiestas throughout the country. It's not uncommon for the *castillo* to fall over, shooting sky rockets directly into the crowd in a shelling reminiscent of the Battle of Leningrad. The cowardly gringos gen-

Mules cautiously cross a mountain bridge.

erally jump for cover behind the plaza fountain, but the Ecuadorians love it.

Ancient center: The 65-km (40-mile) trip via the Pan-American highway from Ambato to **Riobamba**, capital of Chimborazo Province, takes about an hour. The Pana climbs up to the *páramo* past the small town of Mocha, skirting the eastern slopes of Carihuairazo and Chimborazo, crosses the pass and then drops down into the Riobamba Valley.

In 1541 a Spaniard, Pedro de Cieza de León, began an epic 17-year horseback journey in Pasto, Colombia, riding south along the Royal Inca Highway through Ecuador, Peru and Bolivia. By 1545 Cieza was in central Ecuador heading for Riobamba. "Leaving Mocha," he wrote, "one comes to the lodgings of Riobamba, which are no less impressive than those of Mocha. They are situated in the province of the Puruhás in beautiful fair fields, whose climate, vegetation, flowers, and other features resemble those of Spain." Chimborazo is still primarily an agricultural province, growing wheat, barley, potatoes and carrots, with some sheep, llama and cattle herds.

It's only an hour from Ambato to Riobamba, but for each half hour of travel you feel as if you were going back a century. Two more completely unlike provincial capitals located so close to each other would be hard to imagine.

Although Riobamba, at 2,750 meters (8,993 ft) is only 180 meters (589 ft) higher than Ambato, it feels much colder, perhaps because of the wind sweeping down off the glaciers of Chimborazo.

The original Riobamba, the city the Spanish founded on the site of a major Inca settlement, was located 21 km (13 miles) away where the modern town of Cajabamba stands, but old Riobamba was flattened by an earthquake in 1797 and a new location was chosen. The new Riobamba (population 70,000) has the architecture and ambience of an 18th-century town; stately, quiet and slow – except, of course, on market day.

Indigenous peoples: Chimborazo Province was the pre-Inca territory of the Puruhá tribe. Such modern towns as

The town of Riobamba, beneath Mount Chimborazo.

Guano, Chambo, Pungalá, Licto, Punin, Yaruquies, Alausí, Chunchi and Chimbo were Puruhá settlements. As they did throughout the empire, the Incas moved people around. For example, they settled *indígenas* from Cajamarca and Huamachuco, Peru, in the Chimbo region and moved many Puruhá people to the south.

Today Chimborazo has an amazing mixture of people who wear different kinds of traditional dress. There aren't necessarily special names for all these groups, however; they simply call themselves *indígenas* or *Quichuas de...* (indigenous people or Quichuas from...) a particular place. Chimborazo was the site of many *obrajes* (textile sweatshops) in colonial times and the more recent locale of *haciendas* with enormous landholdings, so that the indigenous population became increasingly impoverished and marginalized through succeeding centuries as they were pushed by new settlers into the mountains or became attached to the country *haciendas* as *wasipungeros* (serfs).

The Chimborazo *indígenas* did not take mistreatment and injustice lying down. There have been many revolts over the centuries including an uprising of 8,000 *indígenas* around Riobamba in 1764, a revolt in Guano in 1778, and a rebellion in Columbe and Guamote in 1803. Land shortages are still a problem and men from many communities frequently migrate temporarily to the larger cities in search of work. Chimborazo has also seen intensive Protestant Evangelical missionizing, which has often exacerbated ethnic tensions.

The most obvious ethnic marker in Chimborazo is hats. While *indígenas* are increasingly using dark, commercially made fedoras, a large number still wear the handmade white felt hats, especially for fiestas and other special occasions.

In the Guamote market you can spot as many as 15 different kinds of white, handmade hats being worn. Such variations as the size and shape of the brim and crown and the color and length of the streamers, tassels or other decora-

The main plaza of Riobamba.

tions all indicate the wearer's community or ethnic group.

Two areas of the Riobamba market are of special interest to travelers. Traditional indigenous garments, including such items as hats, belts, ponchos, ikat shawls, fabric, *shigras,* hats and old jewelry (beautiful beads, earrings and *tupus*) are sold in the **Plaza de la Concepción** on Orozco and 5 de Junio, along with baskets and ikat blankets. In one corner of this plaza people set up their treadle sewing machines and mend clothes or sew the collars on ponchos, while other vendors sell aniline dyes. Just south of this plaza on Calle Orozco is a small cooperative store selling crafts made by the *indígenas* of Cacha.

Another important craft of the Riobamba region is tagua nut carving. The egg-sized seeds of the lowland tagua palm are soft when first exposed to air but then harden to an ivory-like consistency. Tagua is carved into jewelry, chess sets, buttons, rings, busts and tiny kitchen utensils. Stores opposite the railroad station located on Avenida Primera Constituyente sell tagua crafts. (The Avenue of the First Constitution got its name because, after winning its war of independence from Spain, Ecuador's first constitution was written and signed in Riobamba on August 14, 1830.)

About eight blocks northeast of the *artesanías* plaza is the **Plaza Dávalos**, where *cabuya* fiber (made from Agave americana cactus, the century plant) and products are sold. *Cabuya* crafts have been an important local industry in the region since colonial times. *Indígena* women spin the fiber into cordage, which is used for such items as the soles of *alpargatas,* rope, *shigras,* saddle bags and vegetable sacks.

After the market the town empties rapidly and lapses into somnolence for another week. This is your opportunity to visit the Religious Art Museum in the **Covento de la Concepción** on Calle Orozco at España. Among the items on display are statues, vestments and a fabulous gold monstrance encrusted with diamonds and pearls (the museum is open from 9am to 12.30pm and from 3pm to 6.30pm Tuesday to Saturday and from 9am to 12.30pm on Sunday).

Riobamba is home to three other small museums. The museum in the **Colegio Nacional Pedro Vicente Maldonado** on Avenida Primera Constituyente 2412 has natural history exhibits. The **Museo de la Escuela Politécnica Superior de Chimborazo** has archaeology and contemporary art, while the **Museo del Banco Central**, in the new bank building downtown, has ethnographic and modern art exhibitions. Riobamba also has a number of majestic old churches, including the **cathedral** on 5 de Junio and Veloz and the completely round **Basilica** (the only such church in Ecuador) on Veloz and Alvarado in the Parque La Libertad.

At sunset climb to the top of the **Parque 21 de Abril** (located on Calle Argentinos north of the center of town). With luck you can catch the last light on mountains Chimborazo, Carihuairaso, Tungurahua and **Altar** (5,319 meters, 17,457 ft). Altar, the brooding hulk south of the city in the Eastern Cordillera, is also known in Quichua as *Capac Urcu*

Elegant park and statue, Riobamba.

(meaning Great or Powerful Mountain).

Exploring the region: Naturally Riobamba makes an excellent base for excursions to the rest of Chimborazo Province. For a day trip to buy rugs and visit the artisans at work, catch a bus or cab 12 km (7 miles) north on a subsidiary road, not the Pan-American highway, to **Guano**. The town is known for its cottage-industry production of fine rugs, which are handknotted on huge vertical frame looms. Most of the shops have a workshop attached where you can watch the weavers.

Just a kilometer or two beyond Guano is the small town of **Santa Teresita**, which specializes in the production of carrot or potato sacks woven from *cabuya* fiber. Many of the weavers have enormous warping frames in their yards, with hundreds of meters of *cabuya* on them, and you may also see the woven yardage stretched out along the road. At the edge of town is the **Balneario Las Elenas**, with two cold-water swimming pools, one warmer pool, and a cafeteria.

Most of Chimborazo Province lies to the south of Riobamba, and it's a part of Ecuador worth exploring. The road to Licto climbs above Riobamba and offers good views of the city and the volcanoes.

Another quiet, but extremely traditional Sunday market, drawing *indígenas* from the Laguna Colta area and the usual assortment of vendors, is held in **Cajabamba**, 13½ km (8 miles) south of Riobamba on the Pan-American highway. This was the site of the old Riobamba, which was originally a Puruhá community and then the Inca settlement of Liripamba. Sounds confusing? *Pampa* or *bamba* means "plains" in Quichua; but the prefix changed through the centuries. In Inca times Liripamba had fine mortarless stonework, including a temple of the sun, a house of the chosen women and a royal *tambo*. The stones from the Inca buildings were incorporated into the Spanish town, which was destroyed in the 1797 earthquake and subsequent landslide. The only building surviving from the 18th century is the chapel.

Man and parrot, Riobamba.

About 2 km (just over a mile) beyond Cajabamba is the tiny town of **Balvanera** (also spelled Balbanera), on the shores of **Laguna Colta**. Colta *indígenas* graze their cattle and sheep along the marshy shores of the lake, and use the totora reeds in the lake to make mats *(esteras)* and baskets *(canastas)*.

Legend holds that the little church, with its image of the Virgin of Balvanera, is the oldest church in Ecuador, constructed by the conquistador Sebastián de Benalcázar and his troops after a victory over the Inca forces, but there is no documentary evidence to support this. Still, it's a nice story.

If the journey to Ambato to Riobamba takes you back two centuries, the trip to the Guamote market (51 km, 32 miles south of Riobamba) is yet another time warp. The Thursday market is the major weekly fair for the southern part of the province. *Indígenas* on horseback or leading llamas laden with produce arrive from communities where no road reaches. At the animal market much of the bargaining takes place in Quichua,

but at the food and clothing markets more vendors speak Spanish. You will see more *indígenas* in different kinds of traditional dress here than at any other market in Ecuador.

From here, the highway drops down past Tixan and into **Alausí** (2,356 meters, 7,704 ft). Alausí in its heyday was a highland resort for people from Guayaquil, but now most Guayaquileños visit Cuenca, so that Alausí has the feel of a place past its prime. Alausí has a Sunday market attended by *indígenas* from the Chimborazo-Cañar provincial border region.

A few miles southwest of Alausí is **Sibambe**, a stop on the Guayaquil-Riobamba-Quito railway line. Between Alausí and Sibambe the famous Nariz del Diablo (Devil's Nose) railway switchbacks zig-zag back and forth dropping precipitously to Sibambe, and on to the coast. The switchbacks were washed out in the storms of 1982–83, but the railroad has been repaired and trains are again making the amazing trip between Guayaquil and the highlands.

Train leaving Alausí station.

THE SOUTHERN SIERRA

The southern Sierra, consisting of Cañar, Azuay and Loja Provinces, is the least visited part of the highlands, mainly for reasons of accessibility rather than for lack of attractions. The Andes broaden and flatten out somewhat here, with none of the dramatic snowcaps of the central and northern highlands, but with plenty of stunning, green vistas and mountain roads guaranteed to give you an adrenaline rush.

Hub of the south: The jumping off point for most trips in the south is **Cuenca**, capital of Azuay Province. Until about 35 years ago, Cuenca was isolated from the rest of Ecuador by the lack of good roads, but now it is connected to both Guayaquil and the northern Sierra by paved highways. Cuenca (population about 153,000, which makes it Ecuador's third largest city) has daily flights to Quito and Guayaquil, and (when the railway is working) it also has *autoferro* connections with the Guayaquil-Ríobamba-Quito line at Sibambe.

The Cuenca basin is a major *artesanías* center, producing ceramics, *paja toquilla* (Panama) hats, baskets and Christmas ornaments, gold and silver jewelry, and ikat shawls, ponchos and blankets. Other industries include textiles, furniture and automobile tires. The city is the economic center of the southern Sierra, and an intellectual center as well, with a state university and a long history as the birthplace of Ecuadorian artists, writers, poets and philosophers.

Most Ecuadorians consider Cuenca to be their country's most beautiful city and it's hard to find anyone who would argue. Cuenca means river basin or bowl in Spanish, and the city is situated at 2,549 meters (8,335 ft) on the banks of the Tomebamba River. The city has retained its colonial architecture and feel, with new construction in a neo-colonial style that is compatible with existing structures. No boxy skyscrapers to obliterate the surrounding mountains! Instead, the blue domes of the new cathedral dominate the skyline.

Because of its cobblestone streets, interior patios and public plazas overflowing with flowers and greenery, and whitewashed buildings with huge, old wooden doors and ironwork balconies, Cuenca is a walker's delight. In fact, you really need to wander at a slow and gentle pace to appreciate and absorb the details of the city.

Originally, Cuenca was a major Cañari settlement. After the Inca conquest, it became an important Inca city called *Tumipampa*, the Plain of the Knife (Hispanicized as Tomebamba). *Tumipampa* was intended to be the Cuzco of the north, with construction carried out under Tupac Inca Yupanqui (also called Topa Inca) and his son, Huayna Capac.

Pedro de Cieza de León visited the city not long after the Spanish conquest and observed that: "The lodgings of Tomebamba are situated at the joining of two small rivers... The temple of the sun was of stones put together with the subtlest skill, some of them large, black, and rough, and others that seemed of

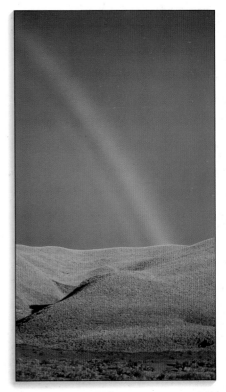

Preceding pages: patchwork fields of the southern Sierra. *Left,* colonial streets of Cuenca. *Right,* after a storm on the *páramo.*

jasper… The fronts of many of the buildings are beautiful and highly decorated, some of them set with precious stones and emeralds, and, inside, the walls of the temple of the sun and the palaces of the Lord-Incas were covered with sheets of the finest gold and incrusted with many statues, all of this metal."

Unfortunately, very little of that Inca city remains. If you follow Calle Larga southeast as it goes downhill along the Tomebamba River (near the junction of Calle Tomas Ordoñez with Calle Larga) you will come to the ruins of **Todos Santos**. This small site includes four perfect Inca trapezoidal mortarless stonework niches, and the remains of the colonial mill of Todos Santos, which was constructed with stones taken from Inca buildings. There are remains of Inca walls on the hillside above the mill, where ceramics and other evidence of Inca occupation were excavated.

Ancient relics: Workers frequently uncover Inca artifacts during the construction of houses in this neighborhood, which was obviously a central part of

the Inca settlement. The area may have been part of Huayna Capac's Puma Punku (Puma's Gate) Palace.

In the 1980s the Banco Central del Ecuador undertook excavations along the river, uncovering more Inca structures and tombs with skeletons and gold, silver and ceramic artifacts. The new **Museo del Banco Central** is located on Avenida Huayna Capac across Calle Larga, above excavations of more Inca walls. The museum has permanent archaeological, ethnographic, colonial and republican art collections, as well as old photographs of Cuenca.

The Museo del Banco Central inherited the collection of the late Father Crespi, a Salesian priest who died in the late 1980s. Father Crespi's artifacts consist of an amazing variety of pieces from pure junk to fine pre-Inca ceramics, which the Museo is in the process of sorting and dating. Father Crespi held the bizarre theory that the Phoenicians sailed up the Amazon and reached Cuenca, but there is nothing in the archaeological record to support this. Still, when

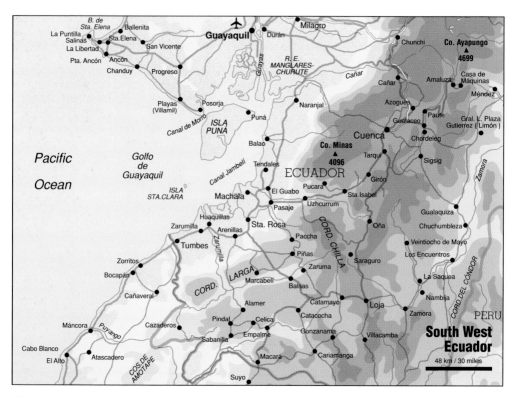

he was alive it was great fun to listen to him expound his version of the pre-Hispanic past as he gave a guided tour of his collection.

In 1532 the Inca armies retreated north before the advancing forces of Sebastian de Benalcázar, who was marching up from Piura on the coast of Peru, with thoughts of looting Quito on his mind. Benalcázar rested in Tomebamba for a week, forming an alliance with the Cañari *indígenas* to fight against the Quito Incas. The Spanish city of Cuenca was founded on this site 23 years later, in 1557, by the conquistador Ramirez Dávalos and named Santa Ana de los Cuatro Ríos de Cuenca.

As soon as the Spanish arrived in an area they built a church, and Cuenca was no exception. The **Catedral Vieja** (Old Cathedral), on the east side of the main plaza, the Parque Calderón, was started in 1557, the year the city was founded. But the city outgrew this simple old church and construction on the **Catedral Nueva** began in 1880. The new church, dedicated to the Immaculate Conception of the Virgin Mary, was built to hold 10,000 celebrants during religious events and is opposite the old cathedral on the Parque Calderón.

The neo-Gothic New Cathedral was intended to be 42½ meters (141 ft) wide and 105 meters (351 ft) tall, which would have made it the largest church in South America. It is constructed from alabaster and local marble with floors of pink marble imported from Carrara, Italy. But the architect miscalculated and designed bell towers that are too heavy for the structure to support, so work on the towers was halted in 1967. The bells donated by Germany remain at the entrance to the nave.

The **Parque Abdón Calderón** is Cuenca's main square, with the Municipo (town hall) on the south side. Just off the southwest corner of the Parque, on Calle Sucre, is the **Casa de la Cultura Ecuatoriana**, similar to those found in other cities. This small colonial-style building frequently has good exhibitions of local art. At the end of Calle Sucre on the same block is the **Church**

Cupolas in Cuenca.

and Monastery of el Carmen de la Asunción, founded on August 1, 1682. The church has a fine old carved stone facade and the pulpit is gilded and embellished with mirrors, but the building is often closed, so you may have to be content with the exterior architecture. A daily flower market is held in the tiny plaza in front of the church and for a few sucres you can brighten your hotel room considerably.

If you're not tired of churches (Cuenca has 27), walk one block south toward the river to Calle Presidente Cordova, then four blocks east to Calle Hermano Miguel 6-33 to the **Church, Convent and Museum of La Concepción**. The entrance to the church contains 17th-century tombstones. The cloister, built between 1682 and 1729, was recently restored by the Banco Central. The cloister's museum contains an unusual collection of religious art including toys presented to the convent by novices entering the order, a silver nativity scene, and an altarpiece of carved wood and gold by the sculptor Manuel Machina.

As for other museums, the **Municipal Museum Remigio Crespo Toral**, on Calle Larga 707 at the intersection with Borrero, gives new meaning to the word decrepit. The building is ancient, with creaking stairways and crumbling plaster, but somehow it's the perfect setting for all kinds of old artifacts, from pre-Hispanic ceramics and goldwork from the Cañari and Chordeleg cultures to colonial paintings, furniture and religious sculptures.

Also try the **Museo de las Culturas Aborigines** at Av 10 de Agosto 4-70, on the south side of the river Tomebamba. It holds a fascinating private collection of pre-colombian archaeology from various cultures throughout Ecuador.

Is modern art more to your taste? The **Museo de Arte Moderno** (Modern Art Museum) is on Calle Sucre at Coronel Talbot. This museum has rotating exhibitions of contemporary art as well as art workshops for children.

Indigenous groups: Many of the people of the Cuenca valley occupy an intermediate position between *indígenas* and

Art in Cuenca, past and present: <u>left</u>, cathedral door, <u>right</u>, mural in El Turi.

whites. They are generally artisans and country people and are called *Cholos Cuencanos* (Cuenca cholos). Undoubtedly garrison populations were settled in this area to help secure Inca rule, so contemporary *cholos* probably represent a mixture of Inca, Cañari, and Spanish blood. This old and rich *cholo* culture is slowly disappearing as more and more young people adopt modern-style clothing and move to the cities or to work in the United States.

In rural areas and especially at the markets in Sigsig, Gualaceo, Chordeleg, and sometimes in Cuenca you will still see people in traditional *cholo* costume, which includes "Panama" hats for both men and women and ponchos of various colors for men, especially burgundy and red. For fiestas many *cholo* men wear beautiful handwoven ikat ponchos (see the chapter on *Artesanías* for details).

If you're in Cuenca mid-week for the Thursday weekly fair or for the smaller Saturday market, check out the plaza between Calle Mariscal Lamar and Sangurima off Calle Hermano Miguel,

Artists at work in El Turi, Cuenca.

where *artesanías* are sold, including baskets, wool and ikat shawls (*paños*). The permanent food market is on the other side of town, on Calle Cordova off Padre Aguirre.

On Sunday there is a market for the raw material for "Panama" hats; *paja toquilla* (*toquilla* straw) comes from the leaves of the shrubby, palm-like tree the *Carludovica palmata*, which grows in the western lowlands around Montecristi and Jipijapa. The fiber is trucked up to Cuenca and distributed to smaller outlying markets where most of the hats are made. The hats are then brought into Cuenca for blocking and finishing.

Southern Ecuador is well-known for its crafts. The Organization of American States has a permanent center in Cuenca for the preservation and promotion of traditional *artesanías:* the Centro Interamerico de Artesanías y Artes Populars (CIDAP). The offices of CIDAP and their Museo de Artes Populares (Museum of Popular Art) is located on the stairs where Calle Hermano Miguel intersects with Calle Larga and descends

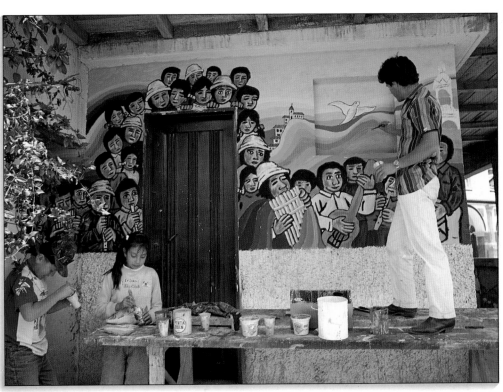

to the Tomebamba River. The address is Hermano Miguel 3-23 and visiting hours are Monday–Friday 8am–1pm and 2–4pm. The store is open Monday–Friday 9am–1pm and 3–5pm.

Excursions into the countryside: A visit to the CIDAP museum is good preparation for a trip to several small communities outside Cuenca where many of the crafts are made. **Gualaceo** is about 36 km (22 miles) west of Cuenca on paved roads. Buses run regularly between the two places, heading north of Cuenca on the Pana, turning east at El Descanso and following the Río Paute.

Gualaceo is a pretty town situated on the banks of the Río Gualaceo and is the site of *quintas*, or summer homes for people from Cuenca and Guayaquil. The slightly lower elevation makes it ideal for growing peaches, apricots, apples, cherries, guayabas and cherimoyas. There are several good restaurants along the river, and an inn, the **Parador Turistico Gualaceo**, which has comfortable rooms, a restaurant and a heated swimming pool. (Tel: 07-828 661).

Chordeleg, an old pre-Inca Cañari town, has artisans of all kinds: ikat poncho weavers, *paja toquilla* hat and basket weavers, potters, embroiderers and jewelers. The town is just a few kilometers up the mountain south of Gualaceo, a ten-minute trip in the local bus. The road leading into Chordeleg from Gualaceo is lined with jewelry stores selling silver and gold jewelry at very reasonable prices in styles ranging from colonial filigree to modern. Other local *artesanías* (and textiles from Otavalo) are sold in gift shops around the main plaza. CIDAP has a small but excellent ethnographic museum on the plaza, with displays of local crafts and a gift shop. The exhibit showing the process used in making ikat textiles is especially informative.

There are pre-Inca ruins in the Chordeleg area, including an enormous snake-shaped stone walkway near the entrance to the town, and sites on nearby hilltops which have been archaeologically excavated. Chordeleg has a small Sunday market, but most people from the town attend the larger market in Gualaceo. From the plaza in Chordeleg you can catch a bus to **Sigsig**, 20 km (12 miles) farther south. Sigsig is a tiny colonial town with an equally tiny Sunday market, but the trip along the river is gorgeous. Two archaeological sites, Chobshi and Shabalula are close by; ask residents for directions.

For those with interests running more to wilderness adventures consider visiting the **Cajas National Park** 30 km (19 miles) northwest of Cuenca. The park contains hundreds of clear, cold lakes, streams and rivers at altitudes from 3,500 to 4,200 meters (9,000 to 13,000 ft) on the *páramo* beneath jagged mountain cliffs. You can go swimming (if you're brave), but the fishing for rainbow trout is even better and there are miles of hiking trails, camp grounds and a small refuge. Recently the park's management has brought in herds of llamas and alpacas as part of a breeding program to re-introduce these animals to the southern highlands.

You need a permit to visit the park, which can be obtained from the office of **Pots for sale.**

the Ministry of Agriculture (Ministerio de Agricultura y Ganadería, or MAG) in Cuenca. The MAG office is located above the Banco de Azuay on Calle Simón Bolívar near the corner of Hermano Miguel. Space at the refuge should be booked at MAG, which will also provide maps and information about the park.

Buses to El Cajas (as the park is called) leave at 6 and 6.30am from the Church of San Sebastian in Cuenca and return to Cuenca late in the afternoon (San Sebastián is located six blocks west of the Parque Calderón at the corner of Simón Bolívar and Talbot).

Independent traditions: North of Cuenca is **Cañar Province**, ancestral and modern home of the Cañari *indígenas*, with the largest and the most complete accessible Inca ruins in Ecuador. (There are also a number of small Inca fortresses on the slopes of Cayambe, some Inca ruins on private property in central Ecuador and unexcavated ruins around Saraguro.) While Cañar is considered a highland province, about a third of its territory is in the western lowlands, where sugar cane, cocoa, bananas and other tropical fruits are grown. In both the lowlands and Sierra, extensive territory is given over to cattle grazing on large tracts of land own by *haciendas*, despite the agrarian reform of 1964.

The Cañaris have never had an easy time of it, at least not since the arrival of the Incas in the 15th century. The Cañaris were once the principal indigenous group in all of southern Ecuador. They resisted the Incas fiercely, at one time defeating them and throwing them back to Saraguro. When the Cañaris were finally overcome, the Inca Tupac Yupanqui attempted to smash Cañari opposition by removing the population of whole villages such as Cojitambo and Chuquipata to Peru and replacing them with loyal *mitmakuna*. The Inca Huayna Capac built the fortress of Ingapirca near Cañar and stationed forces there to keep an eye on the rebellious locals.

A group of Peruvian Cañaris eventually became the personal bodyguard in Cuzco of Huascar, a son of Huayna Capac. When Huayna Capac died in

Laundry drying on the outskirts of Cuenca.

Quito in 1527 civil war broke out between the two claimants to the throne, his son Atahulapa in Quito and Huascar in Cuzco. The Cañaris sided with Huascar. Atahualpa routed Huascar's army in a battle at Ambato, Ecuador, and in revenge killed most of the men and boys of the Cañari tribe, despite their surrender and pleas for mercy.

A year after the Spanish captured and killed Atahualpa in Cajamarca, a Spanish force under Sebastián de Benalcázar marched north to plunder Quito. When Benalcázar reached Tumipampa he was joined by three thousand Cañari warriors, eager for revenge against the Quito Inca forces. The Cañaris fought with the Spanish throughout the conquest of Ecuador. They received scant recognition from the Spanish for their help, however. By 1544 many thousand Cañari men were working in the gold and silver mines of southern Ecuador. The tribe was so decimated that in 1547 a Spaniard, Pedro de Cieza de León, noted that the ratio of women to men was 15 to 1.

Currently there are about 40,000 Quichua-speaking Cañari *indígenas* scattered throughout Cañar, the highest province in Ecuador. Most Cañari *indígenas* are farmers, but some are sheep and cattle herders. Understandably, the Cañaris are, on the whole, averse to outsiders. They have a reputation among both whites and other *indígenas* as being *bravo,* or belicose.

Cañari men's dress includes the *kushma,* a fine ikat poncho for fiesta use, black wool pants, a white cotton shirt with embroidery on the sleeves and collar and an extremely fine double-faced belt with motifs from local life including animals, Inca pots and skeletons, buses and trains, and designs taken from children's school books. Like the men of Saraguro and Otavalo, Cañari men wear their hair in a long braid. Because some Cañaris are herders, many men also wear sheepskin chaps and carry a small whip with a wooden handle, which is worn over their shoulder when they come into Cañar for the Sunday market. The typical Cañari hat, worn by both

Hoof-cutting in the Sierra near Cuenca.

men and women, is handmade of white felt with a small round crown and narrow brim, turned up in front. Cañari women wear an embroidered blouse, a shoulder wrap held shut with a *tupu,* and a wool *pollera* skirt in various colors.

Exploring Cañar: The Pan-American highway climbs out of Cuenca to **Azogues**, the capital of Cañar Province with 30,000 people. Azogues has a quiet colonial air, with wooden balconies and shutters aslant on ancient whitewashed houses. *Azogue* means mercury in Spanish and the town was named after the mercury mines in the area.

The **Church and Convent of San Francisco** tower above Azogues on a hill to the southeast. The Spanish practice of building churches on pre-Hispanic Inca holy places (*wakas),* many of which were located on mountain-tops, accounts for the large number of churches that are perched at ridiculous heights. If you need the exercise and want the view, it's a half-hour climb to the top. As befits a provincial capital, Azogues has two museums. The **Museo Ignacio** Neira in the Colegio Julio Maria Matavalle has zoology, archaeology, and minerology displays, but is open only on request. The **Museo del Colegio de los Padres Franciscanos** houses religious art and archaeological artifacts. This region was all Cañari territory before the arrival of the Incas and is rich in both Cañari and Inca pieces.

The Pan-American highway winds past Azogues and into **Cañar**, which is 65 km (40 miles) from Cuenca and 36 km (22 miles) from Azogues. Cañar is high and chilly at 3,104 meters (10,150 ft); this is barley, potato, quinua and cattle country. The town has an absolutely fascinating market on Sundays, when *indígenas*, including mounted Cañaris with ikat ponchos, whips (*chicotes*) and sheepskin chaps (*zamarro*), come down off the *páramo* to buy, sell and trade.

The Cañari men's belts are extremely fine, made in a complex intermesh double-faced technique with all kinds of motifs representing local life and folklore. The best place in town to buy belts is the jail (*la carcel*), where *indígenas* doing time don't waste time, but spend it weaving. The jailer will unlock the door and let you into the main patio where you will be besieged by friendly prisoners with belts and sometimes ponchos to sell.

Ecuador's greatest ruins: Many people visit Cañar for the market and then go on to **Ingapirca**. The ruins are not easy to reach as there are no buses, and trucks run infrequently. You can chance it and wait by the side of the road for a truck to come along or you can rent a taxi and driver for the day in Cuenca, rent your own vehicle in Cuenca or go on an organized tour. Ingapirca can be reached by roads on either side of Cañar. About 2 km (1 mile) south of Cañar a sign on the east side of the Pana announces the ruins, which are 15 km (9 miles) down an unpaved road. A kilometer north of Cañar a better, shorter, road goes east through El Tambo 8 km (5 miles) to Ingapirca.

Ingapirca means Inca Stone Wall; the name was given to the site by the Cañaris. We know that the Inca Huayna Capac

Woman from Cañar.

built Ingapirca in the 15th century on the royal highway that ran from Quito to Cuzco and stationed soldiers there to keep the Cañaris under control. Throughout the Inca empire outlying Inca settlements had multiple functions and were intended to be models of Cuzco on a much smaller scale. From what remains of Ingapirca, the site probably had storehouses, baths, a royal *tambo* or inn for the Inca, dwellings for soldiers and others, and a sun temple, the remains of which can be seen in the beautiful elipse, made of green diorite and modeled after the Kuricancha (also spelled Coricancha), the main temple in Cuzco. The high-quality stonework indicates that Ingapirca was an important site.

Not surprisingly, the Incas often chose hilltops for their settlements, both for defensive reasons and to free flat valley land for cultivation. The debates about whether Ingapirca was a fortress, *tambo* or temple miss the point: it was probably all three. Much of Ingapirca was dismantled over the centuries by local people who used the stones in their own buildings. The site has been excavated by various archaeological teams including a Spanish group in the early 1970s, which discovered what were probably pre-Inca Cañari burials on the Pilaloma, a small hill facing the temple.

Various other remains surround the main buildings. The names of these places are modern and their function is still the topic of debate. The Ingachungana, or Inca's playground, is a large rock with carved channels; similar rocks exist in Peru. The Ingachungana may have been used for offerings or for divination, with water, chicha or the blood of sacrificed llamas or guinea pigs poured in the channels. Near the Ingachungana is a chair or throne cut in the rock and called, logically, the **Sillón del Inga** (the Inca's Chair). Below in the gorge are several zoomorphic rock carvings which appear to be a monkey and a turtle, and the **Cara del Inca** (the Inca's Face), a large stone outcropping that is probably natural, rather than carved. The site also houses a small museum with ethnographic and archae-

Ruins of Ingapirca, Ecuador's major Inca site.

ological exhibits. The archaeology displays include such artifacts from the Cañari and Inca cultures as ceramics, jewelry and textile fragments. Less than a mile away is the **village of Ingapirca,** which has a crafts cooperative store next to the church and a basic restaurant where the food looks better and better as the day goes on.

The far south: Tucked away deep in southern Ecuador between Azuay Province and the border with Peru, **Loja Province** is the least visited of the highland provinces, mainly because of its isolation. There are flights to the capital city, Loja, from Quito and Guayaquil, but not from Cuenca, so travelers heading directly south from Cuenca must go overland along the paved Pan-American highway (the Pana). Loja is primarily rural and agricultural and there are only a few small towns along the road.

Fine Inca masonry at Ingapirca ruins.

The Pana south of Cuenca passes through rich, green valley land until **Cumbe** (14 km, 9 miles), where it begins to climb to **Tinajilla Pass** at 3,500 meters (11,445 ft). The Pana traverses the *páramo* of **Gañadel**, which is usually misty and fogged in. In the middle of this wilderness, figures bundled in shawls and ponchos will appear out of the fog to flag down the bus. The clouds sometimes part to surprise you with extensive views of the Western Cordillera and sunlight streaming through in the distance, a sight that looks like the dawn of creation.

From here the road twists a few miles to **Saraguro**, a high, chilly town of about 3,000 inhabitants, mainly *mestizos* and whites. It is the social and commercial center for the Saraguro *indígenas,* relatively prosperous farmers and cattle traders who live in a number of smaller communities (called *barrios)* surrounding the town.

According to their own legends, the Saragureños are descendents of the Inca conquerors of Ecuador, who were brought to the region after the Inca Tupac Yupanqui's conquest of the region around AD 1455. They replaced the indigenous Palta people, who were removed to Bolivia, except for the resi-

dents of a few communities. While there is no documentary evidence to confirm or deny that the Saragureños are descendents of *mitmakuna,* their Quichua including their loom terminology is consistent with an origin in southern Peru. Under Inca rule, each ethnic group was required to retain its traditional costume, especially its headdress and hairstyle. The Spanish outlawed certain kinds of Inca head gear and introduced brimmed hats, but in typically conservative fashion each ethnic group insisted on wearing a distinct style, which accounts for the plethora of hat styles seen in the Andes today.

The *indígenas* of Saraguro were never serfs on the *haciendas* or laborers in textile sweatshops. They have survived as farmers and cattle traders, supplying much of the beef for southern Ecuador. Because of a shortage of pasture in the Saraguro region the Saragureños drive their cattle over the continental divide and down unto the jungle around Yacuambi. The cattle are fattened and driven back up over the Andes to be sold at the Sunday Saraguro market. The Saragureños value education and are among the best educated *indígenas* in Ecuador, with their own high school in Saraguro, and Saragureños attending the universities in Cuenca and Quito. The community now has its own indigenous doctor and nurse.

Remembering the Inca: Saraguro dress is black or dark indigo-blue wool, which many *indígenas* say they wear in mourning for the death of the Inca Atahualpa (who was killed by the Spanish in Cajamarca, Peru, in 1533). Most of the dress is handspun and handwoven and everywhere you travel in the Saraguro region you will see women and girls with distaffs and spindles, spinning wool for their family clothing.

Most striking, though, is the women's jewelry. Several white jewelers in Saraguro specialize in making the large nickel or silver shawl pins *(tupus)* which females use to close their shoulder wraps. Fine silver *tupus* are heirlooms, passed down from mother to daughter, as are filigree earrings. Females also wear **Skipping Mass in Saraguro.**

beaded necklaces. One style has rows of tiny, seed beads strung in zig-zags, and the colors of the beads and number of rows indicates her community.

Saraguro has two very basic pensiones and a couple of bad restaurants, but is worth visiting for the Sunday market which draws *indígenas* and white farmers from the region. Some crafts, especially such traditional jewelry as silver filigree earrings, tupus, seedbead necklaces, and handwoven belts are sold in small shops in the main market building and surrounding streets.

Saraguro was also an Inca settlement and there are extensive ruins, which are impossible to find without a guide, outside the town in the forests on the slopes of Mount Acacana. The ruins, called **Inga Iglesia** (Inca Church), are large, but overgrown, and contain fine mortarless stonework walls and channels carved in the rock for the water system.

The Cuenca-Loja bus continues on to Loja after a stop in Saraguro to pick up passengers. If you decide to stay in Saraguro a local Saraguro-Loja bus also makes the roundtrip between the two places several times a day. Loja is another 61 km (38 miles) from Saraguro, an hour and a half to two hour ride over a dizzying, corkscrew road.

Colonial center: Loja is the provincial capital of the province of the same name, and provincial it is; provincial and old. Because the Spanish invasion of Ecuador began in Piura on the north coast of Peru, Ecuador was conquered and settled from south to north. Loja was founded in 1548 by a conquistador, Alonso de Mercadillo, which makes it one of the oldest Ecuadorian cities. Cieza de León commented on the prosperity of the region and on the vast herds of llamas, vicuñas and guanacos when he rode through Loja on the Royal Inca Highway, but the Spanish soon hunted them to extinction.

Loja has about 95,000 inhabitants and is nestled among the mountains at a pleasant 2,225 meters (7,275 ft). Because it is so close to the Oriente it is a major entry point to the southern jungle and the Province of Zamora-Chinchipe.

Saraguro women at a bus stop.

The city has two universities, one of which has a law school and a music conservatory. It has the inevitable colonial art collection housed in the **Convento de las Conceptas** near the main plaza. A permit from the bishop of Loja is necessary to see this collection, which may lead you to decide that you have already seen enough colonial art. A local branch of the **Museo del Banco Central** recently opened in a colonial mansion at 10 de Agosto and Bernardo Valdivieso and contains archaeological, ethnographic and colonial art collections. Visiting hours are Monday to Friday from 9am to 3.30pm.

As for churches, **Loja Cathedral** and the **Churches of San Martín** and **Santo Domingo** have nicely painted interiors, but are otherwise nothing to write home about. The statue of the Virgin of Cisne is kept in Loja Cathedral from August to November, the time period which includes the fiesta of the Virgin which takes place on September 8th. The religious observances and the accompanying agricultural fair attract pilgrims from throughout northern Peru and the southern part of Ecuador.

Valley of the ancients: For a change of pace there is one more popular excursion using Loja as a base. Certainly one of the most popular nearby destinations is **Vilcabamba**, 62 km (38 miles) due south of Loja.

Vilcabamba gained a certain notoriety in the 1970s as the valley of the ancients, where an unusual percentage of old people were said to live to be 100 to 120 years old. Disappointingly for those looking for the Fountain of Youth, the claims of extreme longevity have turned out to be exaggerated. One book on Vilcabamba, for example contained a document purported to be a birth certificate proving that one old codger was 128 years old. The document, on closer scrutiny, turned out to be a land title in his grandfather's name, which was the same as that of his grandson. There is simply no documentary evidence to support the stories of a large population of centenarians.

Still, there are a number of very healthy, active elders in their 70s, 80s and 90s, bounding around the hilly countryside like wizened mountain goats, and there is good reason for their vitality. Vilcabamba is located at a comfortable, mild 1,500 meters (4,905 ft) and the people lead active lives, farming on the mountainous slopes and eating a balanced, primarily vegetarian, diet. In other words, they follow all the prescriptions Europeans and Americans are given for living to a jolly old age: physical exercise, a strong family life, worthwhile activities that give life meaning, a balanced diet that is low on animal fats, and a relative lack of stress.

The Vilcabamba region is also a visual delight, green, gentle and pretty. PREDESUR, the Ecuadorian government agency responsible for development in the south, has established a recreation area, **Yamburara**, on the river bank about a mile outside Vilcabamba. Here is a small zoo, whose animals gaze wistfully at the hills where they would obviously prefer to be, gardens with many sorts of flowers, including orchids, a swimming pool and fish ponds.

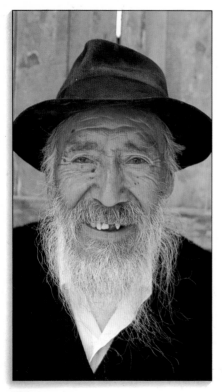

Left, old man from Vilcabamba. **Right**, young cousins in Saraguro.

226

THE WESTERN LOWLANDS

Many visitors to Ecuador claim that the most frightening bus journey in the country is the two and a half hour drive from Quito to **Santo Domingo** in the western lowlands. The road, which is the main link between the capital and the lowlands, drops almost 3,000 meters (10,000 ft) down the western slopes of the Andes and is often shrouded in fog, especially in the afternoons. Truck and bus drivers rely on headlights and horn as they hurtle down the road, paying scant attention to the poor visibility or oncoming traffic. Surprisingly, accidents are rare, but it is not without some sense of relief that the traveler finally arrives.

Home for healers: Santo Domingo's full name is **Santo Domingo de los Colorados**, named after the Colorado Indians who once dominated the area. Their appearance was distinctive: both sexes painted their faces with black stripes and the men plastered down their bowl shaped haircuts with a brilliant red dye of achiote, a local plant. Some of their men, notably the Calazacon brothers, built up a nationwide reputation as *curanderos* (medicine men). Until a decade ago, patients from all over Ecuador came to be treated for a variety of ills, but this custom is now dying out.

Travelers still come to Santo Domingo in the hopes of seeing the Colorados in their authentic finery or perhaps witnessing a curing ceremony. These dreams are bolstered in many tourist centers by the sale of rather garish postcards of the Indians wearing facepaint and red haircuts, but most of the Colorados now wear western dress and have lost interest in their traditional appearance and customs.

Santo Domingo has a tropical climate and is the nearest place for Quiteños to come and enjoy the lowland heat. Hence it has developed a couple of small resort hotels, where visitors can relax by a pool in a tropical garden, or try their luck in the casino. It is also the hub of a network of paved roads radiating out into the western lowlands.

Into banana lands: The road south of Santo Domingo leads through vast plantations of bananas and African oil palms. Until the discovery of petroleum in the Oriente in the late 1960s Ecuador was the archetypal banana republic, with bananas being by far the most important export. Today, Ecuador remains the largest exporter of bananas in the world, with annual exports averaging US$650 million.

Bananas were not always this part of Ecuador's major agricultural export. Friedrich Hassaurek, who served as US minister to Ecuador from 1860 to 1864, reported that then the main export was cacao, used in making chocolate. This crop was raised along the rivers of the western lowlands, and floated down to Guayaquil for export.

In the 1930s, cacao remained the principle export, followed by coffee, also grown in the western lowlands. After the World War II, banana production became increasingly important and ca-

Preceding pages: banana plantations in the western lowlands. Left, chieftain and his wife, Santo Domingo de los Colorados. Right, red-and-green macaws.

cao had dropped to second place by the 1970s. Heavy floods during the *El Niño* phenomenon of 1982–83 severely disrupted the cacao industry, and although it has since recovered, bananas and coffee remain the two most important export crops.

The banana trees in the plantations are arranged in regular rows for ease of harvesting, and travelers driving past are mesmerized by the monotonous repetition of lines of plants. The monotony is broken on occasion by the sight of workers collecting the ripe fruit by means of long-handled shears. Often bunches of bananas are sleeved in large blue plastic bags before harvesting; the polyethylene in the bags acts a chemical signal which makes the fruit inside ripen more quickly.

Market center: An hour and a half drive south of Santo Domingo lies the largest market town of the western lowlands, **Quevedo**. Not only bananas, but cacao, coffee, rice, sugar, African palm oil, citrus and tropical fruits pass through this important center.

Quevedo was founded in the mid-1800s and is thus relatively modern. The city is known as "the Chinatown of Ecuador". Many of Ecuador's Chinese immigrants, some of whom arrived to help in the railway construction around the turn of the century, settled in Quevedo. Most of the better restaurants along the main streets are *chifas*, as Chinese restaurants are locally called.

In the past, produce from the area was able to reach the coast at Guayaquil along the narrow and convoluted River Quevedo which runs a few blocks north of the city's downtown area.

The journey was a difficult and hazardous one, with frequent sand banks, log jams, and shallows to obstruct the unwary. Today, with the construction of a good paved road to Guayaquil, the river is used as a playground by the local children who seek relief from the tropical sun. Although the river port is no longer used, the accompanying street market is still found along the banks of the river.

South of Quevedo, there are many

Left, river valley near Tinalandia. **Right**, the Andean cock-of-the-rock.

BIRDWATCHING

Ecuador is a birdwatcher's paradise. The wide variety of habitats, from tropical rain forests to windswept highlands, from mangrove swamps to hilly forests, provide the avid birder with a wider range of species than any other country in the Americas. Over 1,500 bird species have been recorded here, which is about twice as many as in the United States and Canada combined.

Many birdwatchers begin their adventure by flying into Quito and taking day trips into the surrounding Andean highlands. A visit to the *páramo* habitat of Cotopaxi National Park is high on everyone's list, both figuratively and literally. Elevations well over 4,500 meters (15,000 ft) leave unacclimatised visitors gasping for air and vehicles laboring in first gear. The birds, however, are seemingly unaffected. One of the most surprising sights in this harsh highland environment is a tiny hummingbird, the Andean hillstar, which is able to survive the freezing nights by lowering its body temperature from about 40°C (104°F) in the daytime to about 15°C (59°F) at night – a remarkable feat for a warmblooded animal. At the other end of the size scale is the Andean condor,

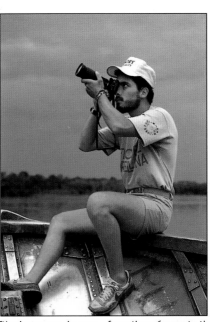

which, with its 3-meter (10-ft) wing span, is one of the largest flying birds in the world.

Other *páramo* species to look for include the carunculated caracara, Andean lapwing, Andean gull, *páramo* pipit, great thrush, and bar-winged cinclodes, all common in the highlands. If you camp overnight in the National Park, you may hear the loud, deep hoots of the great horned owl as it searches for prey. Another nocturnal bird to listen for is the Andean snipe which produces an eerie drumming noise with its outer wing feathers as it careens by in the dark.

The Andes of Ecuador are split into two ranges between which lies the temperate central valley containing Quito and many of Ecuador's principal towns. The less extreme elevation of about 2,800 meters (9,200 ft) ensures a pleasant climate here as it also does on the outer slopes of the Andes. This attracts a variety of fascinating birds.

The favorites of many birdwatchers are the hummingbirds, which begin to increase in number as the elevation drops and the climate becomes milder. Over a fifth of Ecuador's 120 or so species of hummers are found in this highland temperate zone.

The Fundación Natura, Ecuador's leading conservation agency, runs Pasochoa Nature Reserve, scarcely an hour's drive from the capital. Here is one of the last original stands of temperate forest remaining in the central valley and the rewards for the birdwatcher are great. At least 11 hummingbird species, plus a variety of doves, furnarids, tapaculos, tyrant flycatchers, honeycreepers, and tanagers can be seen along the reserve's trails. Many temperate highland species are observed simply by driving down some of the roads which drop down the outside slopes of the Andes.

The Chiriboga road and the Nono road are two little-used roads heading from Quito towards the western lowlands. Any serious birder will spend a couple of days slowly driving down one of these roads looking for the Andean cock-of-the-rock, scarlet-bellied mountain tanagers, Andean guans, and other Ecuadorian specialities.

On the eastern Andean slopes, birders often head to the Amazon basin by driving over the Papallacta pass. This road is also a good choice for birding different zones from the *páramo* to the tropics. Once down in the Amazon, the birding gets a little tricky. Most transport is by dugout canoe. The lush vegetation hides a huge diversity of birds, and to see many of them requires a considerable degree of patience and experience.

For this reason, many birders prefer to hire guides or go on organized tours when visiting Ecuador, particularly the Amazon. Many tours and individuals visit La Selva or Sacha Lodge where guides are on hand to point out some of the approximately 500 birds found in the area. Parrots, toucans, macaws, herons, vultures, kingfishers, puffbirds, antbirds and hummingbirds are all frequently seen. Birders may want to contact CECIA (Fundacion Ornitologia del Ecuador) an organisation devoted to the study and conservation of birds and habitats (Av. Los Shyris 2030 y La Tierra. Tel/fax: 468876). ∎

rivers forming a mosaic across the land which becomes increasingly subject to flooding during the rainy season of January to April. These rivers give the name to one of Ecuador's 21 provinces: **Los Ríos**.

This kind of terrain is admirably suited to the growing of rice, and paddies are often seen. The occasional trees between the fields serve as roosts for flocks of wading birds. The white American egrets are especially pretty at sunset, when they gather like hundreds of huge white flowers virtually blanketing the treetops.

During the dry months, rice is set out to dry on huge open-air platforms of concrete in the many commercial *piladoras* found along the road. *Piladora* is a local word meaning a drying and husking factory. Some of the poorer farmers are unable to afford the cost of the *piladora* and so they spread out their most modest crops on the nearest available flat and dry surface. In many cases, this proves to be the tarmac top of the highway, and drivers do their best to

avoid running over the crops which are spread out on the road to dry.

The rice and other products frequently make their way through **Babahoyo**, the provincial capital of Los Ríos. The city is a modern one with a long history. An Indian settlement existed here before the arrival of the *conquistadores* and Spanish records indicate the presence of a town here as early as 1576. A catastrophic fire wiped out Babahoyo in 1867 and the city was rebuilt at its present location at the confluence of the River Babahoyo and two other rivers.

Before the building of the road, Babahoyo was an important port known as "Bodegas" or store house. There were frequent steam ships linking the coast at Guayaquil with the inland river port of Bodegas. Here, goods were stored to await transport to the highlands and Quito by mule.

Houseboats and stilts: The city is a mere 7 meters (23 ft) above sea level and flooding seems to have been part of the way of life of the inhabitants since early times. Hassaurek, in his visit of 1860, notes how most of the houses were built on stilts to raise the sleeping rooms above the annual floodwaters. Today, some of the inhabitants live in a picturesque floating village of houseboats on the River Babahoyo. Even during the unseasonably high floods of 1983, when the entire population had to wade knee-deep to get anywhere in town, the houseboat village floated safely above the floodwaters.

The western lowlands are an important part of Ecuador's agricultural and tropical life. The exotic crops, equatorial climate, gorgeous birds, and interesting people make this a fascinating area to visit. Yet it is very much off the beaten track. Most travelers do no more than take an express bus through Los Ríos, and Babahoyo is the only one of Ecuador's 21 provincial capitals which didn't merit a mention in the index of one of the most renowned of guidebooks to the continent, *The South American Handbook*.

Ancient forests: The rich agricultural region of the western lowlands was not that way always, of course. At one time

Typical village in the western lowlands.

234

in the past much of the area was covered by dense tropical rainforest.

The famous British mountaineer Edward Whymper, who was the first climber to scale the Matterhorn, arrived in Guayaquil on 9 December, 1879 with the purpose of climbing Ecuador's major peaks. In his *Travels Amongst the Great Andes of the Equator* the mountaineer describes his journey through the western lowlands on his way up to and back down from the Andes. There were "forest-trees rising 150 feet high, mast-like, without a branch, laden with a parasitic growth."

These western forests were very different from the Amazonian forests east of the Andes. The weather patterns of pronounced rainy and dry seasons gave a distinctively unique assemblage of plants and animals which contributed to Ecuador's incredible variety of species. In fact, Ecuador continues to hold the record for the highest biological diversity per unit of land of any country in Latin America.

Some of this biodiversity can be seen at the **Río Palenque Research Station**, about half way between Santo Domingo and Quevedo. Surrounded by plantations, the research station is a small island of tropical rainforest with one of the most accessible and varied assemblages of plants remaining in the western lowlands. This forest island is too small, however, to have saved much of the animal wildlife that once abounded in the area, although some exotic bird species such as the pale-mandibled aracari (a member of the toucan family) can be seen here.

One of the few remaining undisturbed areas is found well north of Santo Domingo. This area has been designated the **Cotocachi Cayapas Ecological Reserve** and as such receives protection from the Ecuadorian government and support from foreign organizations such as Conservation International. With careful management, perhaps, it will prove possible to save some of this unique habitat, as well as allowing Ecuador to continue being the world's foremost exporter of bananas.

Curandero, or healer, at work in Santo Domingo.

THE IBARRA TO SAN LORENZO TRAIN

While most of Ibarra rolls over and pulls the covers closer against the chilly morning, the town's railway station is buzzing. A curling line of hopeful travelers, deprived of sleep and harassed by the mountain wind, fills the platform with plaintive protestation, but the window of the ticket office remains firmly shuttered. Inside, the railway men huddle around a glowing brazier, sipping coffee and joking about the more theatrical of the line's complaints. Then suddenly, with the sun creeping over the Eastern Cordillera, the ticket office opens with a heavy, wooden thud, and the line gives a vote of thanks to God and the president.

Given the gargantuan physical obstacles that a railway must overcome in Ecuador, divine intervention certainly has a role to play. The train for which these people seek tickets travels from Ibarra at 2,210 meters (6,630 ft) to the coastal port of San Lorenzo, cooled by Pacific breezes in the northwestern tip of the country. It passes through no fewer than 20 tunnels, clings to the edges of precipitous valleys and, towards the end of the day, is almost suffocated

by tropical vegetation. Were it not the only means of overland access to San Lorenzo, this railway would have given up the ghost years ago.

Train travel began in Ecuador in 1910, when the Quito-Guayaquil line was opened after more than 30 years' construction. Built with US technical and financial assistance, it was immediately acclaimed as one of the "great railway journeys of the world", and reduced to two days a former nine-day trek along a mule path impassable half the year due to rain. Weather conditions still dramatically affect the route and in 1983 torrential rain and landslides caused by the unpredictable *El Nino* ocean current washed away many kilometers of tracks south of Riobamba, which then took 10 years to repair. Trains do now run along the "Avenue of the Volcanoes" from Quito to Riobamba and then onto the Coast. Both this

route and the Ibarra-San Lorenzo line traverse the physical and cultural barriers between the Andes and the coast, the tracks symbolically linking 98 percent of Ecuador's population.

Amidst great fanfare, the Ibarra–San Lorenzo line was opened in 1957 after two French companies spent five years hacking a way through the wilderness. San Lorenzo was preferred to Esmeraldas as the coastal terminus for its unsurpassed natural harbor; and it was hoped that the railway would bring development to the neglected, untamed northern coast

In fact, little has changed since then, though the easy-going inhabitants of what is called the "wet littoral" now have, with the nightly arrival of the train, a window on the outside world.

Nestled between the frozen peaks of Imbabura and Cotocachi, Ibarra is a sleepy provincial capital with approximately 55,000 residents. Horse-drawn carts laden with Indian families and their vegetables clip-clop along narrow, cobbled streets. The plaza, enclosed by Spanish colonial buildings that house the pillars of society – Church and State – is dotted with ageing photographers, shoe-shine boys, and entranced young lovers. On a clear day, the town's exteriors shine like the drifting snow atop towering Mt Cayambe, Ecuador's third highest mountain at 5,790 meters (17,370 ft), which looms away to the south.

Founded in the early 17th century, Ibarra was the administrative centre of the network of inhumane workshops where the skilful Otavalan Indians produced high-quality textiles for export. Injury was added to insult when, in August 1868, the mountain basin was struck by a devastating earthquake. From an epicenter near Otavalo, a shock wave sped north to the vicinity of Tulcán and rebounded upon Ibarra: in the space of a minute, most of the town's 6,000 inhabitants were killed, and all but a score of its buildings destroyed.

Great chasms split the earth and swallowed up countless victims asleep in their homes; but for the fragile elasticity of the Indians' dwellings, the damage would have been much worse. Edward Whymper, the all-conquering English mountaineer who passed through Ibarra over a decade after the earthquake, found churches, schools, the convent and the town's hospital still in ruins.

Due to its idyllic climate and volcanic fertility, this is one of the most densely populated provinces in Ecuador, which in turn has the highest population density in South America. The train rolls out of Ibarra at 7am past a patchwork of fields of corn, wheat, potatoes and strawberries. *Campesinos* pausing to watch it go by.

Sometimes things are not quite as smooth. Landslides and derailments are not uncommon further down the line, throwing more than just timetables out the window. All passengers can do is wait for normal service to be resumed.

This train is actually a bus on tracks, an *autoferro* ("iron car"). The body of an antiquated Bluebird bus, complete with steering wheel, horn, and brakes that feed on sand, has been mounted on a train's chassis and fitted with a diesel engine. The single cabin seats 56 passengers, while half as many again huddle in the aisle and on the roof. Many of these travelers will disembark en route: for them, the *autoferro* is the only link with the world beyond their tiny, isolated communities.

While the passengers inhale what the poet Henri Michaux called "the opium of high altitude", the *autoferro* begins its steady descent; the distance of 200 km (124 miles) will take all day to cover. For much of the journey, the land provides momentum for the train's onward slide, and when a little speed is gathered, the carriage starts bouncing precariously like a runaway rollercoaster. Mercifully, though, such moments are rare, and the characteristic snail's pace allows the passenger a detailed appreciation of the spectacular scenery that unfolds below.

Passing through the Western Cordillera, the *autoferro* enters the dry, rugged Río Mira valley. In an astonishing feat of engineering, the tracks cling to the ravine's sheer south side, crossing spindly bridges over the Mira's numerous gushing tributaries. The first stop is Salinas, a small, lazy town 30 km (18 miles) from Ibarra at 1,615 meters (4,845 ft), where fields of sugar cane and coffee mingle with rolling paddocks dotted with

Left, heavily loaded *autoferro*. **Above**, a minor adjustment to the track.

dairy cows. In a journey whose setting constantly changes with the elevation and the contours of the land, this lush, irrigated hinterland defies the surrounding barrenness.

At Carchi, another 20 km (12 miles) and 400 meters (1,200 ft) down, the *autoferro* stops before a handful of unadorned dwellings. Here, passengers eat at trackside stalls offering dishes of rice and an unidentifiable meat; for the cautious, there is also fruit.

The locals are black, descendants of African slaves transported by the Spaniards in the 17th and 18th centuries to work on the coastal banana plantations. Today, in this most unlikely of settings, the villagers grow a few crops in a small, dry patch of the riverbed: once again, the higher ground is lifeless stone.

Shortly after Río Blanco, 900 meters (2,700 ft) high and 75 km (46 miles) from Ibarra, the line leaves the course of the Río Mira, which twists onwards and northwards into Colombia. The train's descent continues through the tropical *ennui* of Rocafuerte, the midway junction at Cachaco, and the military checkpoint at Lita, where a religious shrine protects the bridge over a particularly flood-prone tributary of the Mira.

The tracks sweep past vistas of undulating virgin rainforest away to the northern horizon, looking very much like an Amazonian vastness and on past settlements where you can see naked, potbellied, black children staring wide-eyed from the doorways of tiny thatch-roofed huts.

Night falls, the air is warm and humid as the train creeps into San Lorenzo. Flickering street lights reveal a ramshackle tropical town; once-paved streets resemble a rainy moonscape. Life here is nocturnal: as the day's stifling heat dissipates, the makeshift plaza and numerous funky bars start humming. (See pages 243–245 for more on San Lorenzo.)

In these circumstances, conjuring up the genteel, introspective atmosphere of Ibarra is difficult: there is something unreal about traveling between two contrasting worlds in a single day. Everything is different – the people, the climate, the vegetation, the lifestyle – and only the slithering railway, endlessly besieged by the hostile elements, bridges this enormous cultural gulf. ■

THE NORTH COAST

The north coast of Ecuador, extending as far south as Guayaquil, is one of the best places on the continent to take a break from the often demanding rigors of travel. Much of this varied coastline consists of largely empty, palm-fringed beaches, presenting the ideal opportunity to practice one of the foremost customs of ancient Ecuador: the worshipping of the sun.

This area bore the brunt of the devastating *El Niño* floods of 1982–83, when roads, beaches, trees, crops and a significant number of dwellings were washed away. Recovery has in many cases been slow, for in the tropical languor of a sweltering landscape, the tendency to consign things to *mañana* (tomorrow) is pervasive. As a string of holiday resorts springs up along the coast, however, the last signs of destruction fade. This development testifies to Ecuador's growing stature as a tourist destination – partly due to its own charms, and partly to its neighbors' ill-fortunes.

A holiday in Colombia, with its cocaine-related civil disturbances, is not for the faint-hearted, while the Peruvian coastline is endlessly washed by the Humboldt Current, bringing damp, misty weather and ice-cold waters. In this sense, Ecuador has cornered the market in tropical beaches along South America's west coast.

Land of two seasons: The wet season on the Ecuadorian coast runs from December to June, the remainder of the year being dry – or perhaps "not-so-wet". During the wet, when flooding is commonplace and high levels of humidity make life uncomfortably sticky, the beaches – despite being below their best – are well patronized. All things considered, August to October is the best time to visit this relaxed region.

The coastal topography consists of a thin lowland strip which turns from forbidding mangroves in the north to dry scrubland on the Santa Elena Peninsula, west of Guayaquil. A short distance inland runs a range of low, rounded, crystalline hills. The region is cut by numerous rivers slithering down from the Andes, which regularly flood the alluvial plain which lies to the east of the hills. Huge alluvial fans, often consisting of porous volcanic ash eroded from highland basins, spread out from the major river mouths, providing very fertile soil.

The province of Esmeraldas is one of dense, luxuriant rainforest characterized by two main botanical strata: a high canopy of towering evergreen broadleaf species sprinkled with palms; and at eye-level, clusters of giant ferns, shrubs and vines. Amongst these, the spectacular smaller plants such as orchids and bromeliads which proliferate in the Amazonian forest are rarely found west of the Andes.

South of Esmeraldas is a zone of deciduous scrub woodland which drops its leaves during the dry season. A narrow strip of tropical, semi-deciduous forest lies just north of Manta; and from here down to Guayaquil, this mangrove forest is broken only by the infertile

Preceding pages: fishing boats on the tropical coast. Left, oysters and limes on the Atacames beach. Right, enjoying a day by the Pacific.

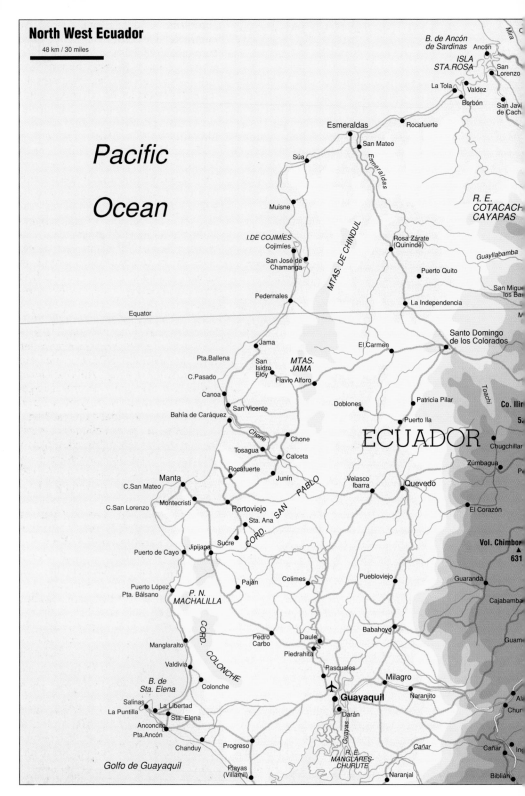

Pacific

Ocean

B. de Ancón
de Sardinas
Ancón
ISLA
STA.ROSA
San
Lorenzo
La Tola
Valdez
Borbón
San Javi
de Cach

Esmeraldas
Rocafuerte
San Mateo

Súa

R. E.
COTACACH
CAYAPAS

Muisne

Esmeraldas

MTAS. DE CHINDUL

I.DE COJIMÍES
Cojimíes
Rosa Zárate
(Quinindé)
Guayllabamba

San José de
Chamanga
Puerto Quito

San Migue
los Bar

Pedernales
La Independencia

Equator

Jama
El Carmen
Santo Domingo
de los Colorados

Pta.Ballena
San
Isidro
Eloy
MTAS.
JAMA

C.Pasado
Flavio Alforo

Toachi

Canoa
Doblones
Patricia Pilar

Co. Ili
5.

Bahía de Caráquez
San Vicente
Puerto Ila

Chone
Chone

ECUADOR
Chugchillar

Tosagua
Calceta
Zúmbagua

Rocafuerte
P

Manta
Junín
Velasco
Ibarra
Quevedo

C.San Mateo

C.San Lorenzo
Montecristi
El Corazón

Portoviejo

Sta. Ana

CORD. SAN – PABLO

Sucre
Vol. Chimbor
631

Puerto de Cayo
Jipijapa

Paján
Colimes
Puebloviejo
Guaranda
Cajabamba

Puerto López
Pta. Bálsano
P. N.
MACHALILLA

Guam

Manglaralto
Pedro
Carbo
Daule
Babahoyo

Valdivia
Piedrahíta

CORD.

COLONCHE

B. de
Sta. Elena
Colonche
Pascuales
Milagro
Ala
Chur

Salinas
La Libertad
Guayaquil
Naranjito

La Puntilla
Sta. Elena
Darán

Anconcito
Pta.Ancón
Guayas

Chanduy
Progreso
Cañar
Cañar
Ing

Golfo de Guayaquil
Playas
(Villamil)
R. E.
MANGLARES-
CHURUTE
Naranjal
Biblián

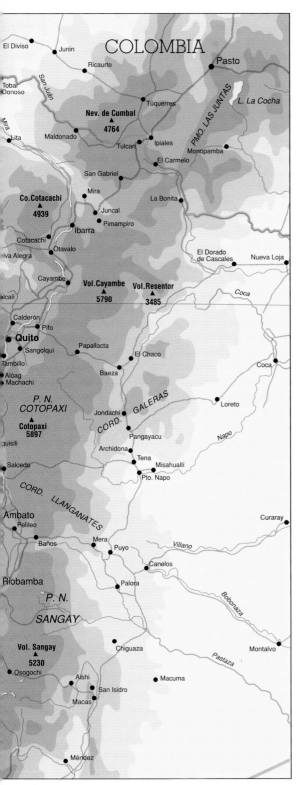

scrubland of Santa Elena. Among the commercially-used plants of the coastal forests are the balsa tree, source of the world's lightest lumber; the ivory-nut palm, used to make buttons; and the *toquilla* reed, from which the renowned Panama hat is manufactured.

The coastal region, which contains almost half of Ecuador's 10 million people, is populated by a veritable melting pot of ethnic groups. Here, more than in the other two regions, the trails of history incorporate all colors of the rainbow. At the time of the Spaniards' arrival, the centers of coastal indigenous habitation were Esmeraldas, Manta, Huancavilca and Puná; these peoples were either exterminated outright, or else they interbred to the point where their racial purity was completely extinguished.

A century or so later, the Spanish-Indian mixture (called *mestizo*) was infused with Negro blood as slaves began arriving from West Africa, creating the *mulatto* (Spanish-Negro mix) and *montuvio* (Indian-Negro mix) races. Indigenous Caribs were also shipped to Ecuador to work the plantations, adding a fourth element to this ethnic conglomeration. *Mestizos* comprise the majority of the coastal population, but the black influence is one of the region's most interesting features, pervading all aspects of life.

From the Colombian border: A journey that begins in **San Lorenzo**, in Ecuador's northwestern corner, can only get drier. The sea is the town's *raison d'être*, and fresh, salty breezes fill the pot-holed streets. The land around San Lorenzo is mostly mangrove swamp, navigated by motorized dugout canoes, while the town itself is frequently sodden with rainwater that has nowhere to run-off. No roads have been constructed through this terra semi-firma: in addition to the canoes, only the Andean railway to Ibarra links San Lorenzo to the world beyond. Most travelers who find themselves in San Lorenzo are at either end of this spectacular, day-long train trip. It should be noted that San Lorenzo has no immigration office, nor any official currency exchange, so crossing the Colombian border to Tumaco is a somewhat risky proposition.

Despite its isolation – during the wet season, even the railway is often impassable – San Lorenzo can generate a certain amount of bustle. It possesses the best natural harbor of the Ecuadorian coast, and a hinterland still largely untouched due to its inaccessibility. The population has grown from 2,000 in 1960 – when, in the days prior to the discovery of oil in the Oriente, this was Ecuador's El Dorado, the alluring, untapped frontier – to 20,000 today. Lumber traders have made profitable incursions into forests rich in mahogany, balsa and rubber, creating industries and bringing itinerant laborers to this long-neglected outpost.

African legacy: Despite this, San Lorenzo still has the feel of a town invented by Gabriel García Márquez. The descendants of people from distant continents have been washed up by history on this forbidding shore, making the most of their displacement. African slaves transported in the 17th and 18th centuries were unloaded in Cartagena (Colombia) and marched southwards to man the coffee, banana and cacao plantations; less than half of this human cargo survived the privations of passage to actually reach their destinations. Despite multifarious interbreeding, the legacy of Africa lives today in the form of ancestor worship and the voodoo rituals of *macumba*, whereby spirits are summoned to cure and curse. Beneath the latinized veneer of regular Sunday mass lies an ancient belief in macabre spirits or *visiones* such as *La Tunda*, who frightens bad children to death and then steals their bodies; or *El Rivel*, who feasts on corpses.

African rhythms anchor the up-tempo beat of *marimba* music, which can be heard at two schools in San Lorenzo. Esmeraldeña *marimba* retains purer links with its origins than does the Colombian style, which has borrowed heavily from the Caribbean jingles of *salsa* and often resembles Western pop music. Talented musicians and dancers of both *marimba* styles can be seen re- **Tranquil waterways near San Lorenzo.**

hearsing on Wednesday nights, and when they hit the downtown bars, San Lorenzo starts jumping. Local men come of age when they begin to *andar y conocer* – literally, "to walk and to know", or "to travel and learn". In black idiom, this commonly-used phrase means "to strut", and is heavily loaded with sexual innuendo.

En route to La Tola, where the coast road begins, lies the island of **La Tolita**, an important ceremonial center from 500 to 100 BC. Tribal chiefs were buried here, their tombs filled with artifacts of gold, silver, platinum and copper. In recognition of its historical significance, La Tolita has been declared an Archaeological National Park and is undergoing extensive excavation.

Like many such sites in South America, La Tolita has been savagely plundered by thieves, its treasures sold on the international black market. Fortunately, however, the government's attention was attracted in time to salvage a substantial portion of the relics, and another gap in the jigsaw-puzzle of ancient Ecuador is slowly being filled.

Frontier town: Opposite La Tolita at the mouth of the Río Santiago is **Limones**, a small town of some importance as the center of the local lumber industry. Timber is floated downriver to the sawmill here, and processed for further distribution.

The lumber camps, isolated in the dense, upriver jungle, were quite notorious in their early days during the 1960s: as in a vision of outpost exploitation worthy of the author Joseph Conrad, the *mestizo* owners forbade their workers – mostly *morenos* (a generic term for blacks) – to leave camp. Instead, prostitutes and alcohol were shipped in each pay-day – a kind of slavery with overpriced fringe benefits.

This delta region is the home of the Cayapa or Chachi Indians, who – along with the Colorados of Santo Domingo – were the only indigenous coastal tribe to evade extermination by the Spaniards. In both cases, survival was due to the inaccessibility of their homelands. Today, the Cayapas number approxi-

Passing the time in the afternoon sun.

mately 4,000. They are sometimes seen selling their finely woven hammocks and basketwork in the markets of Limones and La Tola – and occasionally Esmeraldas – but they prefer the privacy of Borbon and the inhospitable upper reaches of the Río Cayapa.

A turn-off on the La Tola–Esmeraldas road runs to **Borbon**, but this country is decidedly off the beaten track, and travel can be numbingly difficult, especially in the wet season. A better option is to take a motorized dugout from El Bongo restaurant in Limones upriver to Borbon, whence expeditions continue up to **Boca de Onzoles**, at the confluence of the Cayapa and Onzoles rivers. In this far-flung village, a Hungarian émigré called Stefan Tarjany runs a comfortable lodge and organizes trips to the mission stations of **Santa Maria**, **Zapallo Grandea**, and **San Miguel**, the last settlement on the river. At **Punto Venedo** near **San Miguel**, a community of Cayapas still lives in accordance with their traditional customs. They have been fleeing the encroachment of European

civilization for the past 400 years, and like Indians throughout the continent, find the tentacles of business and religion increasingly difficult to evade.

Travel in Ecuador is rarely as adventurous as in these quixotic backwaters, which few visitors make the effort to explore. The Cayapas' counterparts in the Oriente – Stone Age tribes such as the Jivaro and the Huaorani – have received far greater international exposure, which in turn has attracted more tourists. This exposure may, however, prove beneficial as the search for oil in the Amazon basin is a much greater threat to indigenous lifestyles than anything the Cayapas are up against.

Difficult highways: The road from **La Tola** to **Esmeraldas** is rough and never ready: *rancheros*, which are open-sided trucks fitted with far too many wooden benches, take five hours to cover the 100 km (60 miles). The northern half of this road may suffer severe flooding during the wet season, but otherwise it is a carefree, breezy ride past cattle farms and swamps teeming with birdlife. A few small towns are strung out along the way, but offer little reason to pause.

It was near Esmeraldas that the conquistador Bartolomé Ruíz and company landed, the first Spaniards to set foot on Ecuadorian soil. Esmeraldas is named after the precious stone found in bountiful quantities in the like-named river, at whose mouth the city lies. The Cara Indians, who inhabited this area before migrating to the mountain basins around Otavalo during the 10th century AD, worshipped a huge emerald known as Umina. Today, the treasures are more industrial than geological: Esmeraldas is the major port of the north coast, whence lumber, bananas, and cacao are shipped abroad. The 500-km (300-mile) trans-Andean oil pipeline ends here, and the recent construction of an oil refinery has brought new jobs and money to the city.

The treatment of previously fatal tropical diseases has contributed significantly to the growth of Ecuadorian ports, notably Guayaquil, Manta and Esmeraldas. The eradication of yellow fever from these towns early this century was **Fresh coconuts for sale.**

the first step, followed by the discovery and availability of quinine as an antidote for malaria, which as recently as 1942 accounted for one quarter of all deaths in Ecuador. The treatment of tuberculosis, cause of almost one-fifth of fatalities in Ecuador just a generation ago, completed the region's health improvement, providing the basis for growing international maritime trade – and, primarily, improved conditions for the people.

Black capital: Esmeraldas' population of nearly 100,000 consists of mostly *mestizos* and *morenos*, with a surprising minority of mountain Indians looking forlorn and far from home in their bowler hats and thick woollen shawls. Esmeraldas is known as "the capital of rhythm", and is the center of black culture in Ecuador. It is here that the visitor is most likely to encounter a full *marimba* band, complete with huge *conga* drums, led by the *bomero*, who plays a deep-pitched bass drum suspended from the ceiling. Esmeraldas is, like its music, a vibrant, colorful city that embodies the distinctive elements of coastal urban life. The people are gregarious and no-nonsense, playing with far greater enthusiasm than they work. Nothing is high-brow, all culture is popular, and most would rather watch the opposite sex sway by than observe any religious ritual. The energy level on the streets soars as the sun slips down into the Pacific, and bars and restaurants – serving dishes of delicious *cocado*, fried fish in a spicy coconut sauce – fill to overflowing.

For the more cerebrally inclined, the **Archaeological Museum** has exhibits on many of the region's pre-Inca cultures: Bahia, Valdivia, Chorrera and Tuncahuan, as well as some small golden masks from La Tolita. There is also a **House of Ecuadorian Culture** with a collection of colonial and contemporary art, but don't be surprised if you are the only visitor. Discotheques far outnumber museums in Esmeraldas, which is a fair reflection of the hedonistic spirit of the ancient peoples whose suggestive figures now rest on silent shelves.

Guest apartments on the beach at Casa Blanco.

Golden sands and palm trees: To the immediate southwest of Esmeraldas begins a stretch of coastline containing the finest and most peaceful beaches in Ecuador. The beach suburb of **Las Palmas** presents a pleasant alternative to staying in the rather unattractive downtown area of Esmeraldas. The road to the other, less-visited beaches passes the CEPE oil refinery and a luxury hotel, the Hostería La Pradera – complete with swimming pool, tennis courts, and a statue of the Virgin of the Swan in a garden grotto – before reaching the coast.

The small friendly resort town of **Atacames**, 30 km (18 miles) from Esmeraldas, is popular with Ecuadorian and foreign tourists alike. It is relatively undeveloped, with just a string of inexpensive hotels and cabins for rent situated directly on the beach – open the door, and there it is. Predictably, most of the restaurants specialize in fresh seafood, and there is little to be done but sit among the palms and enjoy a plate of fish washed down with a cold beer. Atacames has a cooperative of artisans,

presided over by *"El Tio Tigre"* – "Uncle Tiger" – which manufactures and sells bracelets and chains of black coral, found just offshore a little further south. The purchase of such artifacts cannot be encouraged, however, since in many areas the coral has been pillaged to virtual extinction.

While the beach at Atacames looks harmless enough, there is a powerful undertow. There are no lifeguards, so the current sweeps some swimmers to their deaths each year. Sea snakes washed up on the beach pose a smaller risk: they are venomous and should be avoided. A less avoidable problem is theft, which has been steadily increasing in Atacames in recent years. There have also been several reports of assault on the beach late at night, so a solitary midnight stroll cannot, sadly, be recommended. Despite these warnings, however, the probability of a visitor encountering any trouble remains slim.

Six km (3 miles) further south lies **Sua**, a small, beautifully situated fishing village that is somewhat livelier

A *dorado* makes the latest catch in Atacames.

than Atacames. The fishermen haul their catch right up on to the small beach, which immediately becomes an impromptu market as locals seek out quick bargains. The sky fills with sea birds such as frigates and pelicans, who do a fine job gobbling up fish heads and guts. As a stay in Atacames is chiefly a matter of relishing the elements, Sua offers glimpses of life in a small seaside town with its eye less on tourists than on the next catch.

Luxurious refuge: A further 8 km (5 miles) along the ocean road lies an unpaved side track to the beach of **Same**, perhaps the finest along this stretch. There is little here other than a collection of mostly expensive and tasteful hotels, including the Hotel Casablanca, constructed comparatively recently in Moroccan design. Same does have the air of a place on the verge of overdevelopment, but it remains the quintessential "away-from-it-all-in-comfort" destination in this region.

The completely undeveloped villages of **Tonchigue** and **Galera**, both with lovely beaches nearby, lie a short distance west of Same. At this point, the road leaves the coast and cuts southwards through undulating banana plantations before re-emerging at the shoreline opposite the island of **Muisne**, 83 km (51 miles) from Esmeraldas. Motorized dugouts ply the short distance from the mainland to Muisne and, since few visitors bother to come this far from Esmeraldas for just another beach, Muisne exudes the alluring, timeless languor characteristic of any remote tropical island. The beaches here are enormous and empty; there is a handful of cheap, basic hotels and good seafood restaurants, and nothing more. The ghost of Robinson Crusoe may well haunt Muisne's beaches: if you see another set of footprints in the sand, it must be Friday.

Inland from Muisne hides an isolated community of Cayapa Indians, some of whom may be seen around town at the Sunday market.

From Muisne to **Cojimies**, 50 km (31 miles) to the south, there is no road. One or two motorized dugouts make the two-hour journey each day, some continuing as far as Manta; the boats hug the coastline all the way, making it a safe and picturesque trip. An adventurous alternative is to head off under your own steam: the town of **Bolívar**, whence boats depart for Cojimies, is about 23 km (14 miles) from Muisne, making a feasible day's walk. There are several rivers to be forded en route, but locating a ferry is usually easy, and an early start should bring you to Bolívar, where there are no hotels, in time to catch a boat to Cojimies before dark. The wildlife along this pristine, largely uninhabited coastline is unsurpassed on Ecuador's mainland shore: jellyfish and crabs proliferate, as does the full gamut of pelagic birds, while sea snakes and even the occasional beached whale may be encountered.

Cojimies lies at the northern end of the road that follows the coast down to Manta. It is a quiet and welcoming town, the site of a pre-Columbian settlement that still awaits comprehensive excavation. Transport connections are delight-

Blue waters of the Pacific.

fully whimsical: the unpaved road is impassable in the wet season, and the daily *rancheros* usually run along the beach in a race against the rising tide. Halfway to Pedernales is the inexpensive Hotel Cocosolo, situated on a deserted beach amidst a breezy coconut palm grove. Just south of Pedernales, a town earmarked for tourist development, the road crosses the Equator – marked by a small monument – and then forks. The left-hand turn runs through more farms and plantations to **Santo Domingo de los Colorados**, while the coastal road continues on to the small market town of **Jama**. Another 50 km (31 miles) south lies **Canoa**, center of a fast-developing deep-sea fishing industry.

Scenic roadway: The inland loop through Santo Domingo returns to the coast at **Bahia de Caraquez**, and is a refreshing change for anyone suffering from an overdose of empty, sun-drenched beaches. This route through the heartland of Manabí province is among the most scenic in the entire coastal region, and passes several interesting stop-offs. Just 13 km (8 miles) from Santo Domingo, a right-hand turn leads to Hostería La Hacienda, a country inn with lovely surroundings and all creature comforts. Past more banana plantations and cattle farms, the road runs to **El Carmen**, whereafter densely vegetated hills rise from the plain.

Much of Manabí, particularly the southern area, suffers a dearth of rainfall, due primarily to the lifeless winds of the Humboldt Current. Nevertheless, the province is the agricultural core of Ecuador, with coffee, cacao, rice, cotton and tropical fruits cultivated widely. The Poza Honda Dam, built mostly with West German funds, is fed by the Río Portoviejo and irrigates large areas of previously uncultivatable lowlands.

Chone (population 40,000) prospers on the strength of these industries, as well as the manufacturing of leather saddles and a type of straw hat called *mocora*. The banks of the Río Chone, twisting through the undulating **Balsamo Hills**, sustain increasing numbers of shrimp farms, an indication of Ecua-

Fish lunch by the sea.

dor's modern industrial diversification. The road climbs to a vantage point offering splendid views of Bahia de Caraquez and the mangrove islands dotting the bay, and then slides down to the coast.

The resort village of **San Vicente** stands at the mouth of the Río Chone, opposite Bahia de Caraquez. The recently constructed church of **Santa Rosa** boasts an ornate, eye-catching facade, but otherwise there are few diversions from the pleasures of the beach. Seventy km (43 miles) inland along a typically makeshift road is the important archaeological site of **San Isidro**. The prehistoric inhabitants of San Isidro excelled in the art of ceramics: their beautifully crafted figurines are today sold throughout Ecuador, and have spawned a flourishing trade in well-disguised imitations.

Banana centers: Bahía de Caráquez is named after the Cara Indians who, legend has it, came "by way of the sea" and settled in this bay. Formerly an important export center for bananas and cacao, Bahía entered semi-retirement when the focus of banana exporting – in which Ecuador continues to lead the world – shifted south to Guayaquil and Machala. The cacao industry, in turn, has been steadily declining since it was struck down in its prime by a crippling blight in 1922–23, at which time Ecuador was the world's foremost producer.

A stroll along the palm-fringed riverside Malecón, past rows of stately old mansions – some of them in Victorian "gingerbread" style – reveals remnants of former prosperity. Nevertheless, Bahía's strategic rivermouth location ensures its continued existence as a minor port, and it remains the largest coastal town – with 14,000 inhabitants – between Esmeraldas and Manta.

Much of Bahía's energy is today devoted to tourism: unlike many of Ecuador's north coast towns, it is easily accessible on good roads from Quito, and is one of the most popular resorts in the country. While there are few noteworthy sights in the town, it does offer some simple pleasures. An ascent of **La Cruz hill** is rewarded by sweeping views of

Typical house on the coast.

the river and coastline, and a sojourn at a riverside café affords surprising glimpses of hard work under a burning sun. Ferries across to San Vicente depart frequently, providing a means of transport as well as a scenic way to cool off in the midday sun.

Venturing slightly further afield, launches can be hired to visit **Isla de los Pájaros** and **Isla Corazón** in the bay, which – as the former's name indicates – have raucous sea-bird colonies. Twenty km (13 miles) south of Bahía de Caráquez are the friendly, peaceful fishing villages of **San Clemente** and **San Jacinto**; driving along the beach at low tide may look tempting, but is inadvisable as many cars have died a watery death here. Instead, follow the Portoviejo road and turn off just before **Rocafuerte**: this route leads to San Jacinto, and on to San Clemente 5 km (3 miles) away to the north.

Also along this road, which is notable for the giant ceibo trees lining the way, lies **Cruzita**, a beach resort in the past rarely visited by foreigners but recently becoming known as a perfect spot for paragliding.

Shortly thereafter, and just 15 km (9 miles) east of Manta, is the fishing village of **Jaramijó**, which has twice reared its historical head. It was, firstly, the site of an extensive pre-Columbian settlement – hardly surprising given the beauty of the place. Secondly, Eloy Alfaro, one of Ecuador's best-remembered presidents, lost an important naval battle against conservative forces here in December 1884: the wreck of his ship, the *Alajuela*, can still be seen.

Faded memories: Things blossom quickly in the tropics, and a conscious effort is often required to keep vestiges of the old from being overgrown by the new. In coastal Ecuador, where the *conquistadores* began their epic trek to victory in the relocated Inca capital of Cajamarca, surprisingly little remains of the colonial past. The monuments, which themselves are few and far between, are generally quite recent erections in honor of heroes of the Liberation – Bolívar, Sucre and San Martín – or favorite Republican presidents. It is as if a wilful forgetfulness descended on the pre-Republican centuries: those long years of disease and brutality bequeathed a legacy of military dictatorship and silence.

Descendants of the few hundred *criollo* (pure-bred European) families that have dominated political and economic life since the origins of the *audencia*, still stalk the corridors of power. Since Ecuador returned to civilian government in 1978, however, historians have – without fear or intimidation – cast revealing eyes on the excesses of Spanish colonialism. The people whose transplanted lives are a direct product of that time – all *morenos*, for example – are thus beginning to understand the original forces that have shaped them, their community, and their country.

Given these historical "black holes", the visitor to **Portoviejo** may not be so surprised to learn that it was one of the earliest Spanish settlements in Ecuador. It was founded on March 12, 1535, just three months after Benalcázar re-founded Quito atop abandoned Inca ruins.

At a village dance in Esmeraldas.

Guayaquil, founded in January 1535, was the first Spanish coastal community, but the local Indians, based on the nearby island of Puná, repeatedly launched marauding raids of such ferocity that alternative sites were sought.

The original settlement, founded by Francisco Pacheco on the orders of Francisco Pizarro and Diego de Almagro (who would, a few years hence, more or less, kill each other), was as its name ("Old Port") suggests located on the coast. The omens, however, were far from auspicious: in 1541, a fire destroyed the town, and 50 years later the local Indians staged a fearsome uprising. Finally, when English pirates ravaged the port in 1628, it was decided that a spot further inland would be out of harm's way.

Since then, Portoviejo has existed in the shadow of nearby Manta, though as capital of Manabí Province it remains an important administrative and educational centre. Its population has recently topped the 100,000 mark, most of which **Coastal vista.** is engaged in commerce, industry, and the rich agricultural pickings of the hinterland. Portoviejo's bustling streets are prettily bordered with rows of flora, and a stroll through the **Parque Eloy Alfaro** is perhaps the city's most pleasing pastime. Opposite the park is one of Ecuador's starkest modern cathedrals (could the Catholic Church have been short of cash for once?). Beside it stands a statue of Pacheco.

There are two museums: the **House of Ecuadorian Culture**, with a collection of traditional musical instruments; and the **Archaeological Museum**, which is significantly inferior to its counterpart in Manta. Portoviejo has a few old colonial buildings still standing, but otherwise little testimony to its long and tumultuous history.

Pre-Columbian hedonists: For 1,000 years prior to the arrival of the Spaniards, **Manta** was the center of one of Ecuador's pre-eminent indigenous cultures. It was known as Jocay – literally, "fish house" – by the local Indians, whose exquisite pottery was decorated with scenes of daily life. And what a life

it was! The exuberant hedonism of contemporary coastal Ecuadorians can be traced back directly to the ancient Manteños with their pervasive fertility cult and enjoyment of coca. Their concept of physical beauty was based on the art of *trepining*, whereby children's heads were strapped and bound to increase the backward slope of their chins and foreheads. The desired effect – an exaggeration of the rounded, hooked nose – was quite Neanderthal.

The Manteños sacrificed their prisoners of war by ripping out their still-beating hearts. Their culture was part-settler, part-wanderer as they cultivated fruit and vegetables while also trading with highland Indians – their source of precious metals – and navigating the ocean in rafts and dugouts as far as Panama and Peru, and possibly the Galápagos Islands. Their skill extended to the arts of stonemasonry, weaving, and metalwork – in short, a cultural sophistication of great breadth and depth. (See the chapter entitled *Lost Worlds* on pages 33–36.)

The Spaniard Francisco Pacheco founded the modern settlement of Manta just ten days before Portoviejo in 1535. Nine years earlier, however, Bartolomé Ruíz had encountered a balsa sailing raft with 20 Manteños aboard: 11 of them had leapt into the sea in terror, while the remaining nine served as translators before being set free. Perhaps this rare instance of Spanish tolerance has contributed to the unique character of modern Manta, for it is the most relaxed and livable city of the entire coastal region.

In its previous incarnation as Jocay, the main thoroughfare of Manta was lined with statues of the chieftains and head priests of the "Manta Confederation". Sadly, the Catholic Church ordered their place to be taken by inoffensive jacaranda and poinsiana trees. With a population of approximately 100,000, Manta is a major sea port, with coffee, bananas, cotton textiles and fish comprising the bulk of the exports. For all this, the city feels much smaller than similarly sized Esmeraldas, the pace of

A crushed-ice vendor does a good trade on Atacames beach.

life being much slower due to the presence of large numbers of Ecuadorian tourists.

Manta is divided by an inlet into a downtown and a resort district, the latter called Tarqui. Along the expansive **Tarqui beach**, local fishermen unload and clean their catch – tuna, shark, dorado, eel and tortoise – whipping the attendant gulls and vultures into aerial frenzy. A towering statue of a Manabí fisherman overlooks these proceedings, noticing few material changes from prehistoric times.

The **Municipal Museum** houses the finest collection of Manteño artifacts in Ecuador and is well worth a visit. Manta's outdoor theater is the venue for occasional performances, especially during the agriculture and tourism exposition held each October. **Playa Murciélago** is an unprotected surfing beach a few kilometers west of town, site of the comfortable Hotel Manta Imperial. In Tarqui, the Hotel Haddad Manabí, dating from 1931, offers central accommodation with a slight touch of faded grandeur.

Ecuador's "Panama" hat: Straddling the highway between Manta and Portoviejo is the deceptively non-descript town of **Montecristi**, for more than a century the home of the renowned Panama hat. The majority of Montecristi's 9,000-odd inhabitants are engaged in the weaving of these remarkable headpieces, made from the straw fronds of the *Carludovica palmata*, which grows wild in the nearby hills.

It is the quintessential cottage industry – many houses in Montecristi contain a rudimentary factory and showroom – and the lack of even the remnants of wealth in Montecristi is sad testimony to the inequitable distribution of the industry's hefty profits.

Like Portoviejo, Montecristi owes its existence to pillaging pirates: in 1628, a group of exasperated Manteños departed the coast for a nearby inland refuge. Rows of colonial houses in chronic disrepair line the quiet, dusty streets, and in combination with the non-mechanized weaving, this physical neglect creates the air of a town stuck in another time.

Montecristi's religious atmosphere is similarly dated, as the beautiful church contains a famous statue of the Virgin to which several miracles have been attributed. And Montecristi's favorite son is now long dead: Eloy Alfaro, President of Ecuador at the turn of the century and a committed liberal reformist, was born here. His statue overlooks the main plaza, and his house is now a mausoleum, with his library and many personal effects on display. Almost alone among towns in coastal Ecuador, Montecristi survives as a relic – an impression heightened by the anachronism of tourists and Panama hat dealers roaring into town in search of a bargain.

Montecristi ages gracefully, and also keeps in touch with changing times: whereas every household was engaged in Panama hat production 40 years ago, many have recently switched to making fine wickerwork furniture and decorations. In contrast, **Jipijapa** – a town of 28,000 inhabitants situated another 40 km (25 miles) along the highway to Guayaquil – appears to have been swal-

Ecuadorian belle soaks up the sun.

lowed up by Ecuador's flourishing agricultural industries.

The village of **La Pila**, between Montecristi and Jipijapa, is an interesting stop-off. In the wake of the discovery of exquisite pre-Columbian ceramics in the area, the resourceful inhabitants of La Pila began producing indistinguishable "antique" imitations to cash in on their forebears' artistry. Nowadays, however, they have embraced originality and, to the delight of the experts, have inherited not only the enterprise but also the considerable artistic skill of their ancestors.

At Jipijapa, a side road climbs into the damp, luxuriant hills of southern Manabí before descending to the coast near **Puerto Cayo**, a fishing village with pristine beaches. Fifteen km (9 miles) offshore is **Isla de la Plata**, an ancient Manteño ceremonial center currently undergoing excavation. The island is named after an incident in the late 16th century, when Sir Francis Drake – dispatched by Queen Elizabeth to wreak havoc on the Spanish colonies – captured a silver-laden galleon and made camp on the island to tally his spoils. It is today inhabited only by tortoises and blue-footed boobies, and can be reached by hired motorboat – a trip of two hours.

Watch out for shells of the spondilus oyster, which in pre-Columbian times served as a unit of currency, and as such was regularly interred in the tombs of tribal chieftains.

The well-worn coast road continues on to **Machalilla**, center of the like-named culture which flourished between 1800 and 1500 BC. This area was declared a National Park in 1979 and is rich in archaeological remains, especially in the vicinity of **Salaite** and **Agua Blanca**. A pleasant 45-minute walk from Machililla brings you to the deserted horseshoe beach called, oddly, **"Los Frailes"** (The Friars). A little further south, fleets of heavily-laden fishing boats dock in the village of **Puerto Lopez** each afternoon at about four o'clock: the skippers will happily sell their catch there and then.

South of Puerto Lopez is an interesting ecological resort, **Alandaluz**, built of locally grown and easily replenishable bamboo and palm-leaf thatch. The cabins and towers are set out attractively amongst organic gardens overlooking the sea. Water and rubbish are recycled and innovative bathroom facilities convert human waste, using sawdust, into fertilisers for the flowers.

Digging for the past: Nearby in Salango dozens of scientists, students and local volunteers took part in the largest archaeological dig in the country, providing insights into the fragmentary history of pre-Columbian Ecuador.

The relics of a host of successive cultures – Valdivia, Machililla, Chorrera, Engoroy, Bahía, Guangala and Manteño – which inhabited this fertile stretch of coastline as early as 2000 BC were painstakingly recovered. A museum dedicated to the former balsa-raft sailors of Ecuador, which was opened here in 1987, has been filled with artefacts found in the area. There is more than a touch of irony to such a rich historical yield being offered up by a region with so little apparent interest in its own past.

Left, lone fisherman casts his net. **Right**, statue of Manabí fisherman in Manta.

GUAYAQUIL AND THE SOUTH COAST

Many visitors to Ecuador are surprised to learn that the seaport of **Guayaquil** is the country's largest city, counting a population of some 1.7 million inhabitants, nearly half as large again as Quito. But size is not the only surprise in this bustling commercial city which alternately offers the nation's finest hotels, restaurants and shopping along with one of Ecuador's most thriving red-light districts and plenty of mosquitoes. Guayaquil is not for the meek.

Situated on the west bank of the busy Guayas River, navigable for the biggest of ocean vessels heading in from the Pacific via the Gulf of Guayaquil, this city handles 90 percent of Ecuador's imports and 50 percent of its exports. It has a reputation for being hot and humid with too many inhabitants and few tourist attractions. But that notion – true to some degree – overlooks the rough-and-ready hospitality and gutsiness of Guayaquil and its inhabitants.

During the rainy season, January to April, the heat and humidity are, indeed, oppressive, but from May to December the climate is pleasant with little or no rain and cool nights. And Guayaquil, prosperous despite its rundown facades, is dotted with wide concrete boulevards, spacious parks and colorful gardens, as well as beautiful monuments, attractive residential neighborhoods, museums with rich archaeological and art collections and excellent restaurants.

Its most obvious attraction – a schizophrenic one in this city where good and bad mix with a sometimes delightful, sometimes dubious result – is the **Guayas** itself. The chocolate-colored river teems with ships, small boats, dugout canoes and rafts loaded with produce from the inland villages and plantations. Considered one of the cleanest deepwater ports in this part of the world, it is also a controversial spot. Although Ecuador is not considered a major drug-trafficking country, Guayaquil figured prominently in a drug scandal a couple of years ago when three tons of cocaine in boxes labeled "Ecuadorian cocoa" were shipped from that city to the United States. The persons implicated were two Colombians and two local residents – flashy Carlos Zambrano and his son Julio Cesar, owners of the Cadesa chocolate factory and infamous in Guayaquil for their $1,500 suits.

But the so-called Great Chocolate Cocaine Caper was an exception to the mostly legitimate traffic that moves on the Guayas River. In Guayaquil, a number of travel agencies offer river tours, taking visitors past small settlements, farms and cattle ranches along this lush, tropical river and through locks into the Salado estuary where the city's new seaport area is located.

A name inspired by tragedy: Although Spanish explorer Francisco de Orellana – credited with discovering the Amazon River – claimed to have founded Guayaquil, it was actually inhabited long before the Spanish arrived. The Valdivia Indians flourished in the area around 2000 BC, followed by the Huancavilcas.

Preceding pages: gathering shrimp larvae in Guayas. Left, art sales in Guayaquil. Right, the city's bustling center.

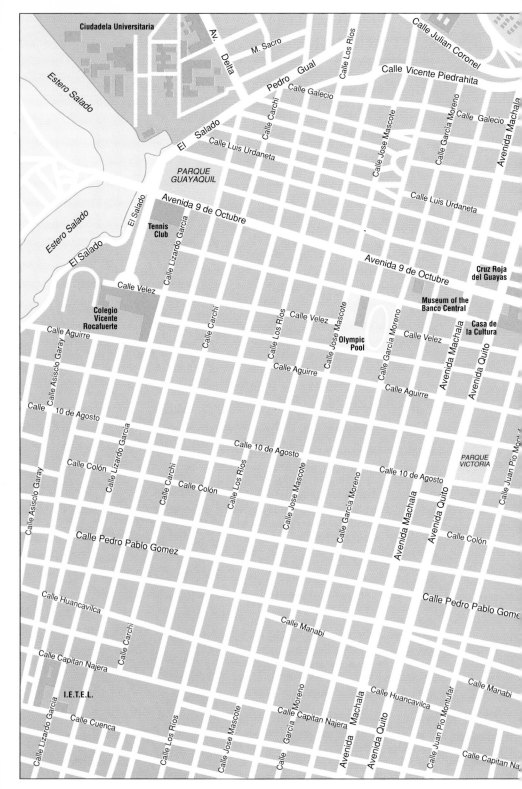

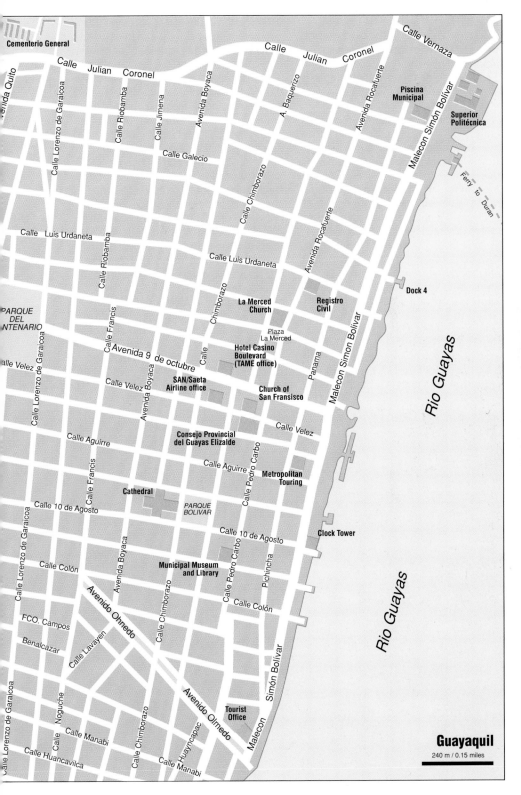

Cementerio General

Calle Julian Coronel

Calle Julian Coronel

Calle Vernaza

Avenida Quito

Calle Lorenzo de Garaicoa

Calle Riobamba

Calle Jimena

Avenida Boyaca

Calle Galecio

A. Baquerizo

Avenida Rocafuerte

Piscina Municipal

Malecon Simón Bolívar

Superior Politécnica

Calle Chimborazo

Ferry to Duran

Calle Luis Urdaneta

Calle Riobamba

Calle Luis Urdaneta

Avenida Rocafuerte

Dock 4

Rio Guayas

PARQUE DEL CENTENARIO

Calle Francis

Chimborazo

La Merced Church

Registro Civil

Calle Lorenzo de Garaicoa

alle Velez

Avenida 9 de octubre

Calle Velez

Avenida Boyaca

Plaza La Merced

Hotel Casino Boulevard (TAME office)

Panama

Malecon Simón Bolívar

Calle

SAN/Saeta Airline office

Church of San Fransisco

Calle Lorenzo de Garaicoa

Consejo Provincial del Guayas Elizalde

Calle Velez

Calle Aguirre

Calle Francis

Calle Aguirre

Calle Pedro Carbo

Metropolitan Touring

Cathedral

Calle 10 de Agosto

PARQUE BOLIVAR

Calle 10 de Agosto

Clock Tower

Calle Lorenzo de Garaicoa

Calle Colón

Avenida Boyaca

Municipal Museum and Library

Calle Pedro Carbo

Pichincha

FCO. Campos

Avenido Ohnedo

Calle Chimborazo

Calle Colón

Benalcazar

Calle Lavayen

Noguche

Rio Guayas

Calle Lorenzo de Garaicoa

Calle

Calle Manabi

Calle Chimborazo

Huayncapac

Avenido Ohnedo

Tourist Office

Simón Bolívar

Malecon

Guayaquil

Calle Huancavilca

Calle Manabi

240 m / 0.15 miles

Legend has it that the Huancavilcas' chieftain, Guayas, killed his beautiful wife Quil then drowned himself so that the Spaniards would not capture them. The tragedy of this doomed couple is supposed to be what inspired the city's name.

While fairly calm and conventional Quito was worrying only about infrequent earthquakes, Guayaquil spent its first 400 years fending fires – maladies that, perhaps, bred the residents' pluckiness and ingenuity. The last major blaze, in 1896, destroyed a large part of Guayaquil's charming wooden houses (some of which had long survived their main enemy – termites). During those ravages, all but one of the city's original neighborhoods remained intact. That is the narrow street along the waterfront known as the "Las Peñas."

The different natures of Quito and Guayaquil – one a sophisticated center for art and culture, the other a rapidly growing center of commerce occupied by tattooed sailors and hard-working, hard-drinking laborers – bred a rivalry between the cities. It is common for competing presidential candidates to be from one or the other and while Quiteños think the Guayaquil residents brutish and unrefined, the Guayaquil dwellers think residents of the capital are dull and backward, not to mention foolish for remaining in a city with no nightlife and no beaches. As the Guayaquileños are quick to say, they make the country's money and the Quiteños spend it.

Brassy wealth: Today Guayaquil, despite its development problems and poorer suburbs, is a growth area, a center of industry with oil and sugar refineries, cement mills, breweries and all types of manufacturing. In many respects, it is an attractive destination for visitors seeking luxurious hotels, fine restaurants, clubs for tennis, golf, yachting and swimming, exciting discotheques and upscale shopping – including a bevy of duty-free stores. The main blotches on its tourism record are crime and an unstable water supply, characterized by sporadic shortages in some of the downtown neighborhoods.

Guayaquil's urban sprawl.

It is the Guayas River that made Guayaquil what it is today, and it is the Guayas River where visitors should start exploring this eclectic city. The seawall area along the water, **Malecón Simon Bolívar**, offers a microcosmic view of the city's light and dark sides. Children selling slices of fresh pineapple and vendors with soft drinks as armor against the hot sun share the same benches as idle sailors. This area is always filled with people, from beer-bellied shirtless men exchanging stories and couples embracing under trees to pickpockets. Across the street and down a handful of blocks along the Malecón is the beginning of the chaotic informal outdoor market where anything from cameras with phony trademarks to misspelled T-shirts are sold. Contraband fuels much of the commerce at this jostling, noisy gathering place. Prostitutes line up along the walls of cut-rate hotels here and theft is common, but there is little physical danger during the day.

The historical Las Peñas district.

One visit here proves that Guayaquil residents are much livelier than those in Quito and are nowhere near as formal.

Near the waterfront, at Aguirre 104 y Malecon, is the national **Tourist Office**, CETUR. At best, visitors may prise a city map out of the staff there but, like much in Guayaquil, the mood is laid back and it is often more effective to explore independently or make city tour arrangements with one of the many private travel agencies.

Along the waterfront are various fountains and a Moorish **clock tower** dating from 1770. Visitors can climb the steep, narrow winding stairway inside its base (which is used as a city office) and go up to the room with the clock workings, even stepping outside onto the little ledge to get a good look at the city. The gardens around the clock are a favorite meeting spot for young couples and in the early evening this area is full of strollers looking for relief from the last blast of daytime heat.

Across the street is the splendid Palacio Municipal, separated from the severe Government Palace by a plaza with a statue dedicated to General Sucre,

hero of Ecuador's independence war.

Meeting place of the liberators: Continuing along the Malecón to the foot of Avenida 9 de Octubre lies the semicircle of **La Rotonda**, with its statue commemorating the historical but enigmatic meeting between the continent's two great liberators, Venezuelan Simón Bolívar and Argentine General José de San Martín. Bolívar had freed the countries to the north and San Martín was responsible for the independence of Argentina and Chile but their final plans differed – Bolívar wanted the countries united under a democracy with an elected president and San Martín envisioned a state headed by a monarch. They met in Guayaquil to see how these differences could be bridged and to decide who would be credited with the independence of Peru – the last Andean country held by Spain.

There was no witness to the exchange between the two men and they refused to reveal the details of their conversation, which ended in the so called "Acuerdo de Guayaquil" (Guayaquil Accord). The only thing historians know for sure is that when the meeting ended, Bolívar took credit for Peru, San Martín exiled himself to France and the plan for a united Gran Colombia crumbled away.

The rotunda is built so that visitors can stand on either side of the statue, whisper, and hear one another. From here, too, you can enjoy an impressive view of the hill known as Cerro El Carmen and, far beyond, the Guayaquil-Duran bridge – the country's largest at 4 km (2½ miles) long and the link to the Duran rail terminal.

At the upper end of the Malecón, past restaurant boats, working docks and the Duran ferry exit, Numa Pompilio Lloma Street mounts the side of Cerro Santa Ana and enters the picturesque bohemian district of **Las Peñas.** Here, the wooden architecture brings to mind the great influence of the principal Pacific naval yards during the Spanish colonization. On the small **Plaza Colón**, where the narrow winding street with its original cobblestone paving begins, two cannons commemorate the defense of the city against the pirate invasions. The romantic 19th-century houses bordered by jasmine bushes are today mostly inhabited by artists; peek into open doors on the way by. There are a few art galleries here and number 186 is the residence of the famous painter Hugo Luis Lara.

From the top of the **Santa Ana hill** there is a spectacular view of the city, salt estuaries, new port and river, although it is not advisable to climb the hill alone. This area also has an open-air theatre – Bogotá – and, just behind, the oldest church in Guayaquil, **Santo Domingo** founded in 1548 and restored in 1938. A patio at the left-hand side of the church's nave contains a spring credited with miraculous healing powers. Meanwhile, stairs to the right of the church and the steep Buitron Street lead to Cerro del Carmen, topped by the religious monument "Cristo del Consuelo." (Because of the isolation of this spot and crime problems, this is best visited on an organized tour.) At the foot of the hill is the dazzling white cemetery, **Cementerio General** with its avenue of royal

The Moorish-style Clock Tower on Guayaquil's Malecón Simón Bolívar.

266

palms leading to the grave of President Vicente Rocafuerte, elaborate marble sculptures and imposing Greco-Roman mausoleums.

The downtown sights are scattered and there is no easy route to see them all, but a good way to start is with a stroll down Avenida 9 de Octubre from the Malecón. Along the way, you will pass the **plaza and church of San Francisco**, built in 1603 and beautifully restored in 1968. You'll also see that many streets in the central district preserve porticos protecting pedestrians from the sun or rain. Farther along the avenue is **Parque Centenario**, the city's largest plaza, covering four city blocks. It is filled with monuments, the most important being the patriotic Liberty monument with the likenesses of Ecuador's heroes and smaller statues representing history, justice, patriotism and heroism.

Pre-Columbian artifacts: Out of the park on Avenida 9 de Octubre 1200 is the Ecuadorian **Casa de Cultura** with a small museum of pre-Columbian arti-facts found in archaeological digs on the country's coast. Reopened following a 1987 fire, this museum once had an impressive collection of gold items in its Carlos Zevallos Menendez Hall – reported to be Ecuador's most valuable pre-colonial gold collection – but many of the items mysteriously disappeared; those that remain at the museum are not publicly displayed. Current exhibits now range from clay whistles known as *ocarines* to molds for casting gold masks and colonial art. Other artifacts and archaeological displays – including ceramics, textiles, gold and ceremonial masks – are located at the **Central Bank museum** on the same street, beside the **Oro Verde Hotel**, the best spot in town for a *gringo* breakfast.

The most intriguing museum contains Jivaro *tzantzas* – or shrunken heads. Located on 9 de Octubre and José de Anteparro, the **Museo Municipal** has a macabre collection of the miniature heads prepared by jungle Indians using secret processes scientists are still unable to unravel. There are, of course,

Waiting bus in San Vicente.

theories on how the human heads were reduced to fist size without losing their original features, but there is no consensus. A 1988 auction at Christie's in London brought in bids of several thousand dollars apiece for such shrunken heads and tourists in Ecuador are occasionally offered *tzantzas* for sale, although authorities say those bargains are not only illegal but are almost certainly monkey – not human – heads. This museum also displays of Inca and pre-Inca ceramics from the Huancavilca and Valdivia Indians, colonial art, modern art and local handicrafts.

Perhaps the most interesting park in the city is **Parque Seminario**, also known as Parque Bolívar, on Calle Chile between 10 de Agosto and Clemente Ballen. This old, well-maintained botanical garden earned its nickname from its equestrian statue of Bolívar; around the statue's base are bas-relief depictions of that mysterious Guayaquil meeting between Bolívar and San Martín. Turtles paddle in the park's pond and iguanas roam free, delighting children who gather to watch them. The pavilion and gates in this nearly century-old park came originally from France.

On one side of the park is the neo-Gothic **cathedral** dating from 1948 with its lovely stained-glass windows and Cuenca marble altar. Its side altars are overwhelmed by innumerable votive candles lit by the devout; some people even hold candles in their hands while walking around the church praying. The original wooden cathedral built in 1547 burned in one of the city's many fires. On another side of the park is the ultramodern **Unicentro Shopping Centre**. The **Unihotel,** at this sparkling indoor gallery of shops and services, has gained a reputation for its cocktails, including its *jipijapa*, a blend of orange aguardiente, grenadine and lemon served with a slice of pineapple.

Beaches of the south: Guayaquil is an important meeting city for business executives but rarely the sole destination of tourists. Rather, it is the jumping-off point for the beaches of Ecuador's southern coast. Except for Sali-

Left, the Pope and the pin-up girl. **Right**, the morning catch at Ayangue.

nas, these are generally undeveloped stretches of sand lapped by warm salt water and toasted by the tropical sun. (People with fair skin should take precautions under these burning rays; sometimes less than half an hour of unprotected sun can cause severe sunburn). Although weekends and the December to April vacation season see much beach activity, the area is all but deserted during the week. There are a few hotels and official camping sites, although camping is allowed everywhere.

The road south from Guayaquil passes through dry scrubland, with the scenery making an astonishing change from wet fields of rice and bananas (farmed in the 1500s by black slaves) to an arid – but attractive – landscape with strange bottle-shaped kapok trees and scattered bright flowers. Traffic on the coastal road, which passes the busy villages of **Cerecita** and **Progreso** about 70 km (42 miles) outside of Guayaquil, is heavy from January to April during local vacation months and on weekends. In Progreso, the official name of which is

Gomez Rendón, the road forks right to Salinas and Santa Elena. A left-hand fork leads to the popular beach resort of Playas, Guayaquil's closest beach at 100 km (60 miles) from the city.

Playas, officially called General Villamil, is an important fishing village and its beaches are lined with old balsa rafts. These rafts, similar to watercraft used in pre-Inca times, are unique to this area and are still used by some of the fishermen who bring in a catch every afternoon.

However, the main focus of this town has turned to tourism and the beaches are the lure for weekend crowds. As an alternative to the main beach with its hotels, including the popular Playas, Rey David and Cattan, and the holiday villas used as escape destinations for Guayaquil residents, is the beautiful beach to the north. Called the Pelado, this is a long and lonely stretch set against the backdrop of a cliff.

For overnight stays at Playas, the best lodgings are to be found in the more expensive *hosterías* Bellavista and Los

Tropical rhythms for sale.

Patios on the main road to Data outside the village.

Heading south along the coast from Playas is **Data de Villamil**, interesting for its traditional wooden shipbuilding industry. An inland road from here passes the old village of Morro with its huge wooden church and farther along is the fishing village of Posorja with commercial boats and hundreds of seabirds wheeling around the **Morro Channel** (Canal de Morro) used by overseas vessels bound for Guayaquil. Shrimp farming caused an economic boom in the village, which has grown rapidly over the past few years, and this is a pleasant stop on a day trip even though the beaches are not really good for swimming.

In front of Posorja is the big island of **Puna**, already settled in pre-Inca times as evidenced by the traces of two Valdivia culture settlements that archaeologists found there. Later, in 1530, Francisco Pizarro stopped at the island on his way to conquer the Incas. Today there is only one village and one basic lodging house on the island and it is difficult to reach Puna. A boat from Capitanía del Puerto or other transportation must be hired at the Yacht Club Guayaquil.

Cactus and tuna: Back at Progreso, the right-hand road leads toward Salinas and an increasingly dry, cactus-covered landscape. At Kilometer 35.6 outside this town is the road to the fishing village of **Chanduy**, a mecca for archaeologists who have made important discoveries while excavating the remains of Valdivia, Machalilla and Chorrera Indian settlements. This is considered the continent's oldest agricultural settlement where ceramics were used and may have been a ceremonial center. Nowadays, like all the fishing villages along this route, the biggest catches are brought close to the shore with the cold Antarctic-born Humboldt Current. The tuna and marlin feed here on smaller, warm-current fish.

Just before reaching Chanduy is the recently inaugurated **Real Alto museum**, which takes the form of two giant huts covered with straw roofs. Poorly marked, it is to the left of a directional sign reading *Fabrica Portuguesa*.

Among the exhibits at this museum is one demonstrating how the local inhabitants of the area now live.

Back to the main roadway, at Kilometer 49.5, a right-hand deviation in the road leads to the **San Vicente thermal baths**, a large complex built by the government tourist board. The water is channeled into swimming pools and mud baths promising to improve ailments. The simple hotel there, the Florida, is clean and reservations can be made in advance in Guayaquil by telephoning 353 316.

Farther down the main road is **Santa Elena**, interesting only for its church and usually bypassed in favor of La Libertad and Salinas. However, on the outskirts of the town near a Mormon temple with a small tower is **Los Amantes de Zumba** (the Lovers of Zumba) archaeological site. Two human skeletons estimated to be 3,500 years old are caught in an afterlife embrace in the grave, which falls under the auspices of the Archaeological Department of the Banco Central in Guayaquil. Roberto Lindao is the warden at the site and special permission must be obtained for the grave to be opened to visitors.

Along the same road, past an oil refinery, is **La Libertad**, the largest town on the peninsula with 45,000 inhabitants. This is a busy port with a bustling market and serves as the hub for bus services to **Manglaralto** – a top destination for surfers – **Puerto Lopez** and **Jipijapa**. On the road to Manglaralto are several fishing villages where Guayaquileños have vacation homes, but there are no restaurants or hotels. However, these are marvelous spots for a day of swimming. **Punta Blanca** boasts an exquisite, isolated beach that attracts shell collectors. **Ayangue**, further north, has white beaches, a gentle slope and no big waves – making it excellent for children.

Valdivia, once the center of Ecuador's oldest culture, is home to an interesting museum (although its best pieces are on display in museums in Quito and Guayaquil). At Manglaralto, at the end of this scenic road, there are basic restaurants and bed-and-breakfast establishments at some of the local homes. La Libertad has the waterfront Samarina Hotel, about a kilometer outside of town, offering guests a bar, pool, restaurants, tennis court and bungalows for families. Travelers with four-wheel-drive vehicles can continue along the coast through lush and dense vegetation to Puerto Lopez, already in Manabí.

Summer beach mecca: But Ecuador's most fashionable resort town – **Salinas** – lies farther along in a half-moon bay on the tip of the **Santa Elena peninsula**, a total of 150 km (90 miles) from Guayaquil. It has a pleasant beaches, tall buildings, fine mansions, excellent hotels, good restaurants, a casino and a yacht club which, together, provide part of the lure for the throngs of swimmers and sun baskers who gather here. It is also the site of a naval base. The best place to stay is the Hotel Miramar, which boasts air-conditioning, a pool and casino. Other hotels are the first-class El Refugio, the modern and reasonable Salinas and the inexpensive but noisy Yulee. Salinas is famous for sport fishing and annually hosts international deep-sea fishing competitions. "Pesca-Tours" organizes ocean fishing trips and provides all the equipment for those looking for king-size dorados and black marlin (*picudos*) weighing in at up to 580 kg (1,300 lb).

About 9 km (5½ miles) from Salinas is **Punta Carnero** with its beach several kilometers long. From the Carnero Inn situated on a cliff, you have a marvelous view of the ocean and the hotel has a good restaurant, pool and bar. Fishing charters can be arranged from here, as well, and one of the biggest marlin ever caught in the area came from a spot near the inn; it topped the scales at more than 635 kg (1,400 lbs). For the best seafood in town, try the Mar y Tierra. And for vigorous nightlife there is the Barba Negra discotheque.

El Oro, the southernmost of Ecuador's provinces, owes its name to the rich gold deposits mined here during the Spanish conquest. It is now Ecuador's leading banana and shrimp-producing region. The fields here are blanketed by

Fish mountain.

massive banana plantations, the ripening fruit protected by light-blue plastic bags, and the main city here – **Machala** – is known as the "World Banana Capital." The International Banana and Agricultural Festival is held here every year in late September and draws large crowds. In fact, with 144,000 inhabitants, Machala is Ecuador's fourth largest city. Although not necessarily attractive, it is a thriving town with some comfortable hotels and an international port, **Puerto Bolívar** near the popular **El Coco beach.**

Some one million tons of banana and shrimp exports pass through Puerto Bolívar annually, and from this city's boat pier motorized dugouts can be taken to the archipelago of **Jambelí**, an extraordinarily beautiful area that is little explored.

Other side trips are available from Machala, including the interesting journey to the pleasant farming center of **Santa Rosa** and then onto the beautiful old coffee-growing town of **Piñas** before reaching the mining town of **Zaruma**. **Santa Anna** is surrounded by banana, coffee and cacao plantations and has a small archaeological museum.

Town amongst the ruins: The main road from Piñas continues to **Portovelo** from where you can see the town of **Zaruma** stuck to the mountainside like a swallow's nest. This mining town of 5,000 inhabitants was founded during the colonial-era gold boom and recently attracted renewed interest with the discovery of pre-Columbian ruins at Chepel, Trencillas, Payama and Pocto. Although the ruins have not yet been fully excavated, they have led archaeologists to conclude that the area was densely populated in pre-Inca times.

South American Development, a US mining company, was still active here during the first half of the 1900s and the town conserves much of its past in its architecture. Its wooden colonial houses with elaborately decorated balconies – unusual in Ecuador – and the church are well worth seeing. From the main plaza and the no-frills Hotel Municipal, there is a fantastic view of the surrounding valley. Visits to an abandoned gold mine can be arranged through the city council – **Consejo Municipal** – and a stop at the **Museo Municipal** with displays of archaeological artifacts, colonial art and Zaruma's history is recommended. The best hotel is the Pedregal, 3 km (1¼ miles) outside Zaruma.

To the far south of Machala, the route ends at **Huaquillas** and the border with Peru – a region whose lines are disputed. Although the border at these two cities is clear, the area to the east is not and appears as Peruvian territory on maps produced in that country and as Ecuadorian territory on Ecuador-printed maps. This border not only marks the beginning of the Peruvian coastal desert but is one of the continent's main cross-border commercial centers – although much of what is bought and sold is contraband. With the outbreak of war between the two countries in January 1995, commercial borders were officially closed for several months. This severely affected not only contraband traders, but also police who would accept ""tips" or rather bribes when suspects were caught. Those foreign tourists not daunted by the conflict continued to cross the border throughout the troubles, the only extra inconvenience for them was having passports checked more often than normal.

Huaquillas is a busy, dusty and unattractive town with stagnant water laying on its rutted roads and a reputation for pickpockets – who generally seek out tourists, sometimes returning stolen passports if a reward is proffered and no charges are pressed. Stolen cash, predictably, is seldom returned. The only decent hotel in town is the government-run Parador Turistico, north of town, with a restaurant and swimming pool, the latter being a welcome relief from the insufferable heat and dust that characterizes this area.

The main street of Huaquillas leads to the **International Bridge** into Peru and is lined with street vendors, aggressive money changers, police and border officers and children and adults alike offering to carry luggage. Travelers must cross the bridge on foot unless they are driving their own car.

A parade in Guayas Province.

THE ORIENTE

An hour east of Quito, the dilapidated bus labors over the snow-covered **Papallacta Pass** – at 4,100 meters (13,400 ft) one of the highest points in Ecuador that can be reached by public transport. Shivering in the early morning cold, the passengers pull their thin clothes tightly about them and comfort one another with the observation that the weather will soon be hot. And indeed it is, for as the narrow gravel road plunges down in a series of ear-popping curves from the snowy pass to the Oriente the temperature rises steadily and the landscape alters dramatically.

The Oriente, as Ecuador's Amazonian region is called, lies less than 100 km (60 miles) away from the Papallacta Pass as the vulture glides. But the eastern slopes of the Andes tumble precipitously, and the road passes lush cloud forests full of giant Andean tree ferns, spiky bromeliads, delicate orchids, and brightly colored birds. This is the very rim of the Amazon basin, and the steepness of the terrain combines with the thick vegetation to make it almost impenetrable.

Into the jungle: Not surprisingly, many visitors to the Oriente prefer to arrive by air. Daily flights dive from Quito in the Andes to the towns of Lago Agrio and Coca deep in the jungle covering in only 30 minutes the same distance that can take 12 gruelling hours by land, as well as providing spectacular aerial views of the changing landscape. The dazzling white of the snow-capped Andes gives way to an endless mattress of green stretching into the horizon. Dozens of rivers snake beneath huge gray clouds, ready to drop their loads of moisture onto the rainforest.

Almost all travelers who have prearranged river tours or visits to jungle lodges (either in Quito or overseas) will arrive by air, leaping suddenly from one climate to another. For those with limited time, or who require some comfort in their visit, previously organized trips are the best way to see the Oriente:

options include a wide range of jungle lodges, the unique Amazon river boat *Flotel Orellana,* or the burgeoning number of "adventure tourism" groups. It's also quite popular amongst younger, independent travelers to organize your own jungle trip once you arrive in the Oriente. This requires liberal amounts of time and energy. It is, however, much cheaper and allows greater freedom.

The highway from Quito: Those travelers who want to observe from the ground the subtle shifts in flora between the Sierra and Oriente gladly sacrifice comfort and speed for a bus window seat along the northern highway (even though almost all elect to return by air).

The heavily forested subtropical slopes of this transitional area are also the haunts of a variety of wildlife, including the spectacled bear, the only bear found in South America. Its name derives from the light markings around the eyes of this otherwise dark animal. It ranges from 200 meters (650 ft) to 13,800 ft (4,200 meters) and is mainly vegetar-

ian, often climbing trees in search of succulent exotic fruits. The spectacled bear is shy and rarely seen which is perhaps why it has survived so long. Nevertheless, as its habitat is encroached upon by colonists, numbers of the bear continue to fall and it is now protected by Ecuadorian law.

Thirty minutes drive past the Papallacta pass is the town of **Papallacta** and its nearby hot springs, a must for anyone in need of a little relaxation. The road drops towards the jungle taking the line of least resistance – a river valley. Amazonian climate patterns ensure heavy rainfall almost year round, and there are hundreds of minor and major rivers flowing down the eastern Andes towards the Oriente. Although at this point they are only 240 km (150 miles) away from the Pacific, these rivers will merge with the waters of the world's greatest river system and finally join the sea at the Atlantic 3,200 km (2,000 miles) away.

At first the road follows the valley of the River Papallacta. It finally ends up in the first important Oriente town. **Bae-za**, near the River Quijos (which is named after an Indian tribe that lived in the region at the time of the conquest). Baeza is small, ramshackle, subtropical outpost whose tin-roofed appearance belies its long and interesting history. Since before the Spanish conquest, lowland forest Indians stopped here on their way to the highlands on trading expeditions. Recognizing the area's strategic importance, the Spaniards founded a missionary and trading outpost there as early as 1548, only 14 years after conquering Ecuador.

Perched on the edge of the Amazon basin at 1,400 meters (4,600 ft) above sea level and 80 km (50 miles) east of Quito. Baeza remained Ecuador's last outpost in the northern Oriente for over four centuries. Today, it is its gateway, and can also be reached by a popular road from Baños futher south, via the jungle town of **Puyo**. Like most towns of this area, it has little of inherent interest, and most travelers will press on in to the newly-opened areas beyond.

Transformed by oil: Until the middle of

Stunningly-colored jungle butterfly.

this century, this Andean rim of the Amazon basin was as far as colonists and travelers regularly went. Wildlife ad Indian groups lived relatively undisturbed further on in to the Oriente. This suddenly changed in the late 1960s with the discovery of oil in the jungle. Almost overnight, a good all-weather road was pushed from Quito beyond Baeza and deep in to the heart of parts of the Oriente which until then could be reached only by difficult river travel or by light aircraft. The new 180 km (110 mile) road stretched from Baeza to **Lago Agrio** (literally "Sour Lake", an oil town built in a trackless region in the middle of the jungle.

For much of its length, the road to Lago Agrio parallels the trans-Ecuadorian pipeline which pumps oil 495 km (310 miles) from the oil fields of the Oriente, up across the Andes and down to the Pacific coast for processing and export. At irregular intervals along the pipeline, little communities have been created. Some are next to an oil pumping station, whilst others have been founded by colonists near a flat piece of land which they have cleared.

The road is the main communication link in the area and the accompanying pipeline has taken on a new and unusual function. Here, where the frequent tropical downpours turn the edges of the road into quagmires, the people use the pipeline as a sidewalk. Groups of boisterous schoolchildren, clad in the gray uniforms worn by pupils of all the local schools, skip and nudge one another as they run precariously along the pipeline, seemingly oblivious to the national wealth flowing beneath their feet. Colonists swinging the ubiquitous machete trudge home from the fields along the pipeline, and even the family dogs trot along behind. The top of the metal tubing has been worn smooth by the many feet treading it every day.

The famous **San Rafael Falls** are on the River Quijos, about half way between Baeza and Lago Agrio. With a height of about 145 meters (475ft), they are the highest falls in the country. They can be glimpsed from the bus from the

The jumping spider.

new road, but for an impressive close up look at the falls one should get off at the UNECEL electricity station at **Reventador**. From here, it is a 20-minute walk down an overgrown trail through lush forest to a viewpoint where, if the wind is right (or wrong, depending on your point of view) you can be sprayed by the light mist caused by the crashing water. Sometimes the spray can be so thick that it obliterates the view of the cascading river; at other times the mists clear for a magnificent sight of the falls.

Lago Agrio itself is one of the fastest growing places in Ecuador, although not much to look at. Its official name is Nueva Loja (or new Loja) after the first Ecuadorian colonists in the area who mainly came from the province of Loja in the south of the country. Homesick North American oilmen working for Texaco nicknamed the town Lago Agrio after the small Texan oil town of Sourlake. Although the official name of the town remains Nueva Loja, everyone now calls it Lago Agrio.

A hot, wet and humid climate pervades the town. Even the newest buildings begin to look decayed within a few months of construction. The unpaved streets are often filled with mud, and rubber boots are the footwear of choice for the inhabitants. Yet it is a lively and progressive place; late model jeeps churn the mud in the streets, the bustling market is thronged with shoppers, and the several banks are always busy. There is a palpable air of civic pride.

For most of its short life, Lago Agrio has lacked political power. It was part of the huge jungle province of Napo, whose capital is **Tena**, an all-day drive away over bad roads. Tena is not an oil town, and the citizens of Lago felt that many political decisions were made which were not in their interests. But the importance of Lago Agrio was made apparent after a major earthquake in the Oriente in 1987 temporarily cut the town off, breaking the oil flow and grinding the economy to a halt. In 1989, Lago Agrio was made capital of Sucumbios, Ecuador's 21st and newest province.

Eco-tourism: Lago Agrio has thrived

Local transport on the Napo River.

on oil, as has Ecuador as a whole (not to mention the multi-national oil companies), but the effect of drilling on the Oriente itself has generally been negative. The environment and wildlife have been devastated in many regions, while the local Indian inhabitants have had their former lands and traditional lifestyles taken away.

The most famous Ecuadorian Amazon tribe is the Huaorani (people), formally know as the Aucas (savages) because of their fierce demeanor towards outsiders and other indigenous groups. They remain among the least-changed tribes of the rainforest because of their isolation to an area around the Cononoco River. Missionaries first visited the Huaorani in the 1950s paddling in dugout canoes or making precarious landings on sandbars to organize the semi-nomadic people into missions.

Although the Huaorani routinely speared these first visitors, much of the tribe eventually accepted a more peaceful and sedentary existence. However with the discovery of oil in the 1960s

and the construction of a road infrastructure, a huge influx of colonists from the highlands is displacing the tribespeople from their traditional lands.

A newly formed political organization (ONHAE) is working with environmental groups, the government and even the oil companies to protect the Huaorani from colonization. They have gained tenuous title to their lands but not the subsurface mineral rights. Consequently a US-based multinational oil company (MAXUS) has been allowed by the Ecuadorian government to punch a road into Yasuni National Park located in the heart of Huaorani territory (see *Black Gold* chapter).

So far colonists have been kept out, but it is difficult to predict whether Ecuador will be able to walk this tightrope between economic development and protecting the Huaorani and the rainforest ecosystem.

Living along the Aguarico River, a small group of Cofan Indians are trying a different survival tactic. Working with the help of US-born Randy Borman,

The air service to Lago Agrio.

they allow groups of foreign tourists to visit their village of **Sabelo** for several days, where they live in a traditional manner, hunting and fishing for food and using the rainforest for materials to build their houses and canoes. The arrangement allows visitors to experience the rainforest and gain a fascinating insight into the Cofan lifestyle.

Visitors to Sabelo sleep on the floor of Cofan style houses, travel in dugout canoes, hike into the jungle in search of medicinal plants, and fish for piranha for dinner. Birdwatching and wildlife observation are favorite pastimes. The money generated from such tourism goes into the pockets of the Cofans, and they are proudly able to use and display their traditional knowledge of the Oriente, both for personal survival and as their own unique contribution to a changing world (see *The Gringo Chief,* page 104).

Amazon lodges: Not every visitor to the Oriente wants to bathe in a jungle river and sleep on the floor of an Indian hut at the end of a hard day of hiking in the jungle. For those wishing to visit the virgin rainforest, yet return to a comfortable room with a private shower at night, there are several well-known options. **La Selva jungle lodge** is one good choice. Owned and operated by an American-Ecuadorian couple, Eric and Magdalena Schwartz, this lodge is certainly the most comfortable and well run in the Oriente, and possibly in the entire Amazon basin.

Getting to La Selva is half the adventure. A twin propeller TAME aircraft flies from Quito to the jungle town of **Coca**, at the confluence of the River Coca with the River Napo.

In Coca, passengers are met by lodge staff who drive them to the River Napo for a two and a half hour boat ride down to the La Selva dock. At this point, 96 km (60 miles) away from Coca, the Napo is about a kilometer wide. Visitors disembark and make a short hike along a rough boardwalk through the rainforest to **Garzacocha** (Heron Lake). Here, they are met by simple dugout canoes and paddled across the lake to the lodge.

The buildings at La Selva, with

Left, cruising in a motorized canoe. Right, young puma.

thatched roofs and on stilts, have been well constructed to withstand extremes of jungle climate. One thing missing though is electricity. Rooms are lit with kerosene lamps, and the lack of a thumping generator outside the cabins ensures that the guests are able to hear the myriad strange and startling sounds of the rainforest. Expert naturalists are on hand to guide the visitor on walks and canoe rides through the jungle.

Sacha Lodge, a little further down the Napo River is another excellent lodge offering a very similar experience. Their observation tower enables you to climb 40 metres (130 ft) into the canopy for an unobstructed view of miles and miles of intact rainforest, close up views of plants, birds and maybe the occasional sloth hanging from a tree-top. After a long day exploring the magic of the rainforest a dip in the Pilchicocha Lagoon in front of the lodge may be welcome.

Floating hotel: Ecuador's most unusual option for seeing the Amazon in style is the unique *Flotel Orellana,* run by Transturi. The tour can be arranged through the company's offices in Quito or through Metropolitan Touring, and involves a flight to Coca (or Lago Agrio, with bus connection to Coca, depending on the weather conditions).

Looking vaguely like a Mississippi riverboat, the three-level Flotel takes some 60 passengers on three and four day trips down the Río Aguarico. The idea is to allow travelers to dip into the rainforest and return to a certain amount of luxury. Small but comfortable rooms provide the amenities of a modern hotel, while the Flotel has a bar, observation deck and dining room where excellent meals are served. Unlike traditional jungle lodges, the slow but sure Flotel allows visits to different parts of the Río Aguarico, and permits deeper penetration of the rainforest (the further away from Lago Agrio, naturally, the more chance of seeing wildlife). Passengers are taken ashore in a motorized dugout canoes, with gumboots, raincoats and insect repellent all provided, for twice-daily forages into the jungle.

Fantastic bird life: Some 500 species of

A spectacled caiman enjoying the sun.

birds alone have been recorded from the Napo region and professional and amateur ornithologists and birdwatchers flock to the area to see species with such exotic names as green and gold tanager, greater yellow-headed vulture, and purple-throated fruitcrow.

For many visitors, the parrots and macaws are favorite birds. One of the highlights in a trip to La Selva or Sacha Lodge is a boat ride further down river to two large patches of soil laden with mineral salts. These natural salt licks attract hundreds of parrots which require the minerals in their diets. Birdwatchers at dawn can witness a magnificent display of hundreds of squawking, squabbling parrots feeding at the *salados*, as the salt licks are known. Species such as the blue-headed, orange-cheeked, and yellow-crowned parrot as well as the dusky-headed parakeet and scarlet-shouldered parrotlet have been observed here.

Mammals of the rainforest: The minerals in the salt licks also attract a variety of jungle mammals. Most of these feed at night and leave only footprints for the curious visitor to observe in daylight. An adventurous person could spend the night by a salt lick and perhaps be rewarded with moonlit glimpses of a variety of mammals. These may include the nine-banded armadillo, or a rodent called the paca which has spotted fur, weighs up to 9 kg (20 lb) and is considered excellent eating by local hunters, or perhaps the capybara, which weighs up to 64 kg (140 lb) and is the world's largest rodent.

Some salt licks attract a huge and strange mammal, the South American tapir. The largest land mammals in Amazonia, tapirs can weigh in excess of 270 kg (600 lb). Their closest relatives are the other odd-toed ungulates, the rhinoceros and the horse. Members of the tapir family are among the most primitive large mammals in the world and are well adapted to life in the jungle. Their short but sturdy legs, thick, strong necks, and barrel-like bodies covered with incredibly tough skin enable them to shove through the dense forest under-

Metropolitan Touring's *Flotel Orellana*.

growth like a living tank. One of their strangest features is a short trunk which gives them an excellent sense of smell and is also used to pull leaves off bushes and into their mouths.

Tapirs are much sought-after game animals. Local Indian hunters are able to feed an entire village if they are fortunate enough to shoot one. Apart from the meat, the tapirs' fatty tissues yield an oil which is much prized for cooking, and the thick skin makes good-quality leather. There are three species of tapir found in Ecuador of which the South American tapir lives in the Oriente lowlands and the mountain tapir inhabits the upper Amazonian basin and the Andean flanks. Hunting is not as much of a threat to these animals as is habitat destruction, and the mountain tapir is regarded as an endangered species by the Ecuadorian conservation organization, the *Fundación Natura*.

Apart from man, the tapir's greatest enemy is the big cat of Amazonia – the jaguar. A fully grown male can reach 113 kg (250 lb) in weight and, when hungry, will attack almost any large animal it comes across. Jaguars will leap onto tapirs' backs and attempt to kill them by breaking their necks in their incredibly powerful jaws. The tapirs' defense is twofold: one is the thick and powerful neck itself which is protected by the tough, leathery skin and a bristly mane. The other is their habit of charging wildly through the dense undergrowth when threatened, thus making it difficult for a predator to hold on long enough to deliver the fatal bite.

Jaguars do not roar, as do most other big cats. Instead, they emit a low, coughing grunt, especially when hunting. Only the luckiest of visitors catch a glimpse of the jaguar in the wild. Generally, jaguars are afraid of man.

Most travelers in the Oriente must be content with foot-prints in the soft earth or thrilling stories told by local residents. The mammals which most visitors do get to see often, however, are the monkeys. The most vocal of these is the very aptly named howler monkey.

The males of this species have a spe-

Jungle settlers.

cialized, hollow, and much enlarged hyoid bone in the throat. Air is passed through the hyoid cavity producing an ear-splitting call which can easily carry for well over a kilometer in the rainforest. This is an astounding feat when one remembers that the forest vegetation has a damping effect on vocalizations. When heard in the distance, the call has been variously described as sounding like the wind moaning through the trees or like a human baby crying. Close up, the call can be quite terrifying to the uninitiated visitor.

The purpose of the call is to advertize a troop's presence in a particular patch of rainforest. This behavior enables troops to space themselves out in the canopy and thus avoid competing as they forage for succulent young leaves. Occasionally, troops do meet in the tree tops and the result is often chaotic with howling chasing, threatening and even fighting. The energy used in these meetings is better expended in feeding and thus it pays for a troop to make its presence known by frequent howling.

Several other species of monkeys are frequently seen, including woolly, squirrel, spider and tarmarin monkeys. Often, the easiest and safest way to observe monkeys is from a dugout canoe floating down a jungle river. A local guide with a trained ear and eye will spot a troop of monkeys early enough to stop the boat in a position which offers a clear view of the animals foraging in trees along the banks. From within the rainforest, on the other hand, animals may be difficult to see in the tree tops. In addition, monkeys may display their displeasure at human intrusion by hurling sticks, fruit, and even faeces down on the unfortunate visitor's head!

A universe of insects: Many people come to the Oriente hoping to see exotic birds and mammals, but also trying to avoid the myriad insects. Yet it is the insects which are the most common and, in many ways, most fascinating creatures of the rainforest. Some are simply beautiful, such as the breathtaking blue morpho butterflies whose huge wings flash a dazzling electric blue as they leisurely flap along jungle rivers. Other species have such complex life cycles that they are still not fully understood by tropical ecologists. Among these are hundreds of ant species, particularly the army ants and leaf-cutter ants, both of which species are commonly observed in the forest.

Colonies of leaf-cutter ants numbering hundreds of thousands live in huge nests dug deep into the ground. Foraging ants search the vegetation for particular types of leaves, cut out small sections, and holding the leaf segments above their heads like small umbrellas, bring them back to the nest. The ants can be quite experimental, bringing back a variety of leaves and even pieces of discarded nylon or plastic wrappers.

Workers within the nest sort out those kinds of leaves which will mulch down into a type of compost; unsuitable material is ejected from the nest after a few days. The composted leaves form a mulch on which a fungus grows. Ants tend these fungal gardens with care, for they provide the main diet for both the adult ants and for the tiny ant young

A traveler plays with an anaconda.

which are being raised inside the nest.

The story, already complex, does not end there. When a particularly good source of leaves has been located, ants lay down a trail of chemical markers, or pheromones, linking the nest with the leaf source, often 100 meters (330 ft) or more away into the forest. People frequently come across one of these trails in the jungle, with hundreds of ants scurrying along them carrying leaf sections back to the next, or returning empty handed for another load.

Other species, for example army ants, may want to prey on this ready and constant supply of foragers. To combat this the leaf cutter ants are morphologically separated by size and jaw structure into different castes. Some specialize in tending the fungal gardens. Others have jaws designed for cutting the leaf segments, and yet others are soldiers, armed with huge mandibles, who accompany the foragers and protect them from attackers. Close observation of the foragers will sometimes reveal yet another caste, a tiny ant which is so small

The notorious piranha.

that it rides along on the leaf segments without disturbing the foragers. The function of these riders is still unclear, but biologists suggest that they act as protection against parasitizing wasps that may try to lay their eggs on the foragers when they are occupied with carrying the leaves.

A colony of leaf cutter ants may last for a decade or more. New colonies are founded by the emergence of a number of potential queens, who mate and then fly off to found another nest. They carry some of the fungus used for food with them. This is essential to "seed" the new nest. The rest of the new queen's life is spent laying tens of thousands of eggs, destined to become gardeners, foragers, soldiers, riders, or perhaps even queens.

It is these kinds of incredibly complicated interactions which make the rainforest so interesting to biologists and tourists alike. A day with a naturalist guide will bring to light many such stories, each one seemingly more amazing than the last.

An Oriente itinerary: Before making

final arrangements, it is worth asking yourself what you want from your trip. How important is comfort, do you need a specialist guide and are you more interested in wildlife, plants or indigenous culture? Also what impact is your visit going to have on the rainforest?

Trips can be organised from Quito or independently arranged from Misahualli, Baños, Tena or Coca. If you are looking for an expert guide or a comfortable lodge, you would do best organising the trip in Quito.

River trips: For the adventurous, the best way to experience primary tropical rainforest is a week long canoe trip down one the rivers of the Oriente. Several qualified guides organize float trips on the Tiputini River or Cuyabeno Reserve where you can see wildlife up close. During the day you will observe woolly and howler monkeys grazing in the trees, toucans or parrots in flight, or if you are lucky an anaconda lazing in the sun. At night you will be serenaded by the symphony of insects and an occasional unidentified animal.

The **Cuyabeno Reserve**, up towards the Colombian border, is well worth making the extra effort to reach. 655,000 hectares (162,000 acres) of the northeast of Ecuador have been turned into a national park. This incredibly biodiverse area consists of much flooded forest and is pretty much intact. Departing from Lago Agrio, it's a full day traveling by bus and motorised canoe to reach the reserve itself. Most companies use *cabanas* (cabins) open-sided platforms or tents as accommodation. Visits to the Siona/Secoya communities are sometimes arranged.

The *Flotel Orellana* drifts down the Aguarico River, with opportunities to penetrate the remote Cuyabeno Reserve. Hikes through the forest, a visit to the Cofan indigenous community, and explanations of local medicinal plants and are just some of the highlights.

Metropolitan Touring also arrange three- to six-day programs staying in their comfortable camps within the Reserve. **Imuya Camp** is by one of the blackwater lakes, home to the pink river

Christ and canoe in a mission chapel.

dolphin and Amazon manatee. The lakes and streams nearby are also home to the paiche, giant catfish, and four species of caiman. **Iripari Camp** is by Iripari Lake, the largest lake in the Ecuadorian Amazon. A perfect spot for birders to either observe hoatsins in their lakeside nests or climb the observation tower into the canopy to see tanagers, cotingas and other birds not seen easily from the forest floor.

Other longer trips travel down the River Napo. One destination is La**go Panacocha,** a beautiful lagoon on the Panayacu River, located in a small protected area of 56,000 hectares (138,400 acres) between the Napo and Aquarico Rivers. Colonists have not taken over here, deterred by so much flooded forest. There is some provision for tourists, with several modest *cabanas* and shelters. Walks along remote trails give a good chance of seeing birds, butterflies and fresh jaguar tracks.

There may be the opportunity on one of these trips to try some piranha fishing. Small pieces of raw red flesh are used as bait on hand-lines, bringing the infamous creature out in their hundreds. These small fish are surprisingly easy to catch, although watch your fingers as you bring them aboard: their small, triangular teeth are razor sharp. Piranhas make a fine meal and you can keep their jaws as a souvenir of the jungle.

Contrary to popular mythology, it is quite possible – if not exactly relaxing – to swim in piranha-infested waters. The variety of piranha found in Ecuador will only ever turn on large mammals like humans and horses if there is a huge quantity of blood in the water. Even so, swimming here is a rather unnerving experience, and many prefer to endure the Amazonian heat rather than test the murky waters.

Red eyes in the darkness: another unforgettable Oriente experience is nighttime caiman-watching. Slip out on a canoe at night and shine a flashlight into the reeds by the lake side: hundreds of red eyes stare back, the reflections from caimans' retinas (rather like the "red eye" effect in flash photography of people). The more adventurous guides will take the boat right in amongst these harmless but vicious-looking reptiles – an experience that can feel a little too adventurous if you happen to be in a unstable dug-out canoe. Some guides will even grab a small caiman by the tail, to bring it alongside the canoe and give everyone a look.

With a few days it is possible to visit **Limoncocha** (Lemon Lake) down river from Coca. Oil exploration nearby seriously threatened this birdwatchers' haven, but protests from the local community and the creation of the **Limoncocha Biological Reserve** pressured oil companies to divert the road. Fortunately the extensive bird population has more or less recovered.

Not far from Limoncocha is the Capuchin Mission of **Pompeya**. A bridge was built to the island by the oil company MAXUS, but access is strictly controlled. Amongst the houses on wooden stilts are an altar with the crucifix above a colored Indian canoe, as well as a curious museum. Here you can handle the various blow pipes used by Amazo-

Red howler monkey.

nian peoples to hunt – many are surprisingly long and heavy, often used to shoot directly upwards into the trees with a dart coated with natural venom that would paralyze the prey.

Opposite Pompeya is **Isla de los Monos** (Monkey Island), where you can wander freely and spot howler monkeys high in the trees above. It takes a little patience, but you will be well rewarded in time – not long ago the island was literally packed with monkeys, but the Ecuadorian Army chose it as the site for survival training, and hundreds of these endangered creatures ended up in the soldiers' stews.

If you are short of time, on a budget and just want a taste of the rainforest there are plenty of trips on offer starting from the small town of **Puerto Misahualli**, in the headwaters of the River Napo. Here guides can be hired for about $30–40 a day. The area has been colonised and the forest here is secondary growth. The large mammals and birds have mainly been hunted out, but a short trip will give you a look at a variety of plants, insects and smaller birds.

Near Misahualli, on the Napo River is **Jatun Sacha Biological Station,** a center dedicated to education and research. Next door are the **Cabanas Alinahui** offering comfortable *cabanas*, canoe trips, visits to nearby indigenous communities and walks along trails in the area. Tourists can visit the station and see field work in progress. For butterfly lovers this area is paradise: besides hundreds of birds and plants a staggering 765 butterfly species have been identified at Jatun Sacha.

One aspect of forest life which can be observed in the environs of Puerto Misahuallí is colonization. Small coffee fincas, oil palm plantations, cattle ranches, and yucca plots can be seen. As you journey down the nearby river, you occasionally notice workers washing and shifting material by the bank. They are panning for gold – modern descendants of the long line of settlers obsessed with dreams of an El Dorado in the jungle.

Gold rush outposts: One place where   **A jungle bar.**

the dreams of the 20th century and those of conquistadors converge is in the south-eastern jungle. In 1549, the colony of **Zamora de los Alcaides** was founded by Spaniards at about 970 meters (3,180 ft) above sea level in the headwaters of the River Zamora in the southern Oriente. This colony was soon wiped out by Indian attacks but, undaunted, the Span-iards pursued their feverish quest for gold. Around 1560, they refounded Zamora with the new fanciful title of the Royal Mining Village of the Rich Hill of San Antonio of Zaruma. Gold was successfully extracted for about 70 years before the colony died out again.

Several attempts were made to re-establish Zamora, the most recent in 1869. It has held on to its existence somewhat precariously since then. In the 1930s there were less than a dozen buildings, but by 1953, Zamora had become the capital of the isolated prov-ince of Zamora-Chinchipe, even though access was still by mule. The first vehi-cle made it to Zamora in 1962.

In the 1980s, a new lode of gold was discovered some 15 km (10 miles) north-east of Zamora, again in the **Nambiji** area, traditional mining grounds of the Incas. Zamora's population has since risen to over 6,000, a new road has been constructed on the south side of the River Zamora, and the area has experi-enced a small gold boom. Ecuadorian prospectors, hoping to strike it rich, make their way to the Zamora area with their ears full of stories about gold. Few of them realize that gold has been ex-tracted here not just this decade, but since the time of the Incas.

Vanishing rainforests: The plight of the world's tropical forests is becoming in-creasingly well known. Huge areas of forest are being logged or burnt every day; so much deforestation is occurring that, at present rates of destruction, most of the world's rainforests will have dis-appeared by early in the next century, a major ecological loss.

Of the almost 2 million known spe-cies of plants and animals, about half live only in the rainforest. Scientific estimates of the number of species yet to

A sluice to filter gold from water, near Zamora.

be discovered vary from 10 million to 80 million. Most of these unknown species live in the tropical forests, which have by far the greatest biodiversity of any region on the globe. Thus deforestation is causing countless extinctions, many of plants and animals that are as yet unknown.

Various medicines have been extracted from forest plants, ranging from malarial prophylactics to anaesthetics, and from antibiotics to contraceptives. Quinine, for example, used as the basis for preventing and curing malaria, was first recorded in the 17th century in the forest of southern Ecuador. Many useful drugs are undoubtedly left to be discovered in the forests, if they are not destroyed first.

The diversity of species growing in the rainforest is also extremely important as a storehouse of wild or new strains of agriculturally important food plants which may be destroyed by disease or drought. For example, if bananas, which are Ecuador's most important crop, were to be threatened by disease,

scientists could search the rainforest for disease-resistant strains to cross into the commercially grown varieties.

The rainforest is also essential for the survival of local indigenous peoples. Not only the Huaorani and Cofan are threatened by rainforest loss, but so are hundreds of other tribal groups living in the jungles of Latin America, Africa, and Asia.

On a worldwide scale, the moderating effect of the rainforest on global climate patterns is only recently becoming understood. Deforestation could cause severe global warming. This would lead to melting ice caps and rising ocean levels, and cause important coastal cities to be flooded. Climates in agricultural regions would be altered to the extent that major crops, such as wheat, would no longer be able to grow.

The main reason why the rainforest is being cut down is simple: money. Ecuador and other Third World countries need to take advantage of the natural resources that the forest has to offer: lumber, cattle pasture, plantations, mineral wealth. This is, however, a short-sighted view. The essential importance of the rainforest in the long term must be recognized, not only by those countries which contain forest, but also by the developed nations who will be affected by deforestation.

Debt-for-nature swaps, whereby foreign debts are paid off by the lender nations in return for protection of the rainforest by the Third World debtor nations, such as Ecuador, are a move in the right direction. These kinds of financial incentives must, however, recognize the full value of the rainforest, and some Ecuadorians feel that debtor nations should be receiving more, in view of the global importance of their natural resource.

Other important financial incentives to protect the rainforest include sustainable use such as rubber-tapping, brazil-nut collection, and the money brought in by eco-tourism.

Rainforests such as the Oriente are vital for our survival. Whatever the methods used to preserve them, it is essential that they are protected.

Left, tree boa ready to strike. **Right**, great egret.

THE GALÁPAGOS ISLANDS

"Seeing every height crowned with its crater, and the boundaries of most of the lava streams still distinct, we are led to believe that within a period geologically recent, the unbroken ocean was here spread out. Hence, both in space and time, we seem to be brought somewhat near to that great fact, that mystery of mysteries – the first appearance of new beings on this earth."
— Charles Darwin, *The Voyage of the Beagle*

The Galápagos Islands had their fame guaranteed in 1835 when the 26-year-old naturalist Darwin landed on one of their black volcanic coasts. Although an unpromising student, Darwin had begun revealing his extraordinary powers of observation during a voyage around the globe on the HMS *Beagle*. No other place would prove to be quite as fertile for his work as the Galápagos. Some 20 years later, Darwin made the unique creatures of the Galápagos a cornerstone of his theory of evolution by natural selection, in one stroke overturning the whole train of western scientific thought.

Wildlife is still the main reason why tens of thousands of visitors fly the 960 km (570 miles) from mainland Ecuador to the Galápagos archipelago every year. Even those who confess to no particular fascination with animals will find themselves reduced to a childlike glee by the experience: the islands are the ultimate natural zoo, where bizarre fauna exist totally free and fearless of man.

Giant lumbering tortoises, blue-footed boobies and equatorial penguins carry on their daily routine, indifferent to watching human visitors only feet away. Baby sea lions play with swimmers in the water, grabbing their flippers and performing somersaults. Approach as close as you like, but the dozens of marine iguanas sunning themselves on black rocks will just sit there and stare blankly back.

Although these animals have been able to thrive on the Galápagos, the islands' landscapes are mostly bleak and sunburnt. Until recently, permanent human settlement had been kept to a minimum – thankfully, no doubt, since human influence on the islands has been almost uniformally for the worse. In 1961, the Ecuadorian government declared the islands a national park and restricted human settlement to the small outposts already established. Today the Charles Darwin Research Station on Santa Cruz has its hands full trying to restore the Galápagos to the days before humans began to upset the delicate ecological balance.

Preceding pages: volcanic eruption near Cerro Azul, Isabela Island; marine iguana colony, Punta Espinosa, Fernandina Island; giant tortoises at Alcedo volcano, Isabela Island. **Left**, sunbathing marine iguanas on the cliffs, South Plaza.

THE GALAPAGOS: DARWIN'S ZOO

The "living laboratory" of the Galápagos archipelago is set in the Pacific Ocean some 960 km (570 miles) west of the Ecuadorian coast. It consists of 13 major islands, six small islands and 42 islets that are barely more than large rocks. All are of volcanic origin and spread over roughly 80,000 sq. km (30,000 sq. miles) of ocean. Their highest point is Volcano Wolf, at 1,707 meters (5,600 ft) on Isabela, which, at 4,600 sq. km (1,800 sq. miles), is by far the largest island.

Visited at different times by explorers from around the world, most of the islands have two or even three different names. British pirates gave them solid, Anglo-Saxon names like Jervis and Chatham; the Spanish dubbed them from their standard stock of place names, such as Santa Cruz and Santa Fe; while the Ecuadorian government in 1892 tried to clear up the confusion by giving the islands official titles: the effort was unsuccessful and each usually has at least two names still in use.

Even the name Galápagos has been changed several times before being officially restored in 1973: taken from a Spanish word for tortoise, it appropriately refers to the giant creatures that most astonished the first explorers to reach their shores.

An eccentric climate: The Galápagos year can be divided into a two "seasons": the "hot" or "wet" season lasts from January to early May with an average temperature of 28°C (82°F); while the "cool" or "dry" season from May to December has an average of 18°C (64°F). The cooler period is also referred to as the *garua* season, after the bank of clouds that generally settle over the islands at this time. Altitude also affects the climate: it can be hot and dry in the low parts of the islands, and almost cold and humid in the highlands (above 22 meters/72 ft). The winds, marine currents and finally the geological formation of the soil can alter considerably the climactic conditions: generally, the beaches with white sands are cooler on the feet, while stretches of black lava can reach temperatures of up to 50°C (120°F).

Two marine currents pass along the archipelago. The cold Humboldt stream originates in the south of Chile and brings the *garua* with it in May – it has a moderating effect on the whole climate of the Galápagos, which, sitting directly on the Equator, should be more punishing than it actually is. The other current is the warm northern stream called *El Niño*. It was dubbed "the Christmas child" because it arrives in December, although its effects are rarely welcome: it brings heavy rains and – on occasion – floods and tidal waves to the Ecuadorian mainland.

Geology of the islands: What we see of the Galápagos islands is actually the tips of various gigantic "shield volcanoes" poking up some 10,000 meters (30,000 ft) from the ocean floor and composed entirely of basalt. Some scientists once believed that the islands

Preceding pages: the lunar landscape of Bartolomé Island. **Left,** the Galápagos islands are a photographer's dream. **Right,** the naturalist Charles Darwin, who visited the islands in the early 1830s.

were the remains of a sunken continental platform that was linked to the South American continent during the Miocene era. But today it is widely accepted that the archipelago was formed mainly by the accumulation of lava from successive underwater volcanic eruptions.

It appears that the earliest of the islands were formed roughly four to five million years ago, and that some of the western islands, such as Fernandina and Isabela are only one million years old.

The process of island formation is in fact still going on. The Galápagos lie on the northern edge of the Nazca tectonic plate – one of the several huge land masses that, over millions of years, slowly move around the earth's surface. Over time, this minute continental drift takes them towards the southeast – precisely over one of the world's so-called "hotspots." These volatile, unmoving points beneath the tectonic plates build up heat over time to eventually create a volcanic eruption that will rise above the ocean's surface. The southeastern islands of the Galápagos were the first formed in this way, and the more recent, western islands still have active volcanoes. The scientist Morrel witnessed an eruption on Fernandina in 1825 that sent the surrounding sea to a temperature of 65°C (149°F). More recently, Volcan Cerro Azul on Isabela erupted in 1979 and again in 1982.

Relatively fresh basalt lava flows can still be seen around the island, often making fascinating patterns. They include "pahoehoe" or "ropy" lava – where the skin of the lava flow has been wrinkled by the heat of the still-flowing lava beneath. Another type is "aa" – pronounced "aah aah" – and looks like twisted black caramel.

Colonization: Obviously, the volcanic lumps that first burst forth from the Pacific four million years ago were utterly devoid of life. Yet now the islands are teeming with often bizarre plants and animals. Somehow they had to have made their way from South America – and, since the islands were never connected to the continent, this fauna and flora must have come out across the

Island transport: luxury cruiser *The Galápagos Explorer*, and a fishing boat.

1,000-km (620-mile) stretch of water.

Only certain types of creatures could survive the journey: this explains the present-day predominance of sea birds (which could fly), sea mammals (which could swim) and reptiles (which apparently floated across from the American coast on accidentally formed vegetation rafts and, unlike amphibians and land mammals, could survive for long periods without food or water). Meanwhile, plant seeds and insects could have come across stuck to birds' wings or in animals' stomach contents.

Then, once they had landed on the bleak islands, only certain animals could survive. Those that did found that their traditional predators had been left behind on the South American coast. The animal's famous lack of timidity probably stems from this general absence of predators – a fact that also explains why recently introduced domestic creatures, like goats and pigs, are able to wreak havoc so easily.

Charles Darwin was the first to observe how each arriving animal species had adapted over time in order to thrive. The most famous case may be "Darwin's finches" – the 13 similar species of finches that probably descended from the one original species. Each modern species has certain differences that suits its particular environment on different Galápagos islands: some have short and thick beaks so that they can split seeds, for example; others have long and thin bills to catch insects.

Many years after his visit to the Galápagos, Darwin attributed the process to natural selection. After their arrival on the Galápagos, each finch produced offspring that were imperceptibly different from the parent. In this strange new environment, some chicks were better able to survive. They were the ones that reached maturity and produced young, passing on new genetic traits to their offspring. Over thousands of generations, some traits were thus "selected" as fitting the finches' new home – until the differences between the new creature from the original qualified it to be re-named as a new species entirely.

Sullivan Bay and Pinnacle Rock, Bartolomé Island.

Darwin propounded this theory in his classic work *Origin of the Species*. It became particularly controversial when applied to man: not only did it suggest blasphemously that the animal kingdom did not spring ready-made from the finger of God, but that man is in most important respects no different from the other forms of animal life.

The human history: There is some possibility that the Inca Tupac-Yupanqui organized an expedition to the Galápagos during his rule in the 1400s. According to this theory, favored by archaeologists like Thor Heyerdahl, two islands may have been called "Ninachumbi" and "Huahuachumbi" in oral Incaic tradition, although no archaeological evidence has yet been produced to prove it.

Most historians accept that the islands were first discovered by accident in 1535 by the Spanish cleric Fray Tomas de Berlanga, bishop of Panama and the highest Catholic representative in Spanish America at the time. On the way to Peru, his boat was becalmed and drifted to the Galápagos. The cleric landed in search of water but "found nothing but seals and tortoises, and such big tortoises that each could carry a man on top of itself" and birds "so silly that they do not know to flee." He dubbed the islands "Las Encantadas," the Bewitched Ones, because they tricked his navigator's eyes and seemed to appear and disappear in clouds of mist.

For the next two centuries, the islands, far from the Spanish trade routes, were a hideaway for Dutch and English buccaneers. They began the practise of killing large numbers of giant tortoises for their meat – having found that the creatures could be stacked upside-down in their ships' holds without food and water for over a year and still be turned into fine soup. This practice was taken up most devastatingly by the 19th-century whalers. Between 1811 and 1844 there were said to be over 700 whaling ships in the Pacific, and many of them called into the Galápagos Islands to stock up on tortoise meat.

The first permanent colonist on the

Gutting fish for dinner on a chartered boat.

Galápagos was an Irish ruffian named Patrick Watkins, who arrived at Floreana in 1812. His story is included in a series of sketches called *The Encantadas* by Herman Melville. Melville's portrait of the islands was not a flattering one: "Take five and twenty heaps of cinders dumped here and there in an outside lot; imagine some of them magnified into mountains, and the vacant lot the sea; and you will have a fit idea of the general aspect of the Encantadas…"

The inhabitants of the islands were no more appealing, turning out to be a collection of lunatics, sadists and megalomaniacs. When the Ecuadorian government claimed the islands in 1832, Floreana was given as a reward for bravery to a local Creole officer. He brought 80 subjects from the mainland and kept them enslaved using giant dogs. But the so-called "Dog King of Charles Island" was forced to flee when his slaves rebelled. A brutal penal colony was set up on San Christóbal in the 1880s, with the prisoners worked to death, flogged mercilessly and ma-

A dip in the warm waters of Bartolomé Island.

rooned on desert islands to slowly die of thirst as punishment for misdemeanors.

In this century, a settlement at Puerto Ayora managed to be founded without too much violence. Norwegians and Germans appeared particularly attracted to the harsh life here, although not without more traces of insanity and murder: in one famous case, a number of German settlers on Floreana died one by one. In a scandal that reached world headlines, a self-styled baroness kept three men as her "sex slaves" using a pearl-handled revolver, before she disappeared without a trace herself.

When the United States entered World War II, it chose the Galápagos as a defense base against attacks on the Panama Canal. An airstrip was built on Baltra Island that is still in use today. In 1958 the last convict colony was closed on the island, and in the 1960s regular passenger flights began to operate. Tourists discovered that the famous islands were now within relatively easy reach and began to make the long journey.

Since then, tourism has been ever-

increasing. In September 1995, the islands were brought to a halt when fed up locals led by the Deputy of the Galapagos, Eduardo Veliz, seized San Cristobal airport, the National Park office and the Charles Darwin Centre. The demands were for more control and benefits from tourism. Some kind of peace was secured, but only after two weeks of fierce protesting, complete suspension of all visits, intense talks in Quito and international attention once again.

Concern for conservation: Scientists had been observing the Galápagos periodically ever since Darwin's work in the mid-19th century. In this century, it was becoming obvious that many of the animals introduced by man had gone feral and were devastating the natural ecology of the islands. Everything from goats to pigs, rats, dogs and cats were breeding furiously. They were taking other animals' food, devouring turtle eggs and baby land iguanas, eroding the soil and destroying the plants.

In 1930 an expedition led by Gifford Pinchot from the United States suggest-

ed for the first time the possibility of creating a wildlife sanctuary in the archipelago. Five years later, the Ecuadorian government decreed laws in order to protect the fauna of the islands, but it was not until 1959 – on the 100th anniversary of the publication of the *Origin of the Species* – that the Galápagos were declared a National Park. Human settlement was restricted to those areas were they existed at that time, while a Marine Resources Reserve was created in 1986 to cover 50,000 sq. km (19,300 sq. miles).

Both the park and reserve were designed to protect the islands and encourage scientific research. Also created in 1959 was the "Charles Darwin Foundation for the Galápagos Islands," an international organization under the auspices of UNESCO and the International Union for the Conservation of Nature. In 1964, the foundation established the Charles Darwin Research Center, with three objectives: scientific, educational and protective. The scientific program provides assistance for experts, as well as foreign and Ecuadorian biology students who visit the islands. The educational program is aimed at improving environmental awareness, particularly amongst students. And the protective program is aimed at overcoming the negative effects of introduced animals, and preventing the reoccurrence of other such man-made disasters.

Various protective programs have been undertaken in cooperation with the National Park administration. So far, they have been successful in eliminating all black rats on Bartolomé, while all wild goats were hunted on Santa Fe, Española (Hood) and Rábida. A campaign against dogs, which attack young tortoises and land iguanas, started recently. The Center also actively boosts the numbers of endangered species.

Tourism takes off: Before the 1960s, a visit to the Galápagos involved a long and uncomfortable sea-voyage on the old ship *Christóbal Carrier*, which ran once a month from Guayaquil to the archipelago. Travel between the islands was spartan and often nearly impossible: travelers sometimes had to wait

Great frigate male with fully inflated pouch.

weeks at a time to find a boat heading where they wanted. Not surprisingly, most visitors were from the ranks of the wealthy who could afford their own yachts and cruise the islands at leisure.

All this changed overnight when regularly scheduled air transportation was made available to the public, and passenger ships began to be run by Ecuadorian tourist agencies. In 1970, an estimated 4,500 tourists arrived; in 1978 the figure was 12,000; now more than 45,000 make the trip every year. This figure is worryingly high. Wildlife and vegetation are in danger of being severely affected if tourism continues at this rate. The Ecuadorian government claims to want to control the number of visitors to the islands, but is not enforcing its restrictions.

Tourism on the islands themselves is strictly controlled. The national park service has made a selection of about 54 visitor sites and 62 marine sites where tourists are allowed outside of towns – and then only in the company of trained guides. Trails are marked with small stakes painted in white. They should not be left, or you risk crushing plants and animals underfoot. They also keep crowds away from crater borders, where serious erosion can occur.

A range of plant life: Every island on the Galápagos is unique, although only a committed naturalist would plan to visit them all. Many are virtual deserts. Others, more mountainous, are relatively lush. Their plants vary from the tall *opuntia* cactus, which makes the islands look like a *Lost in Space* set, to other hanging trees that seem to belong in a Dr Seuss book. Thanks to the icy Humboldt current, the islands are not as hot as they should be on the Equator, but the sun can still be punishing, and not many can stand more than a few hours hiking steep trails.

There are six different vegetation zones on the Galápagos, beginning with the shore and ending with the highlands. The low islands are the driest due to the lack of rainfall – clouds pass by here without discharging. Meanwhile, the mountainous islands often block clouds,

Swimming with sea lions.

which turn into fog, drizzle or rain showers and help flora to thrive.

The area of the shoreline or "Littoral" zone is populated by plants that can tolerate high levels of salt – mangroves, saltbush, myrtles and other minor aquatic plants. Next comes the Arid zone, characterized by thorny plants with small flowers: different types of cactus (particularly *opuntia* and *cereus*), inextricable brushwood (*matorrales*), the ghostly-looking *palos santos*, carob trees (*algarrobos*) and lichens (*liquenes*). In the following Transition zone, perennial herbs and smaller shrubs are dominant, among them the *matasanos*, and the pega pega (*Pisonia floribunda*).

The high humid area – called Scalesia after the zone's dominant tree typically covered with bromeliads, ferns and orchids – extends between 200 and 500 meters (650 and 1,650 ft) above sea level. Several typical plants are found in this zone: locust and guava trees, *passiflora* and fungus. Above 500 meters is the Miconia zone, which is also the main area used for cultivation and pasture on the inhabited islands, where coffee, vegetables, oranges and pineapples are planted.

In the highest zone, called Fern-Sedge, grow mainly ferns and grasses, including the giant Galápagos fern tree which can sometimes grow up to 3 meters (10 ft) in height.

Of the 875 plant species so far recorded on the island, 228 are endemic – that means, they are unique to the Galápagos. But every plant did come originally from the South American continent, and has since adapted to the harsh new environment.

A fascinating wildlife: When it comes to animals, visitors are probably first struck by the incredible range of birds all over the islands.

Fifty-eight resident bird species have been recorded here, of which 28 are endemic. The others are either found in other parts of the world or are migratory, spending some part of the year living or breeding outside of the islands. They can be classified into sea birds and land birds: amongst the latter are the famous **Marine iguana with young.**

Darwin finches, mockingbirds (distinguished by their gray and brown streaks), the Galápagos dove and the endemic Galápagos hawk.

Sea birds tend to be more impressive for non-naturalist visitors. The world's entire population of 12,000 yellow-billed, waved albatross lives on the single island of Española (Hood). These magnificent creatures are famous for their extraordinary courtship displays, dancing about and "fencing" with their beaks – literally, standing face to face and clicking their beaks together at a great rate.

One of the most common birds is the blue-footed booby. While not endemic, they are an unforgettable sight: their feet really are a bold, striking blue. They were named "boobies" after the Spanish word "bobo" (a dunce) by early sailors, who were amazed that the birds would not fly away when men approached to kill them. The boobies also have a somewhat comical courtship ritual: they "dance" towards one another, plodding about with blue feet working up and down, "skypoint" (pushing their wings up to the heavens) and give one another twigs as presents. They are often seen diving into the water from heights of 20 meters (65 ft) to catch fish.

Another common seabird is the frigate bird. They can look quite sinister when hovering overhead, and are not above preying on other birds' young. The males' puffed scarlet chest sack makes an impressive sight when they are mating.

With only 400 pairs still alive, the Galápagos lava gull is said to be the rarest bird species on earth. The Galápagos also boasts the world's only two flightless sea birds: the Galápagos penguin and the flightless cormorant. The penguin is a big favorite, clumsily waddling about above water but speeding like a bullet under the waves. Being on the Equator, they are the most northerly penguin species, probably first coming up from the south with the icy Humboldt current. They are mostly found on Isabela and Fernandina, although they can also easily be seen at Bartolomé.

Flightless cormorant drying its wings, Fernandina Island.

Like the penguin, the endemic flightless cormorant makes an entertaining sight – if you are lucky enough to spot one, since there are only some 700 pairs in existence, found on the remote, far coasts of Isabela and Fernandina. The flightless cormorant has no enemies to fear, so long ago lost its ability to fly – it scampers along flapping what look like the shreds of lost wings. It is, however, a good diver and can easily catch the fish it needs for its food.

Prehistoric creatures: It was Darwin who called the Galápagos "a paradise for reptiles." Most common are the endemic black marine iguanas, often found sunning themselves on cliffs and shorelines. Darwin himself found their dragon-like appearance rather horrifying: he called them "imps of darkness… of a dirty black color, stupid and sluggish in [their] movements."

They are probably relatives of a landgoing reptile species that died out 100 million years ago. But these creatures have adapted themselves to the ocean to feed on seaweed, often diving to 12-meter (40-ft) depths. They have developed unusual glands connected to their breathing systems that accumulate the excess of salt in their bodies. Every so often the salt is snorted out through the nose – not always an attractive sight. While they are usually a suitably devilish black, the males change skin color during mating to some surprising tones of orange, red and blue.

The rarer-to-spot land iguanas are yellow in color and often larger than their sea-going relatives. They have been one of the hardest-hit species by the animals introduced by man. Tiny lava lizards, however, can be found on all of the islands – frequently seen doing somewhat absurd "push-ups" on pathways, a sign that they are marking out their territory against intruders.

Slow-moving giants: No doubt the most famous of the Galápagos reptiles is the giant tortoise. Countless thousands were killed for their flesh by whalers during the 18th and 19th centuries, and now only an estimated 10,000 remain. There were 14 subspecies of giant tortoise

A giant tortoise munches leaves.

here – distinguished most easily by the different shell shapes – but three are now extinct (the last example of one species was found at the turn of the century by an expedition from the San Francisco museum. The scientists promptly despatched the creature to take its shell back for study).

The giant tortoise is one of the most ancient of reptiles, but also amongst the rarest – it only exists here and on the island of Aldabra in the Indian Ocean. Weighing up to 250 kg (550 lb), it has two types of shell; the dome-shaped can be found in humid environments like Santa Cruz, where vegetation is low and abundant. This type of tortoise has short legs and neck. The second type has a shell that resembles a horse's harness and lives on islands with uneven soil and no low grass, such as Española (Hood). These tortoises are more agile (relatively speaking!) and have long legs and necks in order to feed themselves. The shell indentation allows them to protrude their necks further.

Legend has it that these tortoises can live for centuries. One, given to the Queen of Tonga by Captain Cook in the 1770s, is said not to have died until 1966, but there is no certain evidence for them living over 100 years.

Saving these magnificent creatures has been a major task of the Charles Darwin Research Station here – and a program of breeding and reintroducing the animals to their natural habitat seems to be successful. On Española (Hood), only 10 males and two females of a subspecies were still alive – until after years of breeding in captivity, some 100 healthy specimens were returned to the island.

There is only one survivor, however, of one subspecies from the island of Pinta, and he goes by the name of Lonesome George. Despite a US$10,000 reward for a female of the species, no mate has been found for him to carry on the line. But hope has not been surrendered, since in 1981 some tortoise droppings were actually found on Pinta.

Easier to spot in the wild seems to be the Pacific green sea turtle, which snor-

National Park wardens measure and mark a giant tortoise in the wild, Isabela Island.

kelers can often observe underwater. They can also be seen mating in the water, with the male clambering on the female's back and apparently almost drowning her.

Playful sea lions and dolphins: There are fewer land mammals than either birds or reptiles because they were much less likely to survive the journey across from coastal South America. Storms may have blown the hoary bat to the Galápagos, while the rice rat may have made it across on a vegetation raft. Sea mammals, however, simply followed the currents to the islands, and these days they make up some of the Galápagos' most popular creatures with the visitors.

Topping the list is the sea lion, related to the Californian species. The young are incredibly cute and playful – they will swim about snorkelers and tease them, even staring into your goggles and pretending to charge you before turning away. The *machos*, or older males, do, however, stake out their territory very jealously. They can turn ag-gressive and have been known to bite swimmers, so a degree of caution should be used in their presence (guides will know which areas are the preserve of the bull lions).

Fur seals have more hair than sea lions, are smaller and shy: they prefer to live in colonies, on distant and lonesome cliffs. Bottle-nosed dolphins are often seen surfing the bow spray of boats, while seven whale species have been sighted at or near the Galápagos archipelago – although getting a close look is fairly unlikely.

An underwater world: Under the waves, snorkelers will be constantly surrounded by the 307 species of fish recorded in the Galápagos – and more are being discovered every year. Schools of brightly colored tropical fish pass over the sea floor and around rocks, making a spellbinding sight. There is also a variety of sharks that can be seen quite safely in the water. They are much too well fed to bother attacking humans, and apparently have never attacked a swimmer in the Galápagos – if that's any consolation **Galápagos penguin.**

when you see one!) Although the thought is somewhat unnerving, the grace of these creatures is said to be particularly impressive.

Keep an eye out for the different types of rays that glide majestically along the ocean floor. The giant manta ray can sometimes be spotted leaping out of the sea and landing with a loud slap on the waves. None of the rays are dangerous except for the stingray – on some beaches they lie in shallow water beneath a layer of sand, and can let out quite a sting if trodden on. It's worth giving the sand a shuffle with your feet to scare off any basking rays.

Those animals that do not have backbones are called invertebrates – creatures like jellyfish, sponges, molluscs and crabs. The most commonly seen of these is the bright yellow and orange Sally Lightfoot crab, which can be found on almost every rock in the Galápagos. There are also a number of insects, although nowhere near as many as on the South American mainland.

Organizing your trip: These days, al-most all travelers to the Galápagos arrive by air. Unless you have a pre-arranged trip on one of the larger cruisers, which occasionally depart from Guayaquil, there are very few berths on merchant or naval ships to the islands any more.

Flights leave from both Quito and Guayaquil. TAME flies daily to the island of Baltra, from where a bus and ferry will take you across to Puerto Ayora on Santa Cruz. SAN-Saeta has flights four days a week to Puerto Baquerizo Moreno on the island of San Christóbal, where a second airport has recently been built. On arrival, it is important to have your passport ready and US$80 entrance tax to the National Park – without these two essentials, you cannot enter the islands.

Many travelers will have pre-arranged their cruise around the islands on one of the larger luxury ships. The two best are the *Galápagos Explorer*, a liner owned by the airline SAN-Saeta, and which leaves from San Christóbal in conjunction with their new air service; and the

Penguin diving in the tropical waters of the Galápagos.

Santa Cruz, run by the Ecuadorian agency Metropolitan Touring, which leaves from Baltra airport with the TAME flights. Both offer all the comforts of a five-star hotel, with excellent food, swimming pools, evening slide shows and the like. They also have English-speaking guides that are college-trained naturalists. Although the capacity of these ships is 90 people, they operate with groups of no more than 20 – landing them by small dinghies called *pangas* for twice-daily excursions. The large boats have the advantage of covering a lot of territory by night, easily reaching the remoter islands without unduly rough passages.

Independent (and less pecunious) travelers often choose to organize their own cruise on one of the dozens of smaller boats on the islands. This can be arranged in Quito or Guayaquil, but is cheapest when done in Puerto Ayora (some small boats operate from San Christóbal, but still relatively few). The idea is to take your time, meet up with other like-minded travelers, meet a captain, organize a price… and all this usually takes two or three days. Those in a hurry might prefer to have their trip pre-arranged but, by cutting a deal in Puerto Ayora itself, a tour can be set on one of the smaller fishing boats for US$50–60 per day per person, including food. More luxurious yachts set their rates at US$100–200.

The main advantage of organizing your own trip is flexibility: you can pick and choose which islands you want to visit, for how long, and when. However, the guides are rarely well educated on the smaller boats, and often do not speak English, while rough weather can make night journeys on these boats difficult for those with delicate stomachs. Still, for younger, independent travelers, this is definitely an experience not to miss.

A guide to the visitor sites: As mentioned earlier, the National Park service has designated some 54 visitor sites. These are the only places that boats may land at, and even then you must be accompanied by a guide. Some of the more fragile are restricted so that only small groups may visit, or limits are imposed on the numbers per month.

The landing by *panga* is either "wet" or "dry" – your guide will tell you which. Wet landings simply mean that you leap into the water up to your ankles (sometimes up to your knees), so keep your shoes aside; dry landings are at natural or man-made jetties, where you should keep your shoes on.

The most densely populated island in the Galápagos (in human terms), as well as its second largest (at 986 sq. km/380 sq. miles) is **Santa Cruz**. Most tours start here at the township of **Puerto Ayora**, and even those that begin at San Christóbal call to visit the famous **Charles Darwin Research Station**.

With 3,400 people, Puerto Ayora has the air of a relaxed and easygoing fishing village. The wide turquoise **Academy Bay** is full of small boats and makes a picturesque sight, while the town docks are usually crowded with small children running, swimming and playing with sea lions. Ayora has plenty of small hotels and restaurants, with the most eccentric being the **Sol y Mar**; run by a local character by the name of Señor Jimmy Peréz, it sits right on the waterline and its porch is always crowded with marine iguanas (the little beasties will even walk over your feet while your having breakfast if you're not careful, which can be something of a surprise until you get used to it).

The main attraction remains the Charles Darwin Research Station. This is the classic place to have your photo taken with one of the giant tortoises: mature specimens of several subspecies are kept in pens here. They are fascinating, ancient-looking creatures (and in the age of Spielberg, you can't quite get over the impression that they look just like ET). Note that while you often see pictures of tourists riding tortoises, this can actually damage their shells and is prohibited. The station also has a tortoise breeding-house, where young tortoises can be seen, and a small museum and information center where a brief lecture is given by one of the station guides. Paths run from the station into "littoral" vegetation: fine examples of various varieties of cacti can be found,

Siesta hour at the Hotel Sol y Mar in Puerto Ayora.

as well as thick expanses of mangrove.

There are several trails from Puerto Ayaro that are worth exploring if you have the time. Seven km (4 miles) towards the west is **Tortuga Bay** (Turtle Bay), with fine white sands and waters rich in lobsters. You can go here for swimming and relaxing without a guide, although the fish and animals are still protected.

The highland interior of Santa Cruz, in the National Park, offers several attractions: the **Lava Tubes** are long underground tunnels made when lava solidified on the surface of a flow but kept going underneath. Climbing **Cerro Crocker,** an 860-meter (2,800-ft) high hill, shows the range of vegetation zones on the island. And a day excursion can be made to the **Tortoise Reserve** which is one of the few places to see giant tortoises in the wild. Organize your trip beforehand with a tour guide in the town or visit independently: you need to take a jeep and then a two-hour walk to find these creatures wallowing in the mud.

The central islands: The islands close to Santa Cruz are the most often visited, although not necessarily the most interesting for naturalists. Day trips are run by various agencies from Puerto Ayora: this means a lot of traveling time on the water if you want to visit more than one. It is more fun and – if properly organized – only slightly more expensive to visit several on your own cruise.

Only 24 km (15 miles) from Puerto Ayora is **Isla Santa Fe** (also known as Barrington). A wet landing is the start of a short trail into a dry landscape crowded with *opuntia* cactuses. Santa Fe is one of the best places to see the shy land iguana, but the steep path is one of the more difficult on the Galápagos, so a swim from the beach near the landing site comes as a welcome relief.

On the northeastern coast of Santa Cruz is the tiny island of **Plaza Sur**. Only 13 hectares (32 acres) in area, its coast is so crowded with sea lions that everyone on the *panga* needs to clap and shout to clear a landing space. Swimming is not encouraged here, since the *macho* or bull sea lions are particularly

Academy Bay docks, Puerto Ayora.

aggressive. Although tiny, Plaza Sur is unusually crowded with animal life: there are plenty of land iguanas and its impressive black cliffs are populated with sea birds. Nearby is what might be termed a retirement home for bachelor *macho* sea lions: after losing a brawl over territory, they come here to recuperate before returning to the fray.

Isla Seymour is separated from the larger island of **Baltra** by a channel. But whereas Baltra has little to interest a visitor, Seymour is considered one of the Galápagos' best breeding grounds for sea birds. Blue-footed boobies, in fact, are so common on this island that visitors have to be careful not to step on any of the nests that may have been built on the trails.

Then, 10 km (6 miles) away, is the strange, block-shaped island of **Daphne**. Access to this island is restricted to only a few boats a month. Landing here is also difficult, with a leap onto nearly-sheer rocks that becomes somewhat hair-raising in rough weather. But it is worth the effort: at the end of a trail, a large crater is dotted with literally hundreds of blue-footed booby nests, making a decidedly surreal sight. It is curious to imagine that the young boobies grow up here without being able to see the ocean that they will depend on for food.

Volcanic rock and iguanas: One of the larger islands, relatively close to Santa Cruz, is most commonly known as either **Santiago** or **James**, although its official title is **San Salvador**. It has a number of landing sites, although by far the most popular is **Puerto Egas** on the west coast. This is one of the best places to see hundreds of marine iguanas sunning themselves on black volcanic rocks, while fur seals can be spotted swimming nearby. The **Sugarloaf Volcano** dominates the horizon here. Swimming is good at Espumilla Beach and Buccaneer Cove. And, if you are in a small group, be sure to snorkel at the **fur seals' grotto**. You can swim with these characters for hours through their crystal pools that have been formed under natural-stone archways.

Sitting off the west coast of James, the

small (120 hectares/300 acres) island of **Bartolomé** is one of the most photographed in the Galápagos. The centerpiece of a visit is the steep climb up **Cerro Bartholomé**: the view is spectacular, looking over lunar fields of dried lava, craters and out over the jutting, honeycombed **Pinnacle Rock**. The heat is also quite intense, so after working up a sweat most people transfer to the second landing sight, one of the most pleasant beaches on the islands. The snorkeling here is excellent, especially around Pinnacle rock itself: apart from the tropical fish moving in formation, you have a chance of spotting teams of penguins hunting underwater. A path leads over to the other side of the island, where dozens of reef sharks patrol only meters from the edge of the water.

South of James (Santiago) is the island of **Rábida** (also known as Jervis). This is famous for its beach with dark red sand – thanks to its high iron oxide content – along which hundreds of bloated sea lions are lounging. Indolent and clumsy on land, they are surprisingly

energetic in the water: this is a great place to play with the baby sea lions. A path into the interior of the island passes a marshy lake full of bright pink flamingos (the pinker the flamingo, the healthier it is – the color comes from the shrimps they sieve through their beaks and down for food). In the trees by the beach are also a large number of brown pelicans.

Another unusual point on Jervis that is well worth visiting is **Caleta Tortuga Negra** – "Black Turtle Cove." This tidal lagoon leads into a maze of mangroves: it can only be visited by *panga*, cutting the motor and paddling quietly through the natural tunnels made by trees. The brackish waters of the area are full of white-tipped sharks and mustard rays. But it is most famous as a mating spot for the green Pacific turtle. With luck, you can spot the two heads coming up for air during copulation, which lasts for many hours.

When cruising the south coast of Jervis/Santiago, keep an eye out for **Sombrero Chino** – literally "Chinese Hat," named for the island's sweeping conical shape. One of the more recent islands, it has a 400-meter (1,300-ft) path around its circumference, along which sea lions relax in abandonment.

The northern islands: Amongst the more far-flung Galápagos islands are **Marchena**, **Pinta** and **Genovesa** (Tower). Genovesa is where to find the main colony of red-footed boobies and three types of Darwin finch. It is also crowded with everything from red-billed tropicbirds to storm petrels. Besides being the island for bird lovers, there is also some fine diving to be done.

At 4,588 sq. km (1,770 sq. miles), and 120 km (75 miles) in length, **Isabela**, the largest of the Galápagos islands, is still recovering from fires which blazed across the island in 1994. The fires were eventually extinguished, but not without a severe impact on vegetation. One of the island's main attractions, the giant tortoises, were thankfully rescued by helicopter and taken to the other side of the island to a breeding center.

Isabela is also one of the islands that still has volcanic activity, and there are **A tuna catch**.

five cones still visible: **Wolf** at 1,640 meters (5,380 ft); **Alcedo** at 1,097 (3,600); **Sierra Negra** at 1,405 (4,610); **Cerro Azui** at 1,689 (5,540) and **Darwin** at 1,280 (4,200).

Some 950 people live on Isabela, mostly in and around **Puerto Villamil** on the south coast. Cruise ships rarely visit the outpost since it is difficult to enter the bay, especially when the sea is rough. It does, however, boast a fine sandy beach, an old cemetery and several basic hotels and restaurants. Eighteen km (11 miles) away is the village of **Santo Tomas** and the "Wall of Tears" – built in camp "Germany", the convict colony that closed in 1959 (legend has it that the closure was ordered after 30 prisoners were gunned down when trying to escape).

The crater Serra Negra has a diameter of 10 km (6 miles), making it the second largest in the world, while the volcano Alcedo has a still-steaming fumarole and scores of giant tortoises living at its rim. It can be reached by climbing a difficult 10-km (6-mile) trail that leaves from Shipton Cove. It is an overnight project: there is a camping site here but you must bring your own food and water (a special National Park permit is also needed to camp here). The view from the summit is also particularly impressive. For those who want an easier hike, the rim of Sierra Negra is easier to reach (9 km/5 miles from the small village of Santo Tomas).

Most of the visitor sites on Isabela are situated on the west side of the island. Probably the most popular is **Tagus Cove**. Here you can climb up a path to see lava fields stretching for miles before you. Around the bay are the graffiti left by early sailors, who scratched the names of their vessels on the cliffs. A *panga* ride along the cliffs will reveal colonies of penguins, as well as the usual range of sea birds. It is, however, probably also the best place to see the unique flightless cormorant.

Other landings can be made at **Urbina Bay**, **Elizabeth Bay** and **Punta Moreno**. **Punta Garcia** was one place where the flightless cormorant was com-

Below, a colorful Sally Lightfoot crab. **Right**, blue-footed booby.

GUIDELINES FOR VISITORS

Tourism to the Galápagos has been described as a two-edged sword: it can be a force to preserve the islands; or, uncontrolled, it can destroy them. The following are guidelines that will ensure the Galápagos is left unaltered by your visit.

No plant, animal, shell, bone, piece of wood, or other natural objects should be removed or disturbed on the islands. Doing so is illegal and changes the island's ecological conditions.

Be careful not to transport any live material to the islands, or from island to island. Check your boot or shoe soles for dried mud before you leave your boat. This material will frequently contain seeds and spores of plants and animals. Inadvertent transport of these materials represents a special danger to the Galápagos: each island has its own unique fauna and flora, and introduced plants and animals can quickly destroy them. These rules obviously apply to pets and other animals and plants as well: do not bring them to the islands. One of the most destructive forces in Galápagos are domesticated species gone wild.

For the same reasons, do not take any food to the uninhabited islands. Together with the food may come insects or other organisms which might threaten the fragile island ecosystems. Fresh fruits and vegetables are especially dangerous. A dropped orange seed, for example, may become a tree.

Animals may not be touched or handled. All wild animals dislike this and will quickly lose their remarkable tameness if fondled by human invaders. Young animals that have been handled may be rejected by their mothers because of their smell. They soon die as a result.

Animals may not be fed. Not only can it be dangerous to your own person but in the long run it can destroy the animals' social structure and affect their reproduction.

Do not startle or chase any animal from its resting or nesting spot. Exercise extreme caution among the breeding colonies of sea birds such as boobies, cormorants, gulls, or frigate birds.

These birds will fly from their nests if they are startled, often knocking the egg or chick to the ground or leaving it exposed to the sun. (A recently hatched booby chick will die in 20 to 30 minutes if it is exposed to the sun; frigate birds will also eat any unguarded chick.)

Do not leave the areas which are designated as visiting sites. In the more heavily used visitor sites, trails are marked with wooden stakes within which the visitor should remain. The trails are designed to guide the visitor to all of the points of interest within a given visitor site, and at the same time to protect the resource.

Litter of all types must be kept off the islands. Disposal at sea must be limited to certain types of garbage only to be thrown overboard in selected areas. Keep all rubbish (film wrappers, cigarette butts, chewing gum, tin cans, bottles, etc) in a bag or pocket, to be disposed of on your boat. The crew of your vessel is responsible to the National Park for proper trash disposal. You should never throw anything overboard.

Do not buy souvenirs or objects made from plants or animals of the islands, with the exception of articles made from wood. Black coral is a particular problem, now endangered by islanders' carvings. If anyone offers you any of these souvenirs, please advise the National Park.

Camping anywhere within the Galápagos without a permit is against the law. Camping is permitted only in certain sites designated by the National Park. Consult with the central office of the National Park in Santa Cruz for information.

All groups visiting the National Park must be accompanied by a qualified guide approved by the National Park. The visitor is responsible for following the instructions of the guide in any situation, while the guide who is responsible for assuring that the regulations of the National Park related to the conservation of the flora and fauna are complied with.

Notify the National Park service if you see any serious damage being done. You may be a decisive factor in the preservation of the islands. (The National Park office is a 10-minute walk east of the main township of Puerto Ayora. Open: Monday–Friday 8am–noon and 2–6pm; Saturday 8–10am). ∎

mon, although it has become more difficult to sight in recent years.

On the other side of Isabela is **Fernandina Island**. One of the least-visited islands because of its remoteness, it is also the most westerly in the Galápagos. It has one visitor site at **Punta Espinosa**, with some impressive lava flows (this was probably the most recently formed major island, and still boasts some volcanic activity). Along its shores are more penguins and hordes of marine iguanas.

Lust and murder: Towards the south of the archipelago, the island of **Floreana** may be more notorious for its human past than its animal life. In the 1930s, three groups of German settlers came here, and their tragic fate is still a mystery. The first to arrive was an eccentric vegetarian with stainless-steel dentures named Dr Friedrich Ritter. With his romantic, impractical lover, this Nietzchean doctor of philosophy planned to set up an ideal colony in the wilderness. Next to arrive was a solid middle-class German family, the Wittners. Finally,

the self-styled "Baroness de Bousquet" turned up with her three young boyfriends (kept in order, they say, with horse whippings and regular blows to the head and shoulder from her pearl-handled revolver).

The conflict amongst the settlers was bitter and constant. Then the deaths began. First, Dr Ritter died mysteriously after eating boiled chicken – poisoning is suspected. Soon after, the "baroness" disappeared without trace with one of her lovers – they were almost certainly murdered. Finally, another of the lovers was shipwrecked while trying to escape the Galápagos with a local sailor – both died of thirst on one of the more barren islands.

The only one of the original settlers still alive is Mrs Margaret Wittner. She now runs a small hotel and restaurant in the village of **Puerto Velasco** – and, despite years of persistent queries, she's not telling what happened, so the truth of the fascinating chain of events is likely to die with her. That's not stopping speculation, of course, and plenty

of books are still written about the bizarre story.

Modern visitors can still find the remains of these original settlers' houses. Also of historical interest is the post box at **Post Office Bay**, where whalers used to leave mail as early as the late 18th century. Since replaced several times, the post box is still in use. It is the custom to look through the mail and take whatever is addressed to your destination – putting a local stamp on it when you arrive and thereby sending the letter on its way.

Of the visitor sites on Floreana, **Punta Cormorant** is a beach with a greenish tinge from the tiny crystals of olivine in the sand. From here a trail leads to a lagoon, where occasionally some magnificent pink flamingos nest and circle around. Nearby is a second beach with glistening white sands. The **Devil's Crown** is a sunken crater that forms a semi-circle of rocks: this is perhaps the best site for diving in the whole archipelago. Apart from the schools of brilliant tropical fish, you will probably be

joined by some baby sea lions who will race snorkelers through a natural underwater archway.

The southern tip: The most southerly island in the Galápagos is **Española** (Hood). Like the northern island of Tower, Hood is famous for its sea birds – particularly the waved albatross. Twelve thousand pairs nest here, almost the world's entire population. They are aristocratic creatures, that seem to look down their beaks at the clumsy travelers traipsing along the pathways nearby.

If you're lucky, you may catch the albatrosses during the mating season, when they begin "fencing" by knocking their beaks together and waddling about "like drunken sailors," as one observer put it. The whole astonishing range of sea birds can be seen on this island, as well as the beautiful beach of Gardner's Bay. Keep an eye out for the "blowhole," which spouts water 50 meters (165 ft) into the air whenever waves hit.

Finally, at the eastern point of the archipelago, lies **San Christóbal** (Chatham). Five hundred and fifty sq. km (210 sq. miles) in size, it is the second human population center after Santa Cruz: some 2,800 people live in the sleepy town of **Puerto Baquerizo Moreno**. This, in fact, is the provincial capital. The recent introduction of SAN's flights here has meant a development boom, and now several hotels and restaurants service the town. Named after the first Ecuadorian President to visit the Galápagos, Baquerizo Moreno has a small **museum** run by the Franciscan Fathers, a monument to Darwin and – at the entrance to the port – a rock called **Leon Dormido** which can be climbed for a good view of the island.

A road leads from the capital to the village of **El Progresso** and the 730-meter (2,400-ft) high **San Joaquin volcano**. The **El Junco Lagoon** is a freshwater lake within a crater, surrounded by ferns. **Frigatebird Hill**, is, as the name suggests, a good place to see frigate birds and is only a short walk from the town. **La Loberia** is a beach crowded with sea lions and **Puerto Grande** a small cove particularly popular for swimming.

Left, dried lava patterns. **Right**, dolphins ride a boat's spray.

INSIGHT GUIDES
Travel Tips

FOR THOSE
WITH MORE THAN
A PASSING INTEREST
IN TIME...

Before you put your name down for a Patek Philippe watch *fig. 1*, there are a few basic things you might like to know, without knowing exactly whom to ask. In addressing such issues as accuracy, reliability and value for money, we would like to demonstrate why the watch we will make for you will be quite unlike any other watch currently produced.

"Punctuality", Louis XVIII was fond of saying, "is the politeness of kings."

We believe that in the matter of punctuality, we can rise to the occasion by making you a mechanical timepiece that will keep its rendezvous with the Gregorian calendar at the end of every century, omitting the leap-years in 2100, 2200 and 2300 and recording them in 2000 and 2400 *fig. 2*. Nevertheless, such a watch does need the occasional adjustment. Every 3333 years and 122 days you should remember to set it forward one day to the true time of the celestial clock. We suspect, however, that you are simply content to observe the politeness of kings. Be assured, therefore, that when you order your watch, we will be exploring for you the physical—if not the metaphysical—limits of precision.

Does everything have to depend on how much?

Consider, if you will, the motives of collectors who set record prices at auction to acquire a Patek Philippe. They may be paying for rarity, for looks or for micromechanical ingenuity. But we believe that behind each $500,000-plus

bid is the conviction that a Patek Philippe, even if 50 years old or older, can be expected to work perfectly for future generations.

In case your ambitions to own a Patek Philippe are somewhat discouraged by the scale of the sacrifice involved, may we hasten to point out that the watch we will make for you today will certainly be a technical improvement on the Pateks bought at auction? In keeping with our tradition of inventing new mechanical solutions for greater reliability and better time-keeping, we will bring to your watch innovations *fig. 3* inconceivable to our watchmakers who created the supreme wristwatches of 50 years ago *fig. 4*. At the same time, we will of course do our utmost to avoid placing undue strain on your financial resources.

Can it really be mine?

May we turn your thoughts to the day you take delivery of your watch? Sealed within its case is your watchmaker's tribute to the mysterious process of time. He has decorated each wheel with a chamfer carved into its hub and polished into a shining circle. Delicate ribbing flows over the plates and bridges of gold and rare alloys. Millimetric surfaces are bevelled and burnished to exactitudes measured in microns. Rubies are transformed into jewels that triumph over friction. And after many months—or even years—of work, your watchmaker stamps a small badge into the mainbridge of your watch. The Geneva Seal—the highest possible attestation of fine watchmaking *fig. 5*.

Looks that speak of inner grace *fig. 6*.

When you order your watch, you will no doubt like its outward appearance to reflect the harmony and elegance of the movement within. You may therefore find it helpful to know that we are uniquely able to cater for any special decorative needs you might like to express. For example, our engravers will delight in conjuring a subtle play of light and shadow on the gold case-back of one of our rare pocket-watches *fig. 7*. If you bring us your favourite picture, our enamellers will reproduce it in a brilliant miniature of hair-breadth detail *fig. 8*. The perfect execution of a double hobnail pattern on the bezel of a wristwatch is the pride of our casemakers and the satisfaction of our designers, while our chainsmiths will weave for you a rich brocade in gold *figs. 9 & 10*. May we also recommend the artistry of our goldsmiths and the experience of our lapidaries in the selection and setting of the finest gemstones? *figs. 11 & 12*.

How to enjoy your watch before you own it.

As you will appreciate, the very nature of our watches imposes a limit on the number we can make available. (The four Calibre 89 time-pieces we are now making will take up to nine years to complete). We cannot therefore promise instant gratification, but while you look forward to the day on which you take delivery of your Patek Philippe *fig. 13*, you will have the pleasure of reflecting that time is a universal and everlasting commodity, freely available to be enjoyed by all.

Should you require information on any particular Patek Philippe watch, or even on watchmaking in general, we would be delighted to reply to your letter of enquiry. And if you send us

fig. 1: The classic face of Patek Philippe.

fig. 4: Complicated wristwatches circa 1930 (left) and 1990. The golden age of watchmaking will always be with us.

fig. 6: Your pleasure in owning a Patek Philippe is the purpose of those who made it for you.

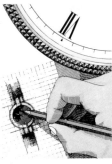

fig. 9: Harmony of design is executed in a work of simplicity and perfection in a lady's Calatrava wristwatch.

fig. 5: The Geneva Seal is awarded only to watches which achieve the standards of horological purity laid down in the laws of Geneva. These rules define the supreme quality of watchmaking.

fig. 7: Arabesques come to life on a gold case-back.

fig. 10: The chainsmith's hands impart strength and delicacy to a tracery of gold.

fig. 2: One of the 33 complications of the Calibre 89 astronomical clock-watch is a satellite wheel that completes one revolution every 400 years.

fig. 11: Circles in gold: symbols of perfection in the making.

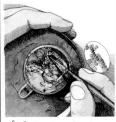

fig. 8: An artist working six hours a day takes about four months to complete a miniature in enamel on the case of a pocket-watch.

fig. 12: The test of a master lapidary is his ability to express the splendour of precious gemstones.

fig. 3: Recognized as the most advanced mechanical regulating device to date, Patek Philippe's Gyromax balance wheel demonstrates the equivalence of simplicity and precision.

PATEK PHILIPPE
GENEVE

fig. 13: The discreet sign of those who value their time.

your card marked "book catalogue" we shall post you a catalogue of our publications. Patek Philippe, 41 rue du Rhône, 1204 Geneva, Switzerland, Tel. +41 22/310 03 66.

Reality check. Call home.

—— *AT&T USADirect® and World Connect®. The fast, easy way to call most anywhere.* ——

Take out AT&T Calling Card or your local calling card.** Lift phone. Dial AT&T Access Number for country you're calling from. Connect to English-speaking operator or voice prompt. Reach the States or over 200 countries. Talk. Say goodbye. Hang up. Resume vacation.

Argentina♦ 001-800-200-1111	Guyana*†† 165
Belize♦...555	Honduras † 123
Bolivia* 0-800-1112	**Mexico**◊◊◊ 95-800-462-4240
Brazil................................000-8010	Nicaragua 174
Chile...........................1-23-0-0311	**Panama**■.......................................109
Colombia 980-11-0010	Paraguay (Asuncion City)† 0081-800
Costa Rica*■.............0-800-0-114-114	**Peru**†...171
Ecuador * 999-119	**Suriname**† 156
El Salvador*■..............................190	Uruguay 00-0410
Guatemala*.......................................190	**Venezuela***■ 80-011-120

AT&T
Your True Choice

**You can also call collect or use most U.S. local calling cards. Countries in bold face permit country-to-country calling in addition to calls to the U.S. World Connect® prices consist of USADirect® rates plus an additional charge based on the country you are calling. Collect calling available to the U.S. only. *Public phones require deposit of coin or phone card. †May not be available from every phone. ††Collect calling only. ♦ Not available from public phones. ◊◊◊When calling from public phones, use phones marked "Ladatel". ■ World Connect calls can only be placed *to* this country. ©1995 AT&T.

For a free wallet sized card of all AT&T Access Numbers, call: 1-800-241-5555.

Getting Acquainted

The Place

Ecuador is located on the northwestern coast of South America, between a latitude of 1° 27' North and 5° South. It owes its name to the equatorial line that runs through the mainland of Ecuador just north of Quito, as well as the Galápagos islands. The country is bordered by Colombia to the north, Peru to the east and south, and the Pacific Ocean to the west.

Ecuador's surface area (excluding the Galápagos and the huge disputed territory in the Oriente, taken from Ecuador by Peru in a 1941 conflict) is approximately 270,670 sq. km (108,268 sq. miles). This makes it the smallest of the so-called Andean countries (a group including Bolivia, Peru, Ecuador, Colombia and Venezuela). Mainland Ecuador is divided by the Andes into three distinct areas: the Sierra (highlands), Costa or coast, and Oriente (Amazon basin).

The Sierra is shaped by two Andean mountain chains, the Eastern Cordillera and Western Cordillera, which create 10 mountain valleys, in which Sierra *indígena* (Indians) live at altitudes between 2,200 and 2,800 meters (6,600 and 7,400 ft).

The inhabitable highland area is often referred to as the *páramo*. Scattered along both the Eastern and Western Cordillera are a number of active volcanoes, prompting the German naturalist Alexander von Humboldt to dub the area "the Avenue of the Volcanoes".

Ecuador's highest peak is Chimborazo at 6,310 meters, or 20,702 ft, followed closely by Cotapaxi, Cayambe, Antisana, El Altar and Sangay.

The Andes drop steeply down to the tropical coastal lowlands on one side and Oriente on the other. The coast manages to escape the icy Humboldt current that washes the beaches of Peru and Chile, so the landscape is lush and swimming a pleasure. Meanwhile, the Oriente, comprising some 30 percent of Ecuador's territory is a mostly flat plainland.

The Galápagos archipelago consists of 17 larger islands and more than 100 smaller ones. They are located 1,120 km (672 miles) west of the mainland, and are famed for their bizarre wildlife and geological formations.

Time Zones

Mainland Ecuador, like the US, is 5 hours behind GMT, with the Galápagos 6 hours behind.

Climate

Located directly on the Equator, Ecuador's climate does not change in the same way as many other nations. Instead of distinguishable summer, fall, winter and spring, Ecuador simply alternates between dry and rainy seasons.

In the inhabited intermountain basin of the Sierra, the temperature changes little between seasons. However, each day runs a gamut of temperatures: the mornings are generally sunny and fresh, becoming warmer towards midday; in the afternoon it often rains, and towards the evenings it gets chilly. The nights are cold. Thus, in Quito, the daily range of temperature is generally 8° to 21° Celsius (46° to 70° Fahrenheit). There is one rainy season in the Sierra, from November to May. At this time there are frequent rainfalls during the afternoon and evening. However, it rains quite often during the dry season also, and the sun shines in the rainy season for at least a couple of hours every day.

Above 3,800 meters (11,400 ft) no plants grow and the temperatures easily reach freezing during the night. Occasional snow storms also occur.

The coastal lowlands and Amazon basin are very hot all year round, with temperatures ranging from 22° C (73° F) at night to 33° C (100° F) during the day. Humidity is extremely high. The rainy season in both areas is from May to December, although the definition is relative: tropical downpours are regular in the dry season also. In the Galápagos islands, there are also two seasons, produced by the ocean currents: the rainy (warm) and dry (cool) season.

During the rainy season, which lasts from January through June, the weather is warm and sunny, while the water temperature is a comfortable 23° C (75° F); heavy, tropical rain showers occur occasionally. This is the best time to visit. For the rest of the year, a mist called the *garua* settles over the islands and makes the day cloudy, and the water begins to cool. It rarely rains, but it can be windy.

The People

Ecuador has an approximate population of 11 million. Some 1.5 million live in Guayaquil and 2.4 million in Quito.

Government

The Republic of Ecuador has been under democratic rule since 1979, when seven years of military government ended. This put Ecuador in the forefront of the general swing back to democracy in Latin America after a period of dictatorships. The new constitution approved by referendum in 1978 allowed the extension of the vote to include all literate citizens over the age of 18 years.

Ecuador has a presidential system. The President and vice-president are elected directly for five-year terms and cannot stand for office again. The 69-person Chamber of Representatives meets for two months of the year. There is a Supreme Court of Justice whose members are chosen by the Congress, and High Courts in every province.

For administrative purposes the country is divided into 21 provinces, each headed by a Governor appointed by the President and a Prefect, elected by the inhabitants. The provinces are subdivided into 103 *cantones* (municipalities), headed by elected *alcaldes* (mayors).

THOMAS COOK MASTERCARD TRAVELLERS CHEQUES...

...HOLIDAY ESSENTIALS

Travel money from the travel experts

THOMAS COOK MASTERCARD TRAVELLERS CHEQUES ARE
WIDELY AVAILABLE THROUGHOUT THE WORLD.

INSIGHT GUIDES

COLORSET NUMBERS

Planning The Trip

What To Wear

Ecuador has three very different climactic zones, so what you wear depends completely on where you are headed.

The Sierra is where most travelers begin. Quito is called the "City of Eternal Spring", although autumn (fall) might be more accurate. When the sun is shining, Sierra days are warm and pleasant, but when the clouds roll in and winds begin to blow, bring a warm sweater. Nights can be quite cold, so a warm coat or parka is recommended.

Note that Quito tends to be more conservative in its dress standards than the rest of the country. Ecuadorians, like most Latin Americans, like to dress up when they go out to restaurants and night spots – men will often wear a coat and tie even in relatively casual surroundings, while women can seem to spend hours on grooming themselves.

Of course, this doesn't apply to many backpacker hangouts. Even in the ritzier establishments, traveling gringos can be forgiven for a more casual appearance than Ecuadorians, but remember that a night out in a restaurant is much more of a big deal for an Ecuadorian, and dressing too unkemptly can seem like an insult to the other clients. If in doubt, err on the side of formality and you can't go wrong.

The coast and Galápagos islands are tropical regions, so dress for the heat. Take a swimsuit, because swimming and snorkeling on the islands are a joy (most boats have snorkelling gear, so you don't need to bring your own unless you want to). Guayaquil and the coast are very casual, so shorts for men are widely accepted (not so widely for women – a light dress is more appropriate) for many social situations. Remember to use protection against the sun.

Dress in the Oriente is even more functional. All clothes should be light, because of the stifling heat, but long trousers and shirts are recommended against insects. Bring some sand-shoes for walking.

Rain can strike in any part of Ecuador whether it's the rainy season or not, so bring a decent rain coat.

Electricity

Ecuador operates on 110 volts, 60 cycles, AC.

Maps

The best selection of maps of Ecuador is produced by the Instituto Geográfico Militar on top of the hill on Avenida T Paz y Mino, off Avenida Colombia in Quito. Some large-scale maps of the whole country, ranging from a 1:1,000,000 one-sheet map to 1:50,000 topographical map are available here. The Sierra has been covered in detail, but the Oriente and parts of the Western Lowlands are not well-served. For a road map, pick up the Guia Vial del Ecuador, with 26 partial maps by Nelson Gomez, Editorial Camino.

Entry Regulations
Visas & Passports

To visit Ecuador as a tourist, all you need is a valid passport (unless you happen to be from China, Cuba, north and south korea, Taiwan or Vietnam, in which case you do need a visa). Ecuadorian Immigration police will give you a free T-3 Tourist Card, which you should keep since it is needed for you to leave the country (stapling it into your passport is not a bad idea). It is usually given for 30 days (unless you ask for more), although you can easily extend it for up to 90 in the Department of Immigration in Quito (Av. Amazonas 2639). Note that tourists can only stay in the country for a maximum of 90 days in any calendar year – a rule that is being strictly enforced, and carries heavy fines if broken.

In theory, Immigration Police can ask for an onward ticket or proof of sufficient funds (US$20 a day) before allowing entry, although this is rare.

You should carry your passport, or a photocopy of it, at all times in Ecuador, since the police are empowered to arrest those without ID should a check be made. Foreigners are unlikely to be bothered in this way in the streets of Quito, but it is very important to have your passport handy on bus trips in the countryside, where checks are common.

Customs

Travelers are allowed to bring a liter of spirits and several bottles of perfume into Ecuador duty free. Foreign cigarettes are not allowed.

Health

No vaccinations are required for Ecuador, although some travelers take a yellow-fever shot if they are heading for the Amazon jungle. This is not really necessary but makes some people feel more comfortable.

The most common illness for tourists is, of course, mild diarrhoea – something that hits most visitors at some stage. Sufferers should have plenty of liquids (hot tea without milk is ideal – definitely no coffee), eat as little as possible and rest as much as they can.

The symptoms of diarrhoea can be stopped with medication like Imodium. This does not cure the ailment, and is really only useful if you have to hop on a long bus or flight and don't want a sudden attack.

If the complaint continues for several days, consult a doctor. Also, if you suffer severe abdominal cramps, fever, nausea or if blood or puss is evident in your stool, you need a test to see if you've caught more serious amoebic dysentery. But in almost all cases, diarrhoea is simply a matter of becoming accustomed to strange foods, and the stomach returns to normal after a couple of days.

To avoid diarrhoea, don't drink the tap water in Ecuador. Ask instead for mineral water (Güitig is the best brand – pronounced Wee-tig). Stay clear of uncooked vegetables, salads that haven't been properly treated or unpeeled fruits.

Most food in the large cities of Ecuador, or in the restaurants that most travelers will eat at, is perfectly safe. Hepatitis is a danger if you eat food prepared in dirty conditions, and some travelers have a gamma globulin shot to protect against this. Although its effectiveness is debated amongst doctors, it does seem that gamma globulin ensures that the most serious strains of hepatitis are less dangerous.

Malaria is currently a risk in surprisingly little of Ecuador, given its large expanses of tropical coast and jungle. Most people do not bother with taking malaria pills unless they are heading into a known malarial area (some obscure parts of Esmeraldas province are currently at risk – not the tourist areas!) If you do elect to take antimalarials however, remember that they should be taken two weeks before your visit until six weeks after. A more everyday health risk is the fierce equatorial sun, a danger even in the cold Sierra. Newcomers to Ecuador should not expose their skin to the sun for long periods, especially during the middle of the day. Bring strong sunscreen lotion. Wearing a hat is a good idea.

Altitude sickness *(soroche)* can sometimes affect travelers arriving by air in Quito from sea level. Most people will need a couple of days to get used to the thin Andean air, so take it easy for the first couple of days: don't go on any strenuous walks, eat light meals and steer clear of excessive alcohol. Drink tea, relax and let your body become accustomed to the height.

Mountain sickness is a more serious problem for climbers, who may be exerting themselves at altitudes over 5,000 meters (15,000 ft). Symptoms can include vomiting, rapid pulse and failing blood pressure. The only real cure is to descend to a lower level.

There are several good private hospitals in Quito and Guayaquil, but they are expensive. It is therefore strongly recommended that travelers take out travel insurance.

Money Matters

Ecuador's currency is the sucre, which devalues fairly rapidly by western standards. It is traded in bills of 100,500, 1,000, 5,000 and 10,000 and coins of 1, 5, 10, 20 and 50 sucres. Some old bills of 5, 10, 20, and 50 do still exist. In early 1996 there were 2,600 sucres to the US dollar.

Foreign currencies can be easily exchanged in banks and casas de cambio (exchange houses) in the business districts of Quito (Av. Amazonas), Guayaquil and Cuenca. The easiest currency to exchange is US dollars (which is the unofficial parallel exchange for all of Latin America), although in Quito and Guayaquil almost any currency can be exchanged. Outside the major cities, however, it becomes difficult to exchange anything but US dollars, usually only in cash form, and at a dismal rate. Change your money before leaving Quito.

On Sundays or holidays, when banks and casas de cambio are shut, you can always exchange money in the major hotels like the Colón in Quito. Most smaller hotels, some shops and even many restaurants will change dollars at a rate slightly lower than the official one.

It is worth bringing most of your money in travelers' checks for safety, as these can be changed almost as easily as cash. Most people also bring a certain amount of cash dollars in manageable denominations (say $20 bills) for times when this is not possible.

Ecuador is one of the easier countries in Latin America to have money transferred to. You can pick up the sum in either US dollars, travelers' checks or local currency.

Major credit cards (particularly Visa and Mastercard) are also accepted here in the larger hotels, restaurants, and tourist-orientated shops.

In Quito and Guayaquil ATM's from which you can withdraw sucres using Visa or Mastercard are becoming more common.

Public Holidays

January

1st – National holiday: New Year's festivities; dances, fancy dressers, masquerades etc.

6th – National holiday: Festival of the Three Kings (Epiphany).

Ambato (Tungurahua): Children's Mass (misas de niños), processions, Christmas carols.

Cuenca (Azuay): Children's Mass, processions, Christmas carols.

Gatazo Grande (Chimborazo): Fireworks, hymns, invitation to share food and drink, election of the "prioste" (Steward of the Festival), kings and ambassadors.

Lican (Chimborazo): Hymns, processions, election of the "prioste" and kings.

Montecristi (Manabí): Bands, dances.

Tisalleo (Tungurahua): High Mass, everybody pays reverence to the Christ child in the crib, folkloric presentation in national costume with dances.

Calpi (Chimborazo): Marimbas, "La Mama Negra" and praises.

15th Quito-Chillogallo (Pichincha): Dances of the Innocent, masquerades, typical bands.

February

1st – Mira (Carchi): Festival of the Virgin of Charity (Virgen de la Caridad); Fireworks, dances, glove ball games (*pelota nacional*), *vaca loca* (crazy cow)-rodeos.

12th – (All-Ecuador): Anniversary of the discovery of the Amazon river (*Dia del Oriente*) – Fairs in Puyo, Tena, Macas and Zamora; day of the province of Galápagos – civic events.

27th – (All-Ecuador): Patriotism and National Unity day to remember the battle of Tarqui in 1829; Oath to the flag by the students, civic events.

Changeable date: Carnival.

March

2nd to 5th – Atuntaqui (Imbabura): Sugarcane and Craftsmanship Festival – dances and *verbenas*.

4th to 10th – Gualaceo (Azuay): Peach Festival. Fruits, flowers and craftsmanship exhibition, dances and masquerades.

April

19th to 21st – Riobamba (Chimborazo): Farming, cattle, handicraft and industrial fair; Folkloric dances, parade, allegorical cars etc.

Changeable date: Holy week. Celebrations and processions on Good Friday and Easter Sunday around Ecuador.

May

1st – (All-Ecuador): Labor day – workers' parades.

2nd – Quito: Festival of Las Cruzes at "La Cruz Verde" quarter (corner of Bolívar and Imbabura Street). Typical band, fireworks, dancing in the streets at night.

3rd – Quito: Festival of La Cruz at Champicruz (Prensa and Sumaco avenues). Dances, fireworks, masquerades and hymns.

Checa (Pinchincha): Patron Saint's day

of the Lord of Good Hope (Señor della Buena Esperanza). Typical band, bonfires, fireworks, serpents, greasy pole climbing and many more attractions.

11th to 14th – Puyo (Pastaza): Farming, cattle and industrial exhibition and fair in the Amazon region.

24th: National civic festivity to remember the battle of Pichincha in 1822 (all over the country). Parades, cultural events.

June

24th – Otavalo (Imbabura), **Tabacundo** (Pichincha), **Guamote** (Chimborazo). Festivity of Saint John (San Juan). Shacks' dancing and other attractions.

24th and following days – Sangolqui (Pichincha). Corn and tourism festivities. Parades, masquerades, craftsmanship exhibition and country bullfights (everybody participates).

24th – Calpi (Chimborazo). "Gallo Compadre", "vaca loca" – rodeos.

28th to 29th – Santo Domingo de los Colorados (Pichincha). Canonization anniversary. Parades, dances, farming exposition.

July

16th – Ibarra (Imbabura): Celebration of Virgen del Carmen. Fireworks, typical music, masquerades.

22nd – Pelileo (Tungurahua): Canonization anniversary. Country bullfights (everybody participates) and many folkloric attractions.

23rd to 25th – Guayaquil: Guayaquil's foundation anniversary. Parades, dancing in the streets, international beauty contest ("pearl of the Pacific"), art expositions and cultural events.

24th: Simon Bolívar's birthday – National Holiday.

29th – Pillaro (Tungurahua): Celebration day of Apostle Santiago the Elder; Country bullfights (everybody participates) and other attractions.

August

3rd to 5th – Esmeraldas: Independence Day. Farming, craftsmanship and industrial fair, processions, dances, marimbas, Afro-American folklore etc.

5th to 7th – Sicalpa (Chimborazo): Festival of the Virgin of the Snow (Virgen de las Nieves). Religious observance, fireworks, clowns, folkloric presentation in national costume with dances.

10th – National Holiday: National civic festival to commemorate independence in 1809. Military and school parades.

Pillaro (Tungurahua): San Lorenzo festivities. Popular bullfights, masquerades.

Yaguachi (Guayas): San Jacinto festivity popular pilgrimages.

25th – Santa Rosa (El Oro): Agricultural fair. Different shows.

September

2nd to 15th – Otavalo (Imbabura): Yamor festivities. Many attractions, typical music, cockfights, parades, folk-singers, beauty contests, dances in national costumes.

5th to 12th – Loja: Patroness Saint's Festival of Virgen del Cisne. Religious observance, fair, typical dances, masquerades, horse races, cockfights, folksongs.

6th to 14th – Cotacachi (Imbabura): Jora festivity. Folkloric dances, typical food and several shows.

11th to 16th – Milagro (Guayas): Agricultural fair. Car races, shows.

8th to 9th – Macara (Loja): Agricultural fair. Folkloric presentations.

8th to 9th – Sangolqui (Pichincha): Bullfights, dances and processions.

20th to 26th – Machala (El Oro): Banana's World Fair. Several attractions.

23rd to 24th – Latacunga (Cotopaxi): Patroness Saint's Festival of Virgen de las Mercedes. Vespers, masquerades, typical bands, fireworks, midnight Mass (*Misa del gallo*) and folkloric festival *La Mama Negra* (shepherds, musicians, native songs, clowns and other typical attractions).

Quito: Festival of Virgen de las Mercedes. Vespers, typical bands, fireworks, midnight Mass, religious procession around the church.

24th – Piñas (El Oro): Production fair. Several events.

24th to 28th – Ibarra (Imbabura): Festivals of the Lakes. Parades, folkloric dances, car races in Yaguarcocha, beauty contests, international agricultural and industrial exhibition.

27th – Espejo (Imbabura): Indian handicrafts fair.

29th – Gonzanama (Loja): Agricultural and industrial exhibition. Several events.

October

9th to 12th – Guayaquil: National civic festival to commemorate the Independence of Guayaquil. International Industrial fair, concerts, regattas, dances, parades, shows and general razzmatazz.

12th – National Holiday: Columbus day (Dia de la raza). To celebrate the European arrival in America.

14th to 18th – Portoviejo (Manabí): Agricultural and industrial exhibition. Many attractions.

November

1st – National Holiday: All Saint's Day.

2nd: All Soul's Day (Dia de los Difuntos). Celebrated all over the country by flower-laying ceremonies in the cemeteries; especially colorful in rural areas, where entire Indian families show up at the cemeteries to eat, drink and leave offerings in memory of their departed relatives; typical food prepared for this occasion: *Guaguas de Pan* (bread rolls) and *Colada morada* (corn fermented syrup).

3rd – Cuenca (Azuay): Civic festivity to remember Cuenca's independence. Processions, expositions, dances and other cultural events.

4th – manta (Manabí): Manta's day. Parades and celebrations.

11th – Latacunga (Cotopaxi): Independence of Latacunga. Parades, several cultural events and popular bullfights.

21st – El Quincha (Pichincha): Patron Saint's Day of Virgen of El Quincha. Religious observance, pilgrimages, commercial fair.

December

1st to 6th – Quito (Pichincha): Foundation anniversary of San Francisco de Quito. Festivities include a series of special bullfights, parades, street dances, greasy pole climbings, election of the Queen of Quito.

25th – National Holiday: Christmas Day. Nativity scenes in churches and homes, illuminations, Christmas carols, midnight Mass, folkloric festival *Pase de Niño* at El Tingo, a village near Quito, and specially in the city of Cuenca.

28th: All Fool's Day. Masquerades, dancing clowns etc.

31st: New Year's Eve celebrations (all over the country). Parades and dances culminate in burning of life-size dolls representing politicians, artists etc., and *el año viejo* (the old year), particularly in Quito, Guayaquil and Esmeraldas.

By Air

Travelers heading to Ecuador from the United States can fly directly to Quito or Guayaquil in Ecuador on daily flights from New York, Miami and Los Angeles with the national airline, SAETA Internacional. Its main competitor, American Airlines, has a regular service to Ecuador, leaving from Miami. In Quito, SAETA is in the Espana building on the corner of Av. Colón and Av. Amazonas.

Reservations with SAETA can be made at the following offices:

Bolivia: *La Paz*, Av. 16 de Julio No. 1800, Edif. Commos, 1er Piso. Tel: (5912) 322-903, 352-079, 376-001. Fax: (5912) 362-697.

Colombia: *Bogotá*, Calle 82 No 11-83 Ofic 402. Tel: (571) 218-7144, 218-2644, 218-9233, 218-5033. Fax: (571) 218-3633.

Medellin, Carrera 34 A No 19 A 87, Local 035, Centro Commercial Automotria. Tel: (574) 262-6400, 262-5906, 262-5868, 262-5786. Fax: (574) 262-3816.

Ecuador: *Quito*, Av. Colón y Av. Amazonas Edifico Espana. Tel: 45-6015, 50-2706. Fax: 44-1507.

Quito Airport: Av. 10 de Augosto y Buenos Aires. Tel: (3932) 44-1506. Fax: (5932) 44-1507.

Guayaquil, Av. Carlos Juilio Arosemena Km 2.5. Tel: (5934) 20-5115, 20-0277. Fax: 20-1153. Vélez 206 y Chile. Tel: (5934) 32-6912, 32-9855, 32-6466. 9 de Octubre 2002 y Los Rios. Tel: 29-6111. Fax: 29-6397.

Guayaquil Airport: Av. las Américas. Tel: (5934) 28-6909, 29-2737. Fax: (5934) 39-7081.

Ambato, Bolívar y Montalvo. Tel: (5932) 326147

Cuenca, Sucre 770 y Luis Cordero. Tel: (5037) 83-1548. Fax: (5937) 835115.

Ibarra, Pedro Moncayp y Olmedo. Tel: (5932) 82-6147.

Peru: *Lima*, Andalucía 174, Mirallores, Lima 18. Tel: (5114) 44-0143, 45-2888. Fax: (5114) 45-5598.

Venezuela: *Caracas*, Av. Libertador, Centro Comercial Libertador, PH.NE. Tel: (582) 761-6530, 761-6630, 762-9905. Fax: (582) 71-9322.

United States: *Chicago*, 6N Michigan Avenue, Suite 1313, Chicago, IL 60602. Tel: (312) 701-0200, 701-0402. Fax: (312) 701-0103.

Los Angeles, Skyview Centre , 6033 West Century Blvd, Suite 375, Los Angeles, CA 90045. Tel: (810) 670-0307, 670-0809. Fax: (810) 670-2058. Toll Free: 1-800-86 SAETA.

Miami, Corporate Center Drive, Suite 402, Miami, FL 33126. Tel: (305) 477-2104. Fax: (305) 477 3945. Toll free: 1-8000-82 SAETA.

Miami Airport: Tel: (305) 526-3310, 526-6613. Fax: (305) 871-4345.

New York, Fifth Avenue, Suite 2030, New York NY 10110. Tel: (212) 302-0004. Fax: (212) 302-4008.

New York Airport: Tel: (718) 558-5622. Fax: (718) 917-5623.

Europe: Air France flies from Paris to Quito several times a week (via French Guiana or Bogotá), Iberia flies from Madrid (via Puerto Rico), KLM from Amsterdam (via Curaçao) and Lufthansa from Frankfurt.

Several Latin American airlines (such as Aerolineas Argentinas, Ladeco, Varig, Viasa and Avianca) offer connecting flights to Ecuador from Europe and the US via their home countries. SEATA operates regular flights from Ecuador to the rest of South America.

In the UK a number of operators offer deals using various flight combinations and packages, and it is best to shop around:

Ecuador Travel, 37–39 Gt Marlborough Street, London W1V HA. Tel: 0171-437-437-7534.Fax: 0171-494-0199.

South American Experience, 47 Causton Street, London SW1P 4AT. Tel: 0171-976-5511. Fax: 0171-976-5908.

Agents and packages: A number of companies also offer tailor-made holidays which are worth considering. These can include yacht charter, jungle trips and excursions to the Galápagos islands. They may also include a stop on the way, for example in Peru.

Animal Watch Wildlife Adventures, Graville House, London Road, Sevenoaks, Kent TN13 1DG. Tel: 01732-74-1612. Fax: 01732-74-0736.

Twickers World, 22 Church Street, Twickenham, TW1 3NW. Tel: 0181-892-7606. Fax: 018-892-7606.

Worldwide Journeys and Expeditions, 8 Coneragh Road, London W14 9HP. Tel: 0171-381-8638. Fax: 0171-381-0836.

Australia, New Zealand, Asia: Travelers have only three options: take the Aerolineas Argentinas transpolar flight from Sydney via Auckland to Buenos Aires, then a connecting flight to Guayaquil; take the Lan Chile flight from Australia to Santiago, then connect with Ecuador; or fly to Los Angeles and pick up one of the several connecting flights from there.

Ecuador's airports: Note that Ecuador has two international airports, Quito and Guayaquil. Business travelers may want to visit Guayaquil, but most tourists will be heading for Quito. You should be aware that the largest airplanes cannot land at Quito airport, and some airlines will only take you as far as Guayaquil, where in theory you take the short 20-minute connection to the capital. Unfortunately, Guayaquil airport can only be described as a hell-hole, and trying to negotiate a ticket oneself is an experience that should be avoided if at all possible.

You should therefore make sure that your carrier either flies direct to Quito, does the connecting leg itself or will at least look after you at the airport. Chile's excellent Ladeco airlines, for example, does not fly to Quito but has a special official at Guayaquil airport to help you find your luggage (no mean task) and ensure that you have a seat to Quito, so you can relax at the bar until the flight leaves. AeroPeru, on the other hand, simply dumps travelers in Guayaquil – leaving you to fight your way onto a waiting list.

Note that there is a 10 percent tax imposed on all air tickets bought within Ecuador, and a US$25 departure tax payable at the airport.

By Sea

It is unlikely that anyone would plan a visit to Ecuador by sea. The only passenger services from Europe are Continental Shipping and Travel, run from 179 Piccadilly, London W1V 9DB, tel: (071) 491-4968; and NAVIS, Billhorner Kanalstr. 69, 2000 Hamburg 28, Germany. The US Grace Line is also said to take passengers to South America.

By Land

It is common for backpacking travelers to travel overland into Ecuador, crossing at either Huaquillas or Macará on the

Peruvian border or Tulcán/Rumichaca on the Colombian side. At both borders, minibuses and trucks run between bus centers on the two opposite sides for a small fee. The borders are usually open from around 8am to 6pm Make sure you get an entry stamp and tourist card when you come in.

REYTUR bus company runs an international service from Quito and Guayaquil to Lima. It is more expensive than buying a ticket to the border, walking across and buying another ticket straight away. And they make you change buses anyway.

Practical Tips

Weights & Measures

The metric system is commonly used throughout Ecuador.

Business Hours

Government offices in Quito are open to the public 8am–4.30pm, Monday–Friday. In Guayaquil, hours are 9am–noon and 3.30–6pm, Monday–Friday.

Banks in Ecuador work a single shift from 9am–1.30pm (although some private banks offer a limited service, called *servicio diferido*, in the afternoon).

Private companies generally work 8am–5pm with an hour for lunch.

Stores are generally open 9am–1pm and 3–7pm, Monday–Friday, then Saturday 9am–1.30pm. Shopping centers and small grocer stores stay open until 8pm. Drug stores (*farmacias*) are open continuously 9am–8pm and some are listed "on duty" 24 hours a day (see the daily newspapers for those rostered to be open that day).

Tipping

A 10 percent service charge is added to bills in restaurants, but it is customary to add on another 10 percent for the waiter. Airport porters can be paid about 50 cents US. Taxi drivers do not expect a tip.

Media

In Quito, there are several decent newspapers to choose from: *El Comercio, Hoy, Tiempo* and *Ultimas Noticias* are the most established. In Guayaquil, you can choose from *Expreso, El Telegrafo, El Universo* and *la Prensa.*

Postal Services

Mail services are not particularly good in Ecuador, and letters are often very slow to be delivered and regularly lost. When sending mail, it is worth having your letters certified *(con certificado)* for about 10 cents – you get a little receipt which won't do much practical good, but means that your letter's existence is recorded somewhere and given safer treatment.

The main post office in Quito is in the old town at Espejo 935 and Guayaquil. This is where the Poste Restante is located. Users of American Express travelers' checks may have their mail sent to the Amex office in the new town operated by Ecuadorian Tours at Amazonas 399. Mail can be sent most safely to Apartado 2605, Quito, Ecuador.

Telecoms

Every town has a long-distance telephone and telex office (EMETEL), although expect to have an hour-long wait. Many people will find it more convenient to call from their hotel – a surcharge is added onto the call, but the time and effort saved is generally worth it. Calls are generally expensive (about US$7 a minute to Europe and the United States). Rates are discounted after 7pm

If you insist on making the call yourself, the main EMETEL office in Quito is on A. 10 de Agosto near Av. Colón.

Photography

Bring sufficient photographic film with you to Ecuador, since it is quite expensive to purchase camera gear within the country and the choice of film is limited. If you are stuck, try one of the photo stores on Quito's Avenida Amazonas and make sure the film date hasn't expired. Processing is unreliable, so wait until returning home.

Equatorial shadows are very strong and come out almost black on photographs, so the best results are often achieved on overcast days.

Not surprisingly, Ecuadorian indígenas resent having a camera thrust in their faces and often proudly turn their backs on pushy photographers. Unless you are taking a shot from a considerable distance, ask permission beforehand. Many will ask for a small fee or "tip" to be photographed – some tourists are surprised by this, but when you think about it there's no reason why not. It is often a much more pleasant way of taking portraits than furtively trying to shoot people without being noticed.

Travel Packages

Ecuador is such an accessible country that tours to any region can be easily organized from the capital Quito. Of course, you can arrange tours through travel agents in the US or Europe if you are on a tight schedule or are traveling in a peak period, but in many cases it is perfectly simple to organize an itinerary once you arrive.

There are dozens of travel agents along Avenida Amazonas in Quito, many of which offer more or less similar programs. The most popular day trips are to Otavalo and the Mitad del Mundo monument. Longer trips can be to the coastal beaches, Oriente jungle, Cuenca or the Galápagos.

The largest and oldest travel agency in Ecuador, and one that can be recommended without reservation, is Metropolitan Touring. Its main office is in Quito near the Hotel Colón:

Metropolitan Touring: Av. Amazonas 239, PO Box 17-17-1649, Quito, Ecuador. Tel: (593-2) 506-650. Fax: (593-2) 560-807.

Also in Guayaquil: **Metropolitan Touring**: Antepara 915, Guayaquil. Tel: (593-4) 320-300. Fax: (593-4) 323-050.

Bookings can be made in the US through: **Adventure Associates**: Suite 110, 13150 Colt Road, Dallas, Texas 75240. Tel: (214) 907-0414, (800) 527-2500. Fax: (214) 783-1286.

Bookings in Europe: **South American Tours**: Adalberstr. 44–48D, 6000 Frankfurt M. 90, Germany. Tel: (069) 770-371-75. Fax: (060) 707-1107.

Metropolitan Touring is a good place to arrange anything from city tours around Quito to week-long trips to the Galápagos. The company also owns the facilities for some of Ecuador's more unusual trips, including:

The *Flotel Orellana*: journeys on a floating hotel into the Amazon for 3–6 days. Also on offer are excursions into remote jungle lodges. Metropolitan Touring also runs "Eco-Tourism" trips into the Oriente. They include staying at the Imuya, Iripari and Aguarico Camps in the Cuyabeno Reserve, with guided treks into the surrounding rain-forest.

Rail adventures through the Avenue of the Volcanoes in the company's own train carriages, includes stays in Riobamba and/or Cuenca and connections to Guayaquil.

The *Santa Cruz* luxury liner on the Galápagos islands organises package tours for 3, 4 or 7 day trips around the islands. The company also arranges trips on smaller luxury yachts.

Oriente

To visit Randy Borman's Cofan village in the Oriente (see chapter "Gringo Chief"), tours must be organized through Wilderness Travel in Berkeley, California. Wilderness Travel offers 17-days trips visiting both the Sierra and Oriente for around US$2,000 plus airfare.

Wilderness Travel also offers adventure-oriented group trips to the Galápagos and combines Ecuador with trips to the Andes of Peru. For further information contact:

Wilderness Travel, 801 Allston Way, Berkeley, CA 94710-9984. Tel: 1 (415) 548-0420, or toll-free within the US 1 (800) 247-6700.

Adventure Tourism

Trekking equipment, rental outfits and mountain guiding:
Safari, Calama 380 y Juan León Mera, Quito, Ecuador. Tel: 552-505, Fax: 220426.
Sierra Nevada Expeditions, Juan León Mera y Ventimilla, Quito, Ecuador. Tel: 542-605. Fax 547-576.
Campo Abierto, 6 de Diciembre y Roca, Quito Ecuador. Tel 230-029. Fax 324-422.
Pamir Adventure Travels, Juan León Mera 721 & Ventimilla, PO Box 17-16-

190 CEQ, Quito, Ecuador. Tel: 54-2605. Fax: 54-7576.
Surtrek Expediciones, Av. Los Shyris y Luis Cordero, Ambato, Ecuador, Postal address: P.O. Box 865, Ambato, Ecuador. Tel: 844-448. Fax: 844-512.

Mountain guiding/excursions only:
Horizontes Ecuatorianos, Pinto 560 y Amazonas, Quito, Ecuador. Tel: 230-463. Fax: 502-399.
Paragliding: Pichincha C&C Alemania 339 & Eloy Alfaro, Quito, Ecuador. Tel 540-347.
White water rafting: Several Ecuadorian companies have developed river rafting companies.
Sierra Nevada: see above.
Andean River Expeditions, 176 Gaspar de Villaroel. Tel 460-154.
Etnotur, Juan León Mera 1238. Tel 564-565.

Tourist Information

The government tourist office CETUR (Corporación Ecuatoriana de Turismo) has its central office at Eloy Alfaro 1214 by Parque Cardina in Quito. Tel: 225-101. It has smaller offices in most Ecuadorian towns.

A unique resource for backpacking travelers in Ecuador is the South American Explorer's Club, located at 1254 Toledo in the La Floresta section of Quito (SAEC), tel: 566-076. This travelers' meeting place keeps up-to-date information on every aspect of Ecuador and is the perfect place to go for advice, especially on trekking or organizing your own trip to the jungle or Galápagos Islands. The club house has a library with books on Ecuador, tea-making facilities and a pleasant environment where you can lounge around and chew the fat with other like-minded folk. Although it sounds like a place that Phileas Fogg might have visited on his travels around the world, the club is a lot of fun. Non-members are allowed to use the place for one visit and are then asked to sign up: membership costs around US$40 a year, which also entitles you to a quarterly magazine ($7 charge for postage outside US). It is well worth the price – they can also help you out if you have an accident, get robbed and so on.

Written enquiries about travel in Ecuador can be sent to the Club at

Apartado 21-431, Eloy Alfaro, Quito, or the US office at 126 Indian Creek Rd Ithaca, NY 14850. Tel: (607) 277-0488.

Note that the SAEC has an up-to-date guide to organizing individual trips to the Galápagos which it sells for US$3.

Getting Around

Domestic Travel

Until the 20th century, transport and communications in Ecuador were poorly developed. As late as 1900 the journey between Quito and Guayaquil entailed a two-week trek on muleback across mountains and through thick forests. When the Guayaquil-Quito railway was completed in 1908, it provided for the first time an effective inter-regional link and cut the travel time between the two cities from 12 days to 12 hours.

The railway still exists, but today it is more a tourist attraction than a commercial link. The total trek length is 1,043 km (646 miles) and at present the Quito-Riobamba, Riobamba-Alausi-Guayaquil and Ibarra-San Lorenzo stretches are in operation for passengers. The Azogues-Cuenca stretch is out of service at present.

The road network, on the other hand, has expanded considerably after World War II, and the main roads are generally very good. Of the 38,000 km (23,560 miles) of highways, about 18,000 km (11,160 miles) are open the year round and 7,000 km (4,340 miles) are paved.

By Air

Air transport is fairly well developed. The Oriente is the one area where airlines are virtually without competition from other forms of transport. There are many villages whose only contact with the rest of the country is by air; besides numerous small strips, 34 airports can handle bigger planes, some of them modern jet aircraft. The only two airports suitable for international traffic are Mariscal Sucre in Quito and Simón Bolívar in Guayaquil.

There are local domestic flights to all the main cities. Airlines SAN, SAETA and TAME connect the principal urban centers of the country – Quito, Guayaquil and Cuenca – by jet service with several flights daily each way. Flying time Guayaquil-Quito is 35 minutes. TAME offers daily service to the Galápagos islands, landing at Baltra, and SAN flies to the archipelago four times a week, landing at San Cristóbal. TAME flies from Quito to Esmeraldas, Manta, Portoviejo, Tulcan and Loja (via Guayaquil) and from Guayaquil to Machala. In the Amazon jungle area, Lago Agrio, Coca and Macas are served.

Ther are military flights in the more remote Amazon areas. TAO flies small aircraft between Puyo (Shell-Mera) and Macas and ECUAVIA operates charter flights. Air taxis (Cessnas or Bonanzas) can be rented. Small airlines' offices are found at the Guayaquil and Quito airports. "Missionary Air Services" in Macas (Servicio Aereo de la Misión Salesiana) may provide occasional flights to remote jungle villages of the Shuar communities.

With the exception of flying to the Galápagos islands, flights are comparatively inexpensive (a return flight Quito-Guayaquil is currently priced at only US$30). Passengers have to show up one hour before the departure of domestic flights, for baggage handling and check-in procedures. Many flights give marvellous views of the snow-capped Andes, so it is worth getting a window seat. Unfortunately, seats are not assigned; but are given on a first come, first served basis. There are no departure taxes for domestic flights.

By Rail

The few trains still operating are rarely comfortable or reliable. Nevertheless the adventurous tourist may try to board the autoferro (like a bus mounted on a railway chassis) that runs from Ibarra in the Northern highlands to San Lorenzo on the coast (carry your own food and watch your luggage!) For more details, see the chapter on the Ibarra-San Lorenzo railway.

Many hundred kilometers of Ecuador's train system were totally destroyed during the 1982–83 floods.

One of the most spectacular train rides in the world, the Quito-Guayaquil railway line, is now working again. It is possible to go with a tren mixto (passengers/freight) from Guayaquil (Durán) to Alausi, a stretch which has been made famous in the British TV series Great Railway Journeys of the World. The train departs from Durán at 6am every morning, arriving at Alausi 12 hours later. The return trip from Alausi departs at 9am and arrives at Durán at 5pm

A more comfortable option is offered by "Metropolitan Touring" in Quito: a railway car refitted with pullman seats, en route meals and a view platform, operates on the railway between Quito and Riobamba.

The agency operates a number of railway adventures starting from Quito: the Quito-Riobamba Expreso (US$288 per person based on twin-share occupancy) lasts for 2 days and 1 night, taking travelers by rail to Riobamba and returning to Quito by bus. The trip can be extended to include a visit to Guayaquil for an extra US$100.

Alternatively a stay in a hacienda can be included on the return to Quito. For more details, contact Metropolitan Touring at Amazonas 239 in Quito, tel: 560-550.

By Road

Traveling by private car is generally more convenient in Ecuador than in other Andean countries; first, because the main roads are in a good state throughout the year; second, because the running costs are economical; and third, because the countryside is safer than in the neighboring republics. Nevertheless, when touring by car, beware the bus drivers who often go very fast and make sure that your car has good ground clearance.

Car rental is as expensive as in Europe or in the United States. Charges are about US$35 a day, with mileage increments. Extra insurance costs may be charged. It is often more economical to hire a taxi for several hours, which will take you to remote areas or to another town: you have to bargain the costs beforehand. A formal shared-taxi system exists only between Guayaquil and Machala (Oro Taxi) and between Quito and Ibarra (Taxis Lagos).

By Bus

Bus travel is not too comfortable, but numerous companies connect all the main towns at frequent intervals (smaller localities are also served) and fares are incredibly low. In general buses leave from central bus terminals; exact schedules exist only in theory, although one can usually buy tickets one or two days in advance and choose the seat number (the front seats have slightly more leg room than the back seats). During long holiday weekends or special fiestas, buses are booked up for several days in advance, so early booking is recommended.

On buses, always carry your passport with you. There are police checks on all the roads leading out of main towns and you can get into serious trouble if you are unable to present your documents.

Four types of buses are used: small buses (busetas) for 22 passengers and fast (sometimes too fast) and efficient; larger coaches (buses) have more space, but take almost twice as long to reach their destinations. Recently new luxury buses have ben introduced on routes between major cities. finally there are trucks which often serve as buses. They have a tin roof, open sides, wooden plank seats and are called rancheros.

All the main towns and cities are served by urban bus lines. The buses are mostly small and usually extremely overcrowded, especially at peak hours (the double-decker buses operating on Quito's Avenida Amazonas which are for the airport and the new large "selectivo" buses running in Quito's town area are a pleasant exception). If you want to get off a local bus, shout Baja! ("Down") or Esquina! ("Corner"), and the driver will stop at the next corner.

By Taxi

Taxis in Ecuador are very cheap because of the low price of gasoline for domestic consumption, but meters are only used by taxi-drivers in Quito. In Guayaquil, meters are installed by law but drivers do not use them: ascertain the fare beforehand, or you could be overcharged. In smaller towns, meters do not exist; at weekends and at night fares are 25 to 50 percent higher.

Where to Stay

Hotels

There is no shortage of hotels in Ecuador. Every little town, no matter how remote, has somewhere to lay one's head. However, if you want hotels of an international standard, the options are more limited. Five star luxury accommodation can be found in Quito, Guayaquil, Cuenca, the resort areas of Esmeraldas and Santa Elena, or the jungle lodges and Flotel Orellana of the Oriente. Most other areas rely on basic but clean country inns (hosterías), pensiones or residenciales.

During the high tourist season (June to September in the Sierra, December and January on the coast) and during fiestas or the night before market days (in Otavalo particularly), finding accommodation can be tight. In those cases, it is worth making a reservation; in other places just turn up.

Luxury hotels charge international rates for their rooms. A room in a first class hotel might cost US$80, while a double with private bath in a perfectly comfortable residencial can be had for US$20. Decent backpacker hotels with shared bathrooms can generally be found for US$3-6 per person in even the remotest area. In most places apart from budget hotels/hostals), service and tax charges of roughly 10 percent each will be added to the bill.

For specific recommended hotels in Quito, Guayaquil, Esmeraldas, Cuenca and the Galápagos, see their respective sections on the following pages.

Eating Out

What To Eat

Ecuador has a very rich, plentiful and varied gastronomic culture, different from that of other Latin American countries. Ingredients, seasonings and experiences from South America and Europe have blended to create some unique tastes.

Well worth trying are the following local dishes:

Cuy: whole roasted guinea pig is a traditional food dating back to Inca times. This dish is certainly not served in fancy restaurants, but rather at markets and street stands.

Tamales: a pastry dough wrapped in a leaf and steamed, made from toasted corn flour or wheat flour and filled with chicken, pork or beef.

Humitas: a pastry (sweet or salty) prepared from corn *(choclo)* crumbled cheese, egg and butter and wrapped in a corn husk.

Tortillas de maíz: tasty fried corn pancakes filled with mashed potatoes and cheese.

Empanadas de morocho: a delicious small pie of white corn stuffed with pork meat and fried, served with hot sauce.

Empanadas de verde: a pie of green plantain, filled with cheese or meat.

Ceviche: raw seafood marinated in lemon, orange and tomato juice and served with popcorn and sliced onions. It can be made from fish, shrimp, mussels, oysters, lobster or octopus. Very popular on the coast.

Locro: a yellow soup prepared from milk, stewed potatoes and cheese, topped with an avocado. *Locro* sometimes contains meat, watercress, lentils, pork skin etc.

Lechón hornado: roasted suckling pig; a speciality of Sangolqui, near Quito.

Llapingachos: mashed potato-and-cheese pancakes usually served with *fritada* – scraps of roast pork and salad.

Seco (stew): It can be based on

chicken *(de gallina)* goat *(de chivo)* or lamb *(de cordero)* and is usually served with plenty of rice.

Fanesca: a kind of fish soup with beans, lentils and corn. Eaten mainly during the Easter week, *fanesca* is filling and rich.

On the coast, there is also an amazing richness of gastronomic combinations. Seafood is very good. The most common types of fish are: white sea bass, called *corvina*, shrimp *(camarones)* and lobster *(langostas)*. Look out for *encocada* (coconut) dishes, and the *sal prieta* of Manabí, a sauce with peanut butter and corn flour. A surprisingly tasty dessert *(postre)* is *helados de paila*, ice cream made with fruit juice and beaten in a large brass pot *(paila)* which is rotated in another pot filled with ice.

For those who prefer international cooking, it should be added that in Quito, and sizeable towns, there are lots of Italian, Spanish, French and Chinese restaurants. Even German and Arabian food is served in some places.

Where To Eat

Quito has a very good selection of restaurants offering everything from local dishes to French, Chinese, German, Spanish and Italian cuisine. Surprisingly, there are few good restaurants in Guayaquil, apart from in the bigger hotels, where excellent food is served. In the provincial capitals and the countryside it is also possible to eat well at reasonable prices. A restaurant need not be too fancy to serve delicious and healthy food, but shabby places should be avoided.

In Quito and Guayaquil there are some very expensive restaurants, but in a good restaurant you can have a full meal for approximately US$5-10 plus 20 percent service charge and tax. If you order a bottle of wine, however, the bill will be much higher, because wine is imported. It is customary to leave an additional tip of 10 percent for the waiter.

Restaurants open for lunch at noon and stay open until about 3pm They often offer inexpensive "executive lunches". For dinner they are open from 7pm and close generally at midnight. In the evening, ordering is à la carte. Most restaurants are closed on

Sundays or Mondays, but hotel restaurants are open every day of the week.

Drinking Notes

There is an amazing choice of juices (jugos) such as mora (blackberry), naranja (orange), maracuya (passion fruit), naranjilla (a local fruit tasting like bitter orange) or papaya. Beers such as Pilsener, Club and Loewenbrau are quite drinkable. All other beers are imported and rather expensive. The usual soft drinks are known as colas and the local brands are very sweet, and the excellent mineral water is called Guitig (pronounced wee-tig) after the best known brand.

Coffee is often served after meals. A favourite Ecuadorian way of preparing coffee is to boil it for hours until only a thick syrup remains. This is then diluted with milk and water. Instant coffee is common. Espresso-machines are only found in the better hotels and in a very few restaurants and cafeterias.

Finally a word about alcoholic beverages: whilst rum is cheap and good (commonly drunk with Coca-Cola in a *cuba libre*); whisky is fairly expensive and imported wines (from Chile and Argentina) cost much more than they do in their country of origin. Local wines cannot be recommended.

Quito A – Z

Airlines

International

(phone code 593-2)

Aeroflot, 18 de Septiembre y Av. Amazonas. Tel: 545-454.

Aerolineas Argentinas, Av. Amazonas 1188 y Calama. Tel: 543257.

Aero Peru, George Washington 718. Tel: 561-699. Fax: 564-871.

Air France, 18 de Septiembre y Av. Amazonas. Tel: 524-201. Fax: 566-415.

Air Panama, no longer operates.

Alitalia, Ernesto Noboa 474 y 6 de Diciembre. Tel: 545-652. Fax: 545-652.

American Airlines, Av. Amazonas 353 y Robles. Tel: 528-166. Fax: 561-425.

Avianca, 6 de Diciembre 511 y 18 de Septiembre.Tel: 508-843. Fax: 502-746.

British Airways, Colón y Amazonas, edif Espana. Tel: 540-000. Fax: 228-933.

Copa, Ventimilla 888 y JL Mera. Tel: 521-013. Fax: 563-358.

Eastern Airlines, no longer operating.

Iberia, Av. Amazonas 239. Tel: 560547. Fax: 566-852.

KLM, Amazonas 3617 y Sanz, edif Xerox. Tel: 455-233. Fax: 435-176.

Lacsa, 12 de Octubre 394. Tel: 505-213. Fax: 223-744.

Ladeco, 18 de Septiembre 238 y R. Victoria. Tel: 508-396. Fax: 566-682.

Lufthansa, 18 de Septiembre 238 y R. Victoria. Tel: 541-300. Fax: 566-682.

Saeta, Colón y Amazonas, edif Espana. Tel: 564-969. Airport: Av 10 de Agosto y Buenos Aires. Tel: 441-506.

Varig, Av. Amazonas y Pinto. Tel: 563-316. Fax: 563-699.

Viasa, Av. Amazonas 1188 y Calama. Tel: 568-262.

Domestic

Helicopteros Nacionales, Av. Gonzalez Suarez 1050. Tel: 525-280.

Saeta, Colón y Amazonas, edif Espana. Tel: 564-969.

Tame, Colón 1001 y Rabida. Tel: 554-905.

Transportes Aereos Orientales, Av. Amazonas y Palora. Tel: 446-780.

Transportes Amazonicos, no longer operating.

Airport

Quito's international airport Mariscal Sucre is situated only 8 km (5 miles) from the center of the city. Taxi-rides to the tourist and business area downtown should cost no more than US$4. Inexpensive double-decker buses run all the way along Av. Amazonas to the airport and back. There is a US$25 departure tax on international flights. There are no luggage deposit boxes at the airport.

The Icaro flying school offers flights in small propeller aircraft along the Avenue of the Volcanoes. A 7-seater plane costs $650 per hour.

Art Galleries

Artists display their works in the Parque, near the big arch on Av. Patria, regularly every weekend.

Art Forum, J.L. Mera 870.

Centro de Promoción de Artistas, Casa Blanca, Parque del Ejido. Tel: 522-410.

Fundacion Exedra, Carrion 243 y Plaza.

La Galeria, Juan Rodriguez 168. Tel: 232-807. Modern art only.

Automobile Club

ANETA is located at Eloy Alfaro 218 y 10 de Agosto. Tel: 237-779/527. Office hours: 9am–1pm and 3–7pm.

Banks

American Express, Av. Amazonas 325. Tel: 560-488.

Bank of London and South America, Av. Carrion y Amazonas. Tel: 564-134.

Banco de Guayaquil, Colón y Reina Victoria. Tel: 566-800 for cash advance on Visa.

Banco del Pacifico, Av. Amazonas y Roca. Tel: 507-348 for cash advance on Master Card.

Banco de Pichincha, Amazonas y Colón. Tel: 547-006 for cash advance on Diners Card.

Citibank, Patria y Juan León Mera. Tel: 551-008.

Filanbanco, Av. Amazonas 530. Tel: 522-366 for cash advance on Visa.

Thomas Cook, Representative is Ecuacambio, Av. de la Republica 192 y Almagro. Te:l 540-129.

Casas de Cambios (exchange houses), **Casa Paz** in old town: Sucre y Venezuela, Galeria Sucre. Tel: 511-364. In new town: Amazonas 370 y Robles. Tel: 563-900.

Apart from changing foreign currencies into *sucres*, these will change travelers checks into US dollars cash (up to US$200 for a small commission).

The airport **cambio** and the exchange desk at the Hotel Colón are the only places in town that will change money on Saturdays and Sundays.

Books & Periodicals

Librería Científica, Juan León Mera y Av. Colón. Tel: 552-854.

Libri Mundi, Juan León Mera 851. Tel:

234-971. Branch at Hotel Colón. Tel: 550-455. Books in English, German, French and Spanish; large selection of maps, international magazines, records.

Buses

Local buses run frequently and are inexpensive. Destinations are shown on the front of the vehicle. Beware of pickpockets. Long-distance buses leave mainly from the "Terminal Terrestre" in the southern Villa Flora district, at Maldonado and Cumandá. There are about two dozen bus companies with offices at the terminal. It is worthwhile booking in advance.

There are many buses a day to major destinations including Ambato (3 hours), Bahía de Caraquez (8 hours), Baños (3½ hours), Coca (12 hours), Cuenca (9–14 hours), Guaranda (5 hours), Guayaquil (8 hours), Lago Agrio (10 hours), Latacunga (2 hours), Loja (14-18 hours), Machala (11 hours), Manta (8 hours), Portoviejo (8 hours), Puyo (7 hours), Riobamba (4 hours), Santo Domingo (2½ hours), Tena (9 hours), Esmeraldas (6 hours), Otavalo (2½ hours), Ibarra (2½ hours) and Tulcán (5½ hours). There are no direct buses to Peru or Colombia. Reytur (E. Gangotena 158 y Orellana, Tel: 546-674) run an "international" bus to Lima, but this still involves a change at the border. It is cheaper to take a bus to Huaquillas, cross the border and take a **taxi colectivo** to Tumbes, where regular buses connect with Lima. Panamericana (Av. Colón y Reina Victoria) opperate a deluxe service from Quito to Huaquillas. Both Reytur and Panamericana offer services to Colombia, though this again involves changing buses at the border.

Car Rental Agencies

Avis Rent a Car, Colón 1741 y 10 de Agosto. Tel: 550-238. A variety of models (including four-wheeled drive vehicles) are available. Most rental agencies prefer credit cards.
Budget Rent a Car, Av. Amazonas y Colón. Tel: 237-026.
Ecuacar, Colón 1280 y Amazonas. Tel: 529-781. The company also has a branch at the airport.
Hertz, Veintimilla 938 y Amazonas. Tel: 560-628.

Consulates & Embassies

Austria, Av. Coruna 1224 y San Ignacio. Tel: 503-456.
Bolivia, C. B Lavayen y Juan Pablo Sanz. Tel: 458-863.
Brazil, Av. Amazonas1429 y Colón, edif Espana, 10th floor. Tel: 563086.
Canada, Av. 6 de Diciembre 2816 y J. Orton. Tel: 543-214.
Chile, Juan Pablo Sanz 3617 y Amazonas. Tel: 249-403.
Colombia, Av. Atahualpa 955 y Republica, 3rd floor. Tel: 458-012.
Germany, Av. Patria y 9 de Octubre, edif Consolidado, 6th floor. Tel: 225-660.
Peru, Av Amazonas 1429 y Colón, edif Espana, 2nd floor. Tel: 527-678.
Sweden, A. Jerves 134 y Orellana. Tel: 509-514.
Switzerland, Av. Amazonas 3617 y Panz, edif Xerox. Tel: 464-948.
United Kingdom, same address. Tel: 560-670/560-671.
United States, Av. 12 de Octubre y Patria. Tel: 562-890.

Day Trips From Quito

The capital Quito makes a good starting point for many day-long excursions into the lush surrounding Andean sierra. Either by hiring a car, taking a tour or using public transport, there are several popular trips into a region crowded with magnificent mountain views, waterfalls, thermal baths, and peaceful villages.
To the Equatorial Line Monument and the crater of Pululahua: Crossing the northern Quito suburb of Cotocollao and the village of Pomasqui, one reaches the valley of the Monjas river, where grapes are grown. These, incidentally, are the only vineyards of the country. Sadly, the wine they produce is difficult to recommend. After 22 km (14 miles) is the Equatorial Line Monument, at an altitude of 2,483 meters (7,200 ft), located right on latitude 0°. It provides an irresistible opportunity to straddle both hemispheres. The monument forms the focal point of a park and leisure area with gift shops, restaurants, etc. (among others, the Equinoccio, which on request distributes certificates recording the traveler's visit to the Equator), and has a good museum inside. A lift leads to the top for fine views; one then walks

down and encounters different Indian cultures every few steps. (Admission Tuesday to Friday, 9am–3pm, Saturdays and Sundays, 10am–1pm).

Outside the monument there are busts dedicated to the members of the French Geodesic mission which visited the country from 1736 to 1742. The exact equatorial line was determined by Charles de la Condamine. Nearby, a small village in Colonial style was created by the provincial authorities of Pichincha.

Buses to the Equatorial Line Monument ("Mitad del Mundo" – Middle of the World) leave every half hour from the market place near La Merced church in Quito's old town, or you can pick it up on Av. America in the new town. Taxis will charge about US$20 for the return trip, including waiting time.

A few miles beyond the monument – towards the village of Calacali at Km 4 to the right – is the biggest volcanic crater of South America, Pululahua. A paved road leads to the rim of the volcano, which is well worth seeing. The view of the farms on the crater floor is rather impressive. There is a rough path down from the rim, and the interior of the extinct crater has its own warm micro-climate and a rich vegetation.
To the valley of Chillos and its thermal springs: The valley of Chillos (Valle de Los Chillos) forms, together with the valley of Tumbaco, the Quito basin (*hoya*) and is a major resort area for the inhabitants of the capital. Quite a number of wealthy Quiteños live here: San Rafael, Conocoto and Sangolqui are the main villages of the valley, which is separated from the valley of Tumbaco by the small mountain Ilaló (3,869 meters, 10,400 ft), an extinct volcano with thermal springs in its surroundings. It is possible to climb the peak of the Ilaló for a lovely view and to relax in one of the semi-private swimming clubs like the Club Campestre Ilaló.

There is a fine descent into the valley on the Via Oriental and a highway called Autopista de Los Chillos (running east of Quito). The highway crosses the main road of the Valle de Los Chillos in San Rafael (12.5 km/8 miles). On the right-hand side, an old road leads back to Quito via Conocoto. Straight ahead lies the village of Sangolqui (18,000 inhabitants), which has a colorful Sunday market with Indians in traditional dresses and thermal baths nearby (try the Club Campestre Los Chillos).

To the south of here are Amaguaña and Tambillo (30 km/22 miles from Quito), where the Pan-American Highway runs. To the north (taking a left at San Rafael) are the thermal springs of Ushimana, El Tingo, La Merced (9 km/6 miles; the Hostería Angamarca has a swimming pool, restaurant and comfortable rooms) and the country club at Ilaló. The Balneario Ushimana is very small, but clean (open only on Saturdays and Sundays, 8.30am–4pm). The thermal springs El Tingo are the oldest in Ecuador (opened in 1928) and overcrowded on weekends. The pools of La Merced, beyond the town of Alangasi have picnic and camping areas nearby. The Club Campestre Ilaló is bigger and has facilities for ball games and rowing.

To the valley of Tumbaco and Papallacta: Just below the Hotel Quito lies the tiny village of Guápulo with its four-century old church. Passing on down the mountain, crossing the Machángara river, the road curves. The next major road on the right (14.3 km/11 miles from Quito) leads to the warm-water swimming pools of Cununyacü (temperature 26°C, open daily from 7am–3.45pm). Back on the main road one reaches the village of Cumbayá (with restaurants), where a road branches off (right-hand) to Guangopolo, a favorite picnic spot along the river and a fine place for birdwatching. It continues to the valley of Chillos, through unpopulated countryside, winding along the San Pedro river.

The next village on the main road is Tumbaco which has a good restaurant, El Tambo, with many weekend-houses of Quiteños attracted to the milder climate. At Km 20 the road crosses the Chiche river. Beyond the river one can turn left to head northwards for Puembo (where the future international airport of Quito may be built) and Quinche (with a sanctuary of the Virgin of Quinche).

The main road (not paved, but well-maintained) ascends the Eastern Cordillera and reaches an altitude of 4,100 meters (12,00 ft) with a statue of the virgin at the highest point. Descending the other side, one has a wonderful view (to the right) of the snow-capped Antisana (5,704 meters/17,000 ft), and snow and sub-tropical forests lie close together, a quite extraordinary sight. At Km 59, the small lake Papallacta is renowned for trout-fishing. Then at Km 60, a narrow road branches off to the hot thermal springs of Huanonumpa (with three small pools; facilities for bathers and a restaurant; overcrowded on weekends).

The village of Papallacta (62 km/36 miles from Quito) is known for the pipeline from the oil fields in the Oriente that emerges here and sometimes snaps because of landslides. The main road continues to Baeza and then northwards to the oil fields and Lago Agrio, the capital of the Amazon province of Sucumbios in the Ecuadorian Oriente.

To the volcano of Antisana: The road to the Antisana mountains (5,704 meters/17,000 ft) begins at the main plaza of the village of Alangasi. From there it leads through the village of Pintag (2,880 meters/8,700 ft; 12 km/7 miles from Alangasi, 33 km/20 miles from Quito), and continues southwards towards the Hacienda Pinantura past some unusual lava formations. To enter the Hacienda you will need special permission from the owner (Carlos Delgado, Av. 6 de Diciembre 1024, Quito). The road which leads to the foot of the Antisana (inside the territory of the Hacienda) is steep and muddy and can only be covered in a 4-wheel drive vehicle. The last few hundred meters have to be covered on foot. Condors, rainbow ducks and other birds may be seen.

The Antisana has three peaks, covered by eternal snow and numerous glaciers, which are very difficult to climb. The whole area is an extraordinary wilderness area and well worth the effort of getting there.

To Nono and the valleys of Mindo and Nanegal: This excursion into an impressive and varied landscape which will appeal to orchid and butterfly lovers is one that very few people from Quito know well.

Proceeding from Quito's northern suburb of Cotocollao and crossing Avenida Occidental, going uphill, you hit the road to Nono (33 km/20 miles). It ascends to an altitude of 3,350 meters/10,000 ft, and then winds down slowly. A few kilometers beyond Nono, the road forks: the right-hand road descends north to Nanegalito (61 km/35 miles. On the way to Nanegalito is the **Maquipucuna Biological Reserve** (office in Quito, Baquerizo 238 y Tamayo, tel: 507-200) consisting of steeply-sloped, undisturbed cloud forest, housing a high diversity of fauna and flora. The **Bellavista Reserve** (for info contact Safari Tours, tel: 552-505) is on the old road to Mindo at km 68, also located in lush forest, with great views over the valley. **Bosque Mindo-Nambillo**, near to the town of Mindo itself is a protected reserve, home to a wide range of birds, orchids and bromeliads.

To the Pasochoa woods: These woods (at 2,700 to 4,400 meters/7,100 to 13,200 ft) are set around a dead volcano and situated in the southeastern extreme of the *hoya* of the Guayllabamba river, a few kilometers from Amaguaña/Valle de Los Chillos (see above).

It is the only area near Quito that has been able to keep its Andean vegetation intact, and the woods are a sanctuary of native plants (orchids bloom from February to May). It is also a refuge for birds and mammals. For these reasons, the Pasochoa has been declared a protection forest and is being administered by the *Fundación Natura* (Nature Foundation), which organizes excursions to this little paradise regularly (offices: Quito, Av. America 5653 y vos Andes, tel: 447-341).

Staying out: One unusual option for exploring the Sierra is to stay at converted colonial *haciendas,* as below:
North of Quito
Hostería Chorla VI, Km 4 Pan-Americana Sur, Ibarra. Tel: 932-222.
Hostería Cusin, Lago San Pablo, Otavalo. Tel: 918-013.
Hostería La Mirage, Cotocahi (Imbabura Province). (P.O. Box 11365 CCNU, Quito). Tel: 915-237.
Hostería San Agustín, Pan-Americana Sur Km 1Y2, Ibarra. Tel: 955-888.
South of Quito
Hacienda La Cienega, Pan-Americana Sur Km 72, Lasso. Tel: 719-182.
Hosteria Guachala, on the road to Cangahua, just south of Cayambe. Make reservations in Quito, Reina Victoria 1138. Tel: 563-748.

Drugstores

Regular medicine can be bought without a prescription in most pharmacies (*farmacias*). The newspapers list *farmacias de turno*, those which are open on Sunday or at night. Most drugstores will give injections as well as the disposable serum needles (beware of non-disposable needles!)

Hospitals & Doctors

Air Ambulance. Tel: 432-368. Most embassies have telephone numbers of recommended dentists, but **Clínica de Especialidades Odontologicas**, Av. Orellana 1782 y 10 de Agosto. Tel: 521-383, can be called in cases of dental emergency 24 hours a day.
Ambulance Service and Blood Bank (Red Cross). Tel: 516-089, 24 hours.
Analisis Médicos Automatizados, Alpellana 477 y Whymper. Tel: 545-945. For amoebic dysentery tests. Tel: 235-350.
Centro Médico Alemania, Alemania 237 y Eloy Alfaro. Tel: 528-044 and 245-098. Dr Klier speaks German and English.
Clínica Pichincha, Veintimilla 1259. Tel: 561-643.
Clínica Santa Cecilia, Veintimilla 1394 (near 10 de agosto). For gamma globulin prescriptions and injections.
Hospital Metropolitano, Av. Marlana de Jesus y Occidental. Tel: 431-520. Best and most expensive in Quito. English speaking doctors available.
Hospital Voz Andes, Villalengua 263. Tel: 241-540. American-run, with an emergency room. Most doctors speak some English.

Hotels
Luxury

Alameda Real, Roca 655 y Av. Amazonas. Tel: 564-185. Numerous suites; gallery of stores; several restaurants and coffee shop, bar etc. Recently renovated.
Colón International, Av. Amazonas y Patria. Tel: 560-666. All rooms have cable TV (US programs); shopping mall; several restaurants and bars; coffee shop; disco; sports facilities (swimming-pool, sauna, gymnasium); hairdresser.
Hotel Quito, Av. Gonzalez Suaréz 2500. Tel: 544-600. All rooms with ca-

ble TV (US programs) several restaurants and bars; coffee shop; night club; sports facilities (heated pool); quiet, with splendid view and very pleasant gardens.
Oro Verde, Av. 6 de Diciembre. Tel: 566-497. Quito's newest luxury hotel. Numerous suites and executive suites; several restaurants; disco; sports facilities (heated pool, fitness center).

First Class

Chalet Suisse, Reina Victoria 312 y Calama. Tel: 562-700. Excellent food, night club, casino etc.
Hotel Sebastian, Almagro 822 y Cordero. Tel: 222-400. Comfortable.
Tambo Real, 12 de Octubre y Patria. Tel: 563-822. Opposite the US embassy.

Very Good & Good Hotels

Ambassador, 9 de Octubre 1052 y Colón. Tel: 561-777. Newly opened, excellent food, clean, spacious, good service.
Cafe Cultura, Reina Victoria y Robles. Tel: 224-271. Converted mansion. Great Danish breakfasts.
Hostal Los Alpes, Tamayo 233 y Washington, behind US embassy. Tel: 561-110. Very comfortable.
Hotel Santa Barbara, 12 de Octubre 2263. Tel: 564-382. Attractive renovated house.
Real Audencia, Bolívar 220 y Guayaquil. Tel: 512-711. Well-furnished, spacious rooms, restaurant has fine view of Old Quito.

Apartment-Hotels

Amaranta, Leonidas Plaza 194. Tel: 527-191. Luxuriously furnished apartments with kitchenette.
Apart Hotel, Rodriguez 175 y Almagro. Tel: 506-834. Well furnished attractive apartments.
Cafecito, Cordero 1124 y Reina Victoria. Tel 234-862. Shared rooms. Cafe downstairs.
El Taxo, Foch 909 y Cordero, near Av. Amazonas. Tel: 225-593. Hostel-like shared rooms, but spotlessly clean, in a former mansion.
Magic Bean, Foch 681 y J.L. Mera. Tel 566-181. Mostly shared rooms, good restaurant, central location in new town.
Mariscal, Robles 958. Tel: 528-833. Well furnished apartments, but noisy.

Inexpensive Hotels for Students and Globetrotters

Marsella, Los Rios y Castro. The pick of the budget hotels, US$6 a double, hot water, friendly atmosphere, rooftop terrace. Tel: 515-884.
Posada del Maple, Rodriguez 148 y 6 de Diciembre. Tel 544-507. Friendly atmosphere with kitchen and cable tv-room.

Language Classes

Quito is considered one of the best places in Latin America to learn Spanish. There are dozens of cheap places offering classes, with their advertisements in the hotels, bars and restaurants frequented by young gringos. Classes can be taken by the hour, by the day or by the week. Also, many organizations offer intensive courses where you actually board with an Ecuadorian family and are usually on a one-to-one basis.

The following have been recommended:
La Lengua: Av. Colón 1001 y J.L. Mera, Edif Av. Maria. Tel: 501-271.
Escuela de Espanol "Simon Bolívar": Andalucia 565 y Salazar. Tel: 502-640.
Academia Latinoamerica de Espanol: Jose Queri 2 y Eloy Alfaro.

Nightlife

Elegant nightclubs and discotheques are **Licorne**, at the Hotel Colón Internacional and **Techo del Mundo** at the Hotel Quito. For great salsa dancing go to **Seseribo** at Edificio El Giron, Veintimilla y 12 de Octubre. **Arribar**, J.L. Mera 1238 y Garcia and **NoBar**, Calama 442 y Amazonas are popular with young people.

Taberna Quiteña, (Amazonas 1259 y Colón, and in the Old Town Calle Manabí y Luis Vargas), has a cellar bar atmosphere and musicians who wander through from table to table.

The *peñas* are popular and good for local folk music. Try Nucanchi Peña, Av. Universitaria 496. There are casinos at the hotels **Chalet Suisse**, **Colón Internacional**, **Quito** and **Oro Verde**.

Police & Fire Department

Firemen (Cuerpo de Bomberos). Tel: 102.
General Emergency. Tel: 131.
Police: Cuenca y Mideres (in old town).
Radio Patrol (Policia). Tel: 101.
Red Cross. Tel: 131.

Post Office & Communications

The main post office for Poste Restante (in Spanish *La Lista de Correos*) service is at Espejo 935 y Guayaquil. The post office in the new town is at Reina Victoria y Colón in the Ecuatoriana building. Packages need to be sent from the branch at Ulloa 273 y Davalos, also in the new town. Letters for mailing may be dropped at the reception desks of the hotels Colón and Quito at any time. Stamps may be purchased in the bookshops of these hotels during store hours.

Faxes can also be sent from both the above hotels or the EMETEL office at Av. Iode Agosto y Colón. Open daily 8am–10pm Long-distance calls can be made from the same office. English-speaking operators are on duty at all times. Telephone calls are less expensive from 7pm–5am and all day on Sunday (with a three-minute minimum charge).

Railways

Quito's train station is 2 km (1 mile) south of the center, on Av. P. Vicente Maldonado near Llanganates. There is a Saturday service to Riobamba. Tickets need to be bought on the Friday morning from the train station itself. For the Sunday train to Cotopaxi tickets are on sale all week at the administration office in the old town, Calle Bolívar 443 y Benalcazar.

Metropolitan Touring (Amazonas 234) operates a tour by train which includes an overnight at a first-class Riobamba hotel (Tuesdays, Thursdays and Saturdays); and another train service which includes Cuenca.

Religious Services

Roman Catholic services are held regularly in Quito's churches. Services other than Catholic are held at:
Carolina Adventist Church, Av. 10 de Agosto 3929. Tel: 239-995. Meetings on Saturdays at 9am.
Central Baptist Church, Rios 1803. Tel: 513-074. Sunday services 9am and 6pm.
Church of Jesus Christ of the Latter Day Saints, Almagro y Colón. Tel: 529-602. Sunday service 9.30am.
Lutheran Church, Isabel la Católica 1431. Tel: 234-391. Sunday services: 9am in English; 10.15am in German; 11.30am in Spanish.
Synagogue, Versalles y 18 de Septiembre. Services Friday 7pm.

Restaurants

Most of the best restaurants are in the New Town, around Amazonas, Colón and 6 de Diciembre. There are several outdoor cafés along Amazonas where you can take in the sun and street life during the day. At night, a stroll along Amazonas is a good start to restaurant-hunting.

International

El Dorado, In the Hotel Colón. Tel: 521-300. Excellent; good breakfast and pastries in the hotel's cafeteria.
Excalibur, Calama 380 y Juan León Mera. Tel: 541-272. Very elegant and pricey.
Balcón Quiteño, In Hotel Panecillo. Tel: 517-277. Good food, good service, fine view.
Magic Bean, Foch 681 y Juan León Mera. Tel: 566-181. A well known place for younger people to hang out. Good salads, pancakes, great coffee and cakes.
Oro Verde Hotel. Good food, good service. Also excellent Japanese restaurant.
Pym's, On Calama, not far from Amazonas. A well-known place for younger people to hang out. Excellent hamburgers, and good cheese plates. Chilean wines served; comfortable.
Superpapa, On Juan León Mera 741 between Roca and Robles. Serves huge potatoes with chili; also muesli and fruit for breakfast. Popular with younger travelers.
Techo del Mundo, In Hotel Quito. Tel: 544-600.

Local Dishes

La Choza, 12 de Octubre 1821 y Cordero. Tel: 230-839. Typical food, safe, in nice surroundings.

Las Redes, Amazonas 845 y Veintimilla. Tel: 525-691. Known for its *cebiches* and other seafood specialities in informal surroundings.
La Terraza del Tartaro, Veintimilla 926 y Amazonas. Tel: 527-987. Penthouse elevator in rear of entry, fine view, good food.
Rincon La Ronda, Belo Horizonte 400 y Almagro. Tel: 540-549. Good, typical food, live music at weekends.
Taberna Quiteña, Amazonas 1259 y Cordero. Good Ecuadorian food with live entertainment provided.

French

La Belle Epoque, Eduardo Whymper 925 (between 6 de Diciembre and Diego de Almagro). Tel: 222-506. Expensive but excellent restaurant. Reservation necessary.
Rincón de Francia, General Roca 779 y 9 de Octubre. Tel: 554-668. Very good reputation for French specialities. Reservation necessary.

German

El Ciervo zum Hirsch, Ramirez Dávalos y Paez (near Amazonas). Tel: 543-116. Excellent German and international food.
Taberna Bavaria, Cordero 1313. Tel: 563-380. Good and typical German food, pleasant atmosphere.

Spanish

El Meson de la Pradera, Orellana Y 6 de Diciembre Tel 504-815. Good food and service in elegant converted mansion,
La Paella Valenciana, La República y Diego de Almagro. Tel: 239-681. Deliciously prepared Spanish dishes.

Steak Houses

La Casa de Mi Abuela, Juan León Mera 1649. Excellent Argentinian cuts of beef. Tel: 565-667.
Rincon del Gaucho, Almagro 422 y Calama. Good grilled steaks.
Shorton Grill, Calama 216 y Almagro Tel 523-645.

Italian

Pizza Hut – Espejo, downhill from Plaza Independencia.
– Juan León Mera 566 y Carrion.
– Naciones Unidas y Amazonas.
(Other pizzerias, such as El Hornero, are open along Amazonas).
La Gritta, Belo Horizonte 338 y 6 de

Diciembre. Tel: 230-709. Delicious home made pasta.

La Scala, Salazar 958 y 12 de Octubre. Tel: 229-502. Good food, pleasant atmosphere.

Taberna Piemonte, Calle J Arosemena Tola 173 y Eloy Alfaro. Tel: 433-608. Expensive, but well prepared and typical Italian food.

Chinese

Casa China, Cordero 613 y Tamayo. Tel: 522-115. Good Chnese food.

Hong Kong, Lizardo García y Eduardo Xaua (off 12 de Octubre). Tel: 226-374. Excellent.

Arabian

Tarek, Calama 336. Tel: 425-128. Excellent authentic Arabian food, Syrian style.

Cuban

La Bodega de Cuba, Reina Victoria 1721 y La Pinta. Tel: 542-476. Good food, pleasant setting and atmosphere.

Vegetarian

El Marquez, Calama 443 y Amamzonas. Inexpensive, very popular at lunchtime.

Flying Duchman, La Pinta 146 y Reina Victoria. Tel: 527-842. Imaginative selection of dishes.

Shopping

There are dozens of *artesanías* stores and kiosks in Quito, especially in the Avenida Rio Amazonas area. Several have outstanding selections of high quality folk art and clothing. They include:

Almacén Folklore Olga Fisch, Av. Colón 260. There is also a branch in the Hotel Colón.

Centro Artesanal, Calle Juan León Mera 804.

Exedra, Carrion 243 y Plaza. *Artesania* centre.

Galería Latina, Calle Juan León Mera 833.

La Bodega Artesanías
– Calle Juan León Mera 614.

Sports

There is a public swimming pool at Av. Universitaria y Nicaragua and also one at Cochapata, near Villarroel y 6 de Diciembre. The El Condado Country Club is for golf players (temporary membership is available); it has an 18-hole course, a heated swimming pool and riding facilities. Fuente de Juventud, Republica 855 y Eloy Alfaro, open Tuesday–Sunday, 9am–9pm, has an indoor pool, whirlpool sauna, steam room, weight lifting and other gym equipment. Tel: 247-722/ 529-152. The Municipal Tennis Club, Amazonas y Atahualpa (tel: 242-918) has recently added a swimming pool and sauna that can be used by non-members.

Theaters & Cinemas

Teatro Prometeo, Adjoining the Casa de la Cultura Ecuatoriana.

Teatro Sucre, Calle Flores y Guayaquil. Tel: 216-668. The most fancy and also the most traditional of the theaters (plays, concerts, shows).

There are about 20 cinemas. The **Colón**, (10 de Agosto y Colón), **República** (Av. República) and **Universitário** (Av. America) have the best films. Check newspapers for listings. **The Casa de la Cultura** also shows good films.

Travel Agencies

There are travel agencies all over Avenida Amazonas and in the major hotels. As mentioned elsewhere in this section, a reliable bet is **Metropolitan Touring** on Amazonas 239. Tel: 506-650, Fax: 560-807. Other options include:

Angermeyers, Foch 726 y Amazonas. Tel: 569-960, Fax: 569-956.

Ecuadorian Tours, Amazonas 339. Tel: 560-488, Fax: 501-067.

Etnotur, Juan León Mera 1238. Tel: 564-565.

Explorer Tours, García y Reina Victoria. Tel: 522-220.

Galasam, Pinto 523 y Amazonas. Tel: 561-470, Fax: 567-662.

Nuevo Mundo Expediciones, Amazonas 2464. Tel: 552-617, Fax: 565-261.

Cuenca A – Z

Airlines

SAETA, Benigno Malo 727. Tel: 839-090, Fax: 835-5113.

TAME, 9 de Octubre 424. Tel: 561-751, Fax: 562-279. (Daily connections with Quito and Guayaquil.)

Buses

The **Terminal Terrestre** is in Av. España, northwest of the City center. All long-distance buses leave from here. (To Riobamba 5½ hours; Ambato 7½ hours; Quito 10½ hours; Loja 4 hours; Guayaquil 5 hours; Macas 11 hours; Gualaquiza 7 hours).

Hotels

Luxury

El Dorado, Gran Colombia y Luis Cordero. Tel: 831-390. The best hotel downtown, excellent restaurant, discotheque, sauna, pastry-shop and cafeteria.

Oroverde, Av. Ordoñez Lasso. Tel: 831-200. Brand-new, out of town, beautifully situated on lake with rowing-boats; belongs to a Swiss hotel chain; excellent restaurant "La Cabaña Suiza", heated open-air swimming-pool, gymnasium, discotheque.

First-Class

Crespo, Calle Largha 793. Tel: 831-837. Great variety of rooms, all very clean and cozy, with private bath, color TV, central heating. Some overlook the Tomebamba river. Swimming-pool, Turkish bath and French restaurant.

Very Good & Good

Conquistador, Gran Colombia 665. Tel: 831-788. Good value; discotheque "Fernando's", cheap for International Youth Hostel Federation members.

President, Gran Colombia 659 y Hermano Miguel. Tel: 831-066. New, with restaurant.

Budget

Cabanas Yanuncay, Calle Canton Gualaceo 2149, between Av. Loja y Av. de las Américas. Tel: 883-716, Fax: 819-681. Cabins, in country setting, 5 mins drive from centre. Guests can be collected from bus station.

Hostal Macondo, Calle Tarqui 1164. Tel: 831-198. Colonial house with kitchen and laundry facilities.

Money Exchange

Cambiazuay, Borrero 838 y Bolívar. Tel: 823-536.

Citibank, Gran Colombia 749, Only accept cash and personal checks.

Other Addresses

Airport: Tel: 862-203

Clinica Santa Ana: Av. Manuel J. Calle 1-104. Tel: 814-068. Good medical centre. 24 hour emergency service.

EMETEL: Benigno Malo y Cordova.

Immigration: Policia Nacional de Migraciones, Benigno Malo y Larga.

Red Cross (Cruz Roja): Antonio Borrero 563. Tel: 862-203.

Regional Hospital: Av. del Paraiso. Tel: 811-099.

Restaurants

El Tunel, General Torres 860. Tel: 823-109. Good local food.

Govinda, Honorato Velasquez 756 y Cordero. Vegetarian, excellent juices, clean.

Jardin, P. Cordova 727. Tel: 821-120. Considered to be one of the best restaurants in Ecuador, international food – nouvelle cuisine.

La Tuna, Gran Colombia. Pizzeria, good and popular.

Los Capulis, Presidente Cordova y Borrero. Lively atmosphere, good food and live music.

Rancho Chileno, Av. España 1317. Tel: 800-657. Chilean dishes, pleasant ambience.

Villa Rosa, Gran Colombia y Tarqui. Tel: 837-942. Attractive setting, excellent international and local food.

Shopping

The handicraft shops along Gran Colombia, near El Dorado Hotel, include **Ocepa**, **Productos Andinos**, **Artesanías**

Atahualpa, **Arte Artesanías**, **Arte del Pacífico** and **Artesanías Paucartambo**. High quality Panama hats are made by **Romero Ortega**, Vega Muñoz 9-53, Tel: 823-429, who exports hats worldwide.

Tourist Office

CETUR, Hermano Miguel 686 y Cordova. Tel: 839-337.

Travel Agencies

Aeromar, Calle Larga 6102 y Hno Miguel. Tel: 835-697.

Ecuadorian Tours, Benigno Malo 747. Tel: 832-328.

Metropolitan Touring, Mariscal Sucre 662. Tel: 831-185.

Rootours, Calle Larga 890 y Benigno Malo. Tel: 835-888.

Esmeraldas A – Z

Airlines

TAME has flights to Quito daily.

A bridge over the river at San Mateo (upstream from Esmeraldas) connects with the General Rivadeneira airport, 25 km (15½ miles) away. The TAME office (at the corner of the main plaza – tel: 71-2663) will help organize a shared-taxi service to the airport.

Boats

Enquire at the Capitania del Puerto about boat departures (occasionally to Guayaquil and Manta, more frequently to Limones).

Buses

There is no central bus terminal. Aerotaxi is the fastest line: leaves for Quito from the main plaza (journey time 5 hours, frequent departures); Panamericana has a luxury service to Quito once a day, leaving from Hotel Casino; Transportes Occidentales or Trans-Esmeraldas, Av. Piedrahita 200, have large, slower buses (to Quito 7 hours, Santo Domingo 3½ hours,

Guayaquil 9 hours, Machala 12 hours); Cooperativa Sudamericana have buses for Ambato (8 hours); Reina del Camino to Portoviejo (9 hours) and Bahia de Caraquez (8 hours).

Provincial buses leave from the *La Costenita*, or waterfront area. Times: Atacames and Sua (1 hour), Muisne (3½ hours) – very frequent departures. Buses run also to La Tola (5 hours). The road is good until Rio Verde; there is a combined bus/boat service to San Lorenzo.

Hotels

Apart Hotel Esmeraldas, Av. Libertad 407 y Ramon Tello. Tel: 728-700. All rooms with private bath, air conditioning and color TV; good restaurant.

Cayapas, Av. Kennedy y Valdez. Tel: 711-022. Transformed mansion in colonial style, nice rooms, restaurant.

Colonial, Plata y L. Tello, Las Palmas. Nicely situated, close to the Las Palmas beach, under French management, excellent food.

Del Mar, Av. Kennedy, Las Palmas. Tel: 713-910. New, close to the Las Palmas beach.

Diana, Manuela Cañizares y Sucre. Tel: 710-333. Rooms with TV and private bath, good value.

Estuario, Av. Libertad y Gran Colombia. Tel: 713-930. Modern and spotlessly clean, air conditioning, good restaurant.

Money Exchange

Casa de Cambio Rodrigo Paz, Bolívar 516. Tel: 710-460. Several banks are represented in Esmeraldas (open until noon).

Other Addresses

CETUR (Tourist Office), Boliviar 517. Tel: 430-868.

Hospital, Av. Libertad y Parada 8. Tel: 710-012.

Immigration office (Migración y Extranjeria), Av. Olmedo y Rocafuerte. Tel: 720-256.

Police, Sucre 1111. Tel: 711-510.

Post office and telecommunications (EMETEL), J. Montaño y Malecón. Tel: 710-000.

Restaurants

Atenas Tiffany, Av. Kennedy 707, recommended.
Budapest, Manuela Cañizarez 216, Hungarian owner.
Chifa Asiatico, Manuela Cañizarez 227, seems to be the best of the Chífas, or Chinese restaurants.
Tia Carmen, Sucre y 9 de Octubre, good but inexpensive. A typical local dish is *encocado* – fish, crabs or shrimp cooked in coconut cream served with rice and plantains.

Guayaquil A – Z

Airlines

International

(*phone code: 5934*)
Aerolineas Argentinas, Pedro Moncayo 707 y V.M. Rendón. Tel: 302-141.
AeroPeru, Chile 329 y Aguirre. Tel: 513-691, Fax: 513-671.
Air France, Aguirre 106. Tel: 320-313, Fax: 320-313.
American Airlines, Cordova 1021 y 9 de Octubre. Tel: 566-902.
AVIANCA, Rendon 416 y Cordova. Tel: 314-091, Fax: 310-713.
British Airways, Vélez 206. Tel: 323-834, Fax: 3265-419.
Copa, Urdesa, Circunvalacion Sur 631-A y Ficus. Tel: 883-751, Fax: 881-528.
Iberia, Av. 9 de Octubre 101. Tel: 326-085, Fax: 327-886.
KLM, Aguirre 411. Tel: 328-028, Fax: 324-130.
Lacsa, Cordova 1040 y 9 de Octubre. Tel: 562-950, Fax: 562-958.
LADEC, Malecón 1400. Tel: 324-360, Fax: 534-575.
Lufthansa, Malecón 1400. Tel: 324-360, Fax: 325-477.
SAETA, Vélez 206 y Chile. Tel: 329-855. CJ Arosemena Km 2.5. Tel: 205-115. Fax: 201-153.
Varig, Pedro Carbo 7 Av. 9 de Octubre. Tel: 560-876, Fax: 561-479.
VIASA, Pedro Moncayo 707 y Rendon. Tel: 562-141, Fax: 302-602.

Domestic

SAETA, Vélez 206 y Chile.
TAME, Av. 9 de Octubre 424. Tel: 300-714.

Airport

Guayaquil's international airport Simón Bolívar is 5 km (3 miles) from the city center. The taxi fare from the airport to town should not cost more than US$6. There is a *casa de cambio* (exchange house) at the airport as well as a CETUR information office (although the latter is rarely open).

Bookshops

Libreria Cervantes, Aguirre 606.
Libreria Científica, Luque 225 y Chile.
Libreria Universitaria, Chile 410.
Nuevos Horizonles, 6 de Marzo 924. Book exchange.

Car Hire

Budget Rent-a-car, García Moreno.
Hertz, Avis and International have offices at the airport and in the main hotels. Tel: 561-591 (Hertz), 285-498 (Avis), 304-393 (International).

Consulates & Embassies

Argentina, Aguirre 104. Tel: 530-767.
Austria, Av. 9 de Octubre 1312. Tel: 282-303.
Bolivia, P. Ycaza 302, office 601. Tel: 564-260.
Brasil, KM 7,5 Via a Duale, Textiles San Antonio. Tel: 252-899.
Canada, Cordova y Rendón. Tel: 563-580.
Chile, J. A. Campos 101 y G. Aviles. Tel: 562-995.
Colombia, Cordova 812 y Rendon. Tel: 563-308.
Denmark, Cordova 604. Tel: 308-020.
France, Aguirre 503 y Chimborazo. Tel: 328-159.
Germany, Av. 9 de Octubre 109. Tel: 512-700.
Great Britain, Cordova 623. Tel: 560-400.
Italy, Baquerizo Moreno 1120. Tel: 563-1360.
Netherlands, Ycaza 454 y Moreno. Tel: 562-777.
Norway, Av. 9 de Octubre 109. Tel: 322-738.
Peru, Av. 9 de Octubre 411, 6th floor. Tel: 322-738.
Spain, Circunvalacion Sur 118. Calle Unica. Tel: 380-265.
Sweden, Via a Daule Km 6.5. Tel: 254-111.
Switzerland, Av. 9 de Octubre 2105. Tel: 453-607.
United States of America, Av. 9 de Octubre y García Moreno. Tel: 323-570.
Venezuela, Chile 329. Tel: 326-566.

Emergencies

Firemen (*Bomberos*). Tel: 526-666.
Police (*Policía*). Tel: 392-230.
Red Cross (*Cruz Roja*). Tel: 300-744.

Exchange

Banco del Pacifico, Fco.P. Ycaza 200. Tel: 311-744.
Banco Popular, Pedro Carbo 555 y Av. 9 de Octubre. Tel: 328-980 (changes traveler's checks into cash dollars without commission).
Citibank, Av. 9 de Octubre y Lorenzo de Garaicoa. Tel: 564-650 (changes cash and personal checks only).
Filanbanco, 9 de Octubre y Cabo. Tel: 322-780.
LLoyds Bank, Calle Pichincha 108-110. Tel: 563-360.
There are several *casas de cambio* on Av. 9 de Octubre and on Av. Pichincha. Most of them accept travelers' checks; on weekends, change money in the larger hotels or at *Wander Cambios* in the airport.

Entertainment

The 18 cinemas in Guayaquil show English-language movies with Spanish subtitles. Enquire in the local newspapers or at the reception desks of the better hotels about what is going on. *Peñas* (folk music evenings) normally take place at weekends: recommended is **Rincón Folklorico**, Malecón 208 y Montalvo.

There are numerous discotheques. One of the most elegant is **Latin Palace**, out of town.

The first-class hotels also have discos; others include **Infinity**, Esrada 805; **Flashdance**, Aguirre 221; and **El Bucanero**, Av. de las Américas. *La Chiva* city tour is a lively open bus with music leaving from Infinity on Friday evenings. Contact Viajes Horizontes.

Local holidays include Bolívar's birthday July 24, followed by Guayaquil Foundation Day (July 25), when the city celebrates with parties and fiestas and it is difficult to get a hotel room. New Year's Eve is a lot of fun: along the Malecón, life-size dolls representing *el año viejo* (the old year) are carried around. At midnight all these figures are set on fire.

Casinos are found at the hotels Oro Verde, Unihotel, Continental and Ramada.

Hotels
Luxury
Continental, Chile y 10 de Agosto. Tel: 329-270.
Grand Hotel Guayaquil, Boyaca y Ballén. Tel: 329-690/329-698. Shares a city block with the cathedral; very comfortable and spacious rooms with air-conditioning and color TV, good restaurant, swimming-pool, sauna, gymnasium.
Oro Verde, Garcia Moreno y Av. 9 de Octubre. Tel: 327-999. Probably the best hotel in town; very comfortable rooms with air-conditioning and color TV; several restaurants serving international cuisine and Swiss dishes; swimming-pool and fitness center.
UNI Hotel, Ballén 400 y Chile. Tel: 327-100. 46 very comfortable table suites, several restaurants, swimming-pool, casino etc.

First-Class
Boulevard, Av. 9 de Octubre 432 y Chimborazo. Tel: 562-888. Situated amidst Guayaquil's commercial and banking area; comfortable rooms, restaurant *La Rotunda* and casino.
Ramada, Malecón y Orellana. Tel: 565-555. Very nice rooms with view of the Guayas river, excellent restaurant, indoor-swimming pool, discotheque, casino.

Very Good & Good
Hotel del Rey, Aguirre y Mann. Tel: 453-037. Comfortable; includes good breakfast.
Palace, Chile 214. Tel: 321-080.
Plaza, Chile 414. Tel: 327-140. Comfortable rooms with air conditioning and TV; good restaurant.
Sol de Oriente, Aguirre 603 y Escobed. Good, Chinese restaurant. Tel: 325-500.

Immigration
Av. Pichincha y Aguirre (Gobernación). Tel: 514-925.

Local Buses
Since taxis are very cheap in Guayaquil, buses and *colectivos* are mostly avoided by foreign visitors. But the *busetas* or minibuses are safe to ride. *Servicio especial* buses, marked with blue and white diagonal stripes are slightly more expensive but relatively efficient.

Long-Distance Buses
The **Terminal Terrestre** (Central Bus Terminal) is near the airport and the bridge over the Guayas river, and all long-distance buses leave from here. Journey times are: to Quito (8½ hours), Cuenca (7 hours), Riobamba (5 hours), Santo Domingo de los Colorados (5 hours), Manta (3 hours), Esmeraldas (7 hours), Portoviejo (3½ hours), Bahía de Caraquez (5½ hours), Machala (3½ hours), Huaquillas (5 hours), Ambato (6½ hours), Alausi (4 hours). There are also frequent buses to Salinas (2½ hours) and Playas/General Villamil (2 hours). There is a shared taxi-service to Machala (2½ hours), leaving from next door to the Hotel Rizzo, downtown.

Medical Services
Av. del Periodista. Tel: 286-963.
Clínica Kennedy, Tel: 396-963. English-speaking doctors, consulting rooms for external patients.
Clínica Santa Marianita, Boyaca 1915 y Colón. Tel: 322-500.
Dr Angel Serrano Saena, Av. Boyaca 821. Tel: 301-373. (English-speaking doctor.)
Dr Jorge Puente, Clemente Ballén 615. Tel: 524-044. (Speaks German)
Hospital Luis Vernaza, Julian Coronel 404. Tel: 300-300.
Emergency:
Aero Ambulance Aguire, 442 y Cordova. Tel: 308-584.

Post Office
Correo Central, Aguirre y Pedro Carbo.

Restaurants
International
Cafeteria Casa Tossi, Aguirre 212 (fifth floor). Good for inexpensive snacks.
El Parque, Top floor of Unicentro. Very good buffet lunch, overlooks Parque Bolívar.
La Posada de las Garzas, Circunalación Norte 536. Tel: 383-256. Exclusive atmosphere, very good international food.
Yacht Club, Malecón Simon Bolívar, (at the foot of Av. 9 de Octubre). Tel: 325-225. Request admission from the manager, excellent food in pleasant surroundings.

Local Food
Barandua Inn, Circunvalación Norte 528 B, at the shore of the Salado estuary. Tel: 389-407. Excellent seafood.
Galeria El Taller, Quisquis 1313, between Esmeraldas and Los Ríos. Tel: 393-904. Very typical Guayaquileño food and ambience, recommended.
Tertulia de Hilda, Hurtado y Tungurahua. Seafood with vegetables; exotic and highly recommended.

Fench
Anderson, Tulcá n 810 y Hurtado. Tel: 369-138.

Italian
La Carbonara, Bálsamos 108 y V.E. Estrada, Urdesa. Tel: 382-714. Delicious pasta and pizzas.
Trattoria da Enrico, Bálsamos 504 y Ebanos, Urdesa. Tel: 387-079. Very pleasant Italian ambience, rustic-elegant, excellent food.
Trattoria da Migliotini, Primera y Las Monjas, Urdesa. Tel: 382-475. Very good food and service.

Spanish
Juan Salvador Gaviota, Francisco Boloña 603, Ciudadela Vieja Kennedy. Tel: 395-621. Good paellas valencianas.

Chilean
El Caracol Azul, 9 de Octubre y Los Riod. Tel: 280-461. Considered to be one of the best seafood restaurants in Guayaquil.

Chinese
Gran Chifa, Pedro Carbo 1018. Tel: 512-488. Fine ambience, not too expensive.

Japanese

Tsuji, V.E. Estrada 813 y Guayacanes, Urdesa. Tel: 387-091. Exquisite Japanese food.

Pizzeria

Pizza Hut, Av. 9 de Octubre. Good and inexpensive.

Shopping

Guayaquil has four shopping centers: the Policentro, Unicentro, Centro Comercial Urdesa and the Alban Borja. To buy handicrafts of good quality **Lo Nuestro** and **Galería Guayasamín** (both at Policentro) are recommended. **Artesanías de Ecuador**, 9 de Octubre 104 y Malecón, is good and reliable. The **Mercado Artesanal** between Av. Loja y Montalia is also good.

Shopping at the Bahía (black market), located along Calles Pinchincha and Olmedo, is very popular with Guayaquileños.

Sports

There are many sports clubs in Guayaquil. Guests of the **Hotel Oro Verde** can use the facilities of the Tennis Club Guayaquil on request. Nearby there is an Olympic swimming pool, open to the public. Guests of the **Gran Hotel Guayaquil** can use the facilities of the Terraza Racquet Club (with two squash courts, gymnasium and sauna).

Telecommunications

EMETEL: Offices are located at Pedro Carbo y Aguirre and L. Urdaneta 426. Public telex booths exist, although it's easiest to do everything through your hotel.

Tourist Information

The CETUR office is located at Aguirre 104 y Malecón. Tel: 328-312. Open: Monday–Friday 9am–4pm CETUR organizes individually guided tours of Guayaquil on request.

Travel Agencies

Ecuadorian Tours, Av. 9 de Octubre 1900 y Esmeraldas. Tel: 287-111. American Express Agent.

Macchiavello Tours, Antepara 802 y 9 de Octubre. Tel: 286-079.

Metropolitan Touring, Antepara 915 y 9 de Octubre. Tel: 320-300, Fax: 323-050. The oldest and largest travel agency network in Ecuador is also probably its most efficient. Tours and ticketing of all kinds can be done here.

Otavalo

Travelers flock here for the Saturday market. Hotels are thus likely to be booked up early on Friday night and empty for the rest of the week.

The best hotel is a converted *hacienda,* slightly out of town, called the Hostería Cusín. It offers comfortable rooms and full board for about US$40 per person per night.

Hostería Cusin, Lago San Pablo, Otavalo. Tel: 918-013.

If you prefer to stay in town, try the comfortable Hotel El Indio, Bolíviar 904, tel: 920-325. Doubles cost $30.

The Galápagos Islands A – Z

Airlines

Flights are heavily booked so you should confirm and reconfirm your seat and check in early at the airport.

TAME has daily flights at 8.30am to Baltra, with connecting buses making the short trip to Puerto Ayora. Many cruises pick up their passengers directly at the airport and return them there. Note that if you are organizing your own cruise around the islands, Puerto Ayora is currently the best place to do it from.

SAETA flies to San Cristóbal Island every morning at 8am except Sundays. These flights coincide with departures of the company's luxury liner the *Galápagos Explorer* and several other tours. Note that if you want to be on Puerto Ayora, it can be quite difficult to get between the islands.

All non-Ecuadorian travelers to the islands must pay a US$80 entrance fee to the national park on arrival at the airport. This can be paid in *sucres* or dollars. Keep the receipt, since you may have to show it again.

Arranging a Cruise

The Galápagos archipelago is almost entirely a national park, and no visitor is allowed to enter it without a qualified guide on an organized tour. There are a range of different ways that this can be done: some travelers choose to take a series of different day trips from Puerto Ayora to the islands nearest Santa Cruz but, while this is cheap, it is not particularly satisfying (tour operators on the island will offer these for about US$30–50 a day). The great bulk of visitors go on a cruise around the islands, taking at least three nights – the more, the better. If you are going to spend the cash to come all this way, it is a pity to miss out on what must be classed as one of the world's great travel experiences.

Large cruisers: For many, a trip on one of the largest cruisers is the most comfortable and convenient way to visit the islands. The two best are the **Galápagos Explorer** run by SAN/Saeta from San Cristóbal island, and the **Santa Cruz** run by Metropolitan Touring. Both ships have all the comforts of a luxury liner, including excellent food in their dining room. By traveling overnight, these cruises can easily reach outer islands that smaller yachts sometimes struggle to get to. The going is naturally much smoother on a large ship too. Both boats make occasional trips from Guayaquil to the islands.

Both take around 80 passengers on three or four day cruises – one covering the northern islands, another the southern. You can also combine both trips to make a seven-day cruise. Passengers visit the islands in groups of 10 on motorboats (*pangas*) accompanied by English-speaking naturalist guides who all have university degrees in their fields.

The cost works out to between US$135 and US$225 per person per night on a twin-share basis (all inclusive, except for bar and airfare), depending on which cabin you select and how long the cruise.

Bookings for the *Santa Cruz* can be made at Metropolitan Touring in Quito or Guayaquil or their US agents Adventure Associates (see Travel Packages section of *Practical Tips* for contact numbers).

Tours with the Galápagos Explorer can be booked in Ecuador at any travel agent or SAETA office. In the United States and Europe, bookings can be made through:

Galápagos Inc, 7800 Red Rd, S Miami, Fl. Tel: 1 (305) 665-0841. Fax: 1 (305) 661-1457. Toll-free in the US: 1 (800) 327-9854.

Smaller yachts: There are literally dozens of yachts operating cruises around the islands, most of which work out of Puerto Ayora, although a growing number are basing themselves in Puerto Baquerizo Morena to deal with the influx of tourists from SAN/Saeta flights. They can take anything from 6–20 people, with the bigger boats being most stable in rough weather.

Tours on these boats can be booked on mainland Quito from a number of agencies. Metropolitan Touring, for example, runs five yachts at a luxury standard – check at their office for rates and availability. These trips are somewhat more costly than on the larger cruisers, but are also more intimate and still very luxurious. The agency can even arrange special scuba-diving trips for those who practise the sport.

Cheaper tours on small boats can be arranged at places like Galasam on Calle Pinto 523 y Av. Amazonas, tel: 561-470. It is worth checking with the South American Explorer's Club in Quito to find what the latest reports are on such smaller operators and thus to make sure you aren't being ripped off. When booking in Quito or Guayaquil, you are likely to pay around US$60 a day including food.

Situr and Ecoventura operate 20-berth boats with cruises from three to seven nights, and can be booked in the US through Galápagos Network, 7200 Corporate Centre Drive, Suite 404, Miami, FL 33126. Tel: (305) 592 2294, toll-free 1-800-633-7972. Fax: (305) 592-6394.

Diving: The following company offers scuba and diving tours, and diving instructions:

Galápago Sub-Aqua, Av. Charles Darwin, Puerto Ayora, Isla Santa Cruz. Tel/fax: 593-4-314510.

Organizing your own tour: This is the cheapest and most flexible way of visiting the islands, and for many independent travelers the most satisfying. Dozens of backpackers simply turn up at Puerto Ayora and begin getting a few people together to charter a boat – if you look like a candidate, travelers are likely to stop you in the street and come up to you in restaurants asking about your plans. The only drawback is that you need a few days to get the required number of people together and arrange a boat, so it's not a good idea to try to set it up in a hurry.

Boats take 8 or 12 people, and cost about US$40 a day with all meals inclusive. The South American Explorer's Club (Toledo 1254, Quito) offers the following hints for travelers doing this:

● Boat owners like to fill their boats to capacity. The group is usally expected to share the cost of any unsold passenger space.

● When dealing directly with the boat owner, bargaining is expected.

● Bottled drinks are not included in the cost of the cruise. Bring as much mineral water as you think you will need; you can buy it at the Puerto Ayora supermarket (at the docks).

● Every tour group should draw up a formal contract that states the planned itinerary – the SAEC leaflet on the Galápagos sold in Quito has a good prototype.

● Boat travel to the outer islands like Española and Genovesa can be quite rough, especially from September to November.

● Make sure the boats have enough sets of snorkelling gear.

The SAEC in Quito keeps lists of reports from travelers indicating which of the many boats are the best.

Camping

There are three official sites on the island of Santa Cruz: near the Darwin Research Station, at the Tortuga Bay and near the *caseta* in the tortoise reserve. Further information about camping sites and special permits can be obtained in the offices of the National Park administration.

Exchange

If you are taking a tour on one of the large cruise ships, there is no problem paying your tab in dollars or Ecuadorian *sucres*, and exchange facilities are available. Independent travelers can change foreign currency in Puerto Ayora, but at a poor rate, so bring whatever you need in *sucres* from the mainland. The Banco Nacional de Fomento does not accept credit cards. The hotel Sol y Mar and Ninfa restaurant accept travelers' checks; they pay about 50 percent less than for cash. Several shops will change US dollar bills. Note, however, that small charter boat owners arrange trips at a US dollar rate so accept cash or travelers' checks.

Hospital

There is a hospital in Puerto Ayora – consultations are free.

Hotels

At Puerto Ayora (Santa Cruz)

Delfin: Situated at the opposite side of Academy Bay, accessible only by boat. First-class, with private beach. Recommended.

Fernandina: budget, run by friendly family.

Gloria: simple and inexpensive.

Hotel Galápagos: First class; comfortable bungalows with private baths, ocean view, good restaurant.

Lirio del Mar: rooms with private bath, pleasant, with cafe.

Sol y Mar: Comfortable, clean, situated on the waterfront. US$20 per double. A good place for a cheap meal or breakfast whilst sitting among tame marine iguanas and a sealion that likes to watch the proceedings. Friendly and highly recommended.

Information

CETUR (Tourist office) in Puerto Ayora, near the pier, is open Monday–Friday 8am–noon and 3–6pm.

Restaurants

At Puerto Ayora

Four Lanterns, facing Pelican Bay. Good.

La Garrapata, popular meeting place for travelers.

Sol y Mar, good place for breakfast on terrace with *iguanas*.

Shopping

Food and drink are available in several stores on the main islands of Santa Cruz, San Cristóbal and Isabela, but medicines, sun lotions and film are either not available or extremely expensive.

Souvenirs made from black coral, turtle and tortoise shell are offered but, as these animals are protected, avoid buying them.

Traveling between the Islands

INGALA (Instituto Nacional de Galápagos) has official inter-island passenger services on Tuesdays and Saturdays from Santa Cruz to San Cristóbal, returning on Mondays and Wednesdays. On Thursday the INGALA boat leaves Santa Cruz for Isabela, on Friday Isabela for Floreana, returning to Santa Cruz at 12.

The INGALA office in Puerto Ayora is next to the hospital, in Puerto Baquerizo Moreno on the road leading inland at the edge of the town. Rolf Wittmer runs his boat *Tip Top* from Puerto Ayora to Puerto Velasco Ibarra (Floreana) regularly.

Further Reading

General

Pre-Columbian Studies

Bushnell, G.M.S., *The Archaeology of Santa Elena Peninsular*, Cambridge, 1951.
von Hagen, Victor Wolfgang (ed), *The Incas of Pedro de Cieza de León*, Oklahoma Press, 1959.

History and Society

Bork, A.W. and Mayer G., *Historical Dictionary of Ecuador*, New York, 1973.
Cavalho-Neto, P., *Diccionario del Folklore Ecuatoriano*, Casa de la Cultura, Quito, 1964.
Cueva Tamariz, A., *La Literatura Ecuatoriana*, Buenos Aires, 1968.
Drekonja, Gerhard, et al, *Ecuador Hoy*, Bogotá, 1978.
Hemming, John, *The Conquest of the Incas*, Penguin, 1987 (the classic account of the Spanish conquest).

Pike, F.P., *The United States and the Andean Republics*, Cambridge (Mass.), 1979.

Birdwatching

Hilty and Brown, *A Field Guide to the Birds of Ecuador*, Princeton, 1986.

Otavalo

Meisch, Lynn, *Otavalo: Weaving, Costume and the Market*, Ediciones Libri Mundi, 1987.

Travel

Whymper, Edward, *Travels Amongst the Great Andes of the Equator*, Peregrine Books, 1987 (amusing memoirs of the famous British mountaineer).

The Galápagos

Darwin, Charles, *The Voyage of the Beagle*, Penguin.
Jackson, M.H., *Galápagos: A Natural History*, University of Calgary Press, 1985 (without doubt the best guide to the islands).
Merlen, A, *Field Guide to the Fishes of the Galápagos*, Ediciones Libri Mundi, Quito, 1988.
Treherne, John, *The Galápagos Affair*, London, 1983 (an entertaining account of the scandals and murder occurring on Floreana in the 1930s).

Other Insight Guides

The *Insight Guides* series now has almost 190 titles, spanning every continent. Apa Publications has also created two companion series of guidebooks. *Insight Pocket Guides* provide short-stay visitors with a range of carefully selected timed itineraries and include full-size pull-out maps. *Insight Compact Guides* are handy mini-encyclopedias, ideal for on-the-spot use.

In the *Insight Guide* series, South America and Latin America are covered by books on *Argentina, Buenos Aires, Belize, Brazil, Rio de Janeiro, Amazon Wildlife, Chile, Costa Rica, Ecuador, Mexico, Mexico City, Peru*, and *Venezuela*.

Insight Guide: South America provides a country-by-country overview of the continent in more than 400 pages of incisive text and stunning photography.

Insight Guide: Costa Rica provides comprehensive coverage, from the coasts of the Caribbean and the Pacific to the rugged highlands and the national parks.

Insight Guide: Amazon Wildlife, one of Apa Publications' *Discover Nature* books, brings together an impressive team of naturalists and nature photographers to explore the wonders of the world's largest tropical rainforest.

Insight Guide: Belize explores the beautiful coral reefs, diving and ecotourism, plus the exciting archaeological discoveries that have helped make this such a popular destination in the 1990s.

Index